THE PENGUIN POETS

THE PENGUIN BOOK OF EVERYDAY VERSE

David Wright's collected poems, *To the Gods the Shades*, appeared in 1976. He has edited *The Penguin Book of Romantic Verse*, *Longer Contemporary Poems*, and *Thomas Hardy: Selected Poems* for the Penguin Poets, and Thomas Hardy's *Under the Greenwood Tree*, Edward Thomas's *Selected Poems and Prose*, Trelawny's *Records of Shelley, Byron and the Author* and De Quincey's *Recollections of the Lakes and the Lake Poets* for the Penguin English Library. He has also translated *Beowulf* and *The Canterbury Tales*, and published an autobiography, *Deafness*.

Social and Documentary Poetry 1250–1916

The Penguin Book of Everyday Verse

Edited with an Introduction
by David Wright

Penguin Books

Penguin Books Ltd, Harmondsworth, Middlesex, England
Penguin Books, 625 Madison Avenue, New York, New York 10022, U.S.A.
Penguin Books Australia Ltd, Ringwood, Victoria, Australia
Penguin Books Canada Ltd, 2801 John Street, Markham, Ontario, Canada L3R 1B4
Penguin Books (N.Z.) Ltd, 182–190 Wairau Road, Auckland 10, New Zealand

First published by Allen Lane 1976
Published in Penguin Books 1983

Printed and bound in Great Britain by
Richard Clay (The Chaucer Press) Ltd,
Bungay, Suffolk
Set in Ehrhardt

Title-page illustration adapted from a woodcut of the Pilgrims from The Canterbury Tales, *Richard Pynson edition, London, c. 1490 (courtesy the Trustees of the British Museum*

CONTENTS

INTRODUCTION

The nature of the anthology that follows should be plain to anyone who thumbs through it, so this will not be a long introduction. The book is an attempt – the first of its kind, I believe – to show how everyday life in England has been reflected in its poetry. What I have done is to pick from the many poems and even more numerous ballads, broadsheets and popular songs that touch upon contemporaneous life, and commemorate or illumine the customs, habits, behaviour, manners and environment of people of all classes. The field includes whatever illustrates the transitory actualities of living as preserved in the poetry of successive eras: work, amusements, education, toilet, dress, food and drink; weddings and funerals, festivals and fashions, voyages and hangings; domestic, urban and rural life, high life and low; beanfeasts and banquets, travel and shipwreck, trades and occupations, sports and junketings, prisons and palaces; life in metropolitan garrets and suburban villas.

The anthology, then, is a selection of what might be called 'documentary' or 'everyday' verse composed between around 1250 – say, a hundred years before the birth of Chaucer – and the end of the nineteenth century, which I take to have been the advent of the First World War. The selection has been made from poetry rather than mere verse; I hope that little has been given a place for no better reason than the interest or curiosity of its subject-matter. One exception might be the extracts from John Russell's *Book of Nurture*, which gives a fascinatingly detailed picture of the *minutiae* of medieval manners and daily life, but is less 'poetry' than the plain, practical verse of the Elizabethan poet–farmer, Thomas Tusser.

Although this book does not set out to be yet another garland of 'popular' poetry, there is much in it that comes under the category of 'light verse' as defined by Auden: 'Poetry . . . having for its subject-matter the everyday social life of the period or the experiences of the poet as an ordinary human being.' Most comic, in the sense of facetious, verse has been avoided. In the case of satire, which is of course a mine of social observation, I have kept away from its more vituperative and moralistic manifestations (though the former adjective probably applies to Swift's 'A Beautiful Young Nymph Going to Bed'. Pastoral verse in the literary tradition – for instance, Spenser's – has been eschewed: real, not idealized, life is what I have been looking for.

Moderate rein has been given to broadsheets and ballads, preference going in the main to the lesser-known. Indeed, some of the more obvious candidates for an anthology of 'documentary verse' have been left out because of their very obviousness – generally to make way for a less familiar poem on a similar theme, for example, Edward Chicken's 'The Collier's Wedding' instead of the very well-known 'A Ballad upon a Wedding' by Sir John Suckling. This may explain why Shakespeare is not represented. In any case, apart from the fact that the wealth of 'documentary' material in Shakespeare is almost all set in prose, I have arbitrarily limited the field by excluding dramatic poetry (though unable to resist an extract from one of the medieval miracle plays). Yet some very familiar poems have their place, including Chaucer's panorama of medieval life, the Prologue to *The Canterbury Tales*, and Andrew Marvell's 'Horatian Ode upon Cromwell's Return from Ireland', which marks the great historical watershed of the Civil War in England, which in turn marks the beginning of the modern era.

The best excuse for making an anthology is to direct readers to poets they might otherwise have missed or to make available poems not otherwise easily got. In these respects I think the present collection will not be found wanting, though some 'major' poets like Spenser and Shelley are not here because they lacked what I sought. (But Shelley's 'Letter to Maria Gisbourne' would have got in had there been room.) On the other hand, poets like Swift get a showing which they are generally denied. And the whole of Skelton's marvellous canvas of low life, 'The Tunning of Elinour Rumminge', is to be found here, as well as Sir David Lindsay of the Mount's contrasting picture of high life, taken from his remarkable *History of Squire Meldrum*. If William Dunbar's unique poem about civic management, 'To the Merchantis of Edinburgh', is now fairly well-known, Sir William Davenant's half-burlesque but vividly realized 'The Long Vacation in London' is not; nor are the poems of Robert Lloyd, the friend of the better-known but less interesting eighteenth-century satirist, Charles Churchill.

What will probably strike anyone who reads the poems in consecutive order (they are arranged more or less chronologically and not by subject-matter) is the vigour and immediacy of medieval poetry wherever it deals with the mundane. Freshness of experience is registered and paralleled in freshness of language. After Marvell some of the bloom and *brio* goes off; neither the plain workmanship of Swift's verse nor the exquisite technique of Pope can quite compensate. After all, the technological world that was nourished in the womb of the Industrial Revolution and born fully armed around 1918 had its conception in Marvell's day. There begins to be something nostalgic, with more consciousness of the past than of the present, in 'documentary' poetry after Marvell. Exceptions seem to be Scots poets like Burns and his almost forgotten forerunner Robert Fergusson. And while the language of English regional poets like Clare, Barnes and Hardy remains fresh, the point of view becomes increasingly backward-looking. This is most apparent in the prophetically elegiac verse of Edward Thomas, with whom the anthology closes.

David Wright

ACKNOWLEDGEMENTS

For permission to reprint poems in copyright we are indebted to:

The University of Newcastle-upon-Tyne for 'Call the Horse, Marrow' and 'The Skipper's Wedding' from their collection of broadsheet ballads (Bell/White 2).

Lawrence & Wishart Ltd for 'Banks of Newfoundland' and 'Poverty Knock' from A. L. Lloyd's *Folk Song in England* (1967).

Macmillan Publishing Co., Inc., for Thomas Hardy's 'Reminiscences of a Dancing Man', 'One We Knew', 'In a Waiting-room', 'The Country Wedding', 'An East-End Curate', 'A Sheep Fair', 'No Buyers' and 'At the Aquatic Sports' from the *Collected Poems* (copyright 1925).

The Executors of the Estate of Mrs George Bambridge and Doubleday & Co., Inc., for Rudyard Kipling's 'The Ballad of the "Bolivar"', 'Danny Deever' and 'M'Andrew's Hymn' from *The Definitive Edition of Rudyard Kipling's Verse*, and the Executors of the Estate of Mrs George Bambridge and Eyre Methuen Ltd for 'Danny Deever' from *Barrack Room Ballads.*

Mrs H. M. Davies, Jonathan Cape Ltd and Wesleyan University Press for W. H. Davies's 'The Sleepers', originally published in *The Complete Poems of W. H. Davies.*

Thanks are also due to Annie Pike of Penguin Books for her assiduous copy preparation.

NOTE ON THE TEXT

All poems composed before 1500 have been glossed and edited by David Burnley, Lecturer in English Language at Sheffield University, for whose help and advice I would like to record my debt of gratitude. A certain amount of modernization and normalization has been imposed on the varying spellings of the Middle English texts, with the occasional substitution of simpler forms for the spelling of the original. Hence the dialectal characteristics of the manuscripts have not been consistently preserved, although certain recognizably Scottish features have been retained in works by Scots authors. Certain spelling changes have, however, been made with regularity. Thus 'þ' appears as 'th'; 'ȝ' as 'gh', 'g', 'y', 'w', or, more rarely, 'z' or 's'; 'y' as 'y' or 'i'; 'sch' as 'sh'. Certain Middle English spelling alterations (f, u, v; u, v, w; i, j) have been normalized in accordance with modern spelling practice.

In the case of poems after 1500 spelling and the use of capitals and italics have been brought into conformity with modern practice.

ANONYMOUS

GRIM THE FISHERMAN AND HAVELOK

Grim was fishere swithe[1] good
And mikel couthe on the flood.[2]
Many good fish therinne he took
Bothe with net and with hook:
He took the sturgiun and the whal
And the turbut and lax[3] with-al;
He took the sele and the el[4]
(He spedde ofte swithe wel);
Keling[5] he took and tumberel,[6]
Hering and the makerel,
The butte,[7] the shulle,[8] the thornebake.[9]
Goode paniers dide he make –
On til him, and other thrinne[10]
Til hise sones – to beren fish inne
Up o lande to selle and fonge[11]
Forbar he neither toun ne gronge
That he ne to yede with his ware;[12]
Cam he nevere home hand-bare,
That he ne broughte bred and sowel[13]
In his shirte or in his cowel,[14]
In his poke benes and corn:
His swink ne havede he nought forlorn.[15]
And when he took the grete laumprey,
Ful wel he couthe the righte wey[16]
To Lincolne, the goode borough:
Ofte he yede[17] it thorough and thorough
Til he havede al wel sold
And ther-fore the penies told.[18]

[1] very [2] and had great experience of the sea [3] salmon [4] eel [5] cod [6] porpoise [7] flatfish [8] plaice [9] skate [10] one for him, and three others [11] carry . . . inland to sell and take [12] there was no village or farmstead he failed to visit with his wares [13] relish [14] cloak [15] he had not wasted his effort [16] direct route [17] went [18] and counted the takings

Then he com thenne he were blithe,[19]
For hom he broughte fele sithe[20]
Wastels, simenels with the horn,[21]
His pokes fulle of mele and corn,
Netes[22] flesh, sheepes, and swines,
And hemp to maken of goode lines,
And stronge ropes to[23] hise nettes,
In the se-weres he ofte settes.[24]
  Thusgate Grim him faire ledde:[25]
Him and his genge[26] wel he fedde
Wel twelf winter[27] other more.
Havelok was war that Grim swank sore
For his mete,[28] and he lay at hom;
Thought he: 'Ich am now no grom;[29]
Ich am wel waxen[30] and wel may eten
More than evere Grim may geten:
Ich ete more, by God on live,
Than Grim and hise children five!
It ne may nought ben thus longe.
Goddot! I wille with thee gonge
For to leren sum good to gete:[31]
Swinken ich wolde for my mete.[32]
It is no shame for to swinken:
The man that may wel eten and drinken
That n'ought ne have but on swink long.[33]
To liggen at hom it is ful strong![34]
God yelde him, ther I ne may,[35]
That haveth me fed to this day!
Gladlike I wille the paniers bere;
Ich wot ne shal it me nought dere[36]
Thei ther be inne a birthen gret
Al so hevy als a net.[37]

[19] when he came back they were pleased [20] many a time [21] fine bread, horn-shaped cakes [22] ox's [23] for [24] he often set them in the channels [25] in this way Grim managed well [26] household [27] years [28] Havelok realized that Grim slaved for his food [29] lad [30] grown [31] God knows! I want to go with you to learn to earn some money [32] I want to work for my food [33] ought not to have it except by hard work [34] to lie at home is too bad [35] may God repay him, since I cannot [36] hurt [37] although there be a great load inside as heavy as an ox

Shal ich nevere lengere dwelle:[38]
Tomorwen shal ich forth pelle.'[39]
  On the morwen, when it was day,
He stirt up soone and nought ne lay,
And cast a panier on his bac
With fish giveled als a stac.[40]
Al so michel he bar him one
So he foure, by mine mone![41]
Wel he it bar and solde it wel:
The silver he broughte hom ilk del,[42]
Al that he ther-fore took –
Withheld he nought a ferthinges nook.[43]
So yede he forth ilke day
That he nevere at home lay,
So wolde he his mester lere.[44]
  Bifel it so a strong dere[45]
Bigan to rise of corn of bred,
That Grim ne couthe no good red[46]
How he sholde his meine[47] fede.
Of Havelok havede he michel drede,[48]
For he was strong and wel moughte ete
More than evere moughte he gete;
Ne he ne moughte on the see take
Neither lenge[49] ne thornebake,
Ne non other fish that doughte
His meine feden with he moughte.[50]
Of Havelok he havede care
Whilgat[51] that he mighte fare –
Of his children was him nought;[52]
On Havelok was al his thought –
And seide: 'Havelok, dere sone,
I wene that we deye mone[53]

[38] delay [39] hurry [40] piled up with fish like a haystack [41] he alone carried as much as the four of them, in my opinion [42] every bit [43] a fraction of a farthing [44] he wished so much to learn his trade [45] a serious shortage [46] Grim had no idea [47] household [48] he was greatly concerned for Havelok [49] ling [50] nor any other useful fish that he could feed his family with [51] how [52] he was not worried about his own children [53] must

For hunger: this dere is so strong,[54]
And oure mete is uten[55] long.
Betere is that thou henne gonge[56]
Than thou here dwelle longe:
Hethen thou maght gangen to late![57]
Thou canst ful wel the righte gate[58]
To Lincolne, the goode borough –
Thou havest it gon ful ofte thorough;
Of me ne is me nought a slo.[59]
Betere is that thou thider go,
For ther is many good man inne;[60]
Ther thou maght thy mete winne.
But wo is me thou art so naked!
Of my sail I wolde thee were maked
A cloth thou mightest inne gongen,
Sone, no cold that thou ne fonge.'[61]
  He took the sheres of the nail
And made him a cowel[62] of the sail,
And Havelok dide it sone on;[63]
Haved he neither hosen ne shon,[64]
Ne none kines other wede:[65]
To Lincolne barfoot he yede.
When he cam ther he was ful wil,[66]
Ne havede he no frend to gangen til.[67]
Two dayes ther fastinde he yede,[68]
That non for his werk wolde him fede.
The thridde day herde he calle:
'Bermen, bermen,[69] hider forth alle!'
Povre[70] that on foote yede
Sprongen forth so sparke on glede.[71]
Havelok shof doun[72] nine or ten
Right amideward the fen,[73]

[54] famine is so fierce [55] exhausted [56] go away from here [57] you might go away too late [58] you well know the quickest way [59] I don't care a jot about myself [60] for there is many a prosperous man in there [61] a garment you could go about in, son, so that you don't catch cold [62] cloak [63] Havelok immediately put it on [64] shoes [65] nor any other kind of garment [66] bewildered [67] to go to [68] he went without eating [69] porters [70] the poor [71] live coal [72] pushed down [73] mire

And stirte forth to the cook,
Ther the erles mete he took
That he boughte at the brigge;
The bermen let he alle ligge[74]
And bar the mete to the castel,
And gat him there a ferthing wastel.[75]
  That other day kepte he ook
Swithe yerne the erles cook,[76]
Til that he sagh him on the brigge
And by him many fishes ligge.
The erles mete havede he bought
Of Cornwalle, and calde oft:
'Bermen, bermen, hider swithe!'[77]
Havelok it herde and was ful blithe
That he herde 'Bermen!' calle.
Alle made he hem[78] doun falle
That in his gate yeden stoode –[79]
Wel sixtene laddes goode;
As he lep the cooke til[80]
He shof hem alle upon an hil
Astirte til him with his rippe[81]
And bigan the fish to kippe.[82]
He bar up wel a carte-lode
Of segges,[83] laxes, of plaices brode,
Of grete laumprees, and of eles;
Sparede he neither tos ne heles
Til that he to the castel cam,
That men fro him his birthen nam.[84]
Then men haveden holpen him doun
With the birthen of his croun,[85]
The cook stod and on him low,[86]
And thoughte him stalworthe man ynow,
And seide: 'Wilt thou ben with me?
Gladlike wille ich feden the.

[74] he left all the porters lying [75] and got himself a farthing cake there [76] the next day he also kept look-out very eagerly for the earl's cook [77] come here quickly [78] them [79] that went and stood in his way [80] as he ran to the cook [81] bounded to him with his basket [82] pick up [83] cuttlefish [84] took [85] with the load from his head [86] smiled

Wel is set the mete thou etes[87]
And the hire that thou getes.'
'Goddot!' quoth he, 'leve[88] sire,
Bidde ich[89] you non other hire,
But yeveth[90] me ynow to ete;
Fir and water I wille you fete,[91]
The fir blow and ful wel maken;
Stickes can ich breken and craken,
And kindlen ful wel a fir
And maken it to brennen shir;[92]
Ful wel can ich cleven shides,[93]
Eles toturven of here hides;[94]
Ful wel can ich dishes swillen,
And don al that ye evere willen.'
Quoth the cook: 'Wille[95] I no more.
Go thou yonder and sit thore,
And I shal yeve[96] thee ful fair bred,
And make thee broÿs in the led.[97]
Sit now doun and et ful yerne –[98]
Datheit who thee mete werne!'[99]
  Havelok sette him doun anon,
Also[100] stille als a ston,
Til he havede ful wel eten –
Tho havede Havelok faire geten!
When he havede eten ynow,
He cam to the welle, water up-drow,[101]
And filde ther a michel so.[102]
Bad he non agein him go,[103]
Bitwen his handes he bar it in
Al him one[104] to the kichin.
Bad he none him water to fete,[105]
Ne fro brigge to bere the mete;

[87] the food you eat will be well-spent [88] dear [89] I ask [90] only give [91] fetch [92] burn bright [93] split firewood [94] skin eels [95] wish for [96] give [97] broth in the pot [98] heartily [99] bad luck to him who denies you food [100] as [101] drew up [102] pail [103] he asked no one to meet him [104] entirely by himself [105] he bade none to fetch water for him

He bar the turves, he bar the star,[106]
The woode fro the brigge he bar;
Al that evere shulden he nitte,[107]
Al he drow and al he kitte:[108]
Wolde he nevere haven rest
More than he were a best.[109]
Of alle men was he most meke,
Laughinde ay and blithe of speke:[110]
Evere he was glad and blithe –
His sorwe he couthe ful wel mithe.[111]

from *The Lay of Havelok the Dane*

A CHOIR TRAINING

Uncomly in cloistre[1] I cowre ful of care;
I looke as a lurdein[2] and – listne til my lare –[3]
The song of the ce-sol-fa dos me siken sare[4]
And sitte stotiand[5] on a song a moneth and mare.

I ga gouland aboute al so dos a gooke.[6]
Many is the sorwful song I singge upon my booke;[7]
I am holde so harde, unnethes dare I looke.[8]
Al the mirthe of this mold[9] for God I forsooke.

I goule on my grayel[10] and rore as a rooke;
Litil wiste I therof when I therto tooke![11]
Somme notes arn shorte and somme a long nooke,[12]
Somme crooken away-ward als a fles-hooke.[13]

[106] sedge for kindling [107] all they could ever use [108] cut [109] beast [110] speech [111] hide

[1] unsuited to the cloister [2] fool [3] listen to my tale [4] singing high C makes me sigh grievously [5] stuttering [6] I go wailing about like a cuckoo [7] in my book [8] I am so severely restrained I hardly dare look up [9] joys of this world [10] wail over my gradual [11] little did I know of this when I began [12] and some a long angle-shape [13] some bend away like a meat-hook

When I can[14] my lesson, to my maister wil I gon
That heres me my rendre he wenes I have wel don.[15]
'What hast thou don, Daun Walter, sin Saterday at noon?
Thou holdest nought a note, by God, in riht ton!

'Way me! leve Walter, thou werkes al til shame,[16]
Thou stumblest and stikes fast as thou were lame!
Thou tones nought the note ilke by his name;[17]
Thou bitest asunder be-quarre, for be-mol I thee blame.[18]

'Way thee! leve Walter, thou werkes al to wonder![19]
As an old caudron biginnest to clonder![20]
Thou tuchest nought the notes, thou bites hem on sunder.[21]
Hold up, for shame! thou letes al under.'[22]

Then is Walter so wo that wel ner wil he blede,[23]
And wendis him til William and bit him wel to spede.[24]
'God it wot', seys William, 'therof hadde I nede!
Now wot I how *judicare* was set in the Crede![25]

'Me is wo so is the bee that belles in the walmes:[26]
I donke upon David til my tonge talmes.[27]
I ne rendrede nought sithen men beren palmes.[28]
Is it also mikel sorwe in song so is in salmes?'[29]

'Ya, by God! thou reddis! and so it is wel werre.[30]
I sol-fe,[31] and singe after, and is me nevere the nerre;[32]
I horle at the notes and heve hem al of herre![33]
Alle that me heres wenes that I erre.[34]

[14] know [15] who hears me rehearse my lesson and expects me to have done well [16] Alas! my dear Walter, your performance is a disgrace [17] you do not sing the designated note clearly [18] you bite B natural apart [i.e., distort the pitch] and I criticize you for B flat [19] Woe to you, my dear Walter, your performance is atrocious [20] rumble [21] bite them in half [22] you are going all flat [23] nearly wants to die [24] and goes to William and wishes him good luck [25] Now I know what 'judgement' means in the Creed! [26] I am as wretched as the bee buzzing in the water [27] I pound out the Psalms until my tongue wearies [28] I have not repeated my lesson since Palm Sunday [29] is there as much misery in music as there is in the Psalms? [30] you've said it! and indeed it's much worse [31] practise the scale [32] I'm never any nearer [33] I rush at the notes and heave them right off their hinges [34] Everyone who hears me knows that I'm going wrong

'Of be-mol and of be-quarre, of both I was wel bare[35]
When I went out of this world and – liste til my lare –[36]
Of ef-fa-uts and e-la-mi ne coud I never are;[37]
I faile faste in the fa, it files al my fare.[38]

'Yet ther been other notes, sol and ut and la,
And that froward file that men clipis fa:[39]
Often he dos me liken ille and werkes me ful wa;[40]
Might I him nevere hitten in tone for to ta.[41]

'Yet ther is a streinant with two longe tailes;[42]
Therfore[43] has oure maister ofte horled my kailes.[44]
Ful litel thou kennes[45] what sorwe me ailes:
It is but childes game that thou with David dailes![46]

'When ilke note til other lepes and makes hem asaut,[47]
That we calles a moison in ge-sol-re-uts en haut.[48]
Il hail were thou boren if thou make defaut;[49]
Then says oure maister "que vos ren ne vaut".'[50]

A POACHER

In the monethe of Maye when mirthes bene fele,[1]
And the sesone of somere when softe bene the wedres,
Als I went to the wodde my werdes to dreghe,[2]
Into the shawes[3] myselfe a shotte me to gete
At ane hert or ane hinde, happen as it mighte:
And as Drighten the day drove[4] from the heven,
Als I abade on a banke be a brime side,[5]
There the grise[6] was grene growen with floures –

[35] I was quite ignorant of B flat and B natural [36] when I left secular life – listen to my tale – [37] of F and E I never knew anything before [38] I am utterly lacking in the 'fa', it blights all my existence [39] and that perverse wretch called 'fa' [40] often he makes me miserable and causes me pain [41] I could never hit him so as to get him in tune [42] there is also a breve with two long tails [43] on its account [44] bowled me out [45] understand [46] what you do with the Psalms is no more than child's play [47] when every note rushes at the other and clashes together [48] that we call a melody in high G [49] bad luck you were born if you make a slip [50] you are worthless

[1] delights are many [2] to try my luck [3] copses [4] the Lord drove the dawn [5] water's edge [6] grass

The primrose, the pervinke, and piliole the riche –[7]
The dewe uppon daiseys donkede[8] full faire,
Burgons[9] and blossoms and braunches full swete,
And the mery mistes full mildely gan falle:
The cukkowe, the cowshote, kene were thay bothen,[10]
And the throstills full throly threpen[11] in the bankes,
And iche foule in that frithe fainere[12] than other
That the derke was done and the daye lightenede:
Hertis and hindes on hillis thay goven,[13]
The foxe and the filmarte[14] thay flede to the erthe,
The hare hurkles by hawes,[15] and harde thedir drives,
And ferkes[16] faste to hir fourme and fatills[17] hir to sitt.
Als I stode in that stede[18] on stalkinge I thoghte;
Bothe my body and my bowe I buskede[19] with leves;
And turnede towardes a tree and tariede there a while;
And als I lookede to a launde[20] a littil me beside,
I seghe ane hert with ane hede, ane heghe for the nones;[21]
Alle unburneshede was the beme, full borely the midle,[22]
With iche feetur as thy fote, for-frayed in the greves,[23]
With auntlers on aithere side egheliche[24] longe;
The ryalls ful richely raughten[25] frome the middes,
With surryals[26] full semely uppon sides twaine;
And he assommet and sett of sixe and of five,[27]
And ther-to borely[28] and brode and of body grete,
And a coloppe[29] for a kinge, cache him who mighte.[30]
Bot there sewet him a sowre[31] that servet him full yerne,[32]

[7] periwinkle, and the noble penny-royal [8] freshened the daisies [9] buds [10] the cuckoo, the woodpigeon, both were active [11] the thrushes fiercely competed with each other [12] and each bird in that wood more jubilant [13] ? made their way [14] polecat [15] crouches by hedges [16] goes [17] settles [18] spot [19] covered [20] clearing [21] I saw a stag with a particularly tall set of antlers [22] the main part was all in velvet, very solid in the centre [23] with each ? point as long as your foot, tattered by rushing through thickets [24] awesomely [25] the second branches extended magnificently [26] 'sub-royals' [i.e., subsidiary branches] [27] and he was fully developed and set with six antlers on one horn and five on the other [28] massive [29] morsel [30] if anyone could take him [31] but a fourth-year stag followed him [32] which served him most conscientously

That woke[33] and warned him when the winde failede,[34]
That none so sleghe[35] in his sleepe with sleghte[36] sholde him dere,[37]
And went the wayes him bi-fore when any wothe tide.[38]
My liame[39] than full lightly lete I doun falle,
And to the bole of a birche my berselett I cowchide;[40]
I waitted[41] wisly the winde by wagginge of leves,
Stalkede full stilly no stikkes to breke,
And crepite to a crabtre and coverede me ther-undere:
Then I bende up my bowe and bownede me[42] to shoote,
Tighte up my tylere and taisede[43] at the hert:
Bot the sowre that him sewet[44] sett up the nese,[45]
And waittede wittyly[46] abowte and windide full yerne.[47]
Then I moste stonde als I stode, and stirre no fote ferrere,
For had I mintid[48] or movede or made any sinis,[49]
Alle my laike[50] hade bene loste that I hade longe waittede.[51]
Bot gnattes gretely me grevede and gnewen myn eghne;[52]
And he stotaide and stelkett and starede full brode,[53]
Bot at the laste he loutted[54] doun and laughte till his mete,[55]
And I hallede to the hokes[56] and the hert smote,
And happened that I hitt him bi-hinde the lefte sholdire,
That the bloode braste owte uppon bothe the sides:
And he balkede[57] and brayed and brushede thurgh the greves,
As alle had hurlede on ane hepe that in the holte longede;[58]
And sone the sowre that him sewet resorte to his feris,[59]
And thay, forfraiede of his fare,[60] to the felles thay hien;
And I hiede to my hounde and hent[61] him up sone,
And louset my liame and lete him umbecaste;[62]
The breris and the brakans[63] were blody be-ronnen;

[33] kept watch [34] dropped [35] crafty [36] cunning [37] harm [38] any danger threatened [39] leash [40] I made my dog lie down [41] watched [42] prepared [43] lifted up my bow-stock and took aim [44] followed [45] raised his nose [46] looked knowingly [47] eagerly sniffed the wind [48] taken aim [49] signs [50] sport [51] long looked for [52] stung my eyes [53] and he hesitated and moved most carefully [54] bent [55] took to his pasture [56] pulled back the catches [57] bellowed [58] as if he would have flattened everything that dwelt in the wood [59] and soon the four-year-old which followed him returned to his companions [60] terrified at his behaviour [61] got [62] and unfastened my leash and made him cast around for the scent [63] briars and bracken

And he assentis to that sewte and seches him aftire,[64]
There he was crepede[65] into a crage and crouchede to the erthe;
Dede als a dore-naile doun was he fallen.

from *The Parlement of the Thre Ages*

SIR GAWAIN ENTERS THE CASTLE

'Goode sir,' quoth Gawain, 'woldes thou go myn erande
To the high lorde of this hous, herber[1] to crave?'
'Ye, Peter,' quoth the porter, 'and purely I trowe[2]
That ye be, wye, welcom to won[3] while you likes.'
Then yede the wye yerne[4] and com ayain swithe,[5]
And folke frely[6] him with to fonge[7] the knight.
Thay let doun the grete draght[8] and derely out yeden[9]
And kneled doun on her knes upon the colde erthe
To welcom this ilk wye as worthy hem thoght.[10]
Thay yolden him the brode yate yarked up wide,[11]
And he hem raised rekenly[12] and rode over the brigge.[13]
Sere segges[14] him sesed by sadel while he light,
And sithen[15] stabeled his stede stif men innowe.[16]
Knightes and squieres comen doun thenne
For to bring this burne[17] with blis into halle.
When he hef up his helme ther hied innowe
For to hent[18] hit at his honde, the hende[19] to serven;
His bronde and his blasoun[20] both thay token.
Then hailsed he ful hendly tho hatheles uchone,[21]
And mony proud mon there presed[22] that prince to honour
All hasped in his high wede[23] to halle thay him wonnen,[24]
Ther faire fire upon flet[25] feersly brenned.

[64] and he approves of that pursuit and seeks after him [65] crept

[1] lodging [2] and certainly I believe [3] that you, knight, will be welcome to stay [4] then the man went briskly [5] quickly [6] courteously [7] receive [8] drawbridge [9] courteously went out [10] to welcome this same knight as he seemed to them to deserve [11] They offered to let him pass through the broad gate, set wide open [12] graciously [13] bridge [14] several men [15] afterwards [16] many trusty fellows [17] knight [18] take [19] the gracious man [20] sword and shield [21] then he courteously acknowledged each of the men [22] crowded [23] clasped in his fine armour [24] brought [25] floor

Then the lorde of the lede loutes[26] fro his chamber
For to meete with menske[27] the mon on the floore.
He said, 'Ye ar welcom to welde as yow likes[28]
That here is; all is your owen, to have at your wille
    And welde.'
  'Grant merci,' quoth Gawain,
  'Ther Crist hit yow foryelde.'[29]
  As frekes that semed fain[30]
  Aither other in armes con felde.[31]

Gawain glight on the gome that goodly him gret,[32]
And thoght hit a bolde burne that the burgh aghte,[33]
A huge hathel for the nones and of highe elde.[34]
Brode, bright was his berd and all bever-hued,
Sturne, stif on the strithe[35] on stalworth shankes,
Felle face as the fire and fre of his speche;[36]
And wel him semed, for sothe, as the segge thoght,
To lede a lordship in lee of ledes ful goode.[37]
The lorde him charred[38] to a chambre and chefly[39] comaundes
To deliver him a lede[40] him lowly to serve;
And ther wer boun at his bode[41] burnes innowe
That broght him to a bright boure ther bedding was noble,
Of cortaines of clene silk with cler golde hemmes,
And covertores ful curious with comlich panes[42]
Of bright blaunner[43] above, enbrawded bisides,
Rudeles rennande on ropes,[44] red golde ringes,
Tapites tight to the wowe of tuly and tars,[45]
And under feete on the flet of folwande sute.[46]
Ther he was dispoiled with speches of mirthe,[47]
The burn of his bruny and of his bright wedes.[48]

[26] comes [27] honour [28] to employ as it pleases you [29] repay [30] men who seemed glad [31] folded [32] Gawain looked at the man who greeted him so warmly [33] owned the castle [34] mature years [35] standing firmly [36] with an aspect as daunting as fire, and noble of speech [37] and he seemed well-suited, indeed, as the knight thought, to hold command in a castle of very bold knights [38] took him back [39] quickly [40] a man to be assigned to him [41] ready at his command [42] and elaborate coverlets with fine fur facings [43] ? ermine [44] curtains running on ropes [45] tapestries of rich red silk and Tharsian silk fastened to the wall [48] and matching on the floor [47] with jesting words, he was stripped [48] of his mail-shirt and his gleaming armour

Riche robes ful rad renkes him broghten[49]
For to charge and to chaunge[50] and chose of the best.
Sone as he one hent and happed therinne,[51]
That sate on him semly with sailande skirtes,[52]
The ver by his visage verayly hit semed
Welnegh to uche hathel,[53] all on hues,
Lowande and lufly[54] all his limmes under,
That a comloker[55] knight never Crist made
    Hem thoght.
  Whethen[56] in worlde he were,
  Hit semed as he moght
  Be prince withouten peere
  In felde ther felle men foght.

A cheier[57] before the chimny, ther charcole brenned,
Was graithed[58] for Sir Gawain graithly with clothes,[59]
Quishines upon queldepointes that coint wer bothe;[60]
And then a mery mantele was on that mon cast
Of a broun bleaunt,[61] enbrawded ful riche
And faire furred withinne with felles[62] of the best,
All of ermin in erde,[63] his hoode of the same.
And he sate in that settel semlich riche
And achaufed him chefly, and then his chere mended.[64]
Sone was telded[65] up a table on trestes ful faire,
Clad with a clene clothe that cler white shewed,
Sanap and salure[66] and silveren spoones.
The wye weshe at his wille and went to his mete.
Segges him served semely innowe
With sere sewes and sete,[67] sesounde of the best,
Doublefelde, as hit falles, and fele kin fishes,[68]
Summe baken in bred, summe brad on the gledes,[69]

[49] men quickly brought him [50] to try on and change [51] as soon as he had taken one and clothed himself in it [52] one that suited him well with flowing skirts [53] by his appearance, it truly seemed almost like spring to every man [54] all in glowing and delightful colours [55] handsomer [56] from wherever [57] chair [58] made ready [59] pleasantly with covers [60] cushions on quilted covers, both of which were intricately worked [61] fine brown cloth [62] pelts [63] in fact [64] and soon warmed himself and then his spirits improved [65] set [66] over-cloth and salt-cellar [67] with various excellent broths [68] in double portions, as is appropriate, and many sorts of fish [69] some grilled over hot coals

Summme sothen, summe in sewe[70] savered with spices,
And ay sawses so sleye[71] that the segge liked.
The freke called hit a fest[72] ful frely and oft
Ful hendely, when all the hatheles rehaited him at ones
    As hende:[73]
  'This penaunce now ye take
  And eft hit shal amende.'[74]
  That mon much mirthe con make
  For wine in his hed that wende.

A DEER HUNT

Ful erly before the day the folk uprisen.
Gestes that go wolde her gromes thay calden,[1]
And thay busken up bilive blonkes to sadel,[2]
Tiffen her takles,[3] trussen her males.[4]
Richen hem[5] the richest, to ride alle arayede,
Lepen up lightly, lachen[6] her brideles,
Uch wye[7] on his way ther him wel liked.
The leve[8] lorde of the londe was not the last
Arayed for the riding with renkes[9] ful mony;
Ete a sop[10] hastily, when he had herde masse,
With bugle to bent-felde he buskes bilive.[11]
By that[12] any daylight lemed[13] upon erthe,
He with his hatheles[14] on highe horses weren
Then thise cacheres that couthe coupled her houndes,[15]
Unclosed the kenel doore and called hem theroute,
Blew bigly in bugles thre bare mote.[16]
Braches[17] bayed therfore and breme[18] noise maked;

[70] some poached, some in broth [71] and always with subtle sauces [72] feast [73] all the men together courteously urged him [74] accept this penance now and things will improve later

[1] guests who wished to depart called their servants [2] and they hasten quickly to saddle horses [3] make their equipment ready [4] pack their bags [5] prepare themselves [6] catch [7] every man [8] beloved [9] men [10] light meal [11] hastens quickly to the hunting-field [12] by the time that [13] gleamed [14] men [15] then these skilled huntsmen put leashes on their hounds [16] three long blasts [17] hounds [18] fierce

And thay chastised and charred on chasing that went,[19]
A hundreth of hunteres, as I haf herd telle,
    Of the best.
  To trysters vewters yod,[20]
  Couples huntes of kest;[21]
  Ther ros for blastes good
  Grete rurd[22] in that forest.

At the first quethe of the quest[23] quaked the wilde;
Deer drof in the dale, doted[24] for drede,
Hied to the highe, bot heterly[25] thay were
Restayed with the stablie, that stoutly ascried.[26]
Thay let the herttes haf the gate,[27] with the highe hedes,
The breme[18] bukkes also with her brode paumes;[28]
For the fre lorde had defende in fermysoun tyme[29]
That ther shulde no mon meve to[30] the male deere.
The hindes were holden in with 'hay!' and 'war!'
The does driven with grete din to the depe slades.[31]
Ther might mon see, as thay slipte, slenting of arewes,[32]
At uche wende under wande wapped a flone,[33]
That bigly bote on the broun[34] with ful brode hedes.
What, thay brayen and bleeden, by bonkes thay deyen;
And ay raches in a res radly[35] hem folwes,
Hunteres with highe horne hasted hem after
With such a crakkande cry as cliffes haden brusten.
What wilde so atwaped wyes that shotten[36]
Was all toraced and rent at the resayt,[37]
By thay were tened at the highe and taised to the wattres,[38]
The ledes were so lerned[39] at the lowe trysteres,[40]

[19] and they whipped in and turned back those that went off on other scents [20] the keepers of greyhounds went to their hunting-stations [21] the huntsmen released leashes [22] din [23] at the first utterance of the hounds on finding a scent [24] dazed [25] vigorously [26] turned back by a ring of beaters who shouted vigorously [27] pass by [28] antlers [29] forbidden in the close season [30] threaten [31] valleys [32] slanting of arrows [33] at every turn in the wood an arrow whizzed [34] that bit mightily into the brown [35] and always hounds in a rush swiftly [36] whatever animal escaped the man who was shooting [37] was pulled down and slaughtered at the receiving stations [38] by the time they had been driven from the high ground and down to the waters [39] the men were so skilled [40] stations

And the grehoundes so grete that geten hem bilive[41]
And hem tofilched[42] as fast as frekes[43] might looke
There right.
The lorde for blisse abloy[44]
Ful oft con lance and light,[45]
And drof[46] that day with joy
Thus to the derk night.

from *Sir Gawain and the Green Knight*

A BOAR HUNT

Sone thay calle of a quest in a kerre side;[1]
The hunte rehaited[2] the houndes that hit first minged,[3]
Wilde wordes hem warp[4] with a wrast[5] noise.
The houndes that hit herde hasted thider swithe[6]
And fellen as fast to the fuit,[7] fourty at ones.
Then such a glaver and glam of gedered raches[8]
Ros that the rocheres[9] rungen aboute;
Hunteres hem hardened[10] with horne and with mouthe.
Then all in a sembly sweyed[11] togeder
Bitwene a floshe in that frith and a foo cragge;[12]
In a knot[13] by a cliffe at the kerre side,
Ther as the rogh rocher unridely was fallen,[14]
Thay ferden[15] to the finding, and frekes[16] hem after.
Thay umbekesten the knarre[17] and the knot bothe,
Wyes, whil thay wisten[18] wel withinne hem hit were
The best that ther breved was with[19] the blodhoundes.

[41] seized them at once [42] and tore them down [43] men [44] carried away with joy [45] very often galloped and dismounted [46] passed

[1] soon they give tongue on the edge of a boggy piece of scrub [2] the huntsman encouraged [3] announced [4] uttered [5] loud [6] quickly [7] trail [8] uproar and din of assembled hounds [9] rocks [10] emboldened [11] all in a pack rushed [12] between a pool in the wood and a forbidding crag [13] rocky knoll [14] where the rough rock had fallen in a jumble [15] moved on [16] men [17] they quartered around the gnarled rock [18] until they knew [19] the beast that there was announced by

Then thay beten on the buskes[20] and bede him uprise,
And he unsoundyly out soght segges overthwert.[21]
One the sellokest[22] swin swenged out[23] there,
Long sithen fro the sounder that seyed for olde;[24]
For he was breme,[25] bor althergrattest,[26]
Ful grimme when he gronied.[27] Then greved mony,
For three at the first thrast he thright[28] to the erthe
And sparred[29] forth good speed boute spit more.[30]
These other halowed 'hyghe!' ful highe and 'hay! hay!' cried,
Haden hornes to mouthe, heterly rechated.[31]
Mony was the mery mouthe of men and of houndes
That buskes[32] after this bor with bost[33] and with noise
    To quelle.[34]
  Ful oft he bides the baye[35]
  And maimes the mute in melle.[36]
  He hurtes of the houndes, and thay
  Ful yomerly[37] yawle and yelle.

Shalkes[38] to shoote at him shoven to then,
Haled[39] to him of her arewes, hitten him oft;
Bot the pointes paired at the pith that pight in his sheldes[40]
And the barbes[41] of his browe bite none wolde;
Thagh the shaven shaft shindered[42] in peces,
The hed hipped ayain[43] wheresoever hit hitte.
Bot when the dintes him dered of her drie strokes,[44]
Then brainwod for bate on burnes he rases,[45]
Hurtes hem ful heterly[46] ther he forth hies,
And mony arwed[47] therat and on lite drowen.[48]

[20] bushes [21] then he disastrously tried to get out through the line of men [22] quite the most marvellous [23] rushed [24] which had long since gone from the herd because of age [25] fierce [26] biggest of all [27] snorted [28] thrust [29] sprang [30] without further harm [31] vigorously blew the recall [32] hastens [33] outcry [34] kill [35] waits at bay [36] and injures the pack on all sides [37] piteously [38] men [39] loosed [40] but the points which struck his hard hide were blunted by the toughness [41] barbs of the arrows [42] splintered [43] bounced off [44] the impact of their hard blows hurt him [45] then infuriated by the struggle he rushes on the men [46] very fiercely injures them [47] were terrified [48] and drew back

Bot the lorde on a light horse launces[49] him after,
As burne bolde upon bent[50] his bugle he blowes;
He rechated and rode thurgh rones[51] ful thik,
Suande[52] this wilde swin til the sunne shafted.[53]

from *Sir Gawain and the Green Knight*

WASTOURE IN LONDON

Chese thee forthe into the Chepe,[1] a chambre thou rere,[2]
Looke thy windowe be wide, and waite[3] thee aboute,
Where any berande potener[4] thurgh the burgh passe;
Teche him to the tonne till he taite worthe;[5]
Doo him drink all nighte that he dry be at morow,
Sithen ken him to the Crete[6] to comforth his vaines
Bringe him to Bred Strete, bikken with thy finger,
Shew him of fatt shepe sholdirs ynewe[7]
Hotte for the hungry, a hen other twaine,
Sett him softe on a sete, and sithen send after,
Bring out of the burgh the best thou may finde,
And loke thy knave have a knoke bot he the clothe spred;
Bot late him paye or[8] he passe, and pik him so clene
That find a peny in his purse, and put oute his eghe.
When that es dronken and don, dwell ther no longer,
But teche him out of the town, to trotte aftir more.
Then passe to the Pultrie, the peple thee knowes,
And ken wele thy katour[9] to knawen thy fode,
The herons, the hasteletes,[10] the hennes wele served,
The pertrikes,[11] the plovers, the other pulled birddes,[12]
The albus, the oselles, the egretes dere.[13]

from *Winnere and Wastoure*

[49] gallops [50] field [51] bushes [52] following [53] set

[1] make your way into Cheapside [2] set up [3] keep watch [4] bearing a purse [5] guide him to the barrel until he gets merry [6] afterwards introduce him to the wine of Crete [7] many [8] before [9] steward [10] spit-roasted delicacies [11] partridges [12] plucked fowls [13] the bullfinches, the ouzels, the herons

WILLIAM LANGLAND

THE FIELD FULL OF FOLK

In a somer seson whan soft was the sunne
I shope me in shroudes as I a sheepe were;[1]
In habite as[2] an heremite unholy of workes
Went wide in this world wondres to here.
Ac on a May morninge on Malverne hilles
Me bifel a ferly, of fairy me thoughte.[3]
I was wery forwandred[4] and went me to reste
Under a brode banke bi a burnes side,
And as I lay and lened[5] and loked in the wateres,
I slombred in a sleping, it sweyved so merie.[6]
  Thanne gan I to meten a merveilouse swevene,[7]
That I was in a wildernesse, wist[8] I never where.
As I bihelde into the est, an hiegh to the sunne,
I seigh a toure on a toft trielich ymaked;[9]
A depe dale binethe, a dongeon thereinne
With depe diches and derke and dredful of sight.
A faire felde ful of folke fonde I there bitwene,
Of alle maner of men, the mene and the riche,
Worching and wandring as the worlde asketh.[10]
Some putten hem to the plow, pleyed ful selde,[11]
In setting and in sowing swonken[12] ful harde,
And wonnen that[13] wastours with glotonye destruyeth.
  And some putten hem to pruyde, apparailed hem thereafter,[14]
In contenaunce of clothing comen disgised.[15]
  In prayers and in penance putten hem manye,
Al for love of oure Lorde liveden ful streite,[16]
In hope forto have heveneriche blisse;[17]

[1] I dressed myself in garments as if I were a sheep [i.e., in wool] [2] dressed as [3] a marvellous thing happened to me, which seemed like magic [4] exhausted from walking [5] rested [6] I dozed into sleep, it sounded so pleasant [7] I began to dream a wonderful dream [8] knew [9] a tower on a hill, excellently constructed [10] as everyday life demands [11] rarely [12] laboured at planting and sowing [13] gained what [14] some devoted themselves to pride, and dressed accordingly [15] went about decked out in ostentatious display [16] austerely [17] bliss of the heavenly kingdom

As ancres and heremites that holden hem in here selles,[18]
And coveiten nought in contre to kairen aboute,[19]
For no likerous liflode her likam to plese.[20]
  And somme chosen chaffare; they cheven the bettere,[21]
As it semeth to oure sight that suche men thriveth;
And somme mirthes to make as minstralles conneth,[22]
And geten gold with here glee giltles,[23] I leve.
Ac japers and jangelers, Judas childeren,
Feynen hem fantasies and fooles hem maketh,
And han here witte at wille to worche, if they sholde;[24]
That Poule precheth of hem I nel nought preve it here;
Qui turpiloquium loquitur etc. is Luciferes hyne.[25]
  Bidders[26] and beggeres fast about yede[27]
With her bely and her bagge of bred ful ycrammed;
Fayteden[28] for here foode, foughten atte ale;
In glotonye, God it wote, gon hi to bedde,
And risen with ribaudye, tho roberdes knaves;[29]
Slepe and sory sleuthe seweth[30] hem evere.
  Pilgrimes and palmers plighted hem togidere[31]
To seeke seint James and seintes in Rome.
They went forth in here wey with many wise tales,
And hadden leve to lie[32] al here lif after.
I seigh somme that seiden they had ysought seintes:
To eche a tale that they tolde here tonge was tempred to lie[33]
More than to sey soth, it semed by here speche.
  Heremites on an heep[34] with hooked staves,
Wenten to Walsingham, and bere wenches after;
Grete lobies[35] and longe that loth were to swinke[36]
Clotheden hem in copes, to ben knowen fram othere,

[18] such as anchorites and hermits that remain in their cells [19] and have no desire to wander about outside [20] pursuing no delectable life, pleasing to their bodies [21] some took to commerce, they were more prosperous [22] and some, as minstrels, know how to compose entertainments [23] and earn gold . . . blamelessly [24] jesters and chatterers . . . who have the wit at their disposal to work if they had to, concoct idle tales and make fools of themselves [25] 'He who speaks obscenities' is the servant of Lucifer [26] mendicants [27] busily went about [28] dissimulated [29] rise with wickedness, those thieving scoundrels [30] follow [31] pledged themselves [32] tell lies [33] attuned to lying [34] in a crowd [35] great, lanky lubbers [36] work

And shopen hem heremites here ese to have.
  I fonde there freres, alle the foure ordres,
Preched the peple for profit of hemselven,
Glosed the gospel as hem good liked,[37]
For coveitise of copes construed it as they wolde.
Many of this maistres freres mowe clothen hem at liking,[38]
For here money and marchandise marchen togideres.
For sith charite hath be chapman and chief to shrive lordes[39]
Many ferlys han fallen[40] in a fewe yeres
But holychirche and hi holde better togideres,
The most mischief on molde is mounting wel faste.[41]
  There preched a pardonere as[42] he a prest were;
Broughte forth a bulle with bishopes seles,
And seide that himself mighte assoilen[43] hem alle
Of falshed of fasting,[44] of vowes ybroken.
  Lewed men leved him[45] wel and liked his wordes;
Comen up kneling to kissen his bulles.
He bunched hem with his brevet[46] and blered here eyes
And raughte with his ragman[47] ringes and broches.
Thus they geven here golde glotones to kepe.
And leveth such loseles that lecherye haunten.[48]
Were the bishop yblissed and worth bothe his eres,[49]
His seel shulde nought be sent to deceive the peple.
Ac it is naught by[50] the bishop that the boy precheth,
For the parish prest and the pardonere parten[51] the silver
That the poraille[52] of the parish sholde have, if thei nere.[53]
  Persones and parish prestes pleined hem[54] to the bishop
That here parishes were poore sith the pestilence time,
To have a licence and a leve at London to dwelle,
And singen there for simonye,[55] for silver is sweete.

[37] Interpreted gospel as suited them best [38] Many of these learned friars clothe themselves as they like [39] For, since charity has become a pedlar and a chaplain to confess lords [40] many wonders have happened [41] the greatest catastrophe in the world is building up quickly [42] as though [43] absolve [44] failure to fast [45] ignorant men believed him [46] he tapped them with his letter of authority [47] collected with his parchment [48] and believe such wretches who live in lechery [49] If the bishop were truly saintly and alert to his duty [50] for [51] share [52] poor [53] if it was not for them [54] complained [55] [i.e., sing masses for the dead in return for payment]

Bishopes and bachelers, bothe maistres and doctours,
That han cure under Criste and crowning in tokne[56]
And signe that thei sholden shriven here paroshienes,[57]
Prechen and prey for hem, and the pore feede,
Liggen in London in Lenten, an elles.[58]
Somme serven the king and his silver tellen;[59]
In cheker and in chancerye chalengen his dettes[60]
Of wardes and wardmotes, weives and streives.[61]
And some serven as servantz lordes and ladyes,
And in stede of stuwardes sitten and demen.[62]
Here messe and here matines and many of here oures[63]
Arn don undevoutlich; drede is at the laste
Lest Crist in constorie acurse ful manye.[64]
I parceived of the power that Peter had to kepe,
To binde and to unbinde as the booke telleth;
How he it left with love, as oure Lorde hight:[65]
Amonges foure vertues the best of all vertues
That cardinales ben called and closing gates,
There Crist is in kingdome to close and to shutte,
And to opne it to hem and hevene blisse shewe.
Ac of the cardinales atte courte that caught[66] of that name
And power presumed in hem a pope to make,
To han that power that Peter hadde inpugnen I·nelle:[67]
For in love and letterure the eleccioun bilongeth –[68]
Forthi I can and can naughte[69] of courte speke more.
Thanne come there a king, knyghthod him ladde,[70]
Might of the comunes[71] made him to regne.
And thanne cam Kinde Witte[72] and clerkes[73] he made
For to conseille the king and the comune save.
The king and knyghthode and clergye bothe

[56] the tonsure as a token [57] they ought to confess their parishioners [58] and other times [59] count [60] to make claims for his debts in the Exchequer and in Chancery [61] from estates and district councils, lost property and estates of deceased aliens [62] make rulings [63] religious observances [64] lest Christ in his consistory court [i.e., at the Day of Judgement] curse very many [65] commanded [66] adopted [67] I do not wish to question that the Cardinals . . . were able to make a pope with the power that Peter had [68] for love and learning are proper to the election [69] I know and am not able to [70] chivalry guides him [71] power of the people [72] innate knowledge [73] learned men

Casten that the comune shulde hemself finde.[74]
  The comune contreved of kinde witte craftes,[75]
And for profit of alle the people plowmen ordeigned
To tilie and travaile as trewe lif asketh.[76]
The kinge and the comune and kinde witte the thridde
Shope lawe and lewte,[77] eche man to knowe his owne.

Piers Plowman (B Prologue)

WILLIAM LANGLAND IN LONDON

Thus I awakede, wot God, when I wonede[1] in Cornehille,
Kitte and I in a cote,[2] yclothed as a lollare,[3]
And litel ylet by, leveth me for sothe,[4]
Amonges lollares of London and lewede[5] hermites;
For I made of tho men as Resoun me taughte.
For as I cam by Consience, with Resoun I mette,
In an hot hervest,[6] whenne I hadde myn hele,[7]
And limes to labory with, and lovede wel-fare,[8]
And no deede to do but to drinke and to sleepe.
In hele and in inwitt, one me apposede,
Rominge in remembraunce thus Resoun me aratede:[9]
'Can thou serven', he saide, 'or singen in a churche,
Or coke for my cokeres, or to the cart piche,[10]
Mowen or mywen, or make bond to sheves,[11]
Repe, or been a ripe-reve,[12] and arise erly,
Or have an horn and be hayward, and ligge theroute nightes,[13]
And kepe my corn in my croft fro pikares[14] and theves,
Or shap shoon or cloth, or sheep and kine keepe,
Heggen or harwen,[15] or swine or gees drive,

[74] determined that the common people should provide for themselves [75] by good sense, the common people invented trades [76] to cultivate and labour, as an honest life demands [77] created law and order

[1] lived [2] hovel [3] idler [4] and little esteemed, believe me indeed [5] ignorant [6] harvest-time [7] health [8] soft living [9] sound in mind and body, as my thoughts wandered, I was questioned: Reason berated me there [10] or make haycocks for my harvesters, or pitch it on to the cart [11] mow or stack or make binding for sheaves [12] head reaper [13] be a hedge-warden and lie outside at night [14] pilferers [15] hedge or harrow

Or eny other kines craft that to the comune nedeth,
That thou betere therby that bileve thee finden?'[16]
'Certes', I saide, 'and so me God helpe,
I am to waik[17] to werke with sikel or with sythe,
And to long, leve me, lowe to stoupe,
To werke as a werkeman eny while to duren.'[18]
'Thenne hast thou londes to live by', quod Resoun, 'or linage riche,
That finde thee thy fode? For an idel man thou semest,
A spendour that spene mot, or a spille-time,[19]
Or beggest thy bileve aboute at mens haches,[20]
Or faitest[21] upon Fridayes or feste-days in churches,
The whiche is lollarne[22] lif, tha litel is prised
Ther[23] Rightfulnesse rewardeth right as men deserveth:
Reddet unicuique iuxta opera sua.
Or thou art broke, so may be,[24] in body or in membre,
Or y-maimed thorgh som mishap wherebythou mighte be excused.'
'When I yong was', quod ich, 'many yer hennes,[25]
My fader and my frendes fonde me to scole,[26]
Til I wiste witterly[27] what Holy Writ menede,
And what is beste for the body, as the Bok telleth,
And sikerest for the soule, by so I wil continue;[28]
And fond I ne're in faith, sith[29] my frendes deyede,
Lif that me likede,[30] but in these longe clothes.
And if I by labour sholde liven and liflode deserven,[31]
That labour that I lerned beste therwith liven I sholde:
In eadem vocacione qua vocati estis, sitis.
And so I live in London and upeland[32] bothe;
The lomes[33] that I labore with and liflode deserve[31]
Is *Pater Noster* and my Primer, *Placebo* and *Dirige*,
And my Sauter som time, and my Sevene Psalmes.
These I segge[34] for here soules of suche as me helpeth;
And tho that finden me my foode vouchen saf, I trowe,

[16] or any other manner of skill necessary to the community, so by it you may benefit those who provide you with a living [17] weak [18] to last any time working as a labourer [19] a spendthrift who must spend, or a time-waster [20] or go about begging your living at men's doors [21] beg falsely [22] idler's [23] where [24] you are crippled, perhaps [25] ago [26] provided for me at school [27] for certain [28] and more secure for the soul, so long as I wish to continue in it [29] since [30] pleased me [31] earn a living [32] in the provinces [33] tools [34] say

To be welcome when I come otherwhile in a monthe,[35]
Now with him, now with her. On this wise[36] I begge,
Withoute bagge or botel but my wombe one.[37]

Piers Plowman (C Passus VI)

THE COVETOUS MAN

And thanne cam Coveitise. Can I him nought descrive,
So hungriliche and holwe sire Hervy him looked.[1]
He was bitelbrowed and baberlipped also,[2]
With two blered eyghen as a blinde hagge;
And as a letheren purs lolled his chekes,
Wel sidder than his chin they chiveled for elde;[3]
And as a bondman of his bacoun his berde was bidraveled;[4]
With an hoode on his hed, a lousy hatte above,
And in a tawny tabarde of twelve winter age,
Al totorne and baudy[5] and ful of lis creepinge;
But if that a lous couthe have lopen[6] the bettre,
She sholde noughte have walked on that welche,[7] so was it thredebare.

'I have ben coveitouse,' quod this caitive, 'I biknowe[8] it here;
For some time I served Simme-atte-stile,
And was his prentis yplighte his profit to waite.[9]
First I lerned to lie a leef other tweyne,[10]
Wikkedlich to weighe was my first lessoun.
To Wy and to Winchestre I went to the faire
With many manere marchandise as my maistre me highte;[11]
Ne had the grace of gile ygo amonge my ware,[12]
It had be unsolde this sevene yere, so me God helpe!

[35] when I come from time to time in the month [36] in this manner [37] except my belly alone

[1] he resembled Sir Harvey [traditional name for a rapacious cheat] [2] thick-lipped also [3] his cheeks sagged lower than his chin and trembled with age [4] his beard was matted with grease from his bacon [5] ragged and dirty [6] unless a louse could improve on its jumping [7] welsh flannel [8] acknowledge [9] his apprentice, contracted to look after his profit [10] first I learned a page or two about lying [11] ordered [12] if my merchandise had not been favoured by fraud

Thanne drowe I me amonges draperes my donet to lerne,[13]
To drawe the lyser alonge, the lenger it semed;[14]
Amonge the riche rayes I rendred a lessoun[15]
To broche hem with a pakneedle, and plaited hem togideres[16]
And put hem in a presse and pinned hem therinne
Til ten yerdes or twelve tolled out threttene.[17]
My wif was a webbe[18] and wollen cloth made;
She spak to spinnesteres to spinnen it oute.
Ac the pounde that she payed by poised a quarteroun more
Than mine owne auncere,[19] whoso weighed treuthe.
I boughte hir barly malte; she brewe it to selle,
Peny-ale and poding-ale she poured togideres[20]
For laboreres and for low folke; that lay by himselve.[21]
The best ale lay in my bowre or in my bedchambre,
And whoso bummed[22] therof boughte it therafter,
A galoun for a grote, God wote, no lesse;
And yet it cam in cupmel;[23] this crafte my wif used.
Rose the regratere[24] was hir righte name;
She hath holden hokkerie[25] al hire lif-time.
Ac I swere now, so the Ik,[26] that sinne wil I lete,[27]
And nevere wikkedliche weighe ne wikke chaffare[28] use,
But wenden to Walsingham, and my wif als,
And bidde the rode[29] of Bromeholme bringe me oute of dette.'
'Repentedestou thee evere,' quod Repentance, 'ne restitucioun madest?'
'Yes, ones I was herberwed,'[30] quod he, 'with an heep of chapmen;[31]
I roos whan they were arest and yrifled here males.'[32]
'That was no restitucioun,' quod Repentance, 'but a robberes thefte;

[13] to learn the basics [14] to pull out the selvage, so that it seemed longer [15] I recited a lesson about handling fine striped cloth [16] tacking them together with strong needle, and folding them [17] pinned them out in a press until ten or twelve yards extended to thirteen [18] weaver [19] but the pound weight she paid them by weighed a quarter more than my own balance [20] Thin ale and thick, she poured from the same source [21] it was kept apart [22] tasted [23] cupful [24] retailer [25] kept to retail-trading [26] so help me! [27] abandon [28] crooked dealing [29] pray the cross of Bromholm [30] lodged [31] company of merchants [32] packs

Thou haddest be better worthy be hanged therfore
Than for al that that thou hast here shewed.'
'I wende riflinge were restitucioun,' quod he, 'for I lerned nevere rede on booke,
And I can[33] no Frenche in feith but of the ferthest ende of Norfolke.'
'Usedestou evere usurie,' quod Repentaunce, 'in alle thi lif-time?'
'Nay, sothly,'[34] he seide, 'save in my youthe.
I lerned amonge Lumbardes and Jewes a lessoun,
To weigh pens with a peis and pare the heviest,[35]
And lene it for love of the crosse, to legge a wedde and lese it;[36]
Suche dedes I did write if he his day breke,
I have mo maneres thorgh rerages than thorgh *miseretur et comodat*.[37]
I have lent lordes and ladies my chaffare,[38]
And ben her brocour[39] after and boughte it myself.
Eschaunges and chevesances,[40] with suche chaffare I dele,
And lene folke that lese wol a lippe at every noble.[41]
And with Lumbardes lettres I ladde golde to Rome,
And tooke it by taille here and tolde hem there lasse.'[42]
'Lentestou evere lordes for love of her maintenaunce?'[43]
'Ye, I have lent lordes loved me nevere after,
And have ymade many a knighte, bothe mercere and drapere
That payed nevere for his prentishoode noughte a peire gloves.
'Hastou pite on poore men that more nedes borwe?'
'I have as moche pite of poore men as pedlere hath of cattes,
That wolde kille hem, if he cacche hem mighte, for coveitise of here skinnes.'
'Artou manliche[44] amonge thy neighbores of thi mete and drinke?'

[33] know [34] truly [35] to weigh coins with a weight and clip the heaviest [36] and lend it for love of the cross, so that the borrower should lay a pledge and lose it [37] . . . deeds I had written that if he does not repay on time, I have more manors through debts in arrears than through lending from pity [*Vulgate*, Psalm 111.5] [38] wares [39] broker [40] money-lending [41] and lend to people who are willing to lose a fraction at every coin they borrow [42] and collected it here as bills of exchange, and counted them up as less there [43] for desire of their support [44] charitable

'I am holden,' quod he, 'as hende as hounde[45] is in kichene,
Amonges my neighbores namelich,[46] such a name ich have.'

Piers Plowman (B Passus V)

THE GLUTTON

Now biginneth Glotoun for to go to shrifte,
And caires him[1] to kirke-ward his coupe[2] to shewe.
Fasting on a Friday forth gan he wende
By Betene hous the brewestere,[3] that bad him good morwen,
And whiderward he wolde[4] the brew-wif him askede.
'To holy churche,' quod he, 'for to here masse,
And sennes sitte and be shrive, and sinege no more.'[5]
'I have good ale, gossip.[6] Glotoun, wilt thou assaye?'[7]
'Hast thou', quod he, 'eny hote spices?'
'I have peper and pionie[8] and a pound of garlek,
A ferthing-worth fenkel-sedes,[9] for fasting-dayes I boughte it.'
Thenne goth Glotoun in, and grete othes after.
Sesse the souteress[10] sat on the benche,
Watte the wernere[11] and his wif dronke,[12]
Timme the tinkere and twaine of his knaves,
Hicke the hackenayman[13] and Hewe the nedlere,[14]
Clarice of Cockes Lane, and the clerc of the churche,
Sire Peres of Prydie and Purnele of Flaundres,
An hayward,[15] an heremite, the hangeman of Tybourne,
Dawe the dikere[16] with a doseine harlotes[17]
Of portours and of pike-purses and of pilede[18] tooth-draweres,
A ribibour and a ratoner, a rakere and his knave,[19]
A ropere and a redingkinge, and Rose the dishere,[20]
Godefray the garlek-monger and Griffith the Walshe,

[45] courteous as a dog [46] in particular

[1] goes [2] sin [3] past Betty the ale-wife's house [4] and where he was going to [5] and afterwards to sit and be absolved and sin no more [6] friend [7] try it [8] peony-seed [9] fennel [10] shoemaker [11] gamekeeper [12] were drinking [13] keeper of horses for hire [14] needle-maker [15] hedge-warden [16] ditcher [17] rascals [18] bald-headed [19] a fiddler, a ratcatcher, a street-cleaner and his boy [20] a ropemaker and a ? horse-soldier, and Rose the dish-seller

And of uphalderes an heep,[21] erly by the morwe
Geven Glotoun with glad chere good ale to hanselle.[22]
Clement the coblere cast off his cloke,
And to the newe faire nempnede forth to selle;[23]
Hicke the hackenayman hit his hood after,[24]
And bade Bitte the bochere[25] ben on his side.
There were chapmen ychose this chaffare to preise,[26]
That who so hadde the hood sholde not have the cloke,
And that the bettre thing, by arbitreres, bote sholde the worse.[27]
Tho risen up rape[28] and rouned[29] togideres,
And preisede this penyworthes apart by hem selve,
And there were othes an heep for on sholde have the worse.
They couthe not, by here consience, accorde for treuthe,
Til Robin the Ropere arise they bisoughte
And nempned him for an oumper, that no debat were.[30]
Hicke the hostiler hadde the cloke,
In covenaunt that Clement sholde the cuppe fille,[31]
And have Hickes hood the hostiler, and holde him yserved;[32]
And who so repentede him rathest[33] sholde arise after
And grete[34] Sire Glotoun with a galon of ale.
There was laughing and lowring[35] and 'Let go the cuppe!'
Bargaines and bevereges bigan tho to awake;
And seten so til evensong, and songen umbywhile,[36]
Til Glotoun hadde y-globbed[37] a galon and a gille.

Piers Plowman (C Passus VII)

[21] and a great number of second-hand dealers [22] cordially gave Glutton good ale as a token of fellowship [23] proffered [his cloak] to exchange in a game of Newmarket [24] tapped his hood [25] butcher [26] merchants were chosen to value these wares [27] so that whoever got the better thing, as judged by the arbiters, should compensate the worse [by buying the difference in value of drinks] [28] quickly [29] whispered [30] nominated him as umpire so that there should be no disagreement [31] on condition that Clement should fill the cup [at Hick's expense] [32] and have Hick the ostler's hood, and consider himself well satisfied [33] soonest [34] reward [35] frowning [36] sang from time to time [37] gulped down

William Langland (1331?–1400?)

ADVICE TO GENTLEFOLK

'This were a wikked way, but whoso hadde a gyde[1]
That wolde folwen us eche a fote,'[2] thus this folke hem mened.[3]
Quod Perkin the plouman: 'bi seint Peter of Rome,
I have an half acre to erie[4] by the heighe way;
Hadde I eried this half acre and sowen it after,
I wolde wende with you and the way teche.'
'This were a longe lettinge,'[5] quod a lady in a sklayre,[6]
'What sholde we wommen worke therewhiles?'[7]
'Somme shal sowe the sakke,' quod Piers, 'for shedyng of
the whete;[8]
And ye lovely ladies with youre longe fingres,
That ye han silke and sendal to sowe, whan time is,
Chesibles for chapelleines[9] cherches to honoure.
Wives and widwes wolle and flax spinneth,
Maketh cloth, I conseille you, and kenneth[10] so youre doughtres;
The nedy and the naked, nimmeth hede how hii liggeth,[11]
And casteth[12] hem clothes, for so comaundeth Treuthe.
For I shal lene hem liflode, but if the londe faille,[13]
Flesshe and bred bothe to riche and to pore,
As longe as I live, for the Lordes love of heven.
And alle manere of men, that thorgh mete and drinke libbeth,
Helpeth him to worke wightliche[14] that winneth youre fode.'
'Bi Crist,' quod a knighte tho,[15] 'he kenneth[10] us the best;
Ac[16] on the teme[17] trewly taughte was I nevere.
Ac[16] kenne me,' quod the knighte, 'and, bi Crist, I wil assaye!'[18]
'Bi seint Poule,' quod Perkin, 'ye profre you so faire[19]
That I shal swinke and swete[20] and sowe for us bothe,
And other laboures do for thi love al my lif-time,
In covenaunt[21] that thow kepe holykirke and myselve
Fro wastoures and fro wikked men that this worlde struyeth;[22]

[1] This would be a difficult route, unless we had a guide [2] accompany us every foot [3] complained [4] plough [5] delay [6] veil [7] do meanwhile [8] some ought to sew up the bag to prevent the wheat from spilling [9] may you have fine silk to sew . . . vestments for chaplains [10] instruct [11] take heed how . . . are situated [12] give [13] For I shall give them sustenance, unless the land is lacking [14] manfully [15] then [16] but [17] subject [18] try [19] you make so fair an offer [20] labour and sweat [21] on condition [22] harm

And go hunte hardyliche[23] to hares and to foxes,
To bores and to brockes[24] that breketh adown mine hegges;[25]
And go affaite the faucones,[26] wilde foules to kille:
For suche cometh to my croft[27] and croppeth my whete.'
Curteislich the knighte thanne comsed thise wordes:
'By my power, Pieres,' quod he, 'I plighte thee my treuthe
To fulfille this forward though I fighte sholde;[28]
Als longe as I live I shal thee maintene.'[29]
'Ye, and yit a poynt,' quod Pieres, 'I preye you of more:
Loke ye tene no tenaunt but Treuthe wil assent.[30]
And though ye mowe amercy hem, late mercy be taxoure[31]
And mekenesse thy maister, maugre Medes chekes;[32]
And though pore men profre you presentes and giftes,
Nim[33] it naughte, an aventure[34] ye mowe it naughte deserve:
For thou shalt yelde[35] it agein at one yeres ende
In a ful perillous place, purgatorie it hatte.[36]
And misbede[37] noughte thy bondemen, the better may thou spede;[38]
Though he be thin underlinge here, wel may happe[39] in hevene
That he worth[40] worthier sette and with more blisse
Than thou, bot thou do bette,[41] and live as thou shulde:
Amice, ascende superius.[42]
For in charnel atte chirche cherles ben ivel to knowe,[43]
Or a knighte fram a knave[44] there, knowe this in thin herte;
And that thou be trewe of thy tonge and tales that thou hatie,[45]
But if they ben of wisdome or of witte, thy werkmen to chaste.[46]
Holde with none harlotes[47] ne here noughte her tales,
And nameliche atte mete[48] suche men eschue:
For it ben the develes disoures, I do the to understande.'[49]

[23] vigorously [24] badgers [25] hedges [26] train falcons [27] patch [28] to fulfil the agreement even though I should have to fight for it [29] support [30] see that you harm no tenant except in accordance with Truth [31] tax them, let mercy be the assessor [32] in spite of the allure of dishonest gain [33] accept [34] in case [35] repay [36] is called [37] offend [38] prosper [39] chance [40] will be [41] amend [42] 'Friend, go up higher.' [43] difficult to distinguish [44] serving-man [45] be honest of speech . . . hate tales [46] unless they are . . . to improve your labourers [47] ne'er-do-wells [48] especially at meal-times [49] For I want to make you understand that they are the devil's minstrels

'I assente, by seint Jame,' seide the knighte thanne,
'Forto worke by thy wordes the while my lif dureth.'[50]
'And I shal apparaille me,' quod Perkin, 'in pilgrimes wise,[51]
And wende with you I wil til we finde Treuthe;
And cast on me my clothes, yclouted and hole,[52]
My cokeres and my coffes for colde of my nailles,[53]
And hange min hoper at min hals in stede of a scrippe;[54]
A busshel of bredcorne bringe me therinne,
For I wil sowe it myself and sitthenes wil I wende[55]
To pilgrimage as palmers don, pardoun forto have.
Ac who so helpeth me to erie[56] or sowen here er I wende,
Shal have leve, by oure Lorde, to lese here in hervest,[57]
And make hem mery theremidde . maugre whoso bigruccheth it.[58]
And alkin crafty men[59] that konne liven in treuthe,
I shal finden hem fode that feithfulliche libbeth,[60]
Save Jakke the jogeloure and Jonet of the stues,[61]
And Daniel the dis-playere[62] and Denote the baude,
And frere the faitoure[63] and foke of his ordre,
And Robin the ribaudoure[64] for his rusty wordes.
Treuthe tolde me ones and bad me tellen it after,
Deleantur de libro viventium;[65] I shulde noughte dele with hem,
For holycherche is hote of hem no tithe to take:[66]
Quia cum iustis non scribantur;[67]
They ben ascaped good aventure;[68] now God hem amende!'

Piers Plowman (B Passus VI)

[50] to act according to your advice as long as I live [51] in the style of a pilgrim [52] put on my clothes, patched and sound [53] my leggings and my mittens to protect my nails from the cold [54] hang my seed-basket at my neck instead of a pilgrim's bag [55] set off [56] plough [57] to glean here at harvest-time [58] and to enjoy it, despite whoever grumbles at it [59] all sorts of skilled men [60] who live honestly [61] except for Jack the clown, and Janet of the brothels [62] gambler [dice-player] [63] brother layabout [64] lecher [65] 'Let them be blotted out of the book of the living [66] is promised to receive no tithe from them [67] 'Because they may not be written with the righteous' [68] they have avoided it by good luck

PIERS PLOWMAN AND HUNGER

'Bihote God,'[1] quod Hunger, 'hennes ne wil I wende
Til I have dined by this day and ydrunke bothe.'
'I have no peny,' quod Peres 'poletes forto bigge,[2]
Ne neither gees ne gris,[3] but two greene cheeses,
A fewe cruddes and creem and an haver cake,[4]
And two loves of benes and bran ybake for my fauntes.[5]
And yet I sey, by my soule, I have no salt bacoun,
Ne no kokeney, by Crist, coloppes forto maken.[6]
Ac I have percil and porettes and many kole-plantes,[7]
And eke a cow and a kalf and a cart-mare
To drawe afelde my dunge the while the drought lasteth.
And by this liflode[8] we mot live til Lammasse time;
And by that I hope[9] to have hervest in my croft;
And thanne may I dighte thy diner as me dere liketh.'[10]
Alle the poore peple tho pesecoddes fetten,[11]
Benes and baken apples they broughte in her lappes,
Chibolles and chervelles[12] and ripe chiries manye,
And profred Peres this present to plese with Hunger.
Al Hunger eet in hast and axed after more.
Thanne poore folke for fere fedde Hunger yerne[13]
With greene poret and pesen;[14] to poisoun Hunger they thoughte.
By that it neighed nere hervest newe corne cam to chepinge;[15]
Thanne was folke faine[16] and fedde Hunger with the best,
With good ale, as Glotoun taughte, and gerte[17] Hunger go slepe.
And tho[18] wolde Wastour nought werke, but wandren aboute,
Ne no begger ete bred that benes inne were,
But of coket or clerematin, or elles of clene whete;[19]

[1] I swear to God [2] to buy pullets [3] pigs [4] only two unripe cheeses, a few curds and cream and an oatcake [5] children [6] nor any small eggs . . . to make ham and eggs [7] parsley and leeks and many green vegetables [8] sustenance [9] then I expect [10] then I shall be able to feed you as I should like to [11] then brought peas [12] stone-leeks and chervil [13] anxiously [14] leeks and peas [15] when it drew near harvest new corn came on to the market [16] happy [17] made [18] then [19] only fine white bread, or bread of pure wheat

Ne none halpeny ale in none wise drinke,
But of the best and of the brounest that in borghe is to selle.
  Laboreres that have no lande to live on but her handes,
Deined nought to dine aday night-olde wortes.[20]
May no peny-ale hem paye ne no pece of bacoun,
But if it be fresh flesh other fishe fried other bake,
And that *chaude* or *plus chaud*, for chilling of here mawe.[21]
  And but if he be heighlich huyred ellis wil he chide,[22]
And that he was werkman wrought waille the time;
Ageines Catones conseille comseth he to jangle:[23]
    Paupertatis onus pacienter ferre memento.[24]
  He greveth him ageines God and gruccheth[25] ageines Resoun,
And thanne curseth he the kinge and al his conseille after,
Suche lawes to looke laboreres to greve.[26]
Ac whiles Hunger was her maister there wolde none of hem chide,
Ne striue ageines his statut, so sterneliche he looked.[27]
  Ac I warne you, werkemen, winneth while ye mowe,[28]
For Hunger hiderward hasteth him faste.
He shal awake with water wastoures to chaste.
Ar five yere be fulfilled suche famin shal arise;
Thorugh floodes and thourgh foule wederes frutes shul faille.
And so saide Saturne, and sent you to warne;
Whan ye see the sonne amis and two monkes hedes,
And a maide have the maistrie and multiplied by eight,
Thanne shal Deth withdrawe and Derthe be justice
And Dawe the diker deie for hunger
But if God of his goodnesse graunt us a trewe.[29]

Piers Plowman (B Passus VI)

[20] would not endure to eat in the morning any vegetables from the day before [21] to avoid a chill on the stomach [22] unless he be highly paid, he will complain otherwise [23] begins to carp [24] 'Be sure to bear patiently the burden of poverty.' [25] grumbles [26] for providing such laws to distress working men [27] nor contest his [Hunger's] decree, he looked so fiercely [28] profit while you may [29] respite

William Langland (1331?–1400?)

THE POOR ARE OUR NEIGHBOURS

The most needy aren oure neighbores, and we nime good heede,[1]
As prisones in pittes,[2] and poure folke in cotes,[3]
Charged[4] with children and chef lordes[5] rente:
That[6] they with spinninge may spare,[7] spenen hit in hous-hire;[8]
Bothe in milk and in mele to make with papelotes,[9]
To aglotie with here gurles[10] that greden[11] after foode.
Also hemselve suffren muche hunger,
And wo in winter-time with wakinge[12] a nightes
To rise to the ruel[13] to rocke the cradel,
Bothe to carde and to cembe,[14] to clouten[15] and to washe,
To ribbe and to reli,[16] rushes to pilie,[17]
That reuthe[18] is to rede othere in rime shewe
The wo of these women that wonieth in cotes;[19]
And of meny other men that muche wo suffren,
Bothe afingrede and afurst to turne the faire outwarde,[20]
And beth abashed for to begge, and wolle nat be aknowe[21]
What hem needeth at[22] here neighbores at noon and at even.
This ich wot witerly, as the worlde techeth,[23]
What other bihoveth[24] that hath meny children,
And hath no catel bote his crafte[25] to clothy hem and to fede,
And fele to fonge therto, and fewe pans taketh.[26]
Ther is pain and peny-ale as for a pitaunce ytake,[27]
Colde flesh and cold fish for veneson ybake;[28]
Fridayes and fasting-dayes a ferthing-worth of muscles
Were a feste for suche folke, other so fele cockes.[29]

[1] if we take proper notice [2] such as prisoners in dungeons [3] hovels [4] burdened [5] landlord's [6] whatever [7] save [8] they spend on rent [9] porridge [10] to satisfy their children with [11] who cry out [12] keeping awake [13] space between the bed and the wall [14] comb (wool) [15] patch [16] to scrape [flax] and to reel [thread] [17] peel [18] pitiful [19] who live in shacks [20] assailed by both hunger and thirst, in order to keep up outward appearances [21] admit [22] need from [23] I know this without doubt, as experience teaches [24] what is required of the other man [25] has no assets but his skills [26] and many drawing from his income, and receives very little [27] there, bread and small beer seems a treat [28] like roast game [29] a farthing's worth of mussels, or as many cockles, would be a feast for such people

These were almes to helpe that han suche charges,[30]
And to comfortie suche cotiers[31] and crookede[32] men and blinde.
Ac beggers with bagges, the whiche brewhouses ben here
churches,[33]
Bote they be blinde other broke[34] other elles be sike,
Thaugh he falle for defaute that faiteth for his liflode,[35]
Reccheth nevere, ye riche, thaugh suche lorelles sterven.[36]
For alle that han here hele[37] and here eyen sighte,
And limes to laborie with, and lolleres lif usen,[38]
Liven agens Godes lawe and lore[39] of Holy Churche.
And yet arn ther other beggers, in hele, as hit semeth,
Ac hem wanteth here witt,[40] men and women bothe,
The whiche aren lunatik lollers and leperes aboute,[41]
And mad as the moone sitt more other lasse.
They caren for no cold ne counteth of no hete,
And arn mevinge after the moone; moneyles[42] they walke,
With a good wil, witlees, meny wide contreys,
Right as Peter dide and Paul, save that they preche nat,
Ne miracles maken; ac meny times hem happeth[43]
To prophecien of the puple, pleyinge, as hit were,[44]
And to oure sight, as hit semeth, sith[45] God hath the mighte
To yeven eche a wight wit, welthe, and his hele,[46]
And suffreth suche so gon, hit seemeth, to myn inwitt,[47]
Hit arn as his aposteles, suche puple, other as his privye
disciples.[48]
For he sente hem forth selverles in a somer garnement,[49]
Withoute bred and bagge, as the Book telleth:
Quando misi vos sine pane et pera.[50]
Barfoot and bredles beggeth they of no man.

[30] it would be a charity to help those that have such burdens [31] cottagers [32] crippled [33] whose churches are public houses [34] unless they are blind or disabled [35] though he should collapse from want, who begs his living under false pretences [36] think nothing of it, you rich men, even though such wasters die [37] health [38] and have limbs to work with, but stick to the life of a wastrel [39] teaching [40] who seem to be in physical health, but are lacking in their minds [41] crazed beggars and vagrants [42] penniless [43] they chance [44] as though in jest [45] since [46] to give every man . . . health [47] to my mind [48] or else like his favoured disciples [49] penniless, in summer clothing [50] 'When I sent you without purse and scrip' [Luke 22.35].

And thaugh he meete with the meire[51] amiddes the streete,
He reverenceth him right nought no rather than another:[52]
Neminem salutaveritis per viam.[53]
Suche manere of men, Mathew us techeth,
We sholde have hem to house and help hem when they come:
Et egenos vagosque induc in domum tuam.[54]
For hit aren merye-mouthede men, minstrales of hevene,
And Godes boyes, bordiours,[55] as the Book telleth:
Si quis videtur sapiens, fiet stultus ut sit sapiens.[56]
And alle manere minstrales, men wot wel the sothe,[57]
To underfonge hem faire be-falleth for the riche,[58]
For the lordes love and ladies that they with lengen.[59]
Men suffren al that suche seyn, and in solas taken,[60]
And yet more to suche men doth er they passe,
Given hem giftes and gold for grete lordes sake.
Right so, ye riche, rather ye sholde, for sothe,[61]
Welcomen and worshepen[62] and with youre goode helpen
Godes minstrales and his messagers and his merye bordiours;[63]
The whiche arn lunatik lolleres and leperes aboute,[64]
For under Godes secre seel here sinnes ben ykevered.[65]
For they bereth no bagges ne none botels under clokes,
The whiche is lolleren lif and lewede eremites,[66]
That looken ful loweliche to lachen mennes almesse,[67]
In hope to sitten at even by the hote coles,
Unlouke his legges abrod, other ligge[68] at his ese,
Reste him, and roste him, and his rig turne,[69]
Drinke drue and deepe,[70] and drawe him thanne to bedde;
And when him liketh and list,[71] his leve[72] is to arise;
When he is risen, rometh out and right wel aspieth[73]

[51] mayor [52] no sooner than anyone else [53] 'Salute no man by the way' [Luke 10.4]. [54] 'And bring the poor and cast-out into your house' [Isaiah 58.7]. [55] God's servants, jesters [56] 'If any man . . . seemeth to be wise . . . let him become a fool, that he may be wise' [I Cor. 3.18]. [57] as everyone knows [58] it falls to the rich to receive them courteously [59] out of esteem for the lords and ladies they serve [60] accept it good-humouredly [61] Just so, indeed, ought you rich people more readily [62] honour [63] jesters [64] crazed beggars and vagrants [65] concealed [66] which is the behaviour of wastrels and worthless hermits [67] who adopt an air of humility to get charity from people [68] lie [69] roast his back [70] drain the cup [71] when he pleases, and it suits him [72] pleasure [73] looks around

Whar he may rathest[74] have a repast other a rounde of bacon,
Sulver other sode mete,[75] and som time bothe,
A loof other half a loof, other a lumpe of cheese;
And carieth it hom to his cote and cast him to live[76]
In idelnesse and in ese and by others travaile.
And what frek of this folde fisketh thus aboute,[77]
With a bagge at his bak, a begeneldes wise,[78]
And can som manere craft, in cas he wolde hit use,[79]
Thorgh whiche craft he couthe[80] come to bred and to ale,
And overmore to an hater to helie with his bones,[81]
And liveth lik a lollere,[82] Godes lawe him dampneth.[83]
'Lolleres living in sleuthe and over-londe strikers[84]
Beeth nat in this bulle,'[85] quath Peers, 'til they ben amended,
Nother beggers that beggen, bote if they have neede.'
The Book blameth alle beggerie and banneth in this manere.[86]
Iunior fui, etenim senui, non vidi iustum
derelictum, nec semen eius querens panem;
et alibi: Infirmata est virtus mea in paupertate.[87]
Hit needeth naught nouthe anon for to preche,
And lere these lewede[88] men what this latin meneth,
For hit blameth alle beggerie be ye ful certein.
For they live in no love, ne no lawe they holden;
They wedde non womon that they with delen,
Bringe forth bastardes, beggers of kinde.[89]
Other the bak other[90] som bon they breken of here children,
And goth afaiting with here fauntes[91] for evere-more after.
Ther arn mo misshapen among suche beggers,
Than of meny other men that on this molde[92] walken.

[74] most readily [75] money or boiled meat [76] dispose himself to live [77] and whatever man on this earth roams about like that [78] like a beggar [79] and who knows some other sort of skill, supposing he wished to employ it [80] would know how to [81] and, moreover, to a garment to cover his body [82] ne'er-do-well [83] condemns [84] aimless wanderers [85] roll [86] and curses it thus [87] 'Youth is past, I have grown old; yet never did I see the good man forsaken, or his children begging their bread' [Ps. 36.25, Vulgate]; and elsewhere: 'My strength has waned in destitution' [Ps. 30.11, Vulgate]. [88] ignorant [89] by birth [90] either the back or [91] and go begging with their children under false pretences [92] earth

Tho that liven thus here lif, leive ye non othere,[93]
They han no part of pardon, of preyers, ne of penaunces.
Ac[94] olde men and hore, that helples beeth and needy,
And wommen with childe, that worke ne mowen,[95]
Blinde men and bedreden,[96] and broken in here membres,[97]
And alle poure pacientes, apayed of Godes sonde,[98]
As mesels and mendinauntes,[99] men yfalle in mischef,
As prisons[100] and pilgrimes, paraunter[101] men yrobbed,
Other bylowe thorgh luthere men, and lost here catel after,[102]
Other thorgh fire other thorgh flood falle to poverte,
That taken these meschiefes meekliche and mildliche at herte;
For love of here lowe hertes[103] oure Lord hath hem graunted
Here penaunce and here purgatorie upon this pure erthe,
And pardon with Peers Plouhman *a pena & a culpa.*
And alle holy hermites have shal the same;
Ac eremites that enhabiten by the heye weyes,[104]
And in borwes among brewesters,[105] and beggen in churches; –
Al that holy eremites hateden and despisede,
As richesses and reverences,[106] and riche mennes almesse,[107]
These lolleres, lacchedraweres, lewede eremites,[108]
Coveiten the contrarie, as cotiers they libben.[109]
For hit beth bote boyes, bollers atten ale,[110]
Neither of linage, ne of lettrure, ne lif-holy as eremites,[111]
That wonede whilom[112] in woodes with beres and liones.
Some had liflode of here linage[113] and of no lif elles;
And some livede by here lettrure and labour of here hondes;
Some hadde foreines to frendes[114] that hem foode sente;
And briddes[115] brouhten to some bred wherby they liveden.
Alle these holy eremites were of hye kinne,[116]
For-soke londe and lordship and likinges of the body.[117]

[93] don't imagine otherwise [94] but [95] may not [96] bedridden [97] limbs [98] and all poor sufferers content with what God sends them [99] such as lepers and beggars [100] such as prisoners [101] perhaps [102] or slandered by villainous men, and lost their belongings as a result [103] humble hearts [104] who lie by the main roads [105] in towns along with brewers [106] such as wealth and honours [107] charity [108] these wasters, door-to-door beggars, good-for-nothing hermits [109] they live as cottagers [110] for they are no more than ruffians, tipplers of ale [111] neither of good family, nor learning, nor devout [112] who once dwelt [113] some drew their livelihood from their family [114] strangers as friends [115] birds [116] of a noble race [117] delights of the flesh

Ac these eremites that edefien[118] thus by the hye weyes,
Whilom were workmen, webbes and taillours,[119]
And carters knaves, and clerkes withoute grace,
Helden ful hungry hous and hadde muche defaute,[120]
Long labour and lite winninge,[121] and atte laste aspiden,[122]
That faitours in frere clothinge[123] hadde fatte cheekes.
For-thi[124] lefte they here laboure, these lewede[125] knaves,
And clothed hem in copes, clerkes as hit were,[126]
Other on of som ordre, othere elles a prophete;
A-gens the lawe he liveth if latin be trewe:
Non licet vobis legem voluntati, sed voluntatem coniungere legi.[127]

Piers Plowman (C Passus X)

GEOFFREY CHAUCER

PILGRIMS TO CANTERBURY

Bifel that, in that seson on a day,
In Southwerk at the Tabard as I lay
Redy to wenden on my pilgrimage
To Caunterbury with ful devout corage,[1]
At night was come into that hostelrye
Wel nine and twenty in a companye,[2]
Of sondry folk, by aventure yfalle[3]
In felawshipe, and pilgrims were they alle,
That toward Caunterbury wolden ride;
The chambres and the stables weren wide,[4]
And wel we weren esed atte beste.[5]
And shortly, whan the sonne was to reste,

[118] build [119] weavers and tailors [120] maintained a very meagre household, and went without a great deal [121] slim gains [122] saw [123] confidence tricksters dressed as mendicant friars [124] therefore [125] ignorant [126] as though they were secular clerks [127] 'It is not lawful to reconcile the law to your will, rather your inclination to the law.'

[1] spirit [2] group [3] of various people, fallen by chance [4] spacious [5] made most comfortable

So hadde I spoken with hem everichon,[6]
That I was of hir felawshipe anon,
And made forward[7] erly for to rise,
To take our wey, ther as I yow devise.[8]
 But natheles, whil I have time and space,
Er that I ferther in this tale pace,
Me thinketh it acordaunt to resoun,[9]
To telle yow al the condicioun[10]
Of ech of hem, so as it semed me,
And whiche they weren, and of what degree;[11]
And eek in what array that they were inne:
And at a knight than wol I first biginne.
 A KNIGHT ther was, and that a worthy man,[12]
That fro the time that he first bigan
To riden out, he loved chivalrye,[13]
Trouthe and honour, fredom and curteisye.[14]
Ful worthy[15] was he in his lordes werre,
And therto hadde he riden, no man ferre,
As wel in Cristendom as hethenesse,
And ever honoured for his worthinesse.
 At Alisaundre he was, whan it was wonne;
Ful ofte time he hadde the bord bigonne[16]
Aboven alle naciouns in Pruce.
In Lettow hadde he reised[17] and in Ruce,
No Cristen man so ofte of his degree.
In Gernade at the sege eek hadde he be
Of Algezir, and riden in Belmarye.
At Lyeys was he, and at Satalye,
Whan they were wonne; and in the Grete See
At many a noble armee[18] hadde he be.
At mortal batailles hadde he been fiftene,
And foughten for our feith at Tramissene
In listes thries, and ay[19] slain his fo.
This ilke[20] worthy knight had been also

[6] every one [7] agreement [8] where I tell you [9] it seems to me proper [10] situation [11] station [12] distinguished man [13] the profession of arms [14] integrity, honour, magnanimity and consideration [15] valiant [16] sat at the head of the table [17] campaigned [18] expedition [19] always [20] same

Somtime[21] with the lord of Palatye,
Agein another hethen in Turkye:
And evermore he hadde a sovereyn pris.[22]
And though that he were worthy, he was wis,
And of his port[23] as meke as is a maide.
He never yet no vileinye ne saide[24]
In al his lif, unto no maner wight.[25]
He was a verray parfit gentil knight.[26]
But for to tellen yow of his array,
His hors were gode, but he was nat gay.
Of fustian he wered a gipoun[27]
Al bismotered with his habergeoun;[28]
For he was late ycome from his viage,[29]
And wente for to doon his pilgrimage.
With him ther was his sone, a yong SQUIER,
A lovyere, and a lusty bacheler,[30]
With lokkes crulle, as they were leyd in presse.[31]
Of twenty yeer of age he was, I gesse.
Of his stature he was of evene lengthe,[32]
And wonderly deliver,[33] and greet of strengthe.
And he had been somtime in chivachye,[34]
In Flaundres, in Artois, and Picardye,
And born him wel, as of so litel space,[35]
In hope to stonden in his lady grace.[36]
Embrouded[37] was he, as it were a mede[38]
Al ful of fresshe floures, white and rede.
Singinge he was, or floytinge,[39] al the day;
He was as fresh as is the month of May.
Short was his goune, with sleves longe and wide.
Wel coude he sitte on hors, and faire ride.

[21] formerly [22] and he had always been regarded with the greatest esteem [23] demeanour [24] spoke insultingly [25] to any kind of person [26] a truly accomplished noble knight [27] he wore a tunic of coarse cloth [28] stained with rust from his coat of mail [29] recently returned from his expedition [30] vigorous young knight [31] hair curled, as if it had been crimped [32] moderate height [33] spritely [34] in a cavalry campaign [35] and conducted himself creditably, considering the brevity [of the campaign] [36] hoping to be regarded favourably by his lady [37] embroidered [38] meadow [39] playing the flute

He coude songes make and wel endite,[40]
Juste[41] and eek daunce, and wel purtreye[42] and write.
So hote he lovede, that by nightertale[43]
He sleep namore than dooth a nightingale.
Curteis he was, lowly, and servisable,[44]
And carf biforn[45] his fader at the table.
  A YEMAN hadde he, and servaunts namo
At that time, for him liste[46] ride so;
And he was clad in cote and hood of grene;
A sheef of pecok-arwes brighte and kene
Under his belt he bar ful thriftily;[47]
(Wel coude he dresse his takel yemanly:[48]
His arwes drouped noght with fetheres lowe),[49]
And in his hand he bar a mighty bowe.
A not-heed[50] hadde he, with a broun visage.
Of wode-craft wel coude he al the usage.[51]
Upon his arm he bar a gay bracer,[52]
And by his side a swerd and a bokeler,[53]
And on that other side a gay daggere,
Harneised[54] wel, and sharp as point of spere;
A Cristofre[55] on his brest of silver shene.[56]
An horn he bar, the bawdrik[57] was of grene;
A forster was he, soothly,[58] as I gesse.
  Ther was also a Nonne, a PRIORESSE,
That of hir smiling was ful simple and coy;
Hir gretteste ooth was but by seint Loy;
And she was cleped[60] madame Eglentine.
Ful wel she song the service divine,
Entuned in hir nose fel semely;[61]
And Frensh she spak ful faire and fetisly,[62]
After the scole of Stratford atte Bowe,
For Frensh of Paris was to hir unknowe.

[40] write poetry [41] joust [42] draw [43] at night-time [44] unassuming and eager to please [45] carved in front of [46] it pleased him [47] prudently carried [48] he well knew how to arrange his gear as a yeoman ought [49] his arrows did not fall short because of poor feathering [50] close-cropped head [51] practice [52] arm-guard [53] round shield [54] mounted [55] medal of St Christopher [56] bright [57] strap [58] truly [59] demure [60] called [61] intoned . . . most becomingly [62] elegantly

At mete[63] wel ytaught was she withalle;
She leet no morsel from hir lippes falle,
Ne wette hir fingres in hir sauce depe.
Wel coude she carie a morsel, and wel kepe,[64]
That no drope ne fille upon hir brest.
In curteisye was set ful muche hir lest.[65]
Hir over lippe wiped she so clene,
That in her coppe was no ferthing[66] sene
Of grece, whan she dronken hadde hir draughte.
Ful semely after hir mete she raughte,[67]
And sikerly she was of greet disport,[68]
And ful plesaunt, and amiable of port,[69]
And peined hir to countrefete chere[70]
Of court, and been estatlich[71] of manere,
And to ben holden digne of reverence.[72]
But, for to speken of hir conscience,[73]
She was so charitable and so pitous,[74]
She wolde wepe, if that she sawe a mous
Caught in a trappe, if it were deed or bledde.
Of smale houndes had she, that she fedde
With rosted flesh, or milk and wastel-breed.[75]
But sore weep she if oon of hem were deed,
Or if men smoot it with a yerde smerte:[76]
And al was conscience and tendre herte.
Ful semely hir wimpel pinched[77] was,
Hir nose tretis;[78] hir eyen greye as glas;
Hir mouth ful smal, and therto softe and reed;
But sikerly[79] she hadde a fair forheed;
It was almost a spanne brood, I trowe;
For, hardily,[80] she was nat undergrowe.
Ful fetis[81] was hir cloke, as I was war.[82]
Of smal coral aboute hir arm she bar

[63] meal-times [64] take care [65] she took great delight in etiquette [66] spot [67] she reached for her food most carefully [68] certainly she was very entertaining [69] of friendly disposition [70] she strove to imitate the manners [71] dignified [72] considered worthy of respect [73] feelings [74] soft-hearted [75] fine, white bread [76] or if someone beat it soundly with a stick [77] pleated [78] well-proportioned [79] certainly [80] indeed [81] well-made [82] as I noticed

A peire of bedes, gauded al with grene;[83]
And theron heng a broche of gold ful shene,[84]
On which ther was first write a crowned A,
And after, *Amor vincit omnia.*
  Another NONNE with hir hadde she,
That was hir chapeleine, and PREESTES THREE.
  A MONK ther was, a fair for the maistrie,[85]
An out-ridere,[86] that lovede venerie;[87]
A manly man, to been an abbot able.[88]
Ful many a deintee[89] hors hadde he in stable:
And, whan he rood, men mighte his bridel here
Ginglen[90] in a whistling wind as clere,
And eek[91] as loude as dooth the chapel-belle
Ther as[92] this lord was keper[93] of the celle.
The reule of seint Maure or of seint Beneit,[94]
Bycause that it was old and somdel streit,[95]
This ilke monk leet olde thinges pace,[96]
And held after the newe world the space.[97]
He yaf nat of that text a pulled hen,[98]
That seith, that hunters been nat holy men;
Ne that a monk, whan he is cloisterlees,
Is likned[99] til a fish that is waterlees;
This is to seyn, a monk out of his cloistre.
But thilke[100] text held he nat worth an oystre;
And I seyde, his opinioun was good.
What[101] sholde he studie, and make himselven wood,[102]
Upon a book in cloistre alwey to poure,
Or swinken[103] with his handes, and laboure,
As Austin bit?[104] How shal the world be served?
Lat Austin have his swink to him reserved.[105]
Therfore he was a pricasour aright;[106]
Grehoundes he hadde, as swifte as fowel[107] in flight;

[83] with green beads at intervals [84] bright [85] an outstanding man [86] an inspector of the monastic estates [87] hunting [88] suitable [89] fine [90] jingling [91] also [92] where [93] supervisor [94] Saint Maur and Saint Benedict [95] rather strict [96] pass away [97] meanwhile [98] he didn't give a plucked hen for that text [99] is comparable [100] that same [101] why [102] mad [103] work [104] St Augustine bids [105] let St Augustine's labour be kept for him alone [106] a proper hard rider [107] bird

Of priking[108] and of hunting for the hare
Was al his lust,[109] for no cost wolde he spare.
I seigh his sleves purfiled[110] at the hond
With grys,[111] and that the fineste of a lond;
And, for to festne his hood under his chin,
He hadde of gold ywroght a curious pin:[112]
A love-knotte in the gretter ende ther was.
His heed was balled, that shoon as any glas,
And eek his face, as he had been anoint.
He was a lord ful fat and in good point;[113]
His eyen stepe,[114] and rollinge in his heed,
That stemed as a forneys of a leed;[115]
His bootes souple, his hors in greet estat.[116]
Now certeinly he was a fair prelat;
He was nat pale as a forpined goost.[117]
A fat swan loved he best of any roost.
His palfrey[118] was a broun as is a berye.
  A FRERE ther was, a wantown[119] and a merye,
A limitour,[120] a ful solempne[121] man.
In alle the ordres foure is noon that can
So muche of daliaunce[122] and fair langage.
He hadde maad ful many a mariage
Of yonge wommen, at his owne cost.
Un-to his ordre he was a noble post.[123]
Ful wel biloved and famulier[124] was he
With frankeleyns overal in his contree,[125]
And eek with worthy[126] wommen of the toun:
For he had power of confessioun,
As seide him-self, more than a curat,[127]
For of his ordre he was licentiat.[128]
Ful swetely herde he confessioun,
And plesaunt was his absolucioun;

[108] riding [109] pleasure [110] trimmed [111] grey fur [112] an elaborate pin, made of gold [113] condition [114] prominent [115] that gleamed like a furnace under a cauldron [116] in fine condition [117] tormented spirit [118] horse [119] mercurial [120] a friar who did pastoral work within fixed geographical limits [121] ceremonious [122] flirtation [123] pillar [124] intimate [125] throughout the area [126] substantial [127] parish priest [128] licensed to hear Confession

He was an esy[129] man to yeve[130] penaunce
Ther as he wiste to han a good pitaunce;[131]
For unto a povre ordre for to yive[132]
Is signe that a man is wel yshrive.[133]
For if he yaf, he dorste make avaunt,[134]
He wiste[135] that a man was repentaunt.
For many a man so hard is of his herte,
He may nat wepe althogh him sore smerte.
Therfore, in stede of weping and preyeres,
Men moot yeve[136] silver to the povre freres.[137]
His tipet[138] was ay farsed[139] ful of knives
And pinnes, for to yeven faire wives.[140]
And certeinly he hadde a mery note;
Wel coude he singe and pleyen on a rote.[141]
Of yeddinges he bar utterly the pris.[142]
His nekke whyt was as the flour-de-lis;[143]
Therto[144] he strong was as a champioun.[145]
He knew the tavernes wel in every toun,
And everich hostiler and tappestere[146]
Bet than a lazar or a beggestere;[147]
For unto swich a worthy man as he
Acorded nat, as by his facultee,[148]
To have with sike[149] lazars aqueintaunce.
It is nat honest, it may nat avaunce[150]
For to delen with no swich poraille,[151]
But al with riche and sellers of vitaille.[152]
And overal, ther as[153] profit sholde arise,
Curteys he was, and lowly of servise.[154]
Ther nas no man no-wher so vertuous.
He was the beste beggere in his hous;
For thogh a widwe[155] hadde noght a sho,[156]
So plesaunt was his '*In principio*,'

[129] accommodating [130] give [131] in cases where he expected to receive a good gift [132] giving to a poor order [133] absolved [134] for if he gave, he dared declare [135] knew [136] may give [137] poor friars [138] hood [139] stuffed [140] pretty women [141] fiddle [142] he carried off the prize for ballads completely [143] lily-flower [144] moreover [145] wrestler [146] every innkeeper and barmaid [147] better than a leper or a beggar [148] in view of his abilities [149] sick [150] no good will come of it [151] poor rabble [152] provisions [153] and specially wherever [154] humbly eager to please [155] widow [156] shoe

Yet wolde he have a ferthing, er he wente.
His purchas was wel bettre than his rente.[157]
And rage he coude, as it were right a whelpe.[158]
In love-dayes ther coude he muchel helpe.
For there he was nat lik a cloisterer,[159]
With a thredbar cope, as is a povre scoler,
But he was lik a maister or a pope.
Of double worsted was his semi-cope,
That rounded as a belle out of the presse.[160]
Somwhat he lipsed,[161] for his wantownesse,[162]
To make his English swete upon his tonge;
And in his harping, whan that he had songe,
His eyen twinkled in his heed aright,[163]
As doon the sterres in the frosty night.
This worthy limitour was cleped[164] Huberd.
A MARCHANT was ther with a forked berd,
In mottelee,[165] and hye on horse he sat,
Upon his heed a Flaundrish[166] bever hat;
His bootes clasped faire and fetisly.[167]
His resons[168] he spak ful solempnely,[169]
Souninge[170] alway th'encrees of his winning.[171]
He wolde the see were kept for any thing[172]
Bitwixe Middelburgh and Orewelle.[173]
Wel coude he in eschaunge sheeldes[174] selle.
This worthy man ful wel his wit bisette;[175]
Ther wiste no wight[176] that he was in dette,
So estatly[177] was he of his governaunce,[178]
With his bargaynes,[179] and with his chevisaunce.[180]
For sothe he was a worthy man withalle,
But sooth to seyn, I noot how men him calle.[181]

[157] his perks exceeded his authorized income [158] he knew how to frolic just like a puppy [159] cloistered monk [160] mould [161] lisped [162] affectation [163] indeed [164] called [165] parti-coloured cloth [166] Flemish [167] elegantly [168] phrases [169] pompously [170] proclaiming [171] profit [172] he wished above all that the sea be kept safe [173] Middelburg, Holland, and Orwell, Suffolk [174] French currency [175] employed his ingenuity [176] no one knew [177] impressive [178] conduct [179] bargaining [180] loans [181] I do not know what he was called

A CLERK ther was of Oxenford also,
That unto logik hadde longe ygo.
As lene was his hors as is a rake,
And he nas nat right fat, I undertake;
But loked holwe, and therto soberly.
Ful thredbar was his overest courtepy;[182]
For he had geten him yet no benefice,[183]
Ne was so worldly for to have office.[184]
For him was lever[185] have at his beddes heed
Twenty bokes, clad in blak or reed,
Of Aristotle and his philosophye,
Than robes riche, or fithele, or gay sautrye.[186]
But al be[187] that he was a philosophre,
Yet hadde he but litel gold in cofre;[188]
But al that he mighte of his freendes hente,[189]
On bokes and on lerninge he it spente,
And bisily gan for the soules preye
Of hem that yaf[190] him wher-with to scoleye.[191]
Of studie took he most cure[192] and most heede.
Noght o word spak he more than was neede,
And that was said in forme and reverence,[193]
And short, and quik,[194] and ful of hy sentence.[195]
Souninge in[196] moral vertu was his speche,
And gladly wolde he lerne, and gladly teche.
A SERGEANT OF THE LAWE, war and wis,[197]
That often hadde been at the parvis,[198]
Ther was also, ful riche of excellence.
Discreet he was, and of greet reverence:[199]
He semed swich, his wordes weren so wise.
Justice he was ful often in assise,
By patente, and by pleyn commissioun;[200]
For his science,[201] and for his heigh renoun

[182] outermost jacket [183] living [184] an administrative post [185] was more pleasing to him [186] fiddle or . . . psaltery [187] although [188] coffer [189] get [190] gave [191] study [192] care [193] correctly and properly formulated [194] pungently [195] significance [196] tending towards [197] shrewd and prudent [198] area in front of a church where lawyers and clients met [199] well-respected [200] by letters-patent [from the king] and by full authority [201] knowledge

Of fees and robes hadde he many oon.
So greet a purchasour[202] was nowher noon.
Al was fee simple[203] to him in effect,
His purchasing mighte nat been infect.[204]
Nowher so bisy a man as he ther nas,[205]
And yet he semed bisier than he was.
In termes hadde he caas and domes alle,[206]
That from the time of king William were falle.[207]
Therto he coude endite,[208] and make a thing,[209]
Ther coude no wight pinche at[210] his writing;
And every statut coude he pleyn[211] by rote.
He rood but hoomly[212] in a medlee[213] cote
Girt with a ceint[214] of silk, with barres[215] smale;
Of his array telle I no lenger tale.
  A FRANKELEYN was in his companye;
Whit was his berd, as is the daiesye.
Of his complexioun he was sangwin.[216]
Wel loved he by the morwe a sop in win.[217]
To liven in delit was ever his wone,[218]
For he was Epicurus owne sone,
That heeld opinioun, that pleyn delit[219]
Was verraily felicitee parfit.[220]
An housholdere, and that a greet, was he;
Seint Julian[221] he was in his contree.
His breed, his ale, was alwey after oon;[222]
A bettre envined man was nowher noon.[223]
Withoute bake mete was never his hous,
Of fish and flesh, and that so plentevous,[224]
It snewed[225] in his hous of mete[226] and drinke,
Of alle deyntees that men coude thinke.

[202] property speculator [203] land owned outright [204] invalidated [205] was not [206] he knew to the letter all the cases and judgements [207] had occurred [208] compose [209] deed [210] find fault with [211] complete [212] unostentatiously [213] parti-coloured [214] belt [215] stripes [216] ruddy [217] in the morning, a piece of toast soaked in wine [218] his custom was to enjoy the pleasures of life [219] complete indulgence [220] truly complete happiness [221] patron saint of hospitality [222] of unvarying quality [223] no man anywhere kept a better cellar [224] copious [225] snowed [226] food

After[227] the sondry sesons of the yeer,
So chaunged he his mete and his soper.
Ful many a fat partrich hadde he in mewe,[228]
And many a breem and many a luce in stewe.[229]
Wo was his cook, but-if[230] his sauce were
Poynaunt[231] and sharp, and redy al his gere.
His table dormant[232] in his halle alway
Stood redy covered al the longe day.
At sessiouns ther was he lord and sire;[233]
Ful ofte time he was knight of the shire.[234]
An anlas and a gipser[235] al of silk
Heng at his girdel, whit as morne milk.
A shirreve hadde he been, and a countour;[236]
Was nowher such a worthy vavasour.[237]
  An HABERDASSHER and a CARPENTER,
A WEBBE,[238] a DYERE, and a TAPICER,[239]
Were with us eek, clothed in o liveree,[240]
Of a solempne and greet fraternitee.[241]
Ful fresh and newe hir gere apyked[242] was;
Hir knyves were ychaped[243] noght with bras,
But al with silver, wroght ful clene and weel,
Hir girdles and hir pouches every-deel.[244]
Wel semed ech of hem a fair burgeis,[245]
To sitten in a yeldhalle[246] on a deis.
Everich,[247] for the wisdom that he can,
Was shaply[248] for to been an alderman.
For catel[249] hadde they ynogh and rente,[250]
And eek hir wives wolde it wel assente;
And elles[251] certein were they to blame.
It is ful fair to been yclept[252] '*ma dame*,'

[227] according to [228] coop [229] pike in his fishpond [230] woe betide his cook unless [231] piquant [232] the long, permanent table [233] he presided at the quarterly sessions [234] member of parliament for the county [235] a dagger and a purse [236] a sheriff... and an auditor [237] member of the landed gentry [238] weaver [239] tapestry-maker [240] uniform [241] an important and dignified guild [242] adorned [243] mounted [244] in every part [245] burgher [246] guildhall [247] each one [248] well-fitted [249] capital [250] income [251] otherwise [252] called

And goon to vigilies[253] al bifore,
And have a mantel royalliche ybore.[254]
A COOK they hadde with hem for the nones,[255]
To boille the chiknes with the marybones,[256]
And poudre-marchant tart, and galingale.[257]
Wel coude he knowe[258] a draughte of London ale.
He coude roste, and sethe,[259] and broille, and frie,
Maken mortreux,[260] and wel bake a pie.
But greet harm was it, as it thoughte me,[261]
That on his shine a mormal hadde he;[262]
For blankmanger,[263] that made he with the beste.
A SHIPMAN was ther, woning fer by weste:[264]
For aught I woot,[265] he was of Dertemouthe.
He rood upon a rouncy, as he couthe,[266]
In a gowne of falding[267] to the knee.
A daggere hanging on a laas[268] hadde he
Aboute his nekke under his arm adoun.
The hote somer had maad his hewe[269] al broun;
And, certeinly, he was a good felawe.[270]
Ful many a draughte of win had he ydrawe
From Burdeux-ward, whil that the chapman sleep.[271]
Of nice[272] conscience took he no keep.[273]
If that he faught, and hadde the hyer[274] hond,
By water he sente hem hoom to every lond.
But of his craft[275] to rekene wel his tides,
His stremes[276] and his daungers him bisides,[277]
His herberwe and his mone, his lodemenage,[278]
Ther nas noon swich from Hulle to Cartage.[279]
Hardy he was, and wis to undertake;[280]
With many a tempest hadde his berd been shake.

[253] vigils [on the eves of church festivals] [254] borne [255] at that time [256] marrow-bones [257] mixed spices, sharp and sweet [258] knew how to recognize [259] boil [260] broth [261] it seemed to me [262] he had an ulcer on his shin [263] diced chicken in white sauce [264] living in the west [265] know [266] he rode, as best he could, upon a cob [267] coarse wool [268] strap [269] colour [270] companion [271] merchant slept [272] fastidious [273] account [274] upper [275] skill [276] currents [277] around him [278] his harbour, the phases of the moon, or his navigation [279] Cartagena [280] he was bold and shrewd in his enterprises

He knew wel alle the havenes,[281] as they were,
From Gootlond[282] to the cape of Finistere,
And every crike in Britaine[283] and in Spaine;
His barge ycleped was the Maudelaine.
With us ther was a DOCTOUR OF PHISIK,[284]
In al this world ne was ther noon him lik
To speke of phisik and of surgerye;
For he was grounded in astronomye.[285]
He kepte[286] his pacient a ful greet del
In houres,[287] by his magik naturel.
Wel coude he fortunen the ascendent
Of his images for his pacient.[288]
He knew the cause of everich maladye,
Were it of hoot or cold, or moiste, or drye,
And where engendred, and of what humour;[289]
He was a verrey parfit practisour.[290]
The cause yknowe,[291] and of his harm the roote,
Anon he yaf the seke man his boote.[292]
Ful redy hadde he his apothecaries,
To sende him drogges and his letuaries,[293]
For ech of hem made other for to winne;[294]
Hir frendschipe nas nat newe to biginne.
Wel knew he th'olde Esculapius,
And Deiscorides, and eek Rufus,
Old Ypocras,[295] Haly, and Galien;[296]
Serapion, Razis,[297] and Avicen;[298]
Averrois, Damascien,[299] and Constantyn;
Bernard, and Gatesden, and Gilbertyn.[300]
Of his diete mesurable[301] was he,
For it was of no superfluitee,

[281] harbours [282] Gotland [in Sweden] [283] inlet in Brittany [284] medicine [285] astrology [286] treated [287] the appropriate astrological hours [288] He knew well how to divine the most favourable position of the stars for the talismans which he made for his patient [289] and where it originated and from what humour [290] he was a thoroughly accomplished practitioner [291] known [292] remedy [293] medicinal preparations [294] profit [295] Hippocrates [296] Galen [297] Rhazes [298] Avicenna [299] John of Damascus [300] Bernard Gordon, John of Gaddesden, and Gilbertus Anglicus [all medical authorities] [301] moderate

But of greet norissing[302] and digestible.
His studie was but litel on the bible.
In sangwin and in pers[303] he clad was al,
Lined with taffata and with sendal;[304]
And yet he was but esy of dispence;[305]
He kepte that he wan in pestilence.
For gold in phisik is a cordial,
Therfore he lovede gold in special.
A good WIF was ther of biside BATHE,[306]
But she was somdel deef, and that was scathe.[307]
Of clooth-making she hadde swiche an haunt,[308]
She passed hem[309] of Ypres and of Gaunt.[310]
In al the parisshe wif[311] ne was ther noon
That to th' offring bifore hir sholde goon;[312]
And if ther dide, certein, so wrooth was she,
That she was out of alle charitee.
Hir coverchiefs[313] ful fine were of ground;[314]
I dorste[315] swere they weyeden ten pound
That on a Sonday were upon hir heed.
Hir hosen weren of fin scarlet reed,
Ful streite yteyd,[316] and shoos ful moiste[317] and newe.
Bold was hir face, and fair, and reed of hewe.
She was a worthy womman al hir live,
Housbondes at chirche-dore she hadde five,
Withouten other companye in youthe;
But therof nedeth nat to speke as nouthe.[318]
And thries hadde she been at Jerusalem;
She hadde passed many a straunge streem;[319]
At Rome she hadde been, and at Boloigne,
In Galice at seint Jame,[320] and at Coloigne.
She coude[321] muche of wandring by the weye:
Gat-toothed[322] was she, soothly for to seye.

[302] nourishment [303] in red and Persian blue [304] silk [305] temperate in expenditure [306] There was a woman of some standing from just outside Bath [307] she was somewhat deaf and that was a pity [308] such experience and skill [309] she surpassed those [310] Ghent [311] woman [312] who should make her offering before her in church [313] head-draperies [314] in texture [315] dare [316] tightly laced [317] soft [318] just now [319] foreign river [320] at St James of Compostela in Galicia [321] knew [322] gap-toothed

Upon an amblere esily she sat,[323]
Ywimpled wel, and on hir heed an hat
As brood as is a bokeler or a targe;[324]
A foot-mantel[325] aboute hir hipes large,
And on hir feet a paire of spores[326] sharpe.
In felawschip wel coude she laughe and carpe.[327]
Of[328] remedyes of love she knew perchaunce,
For she coude of that art the olde daunce.
   A good man was ther of religioun,
And was a povre PERSOUN[329] of a toun;
But riche he was of holy thoght and werk.[330]
He was also a lerned man, a clerk,
That Cristes gospel trewely wolde preche;
His parishens devoutly wolde he teche.
Benigne he was, and wonder[331] diligent,
And in adversitee ful pacient;
And swich[332] he was ypreved ofte sithes.[333]
Ful looth were him to cursen for his tithes,[334]
But rather wolde he yeven,[335] out of doute,
Unto his povre parishens[336] aboute
Of his offring,[337] and eek of his substaunce.[338]
He coude in litel thing han suffisaunce.[339]
Wid was his parishe, and houses fer asonder,
But he ne lafte[340] nat, for reyn ne thonder,
In siknes nor in meschief, to visite
The ferreste[341] in his parishe, muche and lite,[342]
Upon his feet, and in his hand a staf.
This noble ensample[343] to his sheep he yaf,[344]
That first he wroghte,[345] and afterward he taughte;
Out of the gospel he tho wordes caughte;[346]
And this figure he added eek therto,
That if gold ruste, what shal iren do?

[323] she sat comfortably on a gentle horse [324] round shield [325] riding-skirt [326] spurs [327] talk [328] about [329] poor parson [330] deed [331] marvellously [332] such [333] proved many times [334] he was unwilling to excommunicate anyone to gain his tithes [335] give [336] poor parishioners [337] from what he received in offerings [338] own property [339] he knew how to be satisfied with little [340] neglect [341] farthest [342] great and small [343] example [344] gave [345] acted [346] took those words

For if a preest be foul, on whom we truste,
No wonder is a lewed[347] man to ruste;
And shame it is, if a preest take keep,[348]
A shiten[349] shepherde and a clene sheep.
Wel oghte a preest ensample for to yive,
By his clennesse, how that his sheep shold live.
He sette nat his benefice to hire,[350]
And leet[351] his sheep encombred in the mire,
And ran to London, unto seint Poules,
To seeken him a chaunterie for soules,[352]
Or with a bretherhed to been withholde;[353]
But dwelte at hoom, and kepte wel his folde,
So that the wolf ne made it nat miscarie;[354]
He was a shepherde and no mercenarie.
And though he holy were, and vertuous,
He was to sinful man nat despitous,[355]
Ne of his speche daungerous ne digne,[356]
But in his teching discreet and benigne.
To drawen folk to heven by fairnesse
By good ensample, was his bisinesse:
But it were[357] any persone obstinat,
What-so he were, of heigh or lowe estat,
Him wolde he snibben[358] sharply for the nones.[359]
A bettre preest, I trowe that nowher noon is.
He waited[360] after no pompe and reverence,[361]
Ne maked him a spiced conscience,[362]
But Cristes lore,[363] and his apostles twelve,
He taughte, and first he folwed it himselve.
With him ther was a PLOWMAN, was his brother,
That hadde ylad of dong ful many a fother,[364]
A trewe swinker[365] and a good was he,
Livinge in pees and parfit charitee.

[347] simple [348] heed [349] filthy [350] he did not rent out his living to another [351] left [352] an endowment for singing masses for the souls of dead benefactors [353] or to be maintained by a guild [354] come to harm [355] contemptuous [356] disdainful [357] but should there be [358] rebuke [359] then [360] looked for [361] ceremony and deference [362] harboured pretensions of an oversensitive conscience [363] teaching [364] carried many a load of manure [365] worker

God loved he best with al his hole[366] herte
At alle times, thogh him gamed or smerte,[367]
And thanne his neighebour right as himselve.
He wolde thresshe, and therto dyke[368] and delve,
For Cristes sake, for every povre wight,[369]
Withouten hire,[370] if it lay in his might.
His tithes payed he ful faire and wel,
Bothe of his propre swink and his catel.[371]
In a tabard[372] he rood upon a mere.[373]
  Ther was also a Reve and a Millere,
A Somnour and a Pardoner also,
A Maunciple,[374] and my-self; ther were namo.[375]
  The MILLER was a stout carl,[376] for the nones,[377]
Ful big he was of braun,[378] and eek of bones;
That proved wel,[379] for over-al ther[380] he cam,
At wrastling he wolde have alwey the ram.[381]
He was short-sholdred, brood, a thikke knarre,[382]
Ther nas no doore that he nolde heve of harre,[383]
Or breke it, at a renning,[384] with his heed.
His berd as any sowe or fox was reed,
And therto brood, as though it were a spade.
Upon the cop[385] right of his nose he hade
A werte, and theron stood a tuft of heres,
Reed as the bristles of a sowes eres;
His nose-thirles[386] blake were and wide.
A swerd and bokeler bar[387] he by his side;
His mouth as greet was as a greet forneys.[388]
He was a janglere and a goliardeys,[389]
And that was most of sinne and harlotryes.[390]
Wel coude he stelen corn, and tollen thryes;[391]
And yet he hadde a thombe of gold, pardee.[392]
A whit cote and a blew hood wered he.

[366] whole [367] whether he was happy or suffered by it [368] dig ditches [369] poor fellow [370] wages [371] on his own work and on his possessions [372] smock [373] mare [374] steward [375] no more [376] fellow [377] indeed [378] muscle [379] that was evident [380] wherever [381] ram [the prize in the wrestling-match] [382] stocky, broad, a tough nut [383] lift off its hinges [384] by running at it [385] tip [386] nostrils [387] bore [388] oven [389] bletherer and a joker [390] obscenities [391] charge three times over [392] and, by heaven, for a miller he was honest

A baggepipe wel coude he blowe and sowne,[393]
And ther-with-al he broghte us out of towne.
  A gentil MAUNCIPLE was ther of a temple,[394]
Of which achatours[395] mighte take exemple
For to be wise[396] in bying of vitaille[397]
For whether that he paide, or took by taille,[398]
Algate[399] he waited[400] so in his achat,[401]
That he was ay biforn and in good stat.[402]
Now is nat that of God a ful fair grace,
That swich a lewed[403] mannes wit shal pace[404]
The wisdom of an heep[405] of lerned men?
Of maistres[406] hadde he mo than thryes ten,
That were of lawe expert and curious;[407]
Of which ther were a doscin[408] in that hous
Worthy to been stiwardes of rente[409] and lond
Of any lord that is in Engelond,
To make him live by his propre good,[410]
In honour dettelees, but he were wood,[411]
Or live as scarsly[412] as him list desire;[413]
And able for to helpen al a shire
In any cas[414] that mighte falle or happe;
And yit this maunciple sette hir aller cappe.[415]
  The REVE was a sclendre colerik man,[416]
His berd was shave as ny[417] as ever he can.
His heer[418] was by his eres round y-shorn.
His top was dokked[419] lik a preest biforn.[420]
Ful longe were his legges, and ful lene,
Y-lik[421] a staf, ther was no calf y-sene.[422]
Wel coude he kepe a gerner[423] and a binne;
Ther was noon auditour coude on him winne.[424]

[393] sound [394] steward . . . of one of the Inns of Court [395] buyers [396] prudent [397] provisions [398] on credit [399] always [400] took account [401] buying [402] always ahead and in a good position [403] uneducated [404] surpass [405] crowd [406] masters [407] subtle [408] dozen [409] income [410] according to his own means [411] unless he were madly extravagant [412] frugally [413] as he would wish to [414] circumstance [415] made them all look foolish [416] lean man in whom the choleric humour was dominant [417] close [418] hair [419] cropped [420] in front [421] like [422] visible [423] take care of a granary [424] get the better of

Wel wiste[425] he, by the droghte, and by the rein,
The yelding of his seed, and of his grein.
His lordes sheep, his neet,[426] his daierye,
His swin, his hors, his stoor,[427] and his pultrye,
Was hoolly[428] in this reves governing,
And by his covenaunt yaf the rekening,[429]
Sin that[430] his lord was twenty yeer of age;
Ther coude no man bringe him in arrerage.[431]
Ther nas baillif, ne herde, ne other hyne,[432]
That he ne knew his sleighte and his covyne;[433]
They were adrad[434] of him, as of the deeth.
His woning[435] was ful fair upon an heeth,
With grene trees shadwed was his place.
He coude bettre than his lord purchace.[436]
Ful riche he was astored prively,[437]
His lord wel coude he plesen subtilly,
To yeve and lene him of his owne good,[438]
And have a thank,[439] and yet a cote and hood.
In youthe he lerned hadde a good mister;[440]
He was a wel good wrighte,[441] a carpenter.
This reve sat upon a ful good stot,[442]
That was al pomely grey, and highte Scot.[443]
A long surcote of pers[444] upon he hade,
And by his side he bar[445] a rusty blade.
Of Northfolk was this reve, of which I telle,
Biside a toun men clepen Baldeswelle.[446]
Tukked he was, as is a frere, aboute,
And ever he rood the hindreste of our route.[447]
A SOMNOUR was ther with us in that place,
That hadde a fir-reed cherubinnes face,
For sawcefleem[448] he was, with eyen narwe.
As hoot he was, and lecherous, as a sparwe;

[425] knew [426] oxen [427] cattle [428] entirely [429] and according to his covenant, he gave his account [430] since [431] no one could find him in arrears [432] nor shepherd, nor other labourer [433] cunning and deceit [434] afraid [435] dwelling [436] acquire property [437] stocked secretly [438] giving and lending to him from his own property [439] gratitude [440] trade [441] craftsman [442] horse [443] dapple-grey and called Scot [444] overcoat of Persian blue [445] bore [446] that is called Bawdswell [447] the last in our party [448] pimply

With scalled[449] browes blake, and piled[450] berd;
Of his visage children were aferd.[451]
Ther nas quik-silver, litarge, ne brimstoon,
Boras, ceruce, ne oille of tartre noon,[452]
Ne oinement that wolde clense and bite,
That him mighte helpen of his whelkes[453] white,
Nor of the knobbes sittinge on his cheekes.
Wel loved he garleek, oinons, and eek leekes,
And for to drinken strong win, reed as blood.
Than wolde he speke, and crye as he were wood.[454]
And whan that he wel dronken hadde the win,
Than wolde he speke no word but Latin.
A fewe termes hadde he, two or three,
That he had lerned out of som decree;
No wonder is, he herde it al the day;
And eek ye knowen wel, how that a jay
Can clepen[455] 'Watte,' as well as can the pope.
But whoso coude in other thing him grope,[456]
Thanne hadde he spent al his philosophye;[457]
Ay '*Questio quid iuris*'[458] wolde he crye.
He was a gentil harlot[459] and a kinde;
A bettre felawe[460] sholde men noght finde.
He wolde suffre,[461] for a quart of win,
A good felawe to have his concubin
A twelf-month, and excuse him atte fulle:[462]
Ful prively a finch eek coude he pulle.[463]
And if he fond owher a good felawe,
He wolde techen him to have no awe,[464]
In swich cas,[465] of the erchedeknes curs,[466]
But-if[467] a mannes soule were in his purs;
For in his purs he sholde ypunisshed be.
'Purs is the erchedeknes helle,' seide he.

[449] scabby [450] patchy [451] afraid [452] there was no mercury, lead peroxide, sulphur, borax, white lead ointment nor any oil of tartar [453] pimples [454] mad [455] say [456] probe [457] exhausted all his learning [458] always 'I ask, what is the law' [459] scoundrel [460] companion [461] allow [462] entirely [463] he also knew how to pluck a goldfinch on the quiet [i.e., have sexual intercourse with a woman] [464] fear [465] in similar circumstances [466] of excommunication by the archdeacon [467] unless

But wel I woot he lied right in dede;
Of cursing[468] oghte ech gilty man him drede –
For curs wol slee,[469] right as assoilling[470] saveth –
And also war him of a *significavit*.[471]
In daunger hadde he at his owne gyse[472]
The yonge girles[473] of the diocyse,
And knew hir counseil,[474] and was al hir reed.[475]
A gerland hadde he set upon his heed,
As greet as it were for an ale-stake;[476]
A bokeler hadde he maad him of a cake.[477]
With him ther rood a gentil PARDONER
Of Rouncival, his freend and his compeer,[478]
That streight was comen fro the court of Rome.[479]
Ful loude he song, 'Com hider, love, to me.'
This somnour bar to him a stif burdoun,[480]
Was never trompe[481] of half so greet a soun.
This pardoner hadde heer as yelow as wex,
But smoothe it heng, as dooth a strike of flex;[482]
By ounces[483] henge his lokkes that he hadde,
And therwith he his shuldres over-spradde:[484]
But thinne it lay, by colpons oon and oon;[485]
But hood, for jolitee, ne wered he noon,
For it was trussed up in his walet.[486]
Him thoughte, he rood al of the newe jet;[487]
Dischevele,[488] save his cappe, he rood al bare.
Swiche glaringe[489] eyen hadde he as an hare.
A vernicle[490] hadde he sowed on his cappe.
His walet lay biforn him in his lappe,
Bret-ful[491] of pardoun come from Rome al hoot.[492]
A vois he hadde as smal as hath a goot.[493]
No berd hadde he, he never sholde have,
As smoothe it was as it were late yshave;

[468] excommunication [469] slay [470] absolution [471] and also beware of a writ for imprisonment [472] under his dominion, at his own will, he had [473] people [474] secrets [475] adviser [476] inn-sign [477] loaf of bread [478] comrade [479] the Papal Court [480] forceful accompaniment [481] trumpet [482] hank of flax [483] thin strands [484] spread over [485] in strips, one by one [486] pack [487] fashion [488] with hair hanging loose [489] staring [490] a relic of St Veronica [491] cram-full [492] hot [493] goat

I trowe he were a gelding or a mare.
But of his craft, fro Berwik into Ware,
Ne was ther swich another pardoner.
For in his male he hadde a pilwe-beer,[494]
Which that, he seide, was our lady veil:
He seide, he hadde a gobet of the seil
That seint Peter hadde, whan that he wente
Upon the see, til Jesu Crist him hente.[495]
He hadde a croys of latoun,[496] ful of stones,
And in a glas he hadde pigges bones.
But with thise relikes, whan that he fond[497]
A povre person dwelling upon lond,[498]
Upon a day he gat[499] him more moneye
Than that the person gat in monthes tweye.
And thus, with feyned flaterye and japes,[500]
He made the person and the peple his apes.[501]
But trewely to tellen, atte laste,
He was in chirche a noble ecclesiaste.
Wel coude he rede a lessoun or a storie,[502]
But alderbest[503] he song an offertorie;
For wel he wiste,[504] whan that song was songe,
He moste preche, and wel affile[505] his tonge,
To winne silver, as he ful wel coude;
Therefore he song so meriely and loude.

from the Prologue to *The Canterbury Tales*

THE WOOING OF THE CARPENTER'S WIFE

Fair was this yonge wif, and therwithal
As any wesele hir body gent[1] and smal.
A ceynt[2] she werede barred al of silk,
A barmclooth[3] eek as whit as morne milk
Upon hir lendes,[4] ful of many a gore.[5]
Whit was hir smok and brouded al bifore[6]

[494] in his bag, he carried a pillowcase [495] took [496] a brass cross [497] found [498] a poor parson living in the provinces [499] got [500] false flattery and tricks [501] dupes [502] sacred narrative [503] best of all [504] knew [505] sharpen

[1] neat [2] belt [3] apron [4] loins [5] pleat [6] embroidered at the front

And eek bihinde, on hir coler aboute,
Of[7] col-blak silk, withinne and eek withoute.
The tapes of hir white voluper[8]
Were of the same suite of hir coler;[9]
Hir filet brood[10] of silk, and set ful hye:
And sikerly she hadde a likerous ye.[11]
Ful smale y-pulled[12] were hir browes two,
And tho were bent, and blake as any sloo.
She was ful more blisful on to see
Than is the newe pere-jonette[13] tree;
And softer than the wolle is of a wether.[14]
And by hir girdel heeng a purs of lether
Tasseld with silk and perled with latoun.[15]
In al this world, to seeken up and doun,
There nis no man so wis, that coude thenche[16]
So gay a popelote,[17] or swich a wenche.
Ful brighter was the shining of hir hewe
Than in the Tour the noble y-forged newe.[18]
But of hir song, it was as loude and yerne[19]
As any swalwe sittinge on a berne.[20]
Therto she coude skippe and make game,[21]
As any kide or calf folwinge his dame.[22]
Hir mouth was swete as bragot or the meeth,[23]
Or hord of apples leid in hey or heeth.[24]
Winsinge[25] she was, as is a joly[26] colt,
Long as a mast, and upright as a bolt.[27]
A brooch she baar upon hir lowe coler,
As brood as is the bos of a bocler.[28]
Hir shoes were laced on hir legges hye;
She was a primerole, a pigges-nye[29]
For any lord to leggen[30] in his bedde,
Or yet for any good yeman to wedde.

[7] with [8] cap [9] matched her collar [10] broad headband [11] and indeed she had a wanton look [12] narrowly plucked [13] early pear [14] lamb's wool [15] studded with brass [16] imagine [17] doll [18] than the gold noble newly minted in the Tower of London [19] zestful [20] barn [21] be playful [22] mother [23] honeyed ale or mead [24] heather [25] skittish [26] lively [27] straight as an arrow [28] the boss of a round shield [29] a primrose, a petal [30] lay

Now sire, and eft[31] sire, so bifel the cas,[32]
That on a day this hende Nicholas
Fil[33] with this yonge wif to rage[34] and pleye,
Whil that hir housbond was at Oseneye,
As clerkes ben ful subtile and ful queynte;[35]
And prively he caughte hir by the queynte,[36]
And seide, 'ywis, but if ich have my wille,[37]
For derne love of thee, lemman, I spille.'[38]
And heeld hir harde by the haunche-bones,
And seide, 'lemman, love me al at-ones,
Or I wol dien, also[39] god me save!'
And she sprong as a colt doth in the trave,[40]
And with hir heed she wryed[41] faste awey,
And seide, 'I wol nat kisse thee, by my fey,[42]
Why, lat be,' quod she, 'lat be, Nicholas,
Or I wol crye out "harrow" and "allas".
Do wey[43] your handes for your curteisye!'
This Nicholas gan mercy for to crye,
And spak so faire, and profred hir so faste,[44]
That she hir love him graunted atte laste,
And swoor hir ooth, by seint Thomas of Kent,
That she wol been at his comandement,
Whan that she may hir leiser[45] wel espye.
'Myn housbond is so ful of jalousye,
That but ye wayte wel and been privee,[46]
I woot right wel I nam but deed,'[47] quod she.
'Ye moste been ful derne, as in this cas.'[48]
'Nay therof care[49] thee noght,' quod Nicholas,
'A clerk had litherly biset his while,[50]
But-if he coude a carpenter bigile.'
And thus they been acorded and ysworn
To wayte a time,[51] as I have told biforn.

[31] again [32] chance [33] happened [34] sport [35] artful [36] pudendum [37] surely, unless I have my way [38] for secret love of you, darling, I shall die [39] as [40][i.e., frame for restraining a restive horse in the smithy] [41] twisted [42] faith [43] take away [44] pressed her so much [45] opportunity [46] unless you keep your eye open and be discreet [47] I am as good as dead [48] completely secret in this matter [49] worry [50] a scholar would have used his time badly [51] look for an opportunity

Whan Nicholas had doon thus everydeel,
And thakked[52] hir aboute the lendes[53] weel,
He kist hir swete, and taketh his sautrye,[54]
And pleyeth faste, and maketh melodye.
  Than fil it thus, that to the parish-chirche,
Cristes owne werkes for to wirche,[55]
This gode wif wente on an haliday;[56]
Hir forheed shoon as bright as any day,
So was it washen whan she leet[57] hir werk.
  Now was ther of that chirche a parish-clerk,
The which that was ycleped[58] Absolon.
Crul[59] was his heer, and as the gold it shoon,
And strouted[60] as a fanne large and brode;
Ful streight and even lay his joly shode.[61]
His rode[62] was reed, his eyen greye as goos;
With Powles window corven on his shoos,[63]
In hoses rede he wente fetisly.[64]
Y-clad he was ful smal[65] and proprely,
Al in a kirtel of a light wachet;[66]
Ful faire and thikke been the pointes[67] set.
And therupon he hadde a gay surplis[68]
As whit as is the blosme upon the ris.[69]
A mery child he was, so god me save,
Wel coude he laten blood and clippe and shave,
And make a chartre of lond or acquitaunce.[70]
In twenty manere[71] coude he trippe and daunce
After the scole of Oxenforde tho,
And with his legges casten[72] to and fro,
And pleyen songes on a small rubible;[73]
Therto he song somtime a loud quinible;[74]
And as wel coude he pleye on his giterne.[75]
In al the toun nas brewhous ne taverne
That he ne visited with his solas,[76]
Ther any gaylard tappestere[77] was.

[52] patted [53] loins [54] psaltery [55] do [56] feast day [57] left [58] called [59] curled [60] spread out [61] parting [62] complexion [63] the uppers of his shoes were cut open into a shape like the window of St Paul's [64] elegantly [65] neatly [66] in a tunic of light sky-blue [67] fastenings [68] robe [69] bough [70] conveyance or release [71] ways [72] fling [73] fiddle [74] falsetto [75] guitar [76] entertainment [77] where any jolly barmaid

But sooth to seyn, he was somdel squaymous[78]
Of farting, and of speche daungerous.[79]
  This Absolon, that jolif was and gay,
Gooth with a sencer[80] on the haliday,
Sensinge the wives of the parish faste;
And many a lovely look on hem he caste,
And namely[81] on this carpenteres wif.
To looke on hir him thoughte a mery lif,
She was so propre and swete and likerous.[82]
I dar wel seyn, if she had been a mous,
And he a cat, he wolde hir hente[83] anon.
  This parish-clerk, this joly Absolon,
Hath in his herte swich a love-longinge,
That of no wif ne took he noon offringe;
For curteisye, he seide, he wolde noon.[84]
The moone, whan it was night, ful brighte shoon,
And Absolon his giterne hath ytake,
For paramours he thoghte for to wake.[85]
And forth he gooth, jolif and amorous,
Til he cam to the carpenteres hous
A litel after cokkes hadde ycrowe;
And dressed him up by a shot-windowe[86]
That was upon the carpenteres wal.
He singeth in his vois gentil and smal,[87]
'Now, dere lady, if thy wille be,
I preye yow that ye wol rewe on[88] me,'
Ful wel acordaunt to his giterninge.[89]
This carpenter awook, and herde him singe,
And spak unto his wif, and seide anon,
'What! Alison! herestow nat Absolon
That chaunteth thus under our boures[90] wal?'
And she answerde hir housbond therwithal,
'Yis, god wot, John, I here it every-del.'[91]
  This passeth forth; what wol ye bet than wel?[92]

[78] somewhat squeamish [79] haughty [80] censer [81] particularly [82] sensuous [83] seize [84] desired none [85] because of his desire he intended to keep awake [86] and set himself close by a casement [87] refined and delicate [88] have pity on [89] in perfect harmony with his guitar-playing [90] bedroom [91] every bit [92] and so it went; what more could you wish for

Fro day to day this joly Absolon
So woweth[93] hir, that him is wo bigon.
He waketh[94] al the night and al the day;
He kembed hise lokkes brode,[95] and made him gay;
He woweth hir by menes and brocage,[96]
And swoor he wolde been hir owne page;
He singeth, brokkinge[97] as a nightingale;
He sente hir piment, meeth,[98] and spiced ale,
And wafres,[99] piping hote out of the glede;[100]
And for she was of towne,[101] he profred mede;[102]
For som folk wol ben wonnen for richesse,
And som for strokes,[103] and som for gentillesse.
  Sometime, to shewe his lightnesse and maistrye,[104]
He pleyeth Herodes on a scaffold hye.[105]
But what availleth him as in this cas?[106]
She loveth so this hende Nicholas,
That Absolon may blowe the bukkes horn;[107]
He ne hadde for his labour but a scorn;
And thus she maketh Absolon hir ape,[108]
And al his ernest turneth til a jape.[109]

from *The Miller's Tale*

THE MILLER AND HIS WIFE

  At Trumpingtoun, nat fer fro Cantebrigge,[1]
Ther gooth a brook, and over that a brigge,
Upon the whiche brook ther stant a melle;[2]
And this is verray sooth[3] that I yow telle:
A millere was ther dwellinge many a day.
As any pecok he was proud and gay.
Pipen he koude and fishe, and nettes beete,[4]
And turne coppes,[5] and wel wrastle and sheete;[6]

[93] woos [94] stays awake [95] combed his spreading locks [96] he woos her by intermediaries and go-betweens [97] trilling [98] spiced wine [99] wafers [100] embers [101] townswoman [102] reward [103] blows [104] vitality and virtuosity [105] he takes the part of Herod on a high stage [106] circumstance [107] [i.e., Absolom was wasting his time] [108] she makes a fool of Absolom [109] jest

[1] Cambridge [2] stands a mill [3] absolute truth [4] mend [5] turn cups [on a lathe] [6] shoot

Ay by his belt he baar a long panade,[7]
And of[8] a swerd ful trenchant[9] was the blade.
A joly poppere baar he[10] is in his pouche;
Ther was no man, for peril, dorste hym touche
A Sheffeld thwitel[11] baar he in his hose.
Round was his face, and camus[12] was his nose
As piled[13] as an ape was his skulle.
He was a market-betere atte fulle.[14]
Ther dorste no wight[15] hand upon hym legge,[16]
That he ne swoor he sholde anon abegge.[17]
A theef he was for sothe of corn and mele,
And that a sly, and usaunt[18] for to stele.
His name was hoote deynous Simkin.[19]
A wif he hadde, ycomen of noble kin;[20]
The person[21] of the toun hir fader was.
With hire he yaf ful many a panne of bras,
For that[22] Simkin sholde in his blood allye.
She was yfostred[23] in a nonnerye;
For Simkin wolde no wif, as he saide,
But she were wel ynorissed and a maide,[24]
To saven his estaat of yomanrye.[25]
And she was proud, and peert as is a pye.[26]
A ful fair sighte was it upon hem two;
On halydayes[27] biforn hire wolde he go
With his typet[28] bounden aboute his heed,
And she cam after in a gyte[29] of reed;
And Simkin hadde hosen[30] of the same.
Ther dorste no wight clepen hire but 'dame';[31]
Was noon so hardy[32] that wente by the weye
That with hire dorste rage or ones pleye,[33]
But if he wolde be slain of[34] Simkin
With panade, or with knif, or boidekin.[35]

[7] knife [8] from [9] sharp [10] he carried a fine dagger [11] blade [12] snub [13] bald [14] he was a thoroughgoing market-bully [15] nobody dare [16] lay [17] pay for it at once [18] accustomed [19] by name he was called scornful Simkin [20] descended from a good family [21] parson [22] so that [23] brought up [24] unless she was well brought up, and a virgin [25] to be a credit to his position as a yeoman [26] sprightly as a magpie [27] feast-days [28] turban [29] gown [30] stockings [31] nobody there dare call her anything except 'Madam' [32] bold [33] flirt or trifle with her [34] by [35] bodkin

For jalous folk ben perilous[36] everemo;
Algate[37] they wolde hire wives wenden[38] so.
And eek, for she was somdel smoterlich,[39]
She was as digne as water in a dich,[40]
And ful of hoker and of bisemare.[41]
Hir thoughte that a lady sholde hire spare,[42]
What for hire kinrede and hir nortelrie[43]
That she hadde lerned in the nonnerie.

from *The Reeve's Tale*

A LONDON APPRENTICE

A prentis whilom dwelled[1] in oure citee,
And of a craft of vitailliers[2] was hee.
Gaillard[3] he was as goldfinch in the shawe,[4]
Broun as a berye, a propre[5] short felawe,
With lokkes blake, ykembd ful fetisly.[6]
Dauncen he koude so wel and jolily
That he was cleped Perkin Revelour.[7]
He was as ful of love and paramour[8]
As is the hive ful of hony sweete:
Wel[9] was the wenche with him mighte meete.
At every bridale wolde he singe and hoppe;[10]
He loved bet[11] the taverne than the shoppe.
For whan ther any riding[12] was in Chepe,
Out of the shoppe thider wolde he lepe –[13]
Til that he hadde al the sighte yseyn,[14]
And daunced wel, he wolde nat come ayeyn –[15]
And gadered him a meinee of his sort[16]
To hoppe and singe and maken swich disport;[17]

[36] dangerous [37] at least [38] thought [39] somewhat stained [40] as haughty as water in a ditch [41] full of contempt and mockery [42] it seemed to her that a lady should show restraint [43] both on account of her breeding and her education

[1] an apprentice once lived [2] provision merchants [3] merry [4] wood [5] good-looking [6] very stylishly dressed [7] he was called Perkin the playboy [8] desire [9] lucky [10] dance [11] better [12] procession [13] run [14] seen [15] return home [16] and he assembled for himself a band of his own kind [17] merriment

And ther they setten stevene[18] for to meete,
To pleyen at the dis[19] in swich a streete.
For in the toune nas ther no prentis
That fairer koude caste a paire of dis
Than Perkin koude, and therto he was free
Of his dispense, in place of privetee.[20]
That fond his maister wel in his chaffare;[21]
For often time he foond his box ful bare.
For sikerly a prentis revelour[22]
That haunteth dis, riot, or paramour,[23]
His maister shal it in his shoppe abye,[24]
Al have he no part of the minstralcye.[25]
For thefte and riot, they been convertible,[26]
Al konne he pleye on giterne or ribible.[27]
Revel and trouthe, as in a lowe degree,
They been ful wrothe al day,[28] as men may see.
This joly prentis with his maister bood,[29]
Til he were ny out of his prentishood,[30]
Al were he snibbed[31] bothe erly and late,
And somtime lad with revel to Newegate.
But atte laste his maister him bithoghte,
Upon a day, whan he his papir soghte,
Of a proverbe that seith this same word,
'Wel bet' is roten appul out of hoord[32]
Than that it rotie[33] al the remenaunt.'[34]
So fareth it by[35] a riotous servaunt;
It is ful lesse harm to lete him pace,[36]
Than he shende[37] alle the servantz in the place.
Therfore his maister yaf hym acquitance,
And bad him go, with sorwe and with meschance![38]

[18] made an appointment [19] dice [20] and, in addition, he was lavish in his spending in a quiet place [21] and his master certainly discovered that in his trading [22] certainly a roistering apprentice [23] who pursues dice, merry-making or sexual licence [24] pay for [25] although he have no share in the merriment [26] interchangeable [27] guitar or fiddle [28] high living and honesty, in people of humble station, are always at odds [29] remained [30] nearly out of his apprenticeship [31] reproved [32] store [33] rot [34] rest [35] goes with [36] go [37] ruin [38] bad luck

And thus this joly prentis hadde his leve.
Now lat him riote al the night or leve.[39]
And for ther is no theef withoute a lowke,[40]
That helpeth him to wasten and to sowke[41]
Of that he bribe[42] kan or borwe may,
Anon he sente his bed and his array
Unto a compeer[43] of his owene sort,
That lovede dis, and revel, and disport,
And hadde a wif that heeld for contenance
A shoppe,[44] and swived for hir sustenance.[45]

The Cook's Tale

THE POOR WIDOW

A povre[1] widwe, somdel stape[2] in age,
Was whilom[3] dwelling in a narwe[4] cotage,
Biside a grove, stonding in a dale.
This widwe, of which I telle yow my tale,
Sin thilke[5] day that she was last a wif,
In pacience ladde a ful simple lif,
For litel was hir catel and hir rente;[6]
By housbondrye,[7] of such as God hir sente,
She fond hirself, and eek hir doghtren two.[8]
Three large sowes hadde she, and namo,[9]
Three kyn,[10] and eek a sheep that highte[11] Malle.
Ful sooty was hir bour, and eek hir halle,
In which she eet ful many a sclendre[12] meel.
Of poynaunt sauce hir neded never a deel.[13]
No deintee morsel passed thurgh hir throte;
Hir diete was accordant to hir cote.[14]

[39] let it alone [40] accomplice [41] squander and cheat [42] steal [43] companion [44] who kept a shop for appearance's sake [45] and prostituted herself for her living

[1] poor [2] somewhat advanced [3] once [4] little [5] since that very [6] goods and income [7] economizing [8] she provided for herself and also her two daughters [9] no more [10] cows [11] was called [12] frugal [13] she never needed a speck of piquant sauce [14] was in keeping with her cottage

Repleccioun[15] ne made hir never sik;
Attempree diete was al hir phisik,[16]
And exercise, and hertes suffisaunce.[17]
The goute lette[18] hir nothing for to daunce,
Napoplexye shente[19] nat hir heed;
No win ne drank she, neither whit ne reed;
Hir bord[20] was served most with whit and blak,
Milk and brown breed, in which she fond no lak,[21]
Seynd[22] bacoun, and somtime an ey[23] or tweye,
For she was, as it were, a maner deye.[24]
A yerd[25] she hadde, enclosed al aboute
With stikkes, and a drye dich withoute,
In which she hadde a cok, hight[26] Chauntecleer,
In al the land, of crowing, nas his peer.[27]

from *The Nun's Priest's Tale*

THE WIFE OF BATH MARRIES HER FIFTH HUSBAND

My fifthe housbonde, God his soule blesse!
Which that I took for love and no richesse,
He somtime[1] was a clerk[2] of Oxenford,
And had left scole, and wente at hoom to bord[3]
With my gossib,[4] dwellinge in oure toun,
God have hir soule! hir name was Alisoun.
She knew myn herte and eek my privetee[5]
Bet[6] than our parishe preest, so moot I thee![7]
To hir biwreyed I my conseil al.[8]
For had myn housbonde pissed on a wall,
Or doon a thing that sholde han cost his lif,
To hir, and to another worthy wif,

[15] over-eating [16] her only medicine was a moderate diet [17] contentment of heart [18] hindered [19] injured [20] table [21] fault [22] broiled [23] egg [24] a kind of dairywoman [25] yard [26] called [27] there was not his equal

[1] formerly [2] student [3] as a boarder [4] friend [5] secrets [6] better [7] as I may thrive [8] I revealed all my secrets to her

And to my nece, which that I loved weel,
I wolde han told his conseil every deel.[9]
And so I dide ful often, God it woot,[10]
That made his face ful often reed and hoot[11]
For verray shame, and blamed himself for he
Had told to me so greet a privetee.
And so bifel that ones, in a Lente,[12]
(So often times I to my gossib wente,
For ever yet I lovede to be gay,
And for to walke, in March, Averille, and May,
Fro hous to hous, to here sondry tales),
That Jankin clerk, and my gossib Dame Alis,
And I myself, into the feldes wente.
Myn housbond was at London al that Lente;
I hadde the bettre leiser for to pleye,[13]
And for to see, and eek for to seye[14]
Of lusty[15] folk; what wiste I wher my grace
Was shapen for to be,[16] or in what place?
Therefore I made my visitaciouns,
To vigilies[17] and to processiouns,
To preching eek and to thise pilgrimages,
To pleyes of miracles and mariages,
And wered upon my gaye scarlet gytes.[18]
Thise wormes, ne thise mothes, ne thise mites,
Upon my peril, frete hem never a deel;[19]
And wostow[20] why? for they were used weel.
Now wol I tellen forth what happed me.
I seye, that in the feeldes walked we.
Til trewely we hadde swich daliance;[21]
This clerk and I, that of my purveyance[22]
I spak to him, and seide him, how that he,
If I were widwe, sholde wedde me.
For certeinly, I sey for no bobance,[23]
Yet was I never withouten purveyance[24]

[9] bit [10] knows [11] red and hot [12] in Lent [13] the better opportunity to amuse myself [14] seen [15] lively [16] how should I know where my destiny was ordained to be [17] vigils [18] gowns [19] upon my oath, never ate a shred of them [20] do you know [21] amusement [22] foresight [23] without boasting [24] prospect

Of mariage, n'of[25] othere thinges eek.
I holde a mouses herte[26] nat worth a leek,
That hath but oon hol for to sterte to,[27]
And if that faille, thanne is al ydo.[28]
  I bar him on honde,[29] he hadde enchanted[30] me;
My dame[31] taughte me that soutiltee.[32]
And eek I seide, I mette[33] of him al night;
He wolde han slain me as I lay up-right,[34]
And al my bed was ful of verray[35] blood,
But yet I hope that he shal do me good;
For blood bitokeneth[36] gold, as me was taught.
And al was fals, I dremed of it right naught,
But as I folwed ay my dames lore,[37]
As wel of this as of other thinges more.
  But now sir, lat me see, what I shal seyn?
Aha! by God, I have my tale ageyn.
  Whan that my fourthe housbond was on bere,[38]
I weep algate,[39] and made sory chere,[40]
As wives moten,[41] for it is usage,[42]
And with my coverchief covered my visage;
But for that I was purveyed of a make,[43]
I weep[44] but smal, and that I undertake.
  To chirche was myn housbond born amorwe[45]
With[46] neighebores, that for him maden sorwe;
And Jankin, oure clerk, was oon of tho.
As help me God, whan that I saugh him go[47]
After the bere, me thoughte he hadde a paire
Of legges and of feet so clene and faire,
That al myn herte I yaf unto his hold.[48]
He was, I trowe, a twenty winter[49] old,
And I was fourty, if I shal seye sooth;
But yet I hadde alwey a coltes tooth.[50]

[25] nor of [26] life [27] jump into [28] it is all up [29] I maintained [30] bewitched [31] mother [32] trick [33] dreamed [34] stretched out [35] real [36] symbolizes [37] teaching [38] bier [39] anyway [40] and behaved mournfully [41] must [42] custom [43] but since I was provided with a mate [44] wept [45] carried in the morning [46] by [47] when I saw him walking [48] into his keeping [49] years [50] a youthful appetite

Gat-toothed[51] I was, and that bicam me weel;
I hadde the prente of Seint Venus' seel.[52]
As help me God, I was a lusty[53] oon,
And faire and riche, and yong, and wel bigoon;[54]
And trewely, as myne housbondes tolde me,
I had the beste quoniam[55] mighte be.
For certes, I am al Venerien
In felinge, and myn herte is Marcien.[56]
Venus me yaf my lust, my likerousnesse,[57]
And Mars yaf me my sturdy hardinesse.[58]
Myn ascendent[59] was Taur, and Mars therinne.
Allas! allas! that ever love was sinne!
I folwed ay myn inclinacioun[60]
By vertu of my constellacioun;
That made me I coude noght withdrawe
My chambre of Venus from a good felawe.
Yet have I Martes mark upon my face,
And also in another privee place.
For, God so wis be my savacioun,[61]
I ne loved never by no discrecioun,
But ever folwede myn appetit;
Al were he short or long, or blak or whit,
I took no kepe, so that he liked me,[62]
How poore he was, ne eek of what degree.
What sholde I seye, but, at the monthes ende,
This joly[63] clerk Jankin, that was so hende[64]
Hath wedded me with greet solempnitee,[65]
And to him yaf I al the lond and fee[66]
That ever was me yeven therbifore;
But afterward repented me ful sore.

from *The Wife of Bath's Prologue*

[51] gap-toothed [52] I had the print of St Venus' seal [53] lively [54] well-endowed [55] 'whatever' [56] for indeed, in my senses I belong to Venus, and my heart to Mars [57] sensuality [58] boldness [59] ascendant [i.e., sign of the Zodiac] [60] disposition [61] for sure as God is my salvation [62] I took no heed, so long as he pleased me [63] handsome [64] personable [65] ceremony [66] money

ANONYMOUS

THE BLACKSMITHS

Swarte smeked smethes smatered with smoke[1]
Drive me to deth with den of here dintes.[2]
Swech[3] nois on nightes ne herd men never:
What knavene cry[4] and clatering of knockes!
The cammede kongons[5] cryen after 'col, col'
And blowen here bellewes, that al here brain brestes:[6]
'Huf, puf!' seith that on; 'haf, paf!' that other.
They spitten and sprawlen and spellen many spelles;[7]
They gnauen and gnacchen,[8] they grones togedere,
And holden hem hote[9] with here hard hamers.
Of a bulle-hide been here barm-felles;[10]
Here shankes ben shakeled for the fere-flunderes;[11]
Hevy hameres they han, that hard ben handled,
Stark strokes they striken on a steled stokke:[12]
Lus, bus! las, das! rowten by rowe.[13]
Swech dolful a dreme the devil it to-drive![14]
The maister longeth a litel, and lasheth a lesse,
Twineth hem twein, and toucheth a treble:[15]
Tik, tak! hic, hac! tiket, taket! tik, tak!
Lus, bus! lus, das! swich lif they leden,
Alle clothemeres:[16] Crist hem give sorwe!
May no man for bren-wateres[17] on night han his rest.

[1] Grimy black smiths smutty with smoke [2] noise of their blows [3] such [4] shouting of workmen [5] snub-nosed mis-shapes [6] bursts [7] stagger and utter many ? curses [8] grind and gnash [teeth] [9] keep themselves warm [10] leather aprons [11] protected against the fire-sparks [12] they strike hard blows on a steel anvil [13] beating in turn [14] devil take such a terrible discord [15] the master-smith lengthens a small piece, beats out a smaller one, twists the two together, and strikes a treble note [16] horse-tailors [17] water-burners

THOMAS HOCCLEVE

HOCCLEVE IN LONDON

I dar nat telle how that the freshe repeir[1]
Of venus femel[2] lusty children deere,
That so goodly, so shaply were, and feir,
And so plesant of port[3] and of maneere,
And feede cowden al a world with cheere,
And of atir passingly wel biseye,[4]
At Poules heed[5] me maden ofte appeere,
To talke of mirthe and to disporte and pleye.

Ther was sweet win ynow thurghout the hous,
And wafres thikke, for this conpaignie
That I spak of been sumwhat likerous.[6]
Where as[7] they mowe a draght of win espie,
Sweete and in wirkinge hoot for the maistrie[8]
To warme a stomak with, therof they dranke.
To suffre hem paie, had been no courtesie:
That charge I tooke, to winne love and thanke.

Of loves art yit touchid I no deel;
I cowde nat, and eek it was no neede:
Had I a kus,[9] I was content ful weel,
Bettre than I wolde han be with the deede:[10]
Theron can I but smal; it is no dreede:[11]
When that men speke of it in my presence,
For shame I wexe as reed as is the gleede.[12]
Now wole I torne agein to my sentence.[13]

Of him that hauntith taverne of custume,
At shorte wordes the profit is this:
In double wise his bagge it shal consume,
And make his tonge speke of folk amis;

[1] lively gathering [2] female [3] bearing [4] surpassingly well-provided [5] Paul's Head tavern [6] greedy [7] wherever [8] very warming in its action [9] kiss [10] act [11] I know very little about that, never fear [12] I grow red as an ember with embarrassment [13] theme

For in the cuppe selden fownden is,
That any wight his neigheburgh commendith.
Beholde and see what avantage is his,
That god, his freend, and eek him self, offendith.

But oon avauntage in this cas I have:
I was so ferd[14] with any man to fighte,
Clos kepte I me, no man durste I deprave[15]
But rowningly; I spak no thing on highte.[16]
And yit my wil was good, if that I mighte,
For lettinge of my manly cowardise,[17]
That ay of strokes impressid the wighte,[18]
So that I durste medlen[19] in no wise.

Wher was a gretter maister eek than I,
Or bet aqweintid at Westminstre gate,
Among the taverneres namely,[20]
And cookes, whan I cam, eerly or late?
I pinchid nat at hem in min acate,[21]
But paied hem as that they axe wolde;
Wherfore I was the welcomere algate,[22]
And for 'a verray[23] gentil man' y-holde.

And if it happid on the someres day
That I thus at the taverne hadde be,
When I departe sholde and go my way,
Hoom to the privee seel[24] so wowed[25] me
Heete and unlust and superfluitee[26]
To walke unto the brigge and take a boot,[27]
That nat durste I contrarie hem all three,
But dide as that they stired me god woot.

And in the wintir, for the way was deep,
Unto the brigge I dressid[28] me also,
And ther the bootmen took upon me keep,[29]
For they my riot kneewen fern[30] ago:

[14] afraid [15] slander [16] except as a whisper; I spoke nothing out loud [17] I would willingly have done so, despite the restraint of my human cowardice [18] gave me an impression of the weight of blows [19] interfere [20] especially [21] I did not find fault with them in my dealing [22] by all means [23] real [24] Privy Seal Office [25] seduced [26] warmth, disinclination, and excess [27] boat [28] directed [29] took notice of me [30] long

With hem[31] was I y-tugged to and fro,
So wel was him that I with wolde fare;[32]
For riot paieth largely[33] everemo;
He stintith nevere, til his purs be bare.

Othir than 'maistir' callid was I nevere,
Among this meynee, in myn audience.[34]
Me thoghte I was y-maad a man for evere:
So tikelid me that nyce reverence,[35]
That it me made larger of despense
Than that I thoght han been.[36] O Flaterie!
The guise of thy traiterous diligence[37]
Is, folk to mescheef hasten and to hie.

from *La Male Regle de Thomas Hoccleve*

JOHN LYDGATE

FROWARD MAYMOND

A froward knave pleinly to descrive[1]
  And a sloggard shortly to declare:
A precious knave that cast him never to thrive,[2]
  His mouth wel wet, his slevis riht thredbare,
  A turnebroche,[3] a boy for Hogge of Ware,[4]
    With louring face, nodding and slombring,
  Of newe cristened[5] and callid Jakke Hare,
    Wich of a boll can plukke out the lining.[6]

This boy Maymond, ful stuborne of his bonis,[7]
  Sloggy on morwen his lemes up to dresse,
A gentel harlot chose out for the nonis,[8]
  Son and cheef eir to Dame Idelnesse,

[31] by them [32] happy was he whom I would travel with [33] generously [34] among this company, in my hearing [35] indiscriminate respect [36] freer-spending than I intended to have been [37] the way of your treacherous esteem

[1] describe [2] a fine rascal who never puts himself out [3] turnspit [4] a helper for Hodge of Ware [the Cook in *The Canterbury Tales*] [5] newly re-christened [6] who can pluck out the contents of a drinking-bowl [7] thoroughly mulish [8] sluggish in getting up in the morning, an egregious rascal

Cosin to Wecok, brother to Reklesnesse,
Wich, late at eve and morwe, at his rising
Ne hath no joye to do no besinesse,[9]
Save of a tancard to plukke out the lining.

A boy Chekrelik was his sworen brother
Of every dish a lipet[10] out to take;
And Fafyntycol also was another
Of every bribe the cariage for to make.[11]
He can wel waiten on[12] an oven-cake
And of newe ale been at the clensing;[13]
And of purpos his thruste for to slake
Kan of a picher plukke out the lining.

This knave be leiser wil don al his message
And holde a tale with every maner wight;[14]
Ful pale drunk, wel vernished of visage,[15]
Whos tonge ay faileth when it draweth to niht,
Of o candell he weneth two wer light;[16]
As barked[17] lether his face is shining;
Glasy-eied wol cleime of dew right
Out of a boll to plukke out the lining.

He can abedd an horskombe wel shake
Lik as he wold coray[18] his masters hors;
And with his on hand his masters doublet take
And with the tother prevly[19] kutt his purs.
Alle swiche knavis shul have Cristes curs
Erly on morwe at their uprising.
To finde a boy I trow ther be none wors[20]
Out of a pot to plukke out the lining.

He may be sold upon warantise[21]
As for a truant[22] that no thing wil doon:

[9] takes pleasure in no activity [10] morsel [11] to carry out any pilfering [12] look out for [13] purifying [14] This rascal will carry out all his errands in a leisurely way, chatting with all kinds of people [15] with a face all glossy [16] he considers the light of one lit candle as good as two [17] tanned [18] curry-comb [19] quietly [20] I believe there is not a worse servant to be found [21] under guarantee [22] as a miscreant

To selle hors-provendre is his cheef marchaundise,[23]
  And for a chevesaunce[24] can plukke off their shoon,
  And at the dise pley the mony soon,
    And with his winnings he maketh his offring
  At the ale-stakes, sitting agein the moon,[25]
    Out of a cup to plukke out the lining.

L'envoye

Wassail to Maymond and to his jousy pate![26]
  Unthrift[27] and he be togedre met;
Late at eve he wil onspere the gate,[28]
  And grope on morwe yif Riggis bak be wet
  And if the bak of Togace be out-het;[29]
    His hevy noll[30] at midmorwe uplifting
  With onwash hands, not lased his doublet,
    Out of a boll to plukke out the lining.

ANONYMOUS

A HENPECKED HUSBAND

How, hey! It is non les:[1]
  I dare not seyn[2] when she seith 'Pes!'[3]

Ying[4] men, I warne you everichon,
Elde[5] wivis tak ye non;
For I myself have on at hom –
  I dare not seyn when she seith 'Pes!'

When I cum fro the plow at noon,
In a reven dish myn mete is doon;[6]

[23] selling horse-feed is his main business [24] profit on the side [25] at the inn-signs, sitting in the moonlight [26] Here's to Maymond and his soggy pate [27] waste and carelessness [28] leave the door unfastened [29] and grope in the morning to see if Rigg's [the dog's] back be wet, and if Togace's [the cat's] back is very hot [i.e., to see what the weather is, and if the fire is in] [30] head

[1] lie [2] speak [3] Quiet! [4] young [5] old [6] my food is put in a cracked dish

I dare not askin our dame a spoon –
  I dare not seyn when she seith 'Pes!'

If I aske our dame bred,
She takith a staf and brekith myn hed,
And doth me rennin under the led –[7]
  I dare not seyn when she seith 'Pes!'

If I aske our dame flesh,[8]
She brekith myn hed with a dish:
'Boy, thou art not worth a rish!' –[9]
  I dare not seyn when she seith 'Pes!'

If I aske our dame chese,
'Boy', she seith, al at ese,[10]
'Thou art not worth half a pese!' –[11]
  I dare not seyn when she seith 'Pes!'

MY BASELARD

Prenegard, prenegard![1]
Thus bere I myn baselard.[2]

Listenith, lordinges, I you beseke:
Ther is non man worth a leke,
Be he sturdy,[3] be he meke,
  But[4] he bere a baselard.

Myn baselard hath a shede[5] of red
And a clene loket of led;[6]
Me thinkith I may bere up myn hed,
  For I bere myn basėlard.

My baselard hath a wrethin haft;[7]
When I am ful of ale caghte[8]
It is gret dred of manslaghte,[9]
  For then I bere my baselard.

[7] and makes me run under the cauldron [8] meat [9] rush [10] coolly [11] pea

[1] Take care [2] dagger [3] fierce [4] unless [5] sheath [6] neat leaden band [7] twisted handle [8] tipsy with ale [9] homicide

My baselard hath a silver chape;[10]
Therfore I may both gaspe[11] and gape.
Me thinkith I go lik non knape[12]
For I bere a baselard.

My baselard hath a trencher[13] kene,
Fair as rasour, sharp and shene.[14]
Ever me thinkith I may be kene[15]
For I bere a baselard.

As I yede[16] up in the strete
With a cartere I gan mete.[17]
'Felawe', he seide, 'so mot I thee,[18]
Thou shalt forgo thy baselard.'

The cartere his whippe began to take,
And al myn flesh began to quake,
And I was leef[19] for to escape,
And there I left myn baselard.

When I cam forth unto myn damme
Myn hed was brokin to the panne;[20]
She seide I was a prety manne
And wel cowde bere myn baselard!

JOLLY JANKIN

'*Kyrie*', so '*kyrie*',
Jankin singith merie,
With 'aleyson'.[1]

As I went on Yol day[2]
In oure prosession,
Knew I joly Jankin
By his mery ton –
Kyrieleyson.[3]

[10] scabbard plate [11] ? boast [12] menial [13] blade [14] bright [15] brave [16] went
[17] met [18] so help me [19] glad [20] skull

[1] Alison [2] Christmas Day [3] Lord have mercy.

Jankin began the offis
  On the Yol day,
And yet me thinkith it dos me good,
  So merie gan he say
  '*Kyrieleyson*'.

Jankin red the pistil[4]
  Ful faire and ful wel,
And yet me thinkith it dos me good,
  As evere have I sel.[5]
  Kyrieleyson.

Jankin at the *Sanctus*
  Crakith a merie note,[6]
And yet me thinkith it dos me good –
  I payid for his cote.
  Kyrieleyson.

Jankin crakith notes,
  An hunderid on a knot,[7]
And yet he hakketh them smallere
  Than wortes[8] to the pot.
  Kyrieleyson.

Jankin at the *Angnus*[9]
  Berith the pax-brede;
He twinkelid,[10] but said nought,
  And on myn foot he trede.
  Kyrieleyson.

Benedicamus Domino,
  Crist fro shame me shilde![11]
Deo gracias therto –
  Alas, I go with childe!
  Kyrieleyson.

[4] Epistle [5] as ever I may be happy [6] sings in very short notes [7] cluster [8] herbs [9] *Agnus* [10] winked [11] Christ protect me from disgrace!

A SERVANT-GIRL'S HOLIDAY

Ribbe ne rele ne spinne ich ne may[1]
For joye that it is holiday.

Al this day ich han sought;[2]
Spindel ne werve ne fond I nought;[3]
To miche blisse ich am brought
Ayen[4] this highe holiday.

Al unswope is oure flet,[5]
And oure fire is unbet;[6]
Oure rushen ben unrepe yet[7]
Ayen this highe holiday.

Ich moste fechen worten in;[8]
Predele[9] my kerchef under my chin –
Leve[10] Jacke, lend me a pin
To predele me this holiday.

Now it draweth to the none,[11]
And al my cherres[12] ben undone;
I moste a lite solas my shone[13]
To make hem douse[14] this holiday.

I moste milken in this pail;
Ought me bred al this shail;[15]
Yet is the dow under my nail[16]
As ich knad[17] this holiday.

Jacke wol bringe me onward in my wey,
With me desire for to pleye;
Of my dame stant me non ay
On never a good holiday.[18]

[1] I cannot scrape flax nor reel nor spin [2] I've been searching all day [3] I haven't found the spindle nor whorl at all [4] in anticipation of [5] our floor is all unswept [6] not laid [7] rushes are still unprepared [8] I have to fetch vegetables in [9] fasten [10] dear [11] midday [12] chores [13] I must ease my shoes a bit [14] comfortable [15] I ought to lay out all this crockery [16] but the dough is still under my hands [17] kneaded [18] I'm not afraid of my mistress on any good holiday

Jacke wol pay for my scot[19]
A Sonday at the ale-scot;[20]
Jacke wol souse wel my throt[21]
  Every good holiday.

Soone he wol take me by the hond,
And he wol legge me on the lond[22]
That al my buttockes ben of sond
  Upon this highe holiday.

In he pult[23] and out he drow,
And ever ich lay on him y-low:[24]
'By Godes deth, thou dest me wow[25]
  Upon this highe holiday!'

Soone my wombe[26] began to swelle
As gret as a belle;
Durst I nat my dame telle
  What me betidde[27] this holiday.

JOHN RUSSELL

TABLE MANNERS

'Simple condicions[1] of a persone that is not taught,
I will ye eschew, for evermore they be nowght.
Your hed ne bak ye claw, a fleigh[2] as thaugh ye sought,
Ne youre heere ye strike, ne pike to pralle for a fleshe mought.[3]
Glowtinge[4] ne twinkelinge with youre ye, ne too hevy of chere,
Watery winkinge ne droppinge but of sight clere.
Pike not youre nose, ne that hit be droppinge with no peerlis clere,
Sniff nor snitinge[5] hit too lowd, lest youre soverayne hit here.

[19] share of the bill [20] drinking-party [21] throat [22] lay me on the ground [23] thrust [24] beneath him [25] do me wrong [26] belly [27] happened to me

[1] habits [2] flea [3] nor stroke nor pick your hair as if to catch a louse [4] glowering [5] blowing

Wrye not youre nek a doyle, as hit were a dawe,[6]
Put not youre handes in youre hosen youre codware for to clawe,
Nor pikinge, nor trifelinge, ne shrukkinge[7] as though ye wold sawe;
Your hondes frote[8] ne rub, bridelinge with brest upon your crawe;
With youre eris pike not, nor be ye slow of hering;
Areche[9] ne spit too fer, ne have lowd laughinge;
Speke not lowd, be war of movinge[10] and scorninge;
Be no lier with youre mouthe, ne likorous[11] ne drivelinge.
With youre mouth ye use nowther to squirt, nor spowt;
Be not gapinge nor ganinge,[12] ne with thy mouth to powt;
Lik not with thy tonge in a dish, a mote to have owt.[13]
Be not rash ne recheles, it is not worth a clowt.
With youre brest, sighe, nor coughe, nor brethe, youre soverayne before;
Be yoxinge, ne bolkinge,[14] ne groninge, never the more;
With youre feet trampelinge, ne settinge youre leggis a shore;[15]
With youre body be not shrubbinge;[16] jettinge is no loore.[17]
Good son, thy tethe be not pikinge, grisinge, ne gnastinge;[18]
Ne stinkinge of brethe on youre soverayne castinge;
With puffing ne blowinge, nowther fulle ne fastinge;[19]
And alle wey be ware of thy hinder part from gunnes blastinge.
These cuttid galauntes[20] with their codware; that is an ungoodly gise; –[21]
Other tacches as towchinge I spare not to misprave after mine avise, –[22]
When he shalle serve his mastir, before him on the table hit lies;
Every sovereyne of sadnes[23] alle such sort shalle dispise.
Many moo condicions a man might finde than now ar named here,
Therfore every honest servant avoid alle thoo, and worshippe lat him leere.[24]

[6] don't twist your neck askew, as though you were a jackdaw [7] shrugging [8] wring [9] retch [10] causing trouble [11] obscene [12] yawning [13] do not lick a dish with your tongue to get the dust out [14] be neither hiccoughing, nor belching [15] wide apart [16] scratching [17] it is not clever to strut [18] grinding or gnashing [19] neither when you have eaten nor when you are without food [20] short-coated young fellows [21] a deplorable fashion [22] other related sins I do not shrink from condemning according to my opinion [23] every serious-minded lord [24] let him learn honour

Panter, yoman of the cellere, butlere, and ewere,[25]
I wille that ye obeye to the marshalle, sewere, and kervere.'[26]
'Good sir, I yow pray the conninge[27] of kervinge ye will me teche,
And the faire handlinge of a knife, I yow beseche,
And alle wey where I shalle alle maner fowles breke, unlace,
or seche,[28]
And with fish or flesh, how shalle I demene me[29] with eche.'
'Son, thy knife must be bright, faire, and clene,
And thine handes faire washe, it wold thee welle besene.
Hold alwey thy knife sure, thyself not to tene,[30]
And passe not two fingers and a thombe on thy knife so kene;
In midde wey of thine hande[31] set the ende of the haft sure,
Unlasinge and minsinge, two fingers with the thombe that
may ye endure.
Kervinge, of bred leiynge, voidinge of cromes and trenchewre,[32]
With two fingers and a thombe, looke ye have the cure.
Sett never on fish nor flesh, beest, nor fowle, trewely,
Moore than two fingers and a thombe, for that is curtesie.
Touche never with youre right hande no maner mete[33] surely,
But with your lift hande, as I seid afore, for that is goodlye.
Alle-wey with youre lift hand hold your loof with might,[34]
And hold youre knife sure, as I have geve yow sight.
Enbrewe[35] not youre table, for than ye do not right,
Ne ther-uppon ye wipe youre kniffes, but on youre napkin plight.[36]
Furst take a loofe of trenchers[37] in thy lift hande,
Than take thy table knife, as I have seid afore hande;
With the egge of the knife youre trenchere up be ye reisande[38]
As nighe the point as ye may, to-fore youre lord hit leyande;[39]
Right so foure trenchers, oon by another foure square ye sett,
And, upon tho trenchers foure, a trencher sengle without lett;
Than take your loof of light paine,[40] as I have said yett,
And with the egge of the knife nighe your hand, ye kett.[41]

[25] water-bearer [26] bread-cutter [27] skill [28] dismember, divide, or carve [29] conduct myself [30] so as not to harm yourself [31] in the middle of your palm [32] laying bread, removing crumbs and trencher [33] food [34] hold your loaf firmly with your left hand [35] soil [36] on your folded napkin [37] sliced loaf of coarse bread [38] raising up the slice with the edge of the knife [39] laying [40] fine bread [41] cut

Furst pare the quarters[42] of the looff round alle abowt,
Than kutt the upper crust for your soverayne, and to him alowt.[43]
Suffere your parelle to stond stille to the botom and so nighe yspend owt,[44]
So ley him of the cromes a quarter of the looff sauns dowt;[45]
Touche never the loof after he is so tamed,[46]
Put it on a platere or the almes dish therefore named.[47]
Make clene youre bord ever, than shalle ye not be blamed,
Than may the sewere[48] his lord serve and neithur of yow be gramed.[49]

from *The Book of Nurture*

A MEAT DINNER

The First Course

Furst set forthe mustard and brawne of boore, the wild swine,
Suche potage[1] as the cooke hath made of yerbis,[2] spice and wine,
Beeff, moton, stewed feisaund,[3] swan with the chawdwin,[4]
Capoun, pigge, vensoun bake, leche lombard,[5] fruture viaunt[6] fine;

And then a Sotelte:[7]
Maidon Mary that holy virgine,
And Gabrielle gretinge her with an Ave.

The Second Course

Two potages, blanger mangere,[8] and also jely[9]
For a standard, vensoun rost, kid, faune, or cony,[10]
Bustard, stork, crane, pecok in hakille ryally,[11]
Heiron-sew or betowre,[12] with-serve with bred, if that drink be by;

[42] peel the sides [43] bow [44] allow your fellow to remain standing at the foot of the table and, thus, serve it nearly all out [45] give him a good quarter of the centre of the loaf [46] trimmed [47] named after its function of giving alms [48] man who sets out the dishes [49] criticized

[1] broth [2] herbs [3] pheasant [4] sauce [5] baked venison, leche lombard [a spiced pork dish] [6] meat fritter [7] set-piece [8] diced chicken in cream sauce [9] aspic-jelly [10] for a main course, roast venison, kid, fawn, or rabbit [11] peacock, royally served in its skin [12] heron or bittern

Partriche, woodcok, plovere, egret, rabettes sowkere;[13]
Gret briddes, larkes, gentille breme de mere,[14]
Dowcettes, paine puff, with leche, jely ambere,[15]
Fretoure powche,[16] a sotelte folowinge in fere,

The course for to fullfille,[17]
An angelle goodly kan appere,
And singinge with a mery chere,
Unto three shepherdes uppon an hille.

The Third Course

Creme of almondes, and mameny,[18] the thridde course in coost,[19]
Curlew, brew, snites,[20] quailes, sparows, mertenettes rost,[21]
Perche in jely, crevise dewe douce, pety perveis[22] with the moost,
Quinces bake, leche dugard, fruture sage,[23] I speke of cost,

And soteltees fulle solein:[24]
That lady that conseved by the holygost
Him that distroyed the fendes boost,[25]
Presented plesauntly by the kinges of coleyn.[26]
After this, delicatis mo:[27]

Blaunderelle, or pepins, with carawey in confite.[28]
Waffers to ete, ypocras[29] to drink with delite.
Now this fest is finished, void the table quite;[30]
Go we to the fish fest while we have respite,
And then with Goddes grace the fest will be do.

from *The Book of Nurture*

[13] sucking rabbits [14] noble sea-bream [15] batter puddings, pie with leek, amber jelly [16] ? poached fritter [17] complete [18] chicken in almonds [19] in rank [20] snipe [21] roast martins [22] freshwater crayfish, small pies [23] sage fritters [24] solemn [25] pretensions of the devil [26] Cologne [i.e., the three Magi] [27] more delicacies [28] white apples or pippins, sugared caraway seeds [29] spiced wine [30] completely clear the table

DUTIES OF A CHAMBERLAIN

Then pray youre sovereyn[1] with wordis mansuetely[2]
To com to a good fire and aray him ther by,
And there to sitt or stand, to his persone pleasauntly,[3]
And ye ever redy to awaite with maners metely.

Furst hold to him a peticote above youre brest and barme,[4]
His dublet then after to put in bothe his arme,
His stomachere welle ychaffed[5] to kepe him fro harme,
His vampeys[6] and sokkes, then all day he may go warme;

Then drawe on his sokkis and hosen by the fire,
His shoon laced or bokelid, draw them on sure;
Strike his hosen uppewarde his legge ye endure,[7]
Then trusse ye them up straite to his plesure;

Then lace his dublett every hoole so by and bye;
On his shulder about his nek a kercheff there must lie,
And curteisly then ye kembe[8] his hed with combe of ivery,
And water warme his handes to wash, and face also clenly.

Then kneele adown on youre knee and thus to youre sovereyn ye say
'Sir, what robe or gown pleseth it yow to were today?'
Suche as he axeth fore, looke ye plese him to pay,[9]
Then hold it to him a brode,[10] his body ther-in to array;

His gurdelle, if he were, be it strait or lewse;[11]
Set his garment goodly after, as ye know the use;[12]
Take him hoode or hatt for his hed, cloke or cappe de huse;[13]
So shalle ye plese him prestly,[14] no neede to make excuse.

Whether it be feire or foule, or misty alle withe rain,
Or youre mastir depart his place, afore that this be seyn,[15]
To brushen besily about him; looke all be pur and plain
Whether he were satin, sendall, vellewet, scarlet, or greyn.[16]

[1] lord [2] softly [3] as is most pleasing to him [4] chest [5] warmed [6] over-socks [7] smooth his hose upward and firm his leg [8] comb [9] to his satisfaction [10] spread out [11] if he wear one, be it tight or loose [12] fashion [13] indoor cape [14] readily [15] seen [16] satin, silk, velvet, fine-quality red or fast-dyed cloth

Prince or prelate if it be, or any other potestate,[17]
Or[18] he enter in to the churche, be it erly or late,
Perceve all thinge for his pewe that it be made preparate,
Bothe coshyn, carpet, and curtein, bedes and booke, forget not that.

Then to youre sovereynes chambur walke ye in hast;
All the clothes of the bed, them aside ye cast;
The fetherbed ye bete, without hurt, so no fedders ye wast,
Fustian and sheetis clene by sight and sans ye tast.[19]

Kover with a keverlite clenly that bed so manerly made;
The bankers and coshyns,[20] in the chamber see them feire ysprad,
Bothe hedsheete and pillow also, that they be saaff up stad,[21]
The urnelle[22] and bason also that they awey be had.

See the carpettis about the bed be forth spred and laid,
Windowes and cuppeborde with carpettis and cosshyns splayd;[23]
Se ther be a good fire in the chamber conveyed,[24]
With wood and fuelle redy the fire to bete[25] and aide.

See the privehouse for esement[26] be faire, soote, and clene,
And that the bordes ther uppon be kevered withe clothe feire and greene,
And the hoole himself,[27] looke there no borde be sene,
Theron a feire coshyn the ordure no man to tene.[28]

Looke there be blanket, coten, or linen to wipe the nether ende;
And ever when he clepithe, waite redy and entende,[29]
Basoun and ewere, and on your shulder a towelle, my frende;
In this wise worship[30] shalle ye win where that ever ye wende.

from *The Book of Nurture*

[17] important person [18] before [19] under-sheet and sheets visibly clean without trying them [20] the bench-covers and cushions [21] safely set up [22] urinal [23] set out [24] brought [25] mend [26] comfort [27] itself [28] so that the ordure does not trouble anyone [29] listen [30] esteem

HOW TO PREPARE A BATH

If youre soverayne[1] wille to the bathe, his body to washe clene,
Hang sheetis round about the rooff; do thus as I meene;[2]
Every sheete full of flowres and herbis soote[3] and greene,
And looke ye have sponges five or six theron to sitte or lene:
Looke ther be a gret sponge, theron youre soverayne to sitt;
Theron a sheete, and so he may bathe him there a fitte;[4]
Undir his feete also a sponge, if ther be any to putt;
And alwey be sure of the dur,[5] and see that he be shutt.
A basin full in youre hand of herbis hote and freshe,
And with a soft sponge in hand, his body that ye washe;
Rinse him with rose water warme and feire uppon him flashe,
Then let him go to bed, but looke it be soote and neshe;[6]
But furst set on his sokkis, his slippers on his feete,
That he may go feire to the fire, there to take his foote sheete,
Then withe a clene clothe to wipe awey all wete;
Then bring him to his bed, his bales there to bete.[7]

from *The Book of Nurture*

ANONYMOUS

LONDON LICKPENNY

To London once my stepps I bent,
  Where trouth in no wise should be faint,[1]
To Westminster-ward I forthwith went,
  To a man of law to make complaint.
  I said, 'for Marys love, that holy saint,
    Pity the poore that wold proceede.'[2]
    But, for lack of mony, I cold not speede.[3]

And as I thrust the presse amonge,
  By froward[4] chaunce my hood was gone,

[1] lord [2] declare [3] sweet [4] while [5] door [6] see that it be sweet and soft [7] to cure his troubles there

[1] falsified [2] go to law [3] I could do no good [4] evil

Yet for all that I stayd not longe,
  Till at the Kinges Bench I was come.
  Before the Judge I kneled anon,
    And prayd him for Gods sake to take heede.
    But, for lack of mony, I might not speede.

Beneth them sat clarkes a gret rout,[5]
  Which fast did write by one assent;[6]
There stoode up one and cried about,
  'Richard, Robert, and John of Kent!'
  I wist not well what this man ment,
    He cried so thicke there in dede.
    But he that lackt mony might not speede.

Unto the Common Place I yode thoo,[7]
  Where sat one with a silken hoode;
I did him reverence for I ought to do so,
  And told my case as well as I colde,
  How my goodes were defrauded me by falshood,
    I gat not a mum of his mouth for my meed![8]
    And, for lack of mony, I might not speede.

Unto the Rolls I gat me from thence,
  Before the Clarkes of the Chauncerye,
Where many I found earning of pence,
  But none at all once regarded mee.
  I gave them my plaint uppon my knee,
    They liked it well, when they had it reade;
    But, lacking mony, I could not be speede.

In Westminster Hall I found out one,
  Which went in a long gown of raye;[9]
I crowched and kneled before him anon,
  For Maryes love, of help I him praye.
  'I wot not what thou meanest,' gan he say;[10]
    To get me thence he did me bede,[11]
    For lack of mony I cold not speede.

[5] company [6] in unison [7] I then went to the Common Pleas [8] I didn't receive a word from his lips in recompense [9] striped cloth [10] he said [11] bid

Within this hall, nether rich nor yett poor
  Wold do for me ought, although I shold die.
Which seing, I gat me out of the doore,
  Where Fleminges began on me for to cry:
  'Master, what will you copen[12] or by?
    Fine felt hattes, or spectacles to reede?
    Lay down your silver, and here you may speede.'

Then to Westminster Gate I presently went,
  When the sunn was at highe prime,[13]
Cookes to me they tooke good entent,[14]
  And profered me bread with ale and wine,
  Ribbs of befe, both fat and ful fine.
    A faire cloth they gan for to sprede,
    But, wanting mony, I might not speede.

Then into London I did me hie,
  Of all the land it beareth the prise:
'Hot pescodes,' one began to crye;
  'Strabery ripe,' and 'cherryes in the rise!'[15]
  One bad me come nere and by some spice;
    Peper and safforne they gan me bede.[16]
    But, for lack of mony, I might not speede.

Then to the Chepe I gan me drawne,[17]
  Where mutch people I saw for to stand;
One offred me velvet, silke, and lawne;
  Another he taketh me by the hande,
  'Here is Paris thred, the finest in the land.'
    I never was used to such thinges in dede,
    And, wanting mony, I might not speede.

Then went I forth by London Stone,
  Throughout all Canwike Streete;[18]
Drapers mutch cloth me offred anone;
  Then comes me one, cried, 'hot shepes feete.'
  One cried, 'makerell'; 'Rishes grene,' another gan greete.[19]
    One bad me by a hood to cover my head;
    But, for want of mony, I might not be sped.

[12] purchase [13] nine o'clock [14] showed great concern for me [15] on the bough [16] offered [17] made my way [18] Cannon Street [19] another shouted 'green rushes'

Then I hied me into Estchepe.
  One cries, 'ribbs of befe, and many a pie!'
Pewter pottes they clattered on a heape;
  There was harpe, pipe, and minstrelsye.
  'Yea, by cock!' 'Nay, by cock!' some began crye;
    Some sunge of 'Jenken and Julian' for there mede.[20]
    But, for lack of mony, I might not speede.

Then into Cornhill anon I yode,[21]
  Where was mutch stolen gere amonge;
I saw where honge mine owne hoode,
  That I had lost amonge the thronge.
  To by my own hood I thought it wronge –
    I knew it well as I did my Crede;
    But, for lack of mony, I could not speede.

The Taverner tooke mee by the sleve,
  'Sir,' saith he, 'will you our wine assay?'
I answered, 'That can not mutch me greve;[22]
  A peny can do no more then it may.'
  I drank a pint, and for it did paye;
    Yet sore a-hungerd from thence I yede,[23]
    And, wanting mony, I cold not speede.

Then hied I me to Bilingsgate,
  And one cried, 'hoo! go we hence!'
I prayd a barge-man, for Gods sake,
  That he wold spare me my expence.
  'Thou scapst not here,' quod he, 'under two pence;
    I list not yet bestow my almes-dede.'[24]
    Thus, lacking mony, I could not speede.

Then I convayed me into Kent,
  For of the law wold I meddle no more,
Because no man to me tooke entent,[25]
  I dight me to do as I did before.
  Now Jesus that in Bethlem was bore,
    Save London, and send trew lawyers there mede![26]
    For who-so wantes[27] mony, with them shall not speede.

[20] to make money [21] went [22] harm [23] went [24] I've no desire to give charity yet [25] took any notice of me [26] reward [27] lacks

BRING US IN GOOD ALE

Bring us in good ale, and bring us in good ale;
For our blissid Lady sak, bring us in good ale.

Bring us in no browne bred, fore that is mad of brane,
Nor bring us in no whit bred, for therin is no game,[1]
But bring us in good ale.

Bring us in no befe, for ther is many bonis,
But bring us in good ale, for that goth downe at onis,[2]
And bring us in good ale.

Bring us in no bacon, for that is passing[3] fat,
But bring us in good ale, and give us ynough of that,
And bring us in good ale.

Bring us in no mutton, for that is often lene,
Nor bringe us in no tripes, for thei be sildom clene,
But bring us in good ale.

Bring us in no eggis, for ther ar many shelles,
But bring us in good ale, and give us nothing elles,
And bring us in good ale.

Bring us in no butter, for therin ar many hores,[4]
Nor bring us in no pigges flesh, for that wil mak us boris,[5]
But bring us in good ale.

Bring us in no capons flesh, for that is often der,
Nor bring us in no dukkes flesh, for thei slober in the mer,[6]
But bring us in good ale.

THE MONTHS

Januar: By this fire I warme my handis,
Februar: And with my spade I delfe my landis.
Marche: Here I sette my thinge to springe,[1]
Aprile: And here I heer the fowlis singe.

[1] pleasure [2] once [3] too [4] hairs [5] boars [6] pond

[1] at this time I put in my plants to grow

Maii: I am as light as birde in bowe,[2]
Junii: And I weede my corne well ynow.
Julii: With my sithe my mede I mowe,
Auguste: And here I shere my corne full lowe.
September: With my flaill I erne my brede,
October: And here I sowe my whete so redde.
November: At Martinesmasse I kille my swine,
December: And at Cristesmasse I drinke redde wine.

THE SHIRES

Hervordshir, shild[1] and spere;
Wosetershir, wringe pere.[2]
Glowsetershir, shoo and naile;
Bristowshir,[3] shippe and saile.
Oxonfordshir, girde[4] mare;
Warwikshir, binde beare.[5]
London, globber;[6]
Sothery,[7] great bragger.
Shropshir, my shines been sharpe,
Lay wood to the fire, and yef[8] me my harpe.
Lankashir, a fair archer;
Cheshir, thacker.[9]
Northumberland, hasty and hot;
Westmerland, tot for sote.[10]
Yorkeshir, full of knightes;
Lincolnshir, men full of mightes.
Cambridgeshir, full of pikes;
Holland, full of dikes.
Suffolk, full of wiles;
Norfolk, full of giles.
Essex, good houswives;
Middelsex, full of strives.[11]

[2] blithe as a bird on a bough

[1] shield [2] press pear [3] Bristol [4] saddle [5] [i.e., reference to the arms of the Earl of Warwick] [6] glutton [7] Surrey [8] give [9] thatcher [10] fool for fool [11] contention

Kent, as hot as fire;
Sussex, full of mire.
Southampton, drie and wete;
Somersetshir, good for whete.
Devinshir, wight[12] and strong;
Dorcetshir will have no wrong.
Willshir, fair and plaine;[13]
Barkshir, fill vaine.[14]
Harvodshir, full of wood;
Huntingdonshir, corne full good.
Bedfordshir is not to lack;[15]
Buckinghamshir is his mak.[16]
Northampton, full of love
Beneath the girdel and not above.
Nottinghamshir, full of hogges;
Darbyshir, full of dogges.
Leicestershir, full of benes;
Staffordshir, full of shrewd quenes.[17]
Cornewall, full of tinne;
Wales, full of gentlemen.

A VISION OF THE COUNTRY

I lepte[1] forth lightly along by the hegges,
And moved forth merily to maistrie[2] the hilles;
For til I came to the coppe couthe I not stinte[3]
Of the highest hille by halfe of alle other.
  I tourned me twyes and toted[4] aboute,
Beholding hegges and holtz[5] so grene,
The mansions and medwes[6] mowen al newe,
For such was the saison of the same yere.
I lifte up my eye-lides and looked ferther
And sawe many swete sightz, so me God helpe:

[12] bold [13] open [14] ditch [15] not to be despised [16] equal [17] scolding women

[1] ran [2] conquer [3] for I could not stop till I came to the top [4] gazed [5] woods
[6] meadows

The wodes and the waters and the welle-springes,
And trees ytrailed[7] fro toppe to th'erthe,
Coriously[8] ycovred with curtelle[9] of grene;
The flours on feeldes flavring swete,
The corn on the croftes ycropped[10] ful faire,
The renning riviere rushing faste,
Ful of fish and of frie of felefold kinde;[11]
The breris with thair beries bent over the wayes,
As honysoucles honging upon eche half;[12]
Chesteines[13] and cheries that children desiren
Were logged[14] undre leves ful lusty to seen.
The hawthorne so holsum I behelde eeke,
And how the benes blowed and the broome-floures;
Peres and plummes and pesecoddes grene,
That ladies lusty looken muche after,[15]
Were gadred for gomes[16] ere thay gunne ripe;
The grapes growed agrete[17] in gardens aboute,
And other fruitz felefold in feeldes and closes;
To nempne[18] alle the names it nedeth not here.
  The coningz[19] fro covert covred the bankes,
And raughte out a raundon[20] and retourned againes,
Played forth on the plaine, and to the pitte[21] after,
But any hound hente thaim or the hay-nettes.[22]
The hare hied him faste, and the houndes after;
For kissing of his croupe acaunt-wise he wente;[23]
For n'ad he tourned twyes,[24] his tail had be licked,
So ernestly Ector iched[25] him after.
The sheepe fro the sunne shadwed thaimself,
While the lambes laiked[26] along by the hegges.
The cow with hire calfe and coltes ful faire
And high hors in haras hurteled togedre,[27]
And preised the pasture that prime-saute[28] thaim made.
The deere on the dale drowe to thair dennes,

[7] decked [8] elaborately [9] gown [10] reaped in the fields [11] of many different kinds [12] on every side [13] chestnuts [14] sheltered [15] seek diligently [16] men [17] in plenty [18] name [19] rabbits [20] dashed out swiftly [21] warren [22] unless some dog or the rabbit-nets got them [23] to prevent them kissing his rump, he went zig-zagging [24] if he had not turned twice [25] chased [26] played [27] and the noble horses at stud rushed together [28] spirited

Ferked[29] forth to the ferne and felle down amiddes.
Hertz and hindes, a hunthred togedre,
With raindeer and robuc runne to the wodes
For the kenetz on the cleere[30] were un-y-coupled;
And buckes ful burnished that baren good grece,[31]
Four hunthred on a herde y-heeded ful faire,[32]
Layen lowe in a launde along by the pale,[33]
A swete sight for souvrains,[34] so me God helpe.
I moved doune fro the mote to the midwardz,[35]
And so adoune to the dale, dwelled I no longer;
But suche a noise of nestlingz ne so swete notez
I herde not this halfe yere, ne so hevenly sounes
As I dide on that dale adoune among the hegges;
For in every bush was a brid that in his beste wise
Babled with his bille, that blisse was to here,
So cheerly thay chirmed[36] and chaunged thair notes,
That what for flavour of the fruite and of the somer floures,
The smelling smote as spices,[37] me thought,
That of my travail trewly tooke I no kepe,[38]
For al was vanished me fro thorough the freshe sightes.

from *Mum and the Sothsegger*

A PRINCESS'S DIVERSIONS

'To-morowe ye shall on hunting fare,
And ride, my doughter, in a chare;[1]
It shal be covered with velvet reede,
And clothes of fine golde al about your hed,
With damaske white and asure-blewe,
Wel diapred[2] with lillies newe;
Your pomelles[3] shal be ended with gold,
Your chaines enameled many a folde;

[29] went [30] the hunting-dogs in the open [31] and bucks glistening and carrying much fat [32] finely equipped with antlers [33] in a clearing alongside the fence [34] lords [35] down from the crest towards the mid-slope [36] sang [37] the perfume struck me like spices [38] that I took no heed of my cares

[1] carriage [2] patterned [3] ornamental knobs

Your mantel of riche degree,[4]
Purpil palle and ermine free;[5]
Jennettes[6] of Spaine, that been so wight,[7]
Trapped[8] to the ground with velvet bright.
Ye shall have harpe, sautry,[9] and songe,
And other mirthes you amonge.[10]
Ye shall have rumney and malmesine,[11]
Both ypocrasse and vernage wine,[12]
Mountrose and wine of Greke,
Both algarde and respice eke,[13]
Antioche and bastarde,[14]
Piment also and garnarde,[15]
Wine of Greke and muscadell,
Both clare, piment, and rochell;[16]
The reed your stomake to defye,[17]
And pottes of osey[18] set you by.
You shall have venison ybake,
The best wilde foule that may be take;
A lese of grehound with you to strike,[19]
And hert and hinde and other like.
Ye shal be set at such a trist[20]
That herte and hinde shall come to your fist;
Your disease[21] to drive you fro
To here the bugles[22] there yblow,
With their bugles[23] in that place,
And sevenscore raches at his rechase.[24]
Homward thus shall ye ride,
On hauking by the rivers side,
With goshauke and with gentil fawcon,[25]
With egle-horne and merlyon.[26]

[4] quality [5] rich crimson cloth and noble ermine [6] light horses [7] swift [8] decked [9] psaltery [10] and other entertainments all about you [11] sweet Grecian wine and Malmsey [12] spiced wine and sweet Italian wine [13] also both Algarve wine and red wine [14] tonic wine and sweet Spanish [15] spiced wine and ? Granada wine [16] wine of La Rochelle [17] red wine to aid digestion [18] Alsace wine [19] three greyhounds to run with you [20] hunting station [21] melancholy [22] hunting-horns [23] ? beagles [24] sevenscore hounds at his recall [25] noble falcon [26] ? kind of hawk and merlin

'When you come home, your men among,
Ye shall have revell, daunces and songe:
Litle children, great and smale,
Shall sing as doth the nightingale.
Then shall ye go to your evensong,
With tenours and trebles among;[27]
Threescore of copes of damask bright,
Full of perles they shall be pight;[28]
Your aulter-clothes of taffata,
And your sicles[29] all of taffetra.
Your sensours shal be of golde,
Endent with asure many a folde.[30]
Your quere non organ-songe shall want[31]
With countre-note[32] and discant;
The other halfe on orgains[33] playing,
With yonge children full faire singing.
'Then shall ye go to your suppere,
And sitte in tentes in greene arbere,
With clothes of Aras pight to the grounde,[34]
With saphires set and diamounde.
A cloth of golde about your heade,
With popinjayes pight, with pery red;[35]
And officers all at your will
All maner delightes to bring you till.[36]
The nightingale sitting on a thorne
Shall singe you notes both even and morne.
An hundreth knightes truly tolde[37]
Shall play with bowles in alayes colde;[38]
Your disease[39] to drive awaye
To see the fishes in pooles playe,
And then walke in arbere up and downe
To see the floures of great renowne.
'To a draw-bridge then shall ye,
The one half of stone, the other of tre;[40]

[27] surrounded by tenors and trebles [28] adorned [29] brocade hangings [30] censers . . . elaborately inlaid with azure [31] your choir shall not lack part-singing [32] counterpoint [33] organs [34] adorned with Arras tapestries hanging to the ground [35] decorated with parrots, with red gems [36] to you [37] accurately counted [38] cool walks [39] malaise [40] wood

A barge shall mete you full right[41]
With twenty-four ores full bright,
With trompettes and with clariowne,
The freshe water to rowe up and downe.
Then shall ye go to the salte fome
Your maner to see, or[42] ye come home,
With eighty shippes of large toure,[43]
With dromedaryes of great honour,[44]
And caracks[45] with sailes two –
The sweftest that on water may go –
With galyes good upon the haven
With eighty ores at the fore-staven.[46]
Your mariners shall singe arowe[47]
"Hey, how, and rumbylawe".
Then shall ye, doughter, aske the wine,
With spices that be good and fine,
Gentil pottes with ginger grene,
With dates and deinties you betwene;[48]
Forty torches breninge[49] bright
At your bridges[50] to bringe you light.
'Into your chambre they shall you bring
With muche mirthe and more liking.[51]
Your costerdes[52] covered with white and blewe
And diapred[53] with lilies newe;
Your curtaines of camaca all in folde,[54]
Your felioles[55] all of golde;
Your tester-pery[56] at your heed,
Curtaines with popinjayes white and reed;
Your hillinges with furres of armine,[57]
Powdred with golde of hew full fine.
Your blankettes shall be of fustiayne,[58]
Your shetes shall be of clothe of Rayne.[59]
Your head-shete shall be of pery pight[60]
With diamondes set and rubyes bright.

[41] in style [42] to see your manor, before [43] with spacious fighting-tops [44] with splendid battleships [45] galleons [46] bow [47] together [48] about you [49] burning [50] landing-stages [51] delight [52] hangings [53] adorned [54] pleated silk [55] bed-posts [56] ? jewelled head-board [57] quilts with ermine [58] fustian [59] linen of Rennes [60] studded with gems

When you are laid in bedde so softe,
A cage of golde shall hange alofte,
With longe peper faire burning
And cloves that be swete smelling,
Frankensence and olibanum,[61]
That when ye slepe the taste[62] may come.
And if ye no rest may take,
All night minstrelles for you shall wake.'[63]
  'Gramercy, father, so mote I the,[64]
For all these thinges liketh not me.'[65]

from *The Squyer of Low Degre*

THE PLOUGHMAN

I seigh a sely[1] man me by upon the plow hongen,
His cote was of a cloute that cary was ycalled,[2]
His hood was full of holes, and his heer oute,
With his knopped shoon clouted full thikke;[3]
His ton toteden out[4] as he the londe treddede,
His hosen overhongen his hokshines[5] on everiche a side,
Al beslobred in fen[6] as he the plow folwede;
Twey mitenes as mete[7] maad all of cloutes;
The fingers weren for-werd[8] and ful of fen honged.
This wight waselede[9] in the fen almost to the ancle,
Foure rotheren[10] him biforn, that feble were worthen;[11]
Men mighte reken[12] ich a rib, so reufull[13] they weren.
His wif walked him with, with a longe gode,[14]
In a cutted cote,[15] cutted full heighe,
Wrapped in a winwe sheete to weren hire fro weders,[16]

[61] aromatic resin [62] scent [63] stay awake [64] thank you so much, father [65] despite all these things I am still not happy

[1] humble [2] his coat was of a [rough] material called 'cary' [3] his lumpy shoes very thickly patched [4] his toes peeped out [5] gaiters [6] mud [7] scanty [8] worn out [9] this fellow plastered himself [10] heifers [11] which had grown weak [12] count [13] pitiful [14] goad [15] shortened coat [16] wrapped in a winnowing sheet to protect herself from squalls

Barfote on the bare is,[17] that the blood folwede.
And at the londes ende laye a litell crom-bolle,[18]
And theron lay a litell childe lapped in cloutes,
And tweyne of tweie yeres olde upon another side,
And alle they songen o songe, that sorwe was to heren;
They crieden alle o cry, a carefull note.[19]

from *Pierce the Ploughman's Crede*

?JAMES RYMAN

FAREWELL ADVENT!

Farewele Advent! Cristemas is cum;
  Farewele fro us, both all and sum.[1]

With paciens thou hast us fedde
And made us go hungrie to bedde;
For lak of mete we were nighe dedde;
  Farewele fro us, both all and sum.

While thou hast be within oure house.
We ete no puddinges ne no souse,[2]
But stinking fish not worth a louse;
  Farewele fro us, both all and sum.

There was no fresh fish ferre ne nere;[3]
Salt fish and samon was to dere;
And thus we have had hevy chere;[4]
  Farewele fro us, both all and sum.

Thou hast us fedde with plaices thinne,
Nothing on them but bone and skinne;
Therfore our love thou shalt not winne;
  Farewele fro us, both all and sum.

[17] ice [18] and at the end of the patch lay a small wooden bowl [19] a doleful sound

[1] one and all [2] pickled meat [3] far or near [4] dreary fare

With muskilles[5] gaping after the moone
Thou hast us fedde at night and noone
But ones a weke, and that to soone;
  Farewele fro us, both all and sum.

Our bred was browne, our ale was thinne,
Our bred was musty in the binne,
Our ale soure or[6] we did beginne;
  Farewele fro us, both all and sum.

Thou art of grete ingratitude
Good mete fro us for to exclude;
Thou art not kinde but very rude;
  Farewele fro us, both all and sum.

Thou dwellest with us ayenst our wille,
And yet thou givest us not our fille;
For lak of mete thou woldest us spille;[7]
  Farewele fro us, both all and sum.

Above all thinge thou art a meane[8]
To make our chekes both bare and leane.
I wolde thou were at Boughton Bleane!
  Farewele fro us, both all and sum.

Come thou no more here nor in Kent,
For, if thou doo, thou shalt be shent;[9]
It is ynough to faste in Lent;
  Farewele fro us, both all and sum.

Thou mayst not dwelle with none estate;[10]
Therfore with us thou playest chekmate.
Go hens, or we will breke thy pate!
  Farewele fro us, both all and sum.

Thou mayst not dwell with knight nor squier;
For them[11] thou mayst lie in the mire;
They love not thee nor Lent, thy sire;
  Farewele fro us, both all and sum.

[5] mussels [6] before [7] destroy [8] means [9] you will come to harm [10] class [11] as far as they are concerned

Thou mayst not dwell with labouring man,
For on thy fare no skille he can,[12]
For he must ete bothe now and than;
  Farewele fro us, both all and sum.

Though thou shalt dwell with monk and frere,
Chanon and nonne ones every yere,
Yet thou shuldest make us better chere;[13]
  Farewele fro us, both all and sum.

This time of Cristes feest natall
We will be mery, grete and small,
And thou shalt go oute of this hall;
  Farewele fro us, both all and sum.

Advent is gone; Cristemas is cum;
Be we mery now, alle and sum!
He is not wise that will be dum.
  In ortu Regis omnium.

ANONYMOUS

THE PILGRIMS' VOYAGE

Men may leve all gamis[1]
That sailen to Saint Jamis;[2]
For many a man it gramis[3]
  When they begin to saile.
For when they have take the see
At Sandwiche or at Winchilsee,
At Bristow, or where that it bee,[4]
  Their hertes begin to faile.

[12] he cannot work [13] still you should treat us more kindly

[1] men may renounce all pleasures [2] St James of Compostela [3] oppresses
[4] Bristol, or wherever

Anone the master commaundeth fast
To his shipmen in alle the hast
To dresse hem soone about the mast[5]
  Their takeling to make.[6]
With 'howe! hissa!' then they cry,
'What howe, mate! thow standist to ny,[7]
Thy felow may not hale thee by';[8]
  Thus they begin to crake.[9]

A boy or twein anone up styen[10]
And overthwart[11] the saile-yerde lyen;
'Y how! tailia!' the remenaunt cryen
  And pulle with alle their might.
'Bestowe[12] the bote, boteswaine, anon,
That our pilgrims may pley theron;[13]
For som are like to cough and grone
  Or[14] it be full midnight.

'Hale the boweline! Now vere the shete![15]
Cooke, make redy anon our mete;
Our pilgrims have no lust[16] to ete,
  I pray God yeve hem rest!
Go to the helm! What howe! No nere![17]
Steward, felow, a pot of bere!'
'Ye shall have, sir, with good chere[18]
  Anon all of the best.'

'Y howe! trussa! hale in the brailes![19]
Thou halist not, by God, thow failes![20]
O see how welle our good ship sailes!'
  And thus they say among.
'Hale in the wartake!'[21] 'It shal be done'.
'Steward, cover the borde[22] anone
And set bred and salt thereon,
  And tary nat to long.'

[5] and at once take up positions round the mast [6] to arrange their ropes [7] close [8] cannot haul next to you [9] shout [10] climb [11] across [12] load [13] relax on it [14] before [15] unfold the sail [16] desire [17] no nearer the wind [18] with pleasure [19] buntlines [20] you're slacking [21] line [22] table

Then cometh one and seith: 'Be mery!
Ye shall have a storme or a pery.'[23]
'Hold thou thy pees! Thou canst no very;[24]
  Thou medlist wonder sore.'[25]
This mene-while the pilgrims ly
And have their bowles fast them by,
And cry after hot malvesy,[26]
  'Thou helpe for to restore!'

And some wold have a saltid tost,
For they might ete neither sode[27] ne rost;
A man might soone pay for their cost
  As for o day or twaine.[28]
Some laide their bookis on their knee
And rad[29] so long they might not see;
'Allas! mine hede will cleve on three!'
  Thus saith another certaine.

Then commeth our owner like a lorde,
And speketh many a royall worde,
And dresseth him to the high borde[30]
  To see alle thing be welle.
Anone he calleth a carpentere
And biddith him bring with him his gere
To make the cabans here and there
  With many a febil[31] celle.

A sak of straw were there right good,
For some must lig them[32] in their hood –
I had as lefe[33] be in the wood
  Withoute mete[34] or drink;
For when that we shall go to bedde,
The pumpe was nigh our beddes hede:
A man were as good to be dede[35]
  As smell therof the stink.

[23] squall [24] you don't know the truth [25] you're a terrible trouble-maker [26] warm Malmsey [27] boiled [28] for a day or two [29] read [30] and goes on to the top deck [31] wretched [32] lie down [33] I would as soon [34] food [35] might as well be dead

A LETTER TO HIS TRUELOVE

Go, litull bill,[1] and command me hertely[2]
Unto her that I call my trulof and lady,
By this same tru tokenninge[3]
That sho se me in a kirk on a Friday in a morning,
With a sper-hauk[4] on my hand;
And my mone[5] did by her stond;
And an old womon sete her by
That litull cold[6] of curtesy,
And oft on her sho did smile
To loke on me for a wile.
And yet by this another token –
To the kirke she comme with a gentilwomon;
Even behind the kirk dore
Thay kneled bothe on the flore,
And fast thay did piter-pater –[7]
I hope thay said matens togeder!
Yet ones or twyes at the lest,[8]
Sho did on me her ee kest;[9]
Then went I forthe prevely,
And hailsed on thaim curtesly.[10]
Be alle the tokens truly,
Comand me to her hertely.

AT THE TAVERN

Is[1] tell you my mind, Annes Tayliur, dame;
I deem we lak plesur.
Looke here, dame, unloke your dur:[2]
Alacke, we have no likur!

Frend, and we ar fer in dette[3]
For your fine goode wine, God wot,
A short gint[4] has a pint potte:
I drank onis, I wold drinke yette.

[1] note [2] cordially commend me [3] sure sign [4] sparrow-hawk [5] servant [6] knew [7] they whispered furiously [8] at least [9] cast her eye [10] and greeted them amicably

[1] I [2] unlock your door [3] even if we are far in debt [4] ? measure

THE AXE WAS SHARP . . .

The ax was sharpe, the stokke[1] was harde,
In the fourthe yere of King Richarde.

THE SCHOOLBOY

Hay, hay, by this day,
What availeth it me though I say nay?

I wold fain be a clerke,[1]
But yet it is a stronge werke;[2]
The birchen twigges be so sharpe
It makith me have a faint herte.
  What availeth it me though I say nay?

On Monday in the morning when I shall rise,
At six of the clok, it is the gise[3]
To go to scole without avise –[4]
I had lever[5] go twenty mile twise.
  What availeth it me though I say nay?

My master lookith as he were madde:
'Wher hast thou be, thou sory ladde?'
'Milke dukkes my moder badde' –[6]
It was no mervaile though I were sadde.
  What availeth it me though I say nay?

My master pepered my ars with well good spede;
It was worse than finkill sede;[7]
He wold not leve till it did blede –
Miche sorow have he for his dede!
  What availeth it me though I say nay?

I wold my master were a watt,[8]
And my booke a wild catt,

[1] block

[1] scholar [2] cruel labour [3] custom [4] second thought [5] rather [6] my mother told me to milk ducks [7] fennel seed [8] hare

And a brase of grehoundes in his toppe:[9]
I wold be glad for to see that!
  What availeth it me though I say nay?

I wold my master were an hare,
And all his bookes houndes were,
And I myself a joly huntere;
To blow my horn I wold not spare,
For if he were dede I wold not care.
  What availeth it me though I say nay?

JOLY WAT

  Can I not sing but hoy,
  When the joly sheperd made so much joy.

The sheperd upon a hill he satt;
He had on him his tabard and his hat,
His tarbox, his pipe, and his flagat;[1]
His name was called Joly, Joly Wat,
  For he was a gud herdes boy.
    With hoy!
  For in his pipe he made so much joy.

The sheperd upon a hill was laid;
His doge to his girdell was tayd;[2]
He had not slept but a litill broyd[3]
But 'Gloria in excelcis' was to him said.
    With hoy!
  For in his pipe he made so much joy.

The sheperd on a hill he stoode;
Rownd abowt him his shepe they yode;[4]
He put his hond under his hoode;
He saw a star as rede as blood.
    With hoy!
  For in his pipe he made so much joy.

[9] harrying him

[1] flask [2] tied [3] space of time [4] went

'Now farwell Mall, and also Will;[5]
For my love go ye all still[6]
Unto I cum again you till,[7]
And evermore, Will, ring well thy bell.'
With hoy!
For in his pipe he made so much joy.

'Now must I go ther Crist was borne;
Farewell, I cum again tomorn;
Dog, kepe well my shep fro the corn,
And warn well, warroke,[8] when I blow my horn.'
With hoy!
For in his pipe he made so much joy.

The sheperd said anon right,[9]
'I will go see yon farly[10] sight,
Wheras the angell singith on hight,[11]
And the star that shinith so bright.'
With hoy!
For in his pipe he made so much joy.

When Wat to Bedlem cum was,
He swet; he had gon faster than a pace.[12]
He fownd Jhesu in a simpell place
Betwen an ox and an asse.
With hoy!
For in his pipe he made so much joy.

'Jhesu, I offer to thee here my pipe,
My skirte, my tarbox, and my scripe;[13]
Home to my fellowes now will I skipe,
And also looke unto my shepe.'
With hoy!
For in his pipe he made so much joy.

'Now, farewell, mine own herdesman Wat.'
'Ye, for God, lady, even so I hat.[14]

[5] [i.e., names of sheep] [6] quietly [7] until I return to you [8] ? wretch [9] at once [10] marvellous [11] where the angel sings out loud [12] walking-pace [13] kilt, tar-box, and my wallet [14] Yes, before God, lady, just so I am called

Lull well Jhesu in thy lap,
And farewell, Joseph, with thy rownd cap.'
With hoy!
For in his pipe he made so much joy.

'Now may I well both hop[15] and sing,
For I have bene at Cristes bering.
Home to my felowes now will I fling.
Crist of heven to his blis us bring!'
With hoy!
For in his pipe he made so much joy.

CHRISTMAS SPORTS

Make we mery, bothe more and lasse,
For now is the time of Cristmas.

Lett no man cum into this hall,
Grome,[1] page, nor yet marshall,[2]
But that sum sport he bring withall,
For now is the time of Cristmas.

Iff that he say he can not sing,
Sum oder sport then lett him bring,
That it may please at this festing,
For now is the time of Cristmas.

Iff he say he can nowght do,
Then for my love aske him no mo,[3]
But to the stokkes then lett him go,
For now is the time of Cristmas.

[15] dance

[1] serving man [2] steward [3] more

A CHRISTMAS FEAST

Hey, hey, hey, hey!
The bores hede is armed gay[1]

The bores hede in hond I bring,
With garlond gay in porttoring;[2]
I pray you all with me to singe
        With hay!

Lordes, knighttes and squiers,
Persons, pristes,[3] and vicars,
The bores hede is the furst mes,[4]
        With hay!

The bores hede, as I you say,
He takes his leve and gothe his way
Soon after the Twelffith Day,
        With hay!

Then comes in the secund kowrs with mikill pride,[5]
The crannes, and the heyrrouns, the bitteres[6] by ther side,
The partriches and the plovers, the woodcokes and the snit,[7]
        With hay!

Larkes in a hoot sewe,[8] ladys for to pik,
Good drink therto, lucius[9] and fine,
Brewet of allmayn, romnay[10] and wine,
        With hay!

Gud bred, alle, and wine, dare I well say,
The bores hede with musterd armed so gay.

Furmante to[11] pottage, with vennissun fin,
And hombuls of the dow,[12] and all that ever commes in.

Cappons ibake, with peses of the roow,[13]
Reisons of corrans,[14] with othere spises moo.

[1] finely garnished [2] bearing [3] parsons, priests [4] dish [5] great ceremony [6] cranes . . . herons . . . bitterns [7] snipe [8] meat-sauce [9] luscious [10] almond milk, sweet Grecian wine [11] frumenty as [12] umbles of the doe [13] pieces of the roe [14] Corinthian currants

THE GOSSIPS

'Go ye before be twaine and twaine,[1]
Wisly, that ye be not isayne,[2]
And I shall go home and com againe,
  To witte[3] what dothe owre sire.

'For if hit happ he did me se,
A stripe or to[4] God might send me;
Yet she that is aferre,[5] lette her flee,
  For that is nowght be this fire.'[6]

That everiche of hem browght ther dishe;
Sum browght fleshe, and som brought fishe;
Quod Margery meke than with a wishe,
  'I wold that Frankelin the harper were here.'

She hade notte so sone the word isaid,
But in come Frankelin at a braid.[7]
'God save you, mastres,' he saide,
  'I come to make you some chere.'[8]

Anon he began to draw owght his harpe;
Tho[9] the gossippes began to starte;
They called the taverner to fill the quarte
  And lette not for no coste.

Then said the gossippes all in fere,[10]
'Strike up, harper, and make gode chere,
And wher that I go, fere or nere,
  To owre husbondes make thou no boste.'[11]

'Nay, mastres, as mote I thee,[12]
Ye shall never be wrayed for me;[13]
I had lever here dede to be
  As hereof to be knowe.'[14]

[1] two by two [2] prudently, so that you aren't seen [3] know [4] two [5] afraid [6] for nobody is around this fire [7] suddenly [8] give you some entertainment [9] then [10] all together [11] clamour [12] as I may prosper [13] betrayed because of me [14] than for this to be known

They filled the pottes by and by;
They lett not for no coste trully;
The harper stroke up merrely,
  That they might onethe blowe.[15]

They sette them downe; they might no more;
Their legges they thought were passing soore;
They prayd the harper, 'Kepe sum store,[16]
  And lette us drinke a bowght.[17]

'Heye thee,[18] tavernere, I praye thee;
Go fill the pottes lightly,
And latte us drinke by and by,
  And lette the cup go route.'[19]

This is the thowght that gossipes take:
Ones in the weke they will mery make,
And all smalle drinckis they will forsake,
  And drinke wine of the best.

Some be at the taverne ones in the weke,
And some be there every day eke,
And ellse ther hartes will be sekke[20]
  And give her hosbondis evill reste.[21]

When they had dronke and made them glad,
And they shuld reken,[22] then they said,
'Call the tavernere,' anone they bade,
  'That we were lightly hens.'[23]

'I swere be God and by Seint Jame,
I wold notte that oure sire at home
Wiste[24] that we had this game,
  Notte for fourty pens.

'Gader the scote, and lette us wend,[25]
And lette us go home by Lurcas Ende,
For dred we mete note with owre frend
  Or[26] that we come home.'

[15] scarcely breathe [16] take some collection [17] round [18] hurry [19] about [20] sick [21] little peace [22] they ought to settle up [23] so that we may be quickly away [24] knew [25] collect up contributions for the bill, and let us go [26] before

When they had there countes caste,[27]
Everiche of hem spend sixpence at the last;
'Alas,' quothe Ceicely, 'I am aggaste;
We shall be shent[28] evrichone.'

Fro the taverne be they all goone,
And everiche of hem shewith her wisdom,
And there she telleth her husbond anone
She had been at the churche.

Of her werke she taketh no kepe;[29]
She must as for anowe[30] go slepe,
And ells for angeyr[31] will she wepe;
She may no werkes wurche.[32]

Of[33] her slepe when she dothe wake,
Faste in hey then gan she arake,[34]
And clawthe[35] her servantes abowte the bake,
If to her they outhe[36] had said.

Of this proses[37] I make an end
Becawse I wil have women to be my frend;
Of there devosion they wold send
A peny for to drinke at the end.

THE FORESTER

I am a joly foster,[1]
I am a joly foster,
And have ben many a day,
And foster will I be still,
For shoot right well I may,
For shoot ryght well I may.

[27] worked out their debts [28] ruined [29] she doesn't care about her work [30] at this moment [31] ? distress, anguish [32] she can do no tasks [33] from [34] begins to bustle [35] beat [36] anything [37] discourse

[1] forester

Wherfor shuld I hang up my bow upon the grenwod bough?
I can bend and draw a bow and shoot well enough.

Wherfor shuld I hang up mine arrow upon the grenwod linde?[2]
I have strength to mak it fle[3] and kill bothe hart and hind.

Wherfor shuld I hang up my horne upon the grenwod tree?
I can blow the deth of a deere as well as any that ever I see.

Wherfor shuld I tie up my hownd unto the grenwod spray?
I can luge and make a sute[4] as well as any in May.

WILLIAM DUNBAR

TO THE MERCHANTS OF EDINBURGH

Quhy[1] will ye, merchantis of renoun,
Lat[2] Edinburgh, your nobill toun,
For laik[3] of reformatioun
The commone proffeitt tyine and fame?[4]
  Think ye not shame,
That onie uther regioun
Sall with dishonour hurt your name?

May nane pas throw your principall gaittis[5]
For stink of haddockis and of scattis,[6]
For cryis of carlingis and debaittis,[7]
For fensum flyttingis of defame:[8]
  Think ye not shame,
Befoir strangeris of all estaittis[9]
That sic dishonour hurt your name?

[2] tree [3] fly [4] I can find the hiding-place of a deer and make pursuit

[1] why [2] allow [3] lack [4] lose reputation and public welfare [5] streets [6] skate [7] for the shouting and squabbling of old women [8] for nauseous and slanderous invective [9] degrees

Your stinkand Scull,[10] that standis dirk,
Haldis the licht fra your parroche[11] kirk;
Your foirstairis makis your housis mirk,[12]
Lik na cuntray bot heir at hame:
  Think ye not shame,
Sa litill polesie[13] to wirk
In hurt and sclander of your name?

At your hie Croce, quhar[14] gold and silk
Sould be, thair is bot crudis[15] and milk;
And at your Trone bot cokill and wilk,[16]
Panshes,[17] pudingis of Jok and Jame:
  Think ye not shame,
Sen as[18] the world sayis that ilk
In hurt and sclander of your name?

Your commone menstrallis hes no tone[19]
Bot 'Now the day dawis,' and 'Into Joun';
Cunningar men man[20] serve Sanct Cloun,
And nevir to uther craftis clame:[21]
  Think ye not shame,
To hald sic mowaris on the moyne,[22]
In hurt and sclander of your name?

Tailiouris, soutteris, and craftis vill,[23]
The fairest of your streitis dois fill;
And merchandis at the Stinkand Styll[24]
Ar hamperit in ane hony came:[25]
  Think ye not shame,
That ye have nether witt nor will
To win yourselff ane bettir name?

Your burgh of beggeris is ane nest,
To shout thai swentiouris[26] will not rest;

[10] school [11] parish [12] your outside stairs make your houses gloomy [13] civic planning [14] where [15] curds [16] and at your public weighing-machine nothing but cockles and whelks [17] tripe [18] since [19] tune [20] more skilful men must [21] and never lay claim to other skills [22] to support such mockers at the moon [foolish idlers] [23] cobblers and base trades [24] stinking alley [probably Old-Kirk Style] [25] are cramped into a honey-comb [26] those rascals

All honest folk they do molest,
Sa piteuslie thai cry and rame:[27]
  Think ye not shame,
That for the poore hes nothing drest,[28]
In hurt and sclander of your name?

Your proffeit daylie dois incres,
Your godlie workis les and les;
Through streittis nane may mak progres
For cry of cruikit, blind, and lame:
  Think ye not shame,
That ye sic substance dois posses,
And will nocht win ane bettir name?

Sen[29] for the Court and the Sessioun,
The great repair[30] of this regioun
Is in your burgh, thairfoir be boun[31]
To mend all faultis that ar to blame,
  And eschew shame;
If thai pas to ane uther toun
Ye will decay, and your great name.

Thairfoir strangeris and leigis treit,[32]
Tak not over meikle for thair meit,[33]
And gar your merchandis be discreit,[34]
That na extortiounes be, proclame
  All fraud and shame:
Keip ordour, and poore nighbouris beit,[35]
That ye may gett ane bettir name.

Singular proffeit[36] so dois yow blind,
The common proffeit[37] gois behind:
I pray that Lord remeid[38] to find,
That deit into Jerusalem,
  And gar yow shame;
That sum time ressoun may yow bind,
For to [   ] yow guid name.

[27] clamour [28] arranged [29] since [30] meeting-place [31] ready [32] entertain strangers and subjects [33] do not take too much for their food [34] make your merchants be reasonable [35] improve poor neighbours [36] personal advantage [37] public welfare [38] a remedy

ANONYMOUS

THE SHEPHERDS' FEAST

Enter Jak Garcio.

Jak Garcio. Now God gif you care, foles all sam![1]
Saw I never none so fare[2] bot the foles of Gotham.
Wo is hir that you bare! Youre sire and youre dam,
Had she broght forth an hare, a shepe, or a lam,
Had bene well.
Of all the foles I can tell,
From heven unto hell,
Ye thre bere the bell;
God gif you unseill![3]

1 Pastor. How pastures oure fee?[4] Say me, good pen.
Garcio. Thay ar grassed to the knee.
2 Pastor. Fare fall thee!
Garcio. Amen.
If ye will ye may se; youre bestes ye ken. [*Exit Garcio.*
1 Pastor. Sitt we downe all thre, and drink shall we then.
3 Pastor. Yey, turde!
I am lever ete;[5]
What is drink withoute mete?
Gett mete, gett,
And sett us a borde;
Then may we go dine, oure bellys to fill.
2 Pastor. Abide unto sine.[6]
3 Pastor. Be God, sir, I nill![7]
I am worthy the wine, me think it good skill.[8]
My servise I tine;[9] I fare full ill
At youre mangere.
1 Pastor. Trus,[10] go we to mete!
It is best that we trete;[11]
I list not to plete
To stand in thy dangere.[12]

[1] bunch of fools [2] fine [3] misfortune [4] stock [5] I'd rather eat [6] wait until later [7] will not [8] I deserve the wine, it seems quite reasonable to me [9] waste [10] come on [11] come to terms [12] I don't wish to contest it and be in your disfavour

Thou has ever bene curst[13] sin we met togeder.
3 Pastor. Now in faith, if I durst, ye ar even my broder.[14]
2 Pastor. Sirs, let us crib[15] furst, for oone thing or oder,
That thise wordis be purst, and let us go foder
Oure mompins.[16]
Lay forth of oure store:[17]
Lo, here browne of a bore!
1 Pastor. Set mustard afore;
Oure mete now begins.

Here a foote of a cowe well sawsed, I wene,
The pestell[18] of a sowe that powderd has bene,
Two blodingis,[19] I trow, a levering[20] betwene;
Do gladly, sirs, now, my breder, bedene![21]
With more –
Both befe, and moton
Of an ewe that was roton
(Good mete for a gloton);
Ete of this store.

2 Pastor. I have here in my maill sothen and rost.[22]
Even of an ox-taill that wold not be lost –[23]
Ha, ha! goderhaill! I let for no cost;[24]
A good py or we faill:[25] this is good for the frost
In a morning;
And two swine-gronys,[26]
All a hare bot the lonys.[27]
We mister no sponis[28]
Here at oure manging.[29]

3 Pastor. Here is to recorde the leg of a gos,[30]
With chikens endorde,[31] pork, partrik to ros,[32]
A tart for a lorde – how think ye this dos? –
A calf-liver skorde with the veriose:[33]
Good sawse,

[13] perverse [14] you are my equal in that [15] trough [16] To shut away these words, let us go and feed our faces [literally, teeth] [17] provisions [18] haunch [19] black-puddings [20] liver-sausage [21] my brothers, at once [22] in my bag boiled and roast meat [23] from an ox-tail that ought not to be wasted [24] good health! I spare no expense [25] a good pie before we run short [26] pigs' snouts [27] loins [28] we need no spoons [29] meal [30] goose [31] glazed with egg-yolk [32] choice partridge [33] crab-apple juice

This is a restorite
To make a good appete.
1 Pastor. Yee speke all by clerge,[34]
I here by youre clause.

Cowth ye by youre gramery[35] reche us a drink,
I shuld be more mery – ye wote what I think.
2 Pastor. Have good aill of Hely! Bewar now, I wink,
For and thou drink drely,[36] in thy poll will it sink.
1 Pastor. A, so!
This is bote of oure baill,[37]
Good holsom aill. [*Drinks.*
3 Pastor. Ye hold long the skaill;[38]
Now lett me go to. [*Drinks.*

2 Pastor. I shrew those lippis bot thou leiff me som parte.
1 Pastor. Be God, he bot sippis; begilde thou art.
Behold how he kippis![39] [*Second Shepherd snatches the cup.*
2 Pastor. I shrew you so smart,
And me on my hippis, bot if I gart[40]
Abate.
Be thou wine, be thou aill, [*Addresses contents of the cup.*
Bot if my brethe faill,
I shall sett thee on saill;[41]
God send thee good gaite![42] [*Drinks.*

3 Pastor. Be my dam saull,[43] Alice, it was sadly[44] drunken!
[*First Shepherd peers into the cup.*
1 Pastor. Now, as ever have I bliss, to the bothom it is sunken.
2 Pastor. Yit a botell here is –
3 Pastor. That is well spoken;
By my thrift, we must kiss!
2 Pastor. – that had I forgoten.
Bot hark!
Whoso can best sing
Shall have the beginning.

[34] in technicalities [35] grammar [36] for if you drink deeply [37] cure for our ill [38] cup [39] snatches [40] make it [41] on your way [literally, a-sailing] [42] passage [43] by my mother's soul [44] deeply

1 Pastor. Now prais at the parting;[45]
I shall sett you on worke. [*They sing.*

We have done oure parte and songen right weill;
I drink for my parte. [*Drinks.*
2 Pastor. Abide, lett cup reill![46] [*Drinks.*
1 Pastor. Godis forbot thou spart,[47] and thou drink every deill.[48]
3 Pastor. Thou has drunken a quart, therfor choke thee the deill![49]
1 Pastor. Thou ravis;
And it were for a sow
Ther is drink enogh.
3 Pastor. I shrew the handis it drow! [*Examines empty cup.*
Ye be both knavis.

1 Pastor. Nay, we knaves[50] all; thus think me best,
So, sir, shuld ye call.[51]
2 Pastor. Forth let it rest;
We will not brall.
1 Pastor. Then wold I we fest,[52]
This mete who shall into paniere kest.
3 Pastor. Sirs, heris![53]
For oure saules lett us do
Poore men gif it to.
1 Pastor. Geder up, lo, lo,
Ye hungre begers, freris!

2 Pastor. It draes nere night. Trus,[54] go we to rest.
I am even redy dight;[55] I think it the best.
3 Pastor. For ferde we be fright, a crosse lett us kest –[56]
Crist-crosse, benedight[57] eest and west –
For drede.
Jesus onazorus
Cruciefixus,
Morcus, Andreus,
God be oure spede! [*The shepherds sleep.*

from *The Wakefield Plays in the Towneley Cycle*

[45] now praise when it's due [i.e., after singing] [46] go round [47] God forbid you spare it [48] drop [49] devil [50] humble men [51] thus it seems best to me that you should call us such, sir [52] settle [53] listen [54] Come on [55] prepared [56] for fear we be frightened, let us make the sign of the cross [57] blessed

JOHN SKELTON

THE TUNNING OF ELINOUR RUMMINGE

Tell you I chill,[1]
If that ye will
A while be still,
Of a comely Jill
That dwelt on a hill:
But she is not grill,[2]
For she is somwhat sage
And well worne in age,
For her visage
It woldt asuage
A mannes courage.[3]
  Her lothely lere[4]
Is nothing clere,
But ugly of chere,[5]
Droupy and drowsy,
Scurvy and lowsy,
Her face all bowsy,[6]
Comely crinkled,
Woundersly wrinkled,
Like a rost pigges eare,
Bristled with here.[7]
  Her lewde lippes twaine,
They slaver, men sayne,[8]
Like a ropy raine,
A gummy glaire.[9]
She is ugly faire:
Her nose somdele hooked,
And camously crooked,[10]
Never stoppinge,
But ever droppinge;

[1] I wish to tell you [2] fierce [3] spirit [4] face [5] appearance [6] boozy [7] hair [8] say [9] glue [10] snub-nosed

Her skinne, loose and slacke,
Greuyned[11] like a sacke;
With a crooked backe.
  Her eyen gowndy[12]
Are full unsowndy,
For they are blered;
And she gray-hered,
Jawed like a jetty;
A man wolde have pitty
To see how she is gumbed,[13]
Fingered and thumbed,
Gently jointed,
Gresed and anointed
Up to the knuckles;
The bones of her huckels[14]
Like as they were with buckels
Togider made fast.
Her youth is farre past!
Footed like a plane,
Legged like a crane,
And yet she will jet[15]
Like a joyly fet,[16]
In her furred flocket,[17]
And graye russet rocket,[18]
With simper-the-cocket.[19]
Her huke[20] of Lincolne greene
It has been hers, I weene,
More then fourty yere;
And so doth it apere,
For the greene bare thredes
Looke like sere weedes,
Widdered[21] like hay,
The wool worne away.
And yet, I dare saye,
She thinketh herselfe gaye

[11] textured [12] full of matter [13] equipped with gums [14] hips [15] strut [16] elegant lady [17] long-sleeved cloak [18] mantle [19] with affected, simpering manners [20] cape [21] withered

Upon the holy daye[22]
When she doth her aray
And girdeth in her gytes[23]
Stitched and pranked[24] with pletes;
Her kertel, Bristowe red,
With clothes upon her hed
That wey a sowe of led,[25]
Writhen[26] in wonder wise
After the Sarasins gise,[27]
With a whim-wham[28]
Knit with a trim-tram[29]
Upon her braine-pan;
Like an Egypcian[30]
Lapped about.
  Whan she goeth out
Herselfe for to shewe,
She driveth downe the dewe
With a paire of heles
As brode as two wheles;
She hobles as she gose
With her blanket hose,[31]
Her shoone smered with talowe,
Gresed upon dirt
That badeth[32] her skirt.

Fit the First

  And this comely dame,
I understande, her name
Is Elinour Rumminge,
At home in her wonninge;[33]
And as men say
She dwelt in Sothray,[34]
In a certaine stede[35]
Biside Lederhede.

[22] feast day [23] skirts [24] decorated [25] that weigh a pig of lead [i.e., a mass of newly smelted lead] [26] coiled [27] fashion [28] trinket [29] joined with a bauble [30] gipsy [31] woollen stockings [32] befouls [33] dwelling [34] Surrey [35] place

She is a tonnish gib,[36]
The devill and she be sib.[37]

But to make up my tale,
She breweth noppy ale,[38]
And maketh thereof port-sale[39]
To travellars, to tinkers,
To sweters, to swinkers,[40]
And all good ale-drinkers,
That will nothinge spare,
But drinke till they stare
And bringe themselve bare,
With 'Now away the mare,[41]
And let us slay care!'
As wise as an hare!

Come whoso will
To Elinour on the hill,
With 'Fill the cup, fill!'
And sit there by still,
Erly and late.
Thither cometh Kate,
Cisly, and Sare,
With their legges bare,
And also their feete
Hardely[42] full unswete;
With their heeles dagged,[43]
Their kirtelles all to-jagged,
Their smockes all to-ragged,
With titters and tatters,
Bringe dishes and platters,
With all their might runninge
To Elinour Rumminge
To have of her tunninge:[44]
She leneth them on the same,[45]
And thus beginneth the game.

[36] a gross old cat [37] akin [38] strong, sweet ale [39] sale by auction [40] sweaters and labourers [41] Drink up and be merry! [42] certainly [43] muddied [44] brewing [45] she gives to them without discrimination

Some wenches come unlased,
Some huswives come unbrased,[46]
With their naked pappes,
That flippes and flappes:
It wigges and it wagges
Like tawny saffron bagges,
A sorte of foule drabbes
All scurvy with scabbes.
Some be flybitten,[47]
Some skewed[48] as a kitten;
Some with a sho-clout
Binde their heddes about;
Some have no herelace,[49]
Their lockes aboute their face
Their tresses untrussed
All full of unlust;[50]
Some looke strawry,[51]
Some cawry-mawry:[52]
Full untidy tegges,[53]
Like rotten egges.
Such a lewde sort
To Elinour resorte
From tide to tide.
Abide, abide,
And to you shall be tolde
Howe her ale is solde
To mawte and to molde.[54]

Fit the Second

Some have no mony
That thider commy[55]
For their ale to pay.
That is a shrewd aray![56]
Elinour swered, 'Nay,
Ye shall not bere awaye

[46] undone [47] flea-bitten [48] unsteady [49] hair-ribbon [50] repulsiveness [51] rustic [52] homespun [53] shaggy sheep [54] to malt and to go mouldy [55] come there [56] a bad business

Mine ale for nought,
By Him that me bought!'[57]
With 'Hey, dogge, hey!
Have these hogges away!'
With 'Get me a staffè,
The swine eate my draffè![58]
Strike the hogges with a club,
They have dronke up my swilling-tubbe!'[59]
For, be there never so muche prese,[60]
These swine go to the hye dese:[61]
The sowe with her pigges,[62]
The bore his taile wrigges,[63]
His rumpe also he frigges[64]
Against the hye benche.
With, 'Fo, ther is a stenche!
Gather up, thou wenche;
Seest thou not what is fall?
Take up dirt and all,
And bere out of the hall:
God give it ill previnge,[65]
Clenly as ivell 'chevinge!'[66]

But let us turne plaine,
There we lefte againe.
For as ill a patch as that
The hennes run in the mashvat;
For they go to roust
Streight over the ale-joust,[67]
And dunge, when it commes,
In the ale tunnes.[68]
Then Elinour taketh
The mashe-bolle, and shaketh
The hennes' dunge awaye,
And skommeth[69] it into a tray
Whereas the yeest is,
With her maungy[70] fistis:

[57] ransomed [58] swill [59] mixing-tub [60] great throng [61] high dais [62] piglets [63] wags [64] scratches [65] bad end [66] bad luck [67] ale-pot [68] falls in the barrel [69] skims [70] scabby

And sometime she blennes[71]
The dunge of her hennes
And the ale togider,
And sayth, 'Gossip, come hider,
This ale shal be thicker,
And floure[72] the more quicker;
For I may tell you
I lerned it of a Jewe
When I began to brewe,
And I have found it trewe.
Drinke now while it is new:
An ye may it brooke,[73]
It shall make you looke
Yonger than ye be
Yeres two or thre,
For ye may prove it by me.
Behold,' she said, 'and se
How bright I am of ble![74]
Ich am not cast away,
That can my husband say;
When we kiss and play
In lust and in liking[75]
He calleth me his whiting,
His mulling and his miting,
His nobbės and his conny,[76]
His sweeting and his honny,
With "Bas,[77] my prety bonny,
Thou art worth good and monny!"
Thus make I my felyre fonny,[78]
Till that he dreme and dronny:[79]
For, after all our sport,
Then will he rout[80] and snort:
Then swetely togither we ly
As two pigges in a sty.'
  To cease me seemeth best,[81]
And of this tale to rest,

[71] blends [72] froth [73] if you can enjoy it [74] how clear I am of complexion
[75] in pleasure and delight [76] bunny [77] kiss me [78] partner foolish [79] doze
[80] snore [81] it seems best to me

And for to leve this letter
Bicause it is no better,
And bicause it is no swetter;
We will no farther rime
Of it at this time,
But we will turne plaine
Where we left againe.

Fit the Third

In stede of coine and monny
Some brought her a conny,[82]
And some a pot with honny,
Some salt, and some a spoone,
Some their hose, some their shoone;
Some ranne a good trot
With a skellet or a pot;
Some fill their pot full
Of good Lemster woll:[83]
An huswife of trust,[84]
When she is athrust,[85]
Suche a webbe can spin,
Her thrifte is full thin.

Some go streight thider,
Be it slaty or slider:[86]
They hold the hye waye,[87]
They care not what men saye,
Be that as be maye.
Some, lothe to be espide,[88]
Start in at the backe side[89]
Over the hedge and pale[90]
And all for the good ale.
Some renne till they swete,[91]
Bringe with them malte or whete,
And Dame Elinour entrete

[82] rabbit [83] wool [84] an honest housewife [85] thirsty [86] be it muddy or slippery [87] they keep to the open road [88] reluctant to be seen [89] slip in at the back door [90] fence [91] run till they sweat

To birle[92] them of the best.

Then cometh another gest:
She swereth by the roode of rest[93]
Her lippes are so drye
Without drinke she must die,
'Therefore fill it by and by,
And have here a pecke of ry!'

Anone cometh another,
As drye as the other,
And with her doth bringe
Mele, salte, or other thinge,
Her hernest[94] girdle, her weddinge ringe,
To pay for her scot[95]
As cometh to her lot.
Some bringeth her husbandis hood
Bicause the ale is good;
Another brought her his cap
To offer to the ale-tap,
With flaxe and with towe;[96]
And some brought sowre dowe[97]
With 'Hey and with howe,
Sit we down arowe,
And drinke till we blowe,[98]
And pipe tirly tirlowe!'

Some laide to pledge[99]
Their hatchet and their wedge,
Their hekell[100] and their reele,
Their rocke,[101] their spinning-wheele;
And some went so narrowe[102]
They laide to pledge their wharrowe,[103]
Their ribskin[104] and their spindell,
Their needell and their thimbell:
Here was scant thrift
When they made such a shift.

[92] draw [93] cross that brings peace [94] mounted with precious metal [95] bill [96] flax fibre [97] sour dough [98] belch [99] as a pledge [100] flax-comb [101] distaff [102] some got so hard-up for cash [103] the pulley of their spinning-wheel [104] leather apron

Their thrust[105] was so great
They asked never for mete,[106]
But, 'Drinke, still drinke,
And let the cat winke,
Let us wash our gummes
From the drye crummes!'

Fit the Fourth

Some for very nede
Laide downe a skein of threde,
And some a skein of yarne;
Some brought from the barne
Both benes and pease,
Small chaffer doth ease[107]
Sometime, now and than;
Another there was that ran
With a good brasse pan,
Her colour was full wan;
She ran in all the hast,
Unbrased[108] and unlast,
Tawny, swart,[109] and sallowe
Like a cake of tallowe:
I swere by all hallowe[110]
It was a stale[111] to take
The devill in a brake![112]
And then came halting Jone,
And brought a gambone[113]
Of bakon that was resty:[114]
But, Lord, that she was testy,
Angry as a waspy!
She began to yane[115] and gaspy,
And bade Elinour go bet[116]
And fill in good met;[117]

Another brought a spicke
Of a bacon flicke,[118]

[105] thirst [106] food [107] small deals are pleasing [108] unfastened [109] dark [110] all the saints [111] bait [112] trap [113] gammon [114] mouldy [115] yawn [116] hurry up [117] measure [118] a piece of a flitch of bacon

Her tonge was very quicke
But she spake somwhat thicke:
Her felowe did stammer and stut,[119]
But she was a foule slut,
For her mouth foamyd
And her bely groanyd:
Jone saide she had eten a fiest.[120]
'By Christ,' said she, 'thou liest,
I have as sweete a breth
As thou, with shamefull deth!'[121]
  Then Elinour saide, 'Ye calettes,[122]
I shall breke your palettes,[123]
Without[124] ye now cease!'
And so was made the peace.
  Then thider came dronken Ales,
And she was full of tales,
Of tidinges in Wales,
And of Saint James in Gales,[125]
And of the Portingales,[126]
With 'Lo, gossip, ywis,[127]
Thus and thus it is:
There hath ben greate war
Betweene Temple Bar
And the Crosse in Chepe,[128]
And thider came an hepe
Of milstones in a route . . .'
She spake this in her snout,
Sneveling in her nose
As though she had the pose.[129]
'Lo, here is an olde tippet,[130]
And[131] ye will give me a sippet
Of your stale ale,
God sende you good sale!'
And as she was drinkinge
She fell in a winkinge

[119] stutter [120] fart [121] may you come to a bad end [122] hussies [123] heads [124] unless [125] Galicia [126] Portuguese [127] Look, friend, indeed [128] Cheap [129] cold [130] hood [131] if

With a barly-hood,[132]
She pist where she stood.
Then began she to weepe,
And forthwith fell on sleepe.
Elinour tooke her up
And blessed her with a cup
Of newe ale in cornes:[133]
Ales found therin no thornes,
But supped it up at ones,
She founde therein no bones.[134]

Fit the Fifth

Nowe in cometh another rabell:
First one with a ladell,
Another with a cradell,
And with a side-sadell;
And there began a fabell,[135]
A clatteringe and babell
Of a foles filly[136]
That had a fole[137] with Willy,
With 'Jast you!' and 'Gup Gilly!'[138]
She coulde not lie stilly.

Then came in a genet[139]
And sware, 'By Saint Benet,
I dranke not this sennet[140]
A draught to my pay![141]
Elinour, I the pray
Of thine ale let us assaye,[142]
And have here a pilche of graye:[143]
I were skinnes of conny,[144]
That causeth I looke so donny!'[145]

Another then did hiche her,[146]
And brought a pottle-picher,[147]

[132] drunken fit [133] newly drawn [134] she made no bones about it [135] tale [136] of a foolish filly [137] foal/fool [138] Gee up, Gilly! [139] little horse [140] week [141] satisfaction [142] try [143] cloak of skins [144] I wear rabbit-skins [145] that make me look so drab [146] stumble in [147] half-gallon jug

A tonnell,[148] and a bottell,
But she had lost the stoppell:
She cut off her sho-sole,
And stopped therewith the hole.

Amonge all the blommer[149]
Another brought a skommer,[150]
A fryinge-pan, and a slice:
Elinour made the price
For good ale eche whit.[151]

Then sterte in[152] mad Kit
That had litell wit:
She seemed somdele seke
And brought a peny cheke[153]
To Dame Elinour
For a draught of her licour.

Then Margery Milkeducke
Her kirtell she did uptucke
An inche above her knee
Her legges that ye might see;
But they were sturdy and stubbéd,[154]
Mighty pestels and clubbéd,
As faire and as white
As the foote of a kite:
She was somwhat foule,
Crooke-nebbed like an oule;[155]
And yet she brought her fees,
A cantell[156] of Essex cheese,
Was well a foote thicke
Full of magottes quicke:[157]
It was huge and greate,
And mighty stronge meate
For the devill to eate:
It was tart and punyete![158]

Another sorte of sluttes:
Some brought walnuttes,

[148] funnel [149] uproar [150] sieve [151] to the full amount [152] rushed in [153] penny chicken [154] stumpy [155] crook-beaked like an owl [156] cut [157] live [158] pungent

Some apples, some peres,
Some brought their clipping sheres,
Some brought this and that,
Some brought I wote nere what;
Some brought their husbands hat,
Some podinges and linkes,[159]
Some tripes that stinkes.
  But of all this thronge
One came them amonge,
She seemed halfe a leche,[160]
And began to preche
Of the Tewsday in the weke
When the mare doth keke,
Of the vertue[161] of an unset leke,
And of her husbandes breke;
With the feders of a quaile
She could to Burdews[162] saile;
And with good ale barme[163]
She could make a charme
To helpe withall a stitch:
She seemed to be a witch.
  Another brought two goslinges
That were noughty froslinges;[164]
She brought them in a wallet,[165]
She was a cumly callet:[166]
The goslenges were untide,
Elinour began to chide,
'They be wretchockes[167] thou hast brought,
They are shyre shaking nought!'[168]

Fit the Sixth

Maude Ruggy thither skipped:
She was ugly hipped,

[159] puddings and links of black pudding [160] physician [161] properties [162] Bordeaux [163] froth [164] worthless frost-bitten things [165] bag [166] wench [167] weaklings [168] utterly worthless

And ugly thicke-lipped,
Like an onion sided,
Like tan ledder[169] hided:
She had her so guided
Betweene the cup and the wall
That she was there withall
Into a palsey fall:
With that her hed shaked,
And her handes quaked,
Ones head would have aked
To see her naked.
She dranke so of the dregges,
The dropsy was in her legges;
Her face glistring like glass,
All foggy[170] fat she was.
She had also the gout
In all her jointes about;
Her breth was soure and stale,
And smelled all of ale:
Such a bedfellaw
Would make one cast his craw![171]
But yet for all that
She drank on the mashvat.
  There came an old ribibe:[172]
She halted of a kibe,[173]
And had broken her shin
At the threshold coming in,
And fell so wide open
That one might see her token,
The devill thereon be wroken![174]
What neede all this be spoken?
She yelled like a calfe.
'Rise up, on Gods halfe!'
Said Elinour Rumming,
'I beshrew thee for thy cumming!'[175]
And as she at her did pluck,
'Quake, quake!' said the duck

[169] leather [170] flabby [171] vomit [172] crone [173] limped from a blister [174] avenged
[175] I curse you for your entrance

In that lampatrams lap.[176]
With 'Fy, cover thy shap
With sum flip-flap!'[177]
'God give it ill hap,'[178]
Said Elinour, 'For shame!' –
Like an honest dame.
Up she stert, halfe lame,
And skantly could go
For paine and for wo.
  In came another dant,[179]
With a goose and a gant:[180]
She had a wide wesant,[181]
She was nothinge plesant,
Necked like an olifant;
It was a bullifant,[182]
A greedy cormerant.
  Another brought her garlike heddes,
Another brought her bedes
Of jet or of cole
To offer to the ale pole.[183]
Some brought a wimble,[184]
Some brought a thimble,
Some brought a silk lace,
Some brought a pincase,
Some her husbandes gowne,
Some a pillowe of downe,
Some of the napery;[185]

. . .

And all this shifte they make
For the good ale sake.
  'A straw!' saide Bele, 'stande utter,[186]
For we have egges and butter,

. . .

And of pigeons a paire.'
  Then sterte forth a fisgigge,[187]
And she brought a bore pigge,

[176] in that old lamprey's lap [177] rag [178] bad luck [179] loose woman [180] gander
[181] windpipe [182] [fabulous creature] [183] inn-sign [184] veil [185] household linen
[186] stand back [187] Then a silly woman burst in

The fleshe thereof was ranke,
And her brethe strongely stanke;
Yet, or she went, she dranke,
And gat her great thanke
Of Elinour for her ware
That she thither bare
To pay for her share.
Nowe truly, to my thinkinge,
This is a solempne drinkinge![188]

Fit the Seventh

'Soft!' quod one hight[189] Sibbill,
'And let me with you bibbill.'[190]
She sat downe in the place
With a sory face
Whey-wormed about.[191]
Garnished was her snout
With here and there a puscull[192]
Like a scabbed muscull.[193]
'This ale,' said she, 'is noppy;[194]
Let us sippe and soppy
And not spill a droppy,
Foı, so may I hoppy,[195]
It cooleth well my croppy.[196]

'Dame Elinour,' saide she,
'Have here is for me,[197]
A clout of London pinnes.'
And with that she beginnes
The pot to her plucke[198]
And dranke a 'good-lucke'.
She swinged up[199] a quarte
At ones for her parte:[200]
Her paunche was so puffed,
And so with ale stuffed,

[188] imposing drinking-party [189] called [190] drink [191] covered with spots [192] pustule [193] mussel [194] strong and sweet [195] as I may have good luck [196] gullet [197] Here, have this for me [198] pull [199] swilled down [200] share

Had she not hied apace
She had defoyled[201] the place.

Then began the sporte
Amonge that drunken sorte.
'Dame Elinour,' saide they,
'Lende here a cocke of hey
To make all thinge cleane –
Ye wote well what we meane!'

But, sir, amonge all
That sate in that hall
There was a prickemedenty[202]
Sat like a seinty
And began to painty[203]
As though she wolde fainty:
She made it as koye
As a lege-moy:[204]
She was not halfe so wise
As she was peevishe nise.[205]
She saide never a worde,
But rose from the borde
And called for our dame,
Elinour by name.
We supposed, ywis,
That she rose to piss:
But the very grounde[206]
Was for to compound[207]
With Elinour in the spence,[208]
To paye for her expence.
'I have no penny or grote
To paye,' saide she, 'God wote,
For washing of my throte,
But my bedes of amber
Bere them to your chamber.'
Then Elinour did them hide
Within her beddes side.

[201] defiled [202] a particular one [203] feign [204] ? a riotous dance [205] foolishly fastidious [206] real reason [207] settle [208] store-room

But some then sate right sad
That nothinge had
There of their awne,
Neither gelt nor pawne:[209]
Suche were there menny
That had not a penny;
But, when they sholde walke,
Were faine with a chalke
To score on the balke,[210]
Or score on the taile:[211]
God give it ill haile![212]
For my fingers itche,
I have written too mitche
Of this mad mumminge
Of Elinour Rumminge.
Thus endeth the gest[213]
Of this worthy fest.

Quod Skelton, Laureate.

SIR DAVID LINDSAY

SQUIRE MELDRUM IS ENTERTAINED AT A CASTLE

Out throw the land than sprang the fame,[1]
That Squier Meldrum wes cum hame.
Quhen[2] thay hard tell how he debaitit,[3]
With everie man he was sa treitit,[4]
That, quhen[2] he travellit throw the land,
Thay bankettit[5] him fra hand to hand,

[209] neither money nor pledge [210] beam [211] tally-stick [212] bad luck [213] story

[1] rumour [2] when [3] had fought [4] he was so well-treated by everybody [6] banqueted

With greit solace; till, at the last,
Out throw Straitherne the Squier past.
And, as it did approch the nicht,
Of ane castell he gat ane sicht,[6]
Beside ane montane, in ane vaill;[7]
And than, efter his greit travaill,[8]
He purpoisit him to repois,[9]
Quhair[10] ilk man did of him rejois.
Of this triumphant plesand place
Ane lustie ladie wes maistres,
Quhais[11] lord was deid short time befoir,
Quhairthrow hir dolour wes the moir.[12]
Bot yet sho tuke sum comforting,
To heir the plesant dulce talking[13]
Of this young squier, of his chance,[14]
And how it fortunit him in France.
This squier and the ladie gent[15]
Did weshe, and then to supper went.
During that nicht thair was nocht ellis
Bot for to heir of his novellis.[16]
Eneas, quhen[2] he fled from Troy,
Did not Quene Dido greiter joy,
Quhen[2] he in Carthage did arrive,
And did the seige of Troy discrive.[17]
The wonderis that he did reheirs[18]
Wer langsum[19] for to put in vers,
Of quhilk[20] this ladie did rejois.
Thay drank, and syne went to repois.[21]
He fand his chalmer weill arrayit[22]
With dornik work on buird displayit.[23]
Of venisoun he had his waill,[24]
Gude aquavite, wine, and aill,

[6] he caught sight [7] by a mountain, in a valley [8] effort [9] he intended to rest [10] where [11] whose [12] through which she suffered great grief [13] soft speech [14] about his fortunes [15] graceful [16] news [17] describe [18] relate [19] lengthy [20] for which [21] and afterwards went to rest [22] he found his bedchamber well adorned [23] with Flemish tapestry displayed on the table [24] choice

With nobill confeittis, bran, and geill;[25]
And swa the squier fuir richt weill.[26]
Sa, to heir mair of his narratioun,
This ladie come to his collatioun,[27]
Sayand[28] he was richt welcum hame.
'Grandmercie!'[29] than quod he, 'madame.'
Thay past the time with ches and tabill[30] –
For he to everie game was abill –
Than unto bed drew everie wicht;[31]
To chalmer went this ladie bricht,
The quhilk this squier did convoy;[32]
Syne,[33] till his bed he went, with joy.
That nicht he sleipit never ane wink,
Bot still did on the ladie think;
Cupido, with his fyrie[34] dart,
Did peirs him so out throw the hart.[35]
Sa all that nicht he did bot murn it;[36]
Sum time sat up, and sumtime turnit,
Sichand with monie gant and grane,[37]
To fair Venus makand his mane,[38]
Sayand:[28] 'Ladie, quhat may this mene?
I was ane fre man lait yistrene,[39]
And now ane cative[40] bound and thrall
For ane that I think flour of all.
I pray God sen[41] sho knew my mind,
How, for hir saik, I am sa pind.[42]
Wald God I had bene yet in France.
Or I had hapnit sic mischance,[43]
To be subject or serviture[44]
Till ane quhilk takis of me na cure!'[45]
This ladie ludgit neirhand by,[46]
And hard the squier prively,

[25] sweetmeats, brawn and jelly [26] fared very well [27] supper [28] saying [29] Many thanks! [30] chess and backgammon [31] everybody [32] whom this Squire escorted [33] then [34] fiery [35] right through the heart [36] he did nothing but lament it [37] sighing with many a yawn and groan [38] making his plaint [39] late yesterday evening [40] prisoner [41] send [42] tormented [43] before such a misfortune had befallen me [44] servant [45] to one who cares nothing for me [46] this lady had a room close by

With dreidfull[47] hart makand his mone,[38]
With monie cairful gant and grone.[48]
Hir hart fulfillit with pietie,[49]
Thocht sho wald haif of him mercie,
And said: 'Howbeit[50] I suld be slane,
He sall have lufe for lufe agane.[51]
Wald God I micht, with my honour,
Have him to be my paramour!'
This wes the mirrie time of May,
Quhen this fair ladie, freshe and gay,
Start up, to take the hailsum air,[52]
With pantonis[53] on hir feit ane pair,
Airlie into ane cleir morning,
Befoir fair Phœbus uprising,
Kirtill alone, withouttin clok;[54]
And saw the squieris dure unlok.
Sho slippit in, or ever he wist,[55]
And fenyeitlie past till ane kist,[56]
And with hir keyis oppinnit the lokkis,
And maid hir to take furth ane boxe:
Bot that was not hir erand thair.
With that, this lustie[57] young squier
Saw this ladie so plesantlie[58]
Cum to his chalmer quietlie,
In kyrtill of fine damais broun,[59]
Hir goldin traissis hingand[60] doun.
Hir pappis wer hard, round, and quhite,[61]
Quhome to behald wes greit delite.
Like the quhite lillie wes hir lire;[62]
Hir hair was like the reid[63] gold wire;
Hir shankis quhite withouttin hois,[64]
Quhairat[65] the squier did rejois.

[47] anxious [48] sorrowful yawn and groan [49] pity [50] even if [51] love in return for love [52] rose up to take the wholesome air [53] slippers [54] in her gown alone, and without a cloak [55] before ever he knew [56] and pretended to go to a chest [57] amorous [58] charmingly [59] in a gown of fine dark damask [60] hanging [61] her breasts were firm, round and white [62] flesh [63] red [64] her white legs without stockings [65] at which

And said, than: 'Now, vailye quod vailye,[66]
Upon the ladie thow mak ane sailye.'[67]
Hir courlike kirtill[68] was unlaist,
And soone into his armis hir braist,[69]
And said to hir: 'Madame, gudemorne!
Help me, your man that is forlorne.
Without ye mak me sum remeid,[70]
Withouttin dout I am bot deid;[71]
Quhairfoir, ye mon releif my harmes.'[72]
With that, he hint[73] hir in his armes,
And talkit with hir on the flure;[74]
Syne,[75] quietlie did bar the dure.
'Squier,' quod sho, 'quhat is your will?
Think ye my womanheid to spill?[76]
Na, God forbid! it wer greit sin:
My Lord and ye wes neir of kin.
Quhairfoir, I mak yow supplicatioun,
Pas, and seik ane dispensatioun;[77]
Than sall I wed yow with ane ring;
Than may ye leif at your liking:[78]
For ye ar young, lustie, and fair,
And, als,[79] ye ar your fatheris air.
Thair is na ladie, in all this land,
May yow refuse to[80] hir husband;
And, gif ye lufe me as ye say,
Haist to dispens[81] the best ye may;
And thair to yow I geve my hand,[82]
I sall yow take to[80] my husband.'
Quod he: 'Quhill[83] that I may indure,
I vow to be your serviture;[84]
Bot I think greit vexatioun[85]
To tarie upon dispensatioun.'[86]

[66] come what may [67] attempt [68] elegant gown [69] embraced [70] unless you make some cure for me [71] I am as good as dead [72] therefore you must assuage my distress [73] clasped [74] in the middle of the room [75] then [76] do you intend to outrage my womanhood [77] leave off, and seek ecclesiastical permission [78] then you may live as you desire [79] also [80] as [81] seek dispensation [82] and I give you my hand on it [83] while [84] servant [85] nuisance [86] to wait for permission

Than in his armis he did hir thrist,[87]
And aither uther sweitlie kist;
And wame for wame thay uther braissit:[88]
With that, hir kirtill wes unlaissit.
Than Cupido, with his fyrie dartis,
Inflammit sa thir luferis[89] hartis,
Thay micht na maner of way dissever,[90]
Nor ane micht not part fra ane uther;
Bot, like woodbind, thay wer baith wrappit.[91]
Thair tenderlie he hes hir happit,
Full softlie up,[92] intill his bed:
Judge ye gif he hir schankis shed.[93]
'Allace!' quod sho, 'quhat may this mene?'
And with hir hair sho dicht hir ene.[94]
  I can not tell how thay did play;
Bot I beleve sho said not nay.
He pleisit hir sa, as I hard sane,[95]
That he was welcum ay agane.
Sho rais,[96] and tenderlie him kist,
And on his hand ane ring sho thrist;[97]
And he gaif hir ane lufe drowrie,[98]
Ane ring set with ane riche rubie,
In takin[99] that thair lufe for ever
Suld never frome thir twa dissever.[100]
And than sho passit unto hir chalmer,
And fand hir madinnis, sweit as lammer,[101]
Sleipand full sound; and nothing wist[102]
How that thair ladie past to the kist.[103]
Quod thay: 'Madame, quhair have ye bene?'
Quod sho: 'Into my gardine grene,
To heir thir mirrie birdis sang:
I lat yow wit, I thocht not lang,[104]

[87] thrust [88] and belly to belly they embraced each other [89] lovers [90] they could not possibly separate [91] but they entwined together like ivy [92] he has gathered her up very gently [93] whether he parted her legs [94] covered her eyes [95] as I heard tell [96] rose [97] pushed [98] love-token [99] signifying [100] should never depart from the two of them [101] amber [102] and little knew [103] how their lady had gone to the chest [104] I'll have you know it didn't seem long to me

Thocht I had taryit thair quhill noone.'[105]
Quod thai: 'Quhair wes your hois and schoone?[106]
Quhy yeid ye[107] with your bellie bair?'
Quod sho: 'The morning wes sa fair:
For, be him that deir Iesus sauld,[108]
I felt na wayis ony maner of cauld.'
Quod thay: 'Madame, me think ye sweit.'[109]
Quod sho: 'Ye see I sufferit heit;[110]
The dew did sa on flouris fleit,[111]
That baith my limmis ar maid weit:[112]
Thairfoir ane quhile I will heir ly,
Till this dulce[113] dew be fra me dry.
Rise, and gar mak our denner reddie.'[114]
'That salbe[115] done,' quod thay, 'my ladie.'
Efter that sho had tane hir rest,
Sho rais, and in hir chalmer hir drest,
And, efter mes,[116] to denner went.
Than wes the squier diligent
To declair monie sindrie storie[117]
Worthie to put in memorie.
  Quhat sall we of thir luferis say,
Bot, all this time of lustie May,[118]
They past the time with joy and blis,
Full quietlie,[119] with monie ane kis!
Thair was na creature that knew
Yet of thir luferis chalmer glew.[120]
And sa he levit, plesandlie,[121]
Ane certane time, with his ladie;
Sum time with halking and hunting,
Sum time with wantoun hors rinning,[122]
And, sum time, like ane man of weir,[123]
Full galyardlie wald rin ane speir.[124]

[105] even if I had remained there until midday [106] stockings and shoes [107] why did you go [108] sold [109] it seems to me that you are sweating [110] you see I've been subjected to heat [111] flow [112] both my limbs have been made wet [113] sweat [114] and have dinner made ready [115] shall be [116] mass [117] recite many different anecdotes [118] flourishing [119] tranquilly [120] that yet knew of these lovers' bedroom delights [121] so he lived, pleasantly [122] hawking and hunting . . . with spirited horse-racing [123] war [124] most merrily would he run in the lists with a spear

He wan the prise above thame all,
Baith at the buttis[125] and the futeball.
Till everie solace he was abill,[126]
At cartis, and dice, at ches, and tabill.[127]

The History of Squire Meldrum

ALEXANDER BARCLAY

DINING AT COURT

But yet is in court more pain and misery.
Brought in be dishes the table for to fill,
But not one is brought in order to thy will.
That thou wouldst have first and lovest principal
Is brought to the board oft times last of all.
With bread and rude meat when thou art satiate,
Then cometh dishes most sweet and delicate.
Then must thou either despise them utterly,
Or to thy hurt surfeit, ensuing gluttony.
Or if it fortune, as seldom doth befall,
That at beginning come dishes best of all,
Or thou hast tasted a morsel or twain,
Thy dish out of sight is taken soon again.
Slow be the servers in serving in alway,
But swift they be after, in taking thy meat away.
A special custom is used them among,
No good dish to suffer on board to be for long.
If the dish is pleasant, either flesh or fish,
Ten hands at once swarm in the dish.
And if it be flesh, ten knives shalt thou see
Mangling the flesh and in the platter flee:
To put there thy hands is peril without fail,
Without a gauntlet or else a glove of mail.

[125] both at the archery butts [126] he was skilled in every pastime [127] at cards, dice, chess and backgammon

Among all these knives thou one of both must have,
Or else it is hard thy fingers whole to save:
Oft in such dishes in court it is seen,
Some leave their fingers, each knife is so keen.
On a finger gnaweth some hasty glutton,
Supposing it is a piece of beef or mutton.
Besides these in court more pains shalt thou see,
At board men be set as thick as they may be.
The platters shall pass oft times to and fro,
And over the shoulders and head shall they go.
And oft all the broth and liquor fat
Is spilt on thy gown, thy bonnet and thy hat.
Sometime art thou thrust for little room and place,
And sometime thy fellow reboketh[1] in thy face.
Between dish and dish is tarry tedious,
But in the meantime though thou have pain grievous,
Neither mayest thou rise, cough, spit or neese,[2]
Or take other easement, lest thou thy name may lese.[3]

from *Eclogue II*

HOW COURTIERS SLEEP

Hear now what pains have courtiers in sleeping.
They oftentime sleep full wretchedly in pain,
And lie all the night forth in cold wind and rain.
Sometime in bare straw, on boards, ground or stones,
Till both their sides ache, and all their bones.
And when that one side acheth and is weary,
Then turn the other, lo here a remedy.
Or else must he rise and walk himself a space,
Till time his joints be settled in their place.
But if it be fortune thou lie within some town
In bed of feathers, or else of easy down,
Then make thee ready for flies and for gnats,
For lice, for fleas, punaises,[1] mice and rats.

[1] belches [2] sneeze [3] lose

[1] bedbugs

These shall with biting, with stinking, din and sound
Make thee worse easement than if thou lay on ground.
And never in the court shalt thou have bed alone,
Save when thou wouldst most gladly lie with one.
Thy sheets shall be unclean, ragged and rent,
Loathly unto sight, but loathlier to scent.
In which some other departed late before
Of the pestilence, or of some other sore.
Such a bedfellow men shall to thee assign,
That it was better to sleep among the swine.
So foul and scabbed, of hard pimples so thin,
That a man might grate hard crusts on his skin.
And all night long shall he his sides grate,
Better lie on ground than lie with such a mate.
One cougheth so fast, another's breath doth stink,
That during the night scarce mayest thou get a wink.
Sometime a leper is signed to thy bed,
Or with other sore one grievously bested.
Sometime thy bedfellow is colder than ice,
To him he draweth thy clothes in a trice.
But if he be hot, by fevers then shall he
Cast all thy clothes and coverlet on thee.
Either is thy fellow alway to thee grievous,
Or else to him art thou alway tedious.
And sometime these courtiers them more to encumber,
Sleep all in one chamber near twenty in number,
Then it is great sorrow for to abide their shout,
Some fart, some flingeth,[2] and other snort and rout.
Some boke,[3] some babble, some cometh drunk to bed,
Some brawl and some jangle when they be beastly fed.
Some laugh, and some cry, each man will have his will,
Some spew, and some piss, and not one of them is still.

from *Eclogue III*

[2] toss [3] butt

ANONYMOUS

THE DEATH OF QUEEN JANE

Queen Jane was in travail
For six weeks or more,
Till the women grew tired,
And fain would give o'er.
'O women! O women!
Good wives if ye be,
Go, send for King Henrie,
And bring him to me.'

King Henrie was sent for,
He came with all speed,
In a gownd of green velvet
From heel to the head.
'King Henrie! King Henrie!
If kind Henrie you be,
Send for a surgeon,
And bring him to me.'

The surgeon was sent for,
He came with all speed,
In a gownd of black velvet
From heel to the head.
He gave her rich caudle,
But the death-sleep slept she.
Then her right side was opened,
And the babe was set free.

The babe it was christened,
And put out and nursed,
While the royal Queen Jane
She lay cold in the dust.

*

So black was the mourning,
And white were the wands,
Yellow, yellow the torches,
They bore in their hands.

The bells they were muffled,
And mournful did play,
While the royal Queen Jane
She lay cold in the clay.

Six knights and six lords
Bore her corpse through the grounds;
Six dukes followed after,
In black mourning gownds.
The flower of Old England
Was laid in cold clay,
Whilst the royal King Henrie
Came weeping away.

HENRY HOWARD, EARL OF SURREY

PRISONED IN WINDSOR, HE RECOUNTETH HIS PLEASURE THERE PASSED

So cruel prison how could betide, alas,
As proud Windsor? Where I in lust and joy
With a king's son my childish years did pass
In greater feast than Priam's sons of Troy;
Where each sweet place returns a taste full sour:
The large green courts where we were wont to hove
With eyes cast up into the maidens' tower,
And easy sighs, such as folk draw in love;
The stately seats, the ladies bright of hue,
The dances short, long tales of great delight;
With words and looks that tigers could but rue,
Where each of us did plead the other's right;
The palm play[1] where, despoiled for the game,
With dazed eyes oft we by gleams of love
Have missed the ball and got sight of our dame,
To bait her eyes, which kept the leads above;

[1] a game resembling handball

The gravel ground, with sleeves tied on the helm,
On foaming horse, with swords and friendly hearts,
With cheer, as though one should another whelm,
Where we have fought, and chased oft with darts;
With silver drops the mead yet spread for ruth,
In active games of nimbleness and strength
Where we did strain, trained with swarms of youth,
Our tender limbs that yet shot up in length;
The secret groves which oft we made resound
Of pleasant plaint and of our ladies' praise,
Recording oft what grace each one had found,
What hope of speed, what dread of long delays;
The wild forest, the clothed holts with green,
With reins avaled,[2] and swift ybreathed horse,
With cry of hounds and merry blasts between,
Where we did chase the fearful hart of force;
The wide vales eke that harbored us each night,
Wherewith, alas, reviveth in my breast
The sweet accord; such sleeps as yet delight,
The pleasant dreams, the quiet bed of rest;
The secret thoughts imparted with such trust,
The wanton talk, the divers change of play,
The friendship sworn, each promise kept so just,
Wherewith we passed the winter night away.
And with this thought the blood forsakes the face,
The tears berain my cheeks of deadly hue,
The which as soon as sobbing sighs, alas,
Upsupped have, thus I my plaint renew:
O place of bliss, renewer of my woes,
Give me account – where is my noble fere?
Whom in thy walls thou dost each night enclose,
To other lief, but unto me most dear!
Echo, alas, that doth my sorrow rue,
Returns thereto a hollow sound of plaint.
Thus I alone, where all my freedom grew,
In prison pine with bondage and restraint;
And with remembrance of the greater grief
To banish the less, I find my chief relief.

[2] slackened

THOMAS CHURCHYARD

A SERVING-MAID

With merry lark this maiden rose,
And straight about the house she goes,
With swapping besom in her hand;
And at her girdle in a band
A jolly bunch of keys she wore;
Her petticoat fine laced before,
Her tail tucked up in trimmest guise,
A napkin hanging o'er her eyes,
To keep off dust and dross of walls,
That often from the windows falls.
Though she was smug,[1] she took small ease,
For thrifty girls are glad to please;
She won the love of all the house,
And pranked it like a pretty mouse,
And sure at every word she spake,
A goodly curtsy could she make;
A stirring housewife every where,
That bent both back and bones to bear.
She never sleeped much by night,
But rose sometimes by candle-light
To card and spin, or sew her smock;
There could no sooner crow a cock,
But she was up, to sleek her clothes,
And would be sweet as any rose.
Full cleanly still the girl would go
And handsome in a house also,
As ever saw I country wench.
She sweeped under every bench,
And shaked the cushions in their kind;
When out of order she did find
A rush, a straw or little stick,
She could it mend, she was so quick

[1] neat

About her business every hour.
This maid was called her mistress' flower.
She bare the keys of ale and beer,
And had the rule of better cheer.
She was not nice, nor yet too kind,
Too proud, nor of too humble mind,
Too fine, nor yet too brave, I trow.
She had, as far as I do know,
Two fair new kirtles to her back;
The one was blue, the other black.
For holy days she had a gown,
And every yard did cost a crown,
And more by eighteen pence, I guess;
She had three smocks, she had no less,
Four rails[2] and eke five kerchers fair.
Of hose and shoes she had a pair;
She needed not no more to have;
She would go barefoot for to save
Her shoes and hose, for they were dear.
She went to town but once a year,
At Easter or some other day,
When she had licence for to play.
I had forgotten for to tell,
She had a purse she loved well,
That hanged at a ribbon green,
With tassels fair, and well beseen;[3]
And as for gloves and knives full bright
She lacked not, nor trifles light,
As pins and laces of small cost.
I have to you rehearsed most
Of all her goods. Now to the form
And making of this creeping worm.
Her port was low, her face was fair;
It came no sooner in the air,
But it would peel, her cheeks were thin.
God knows she had a tender skin.

[2] nightgowns [3] arranged

The worst mis-shape this minion[4] had,
Her legs were swollen very bad;
Some heavy humour down did fall.
Her foot was narrow, short and small,
Her body slender as a snig;[5]
But sure her buttocks were full big;
That came, I think, from sitting mich;[6]
And in her side she had a stitch,
That made her oft short-winded, sure.
But her complexion was full pure.
She was well made from top to tail;
Yea, all her limbs, withouten fail,
Were fine and feat.[7] She had a hand,
There was no fairer in the land,
Save that with toil it changed hue.
Her fingers small, her veins full blue;
Her nails a little largely grown;
Her hair much like the sun it shone;
Her eyes as black as jet did seem;
She did herself full well esteem.
Her lips were red, but somewhat chapped.
Her tongue was still and seldom clapped.
She spake as she were in a cloud,
Neither too soft nor yet too loud,
And tripped upon the floor as trim,
Ye would have thought that she did swim
As she did go, such was her pace.
She minced fine, like Mistress Grace,
That at the Dagger dwelled once,
Who made good pies of marrow-bones.
I dare depose upon a book,
She was as good a maiden cook,
As ever dressed a piece of meat;
And for a banquet, small or great,
And raising paste, she passed still.
As soon as flour came from the mill,

[4] darling [5] eel [6] much [7] well-made

She made the goodliest cakes thereof,
And baked as fair a household loaf,
As e'er was seen or set on board.
What needs more talk? At one bare word,
The greatest lady in a shire
She might have served seven year.

THOMAS TUSSER

HOUSEWIFERY

Now listen, good housewives, what doings are here
set out for a day as it should for a year.

Morning Works

No sooner some up,
But nose is in cup.

Get up in the morning as soon as thou wilt,
with overlong slugging[1] good servant is spilt.

Some slovens from sleeping no sooner get up,
but hand is in aumbrie,[2] and nose in the cup.

That early is done,
Count housewifely won.

Some work in the morning may trimly be done,
that all the day after can hardly be won.

Good husband without it is needful there be,
good housewife within as needful as he.

Cast dust into yard,
And spin and go card.

Sluts' corners avoided shall further thy health,
much time about trifles shall hinder thy wealth.

[1] lying abed [2] cupboard

Set some to peel hemp or else rushes to twine,
to spin or to card, or to seething of brine.

Grind malt for drink,
See meat do not stink.

Set some about cattle, some pasture to view,
some malt to be grinding against ye do brew.

Some corneth, some brineth, some will not be taught
where meat is attainted, there cookery is naught.

Wife make thy own candle,
Spare penny to handle.

Provide for thy tallow, ere frost cometh in,
and make thine own candle, ere winter begin.

If penny for all thing be suffered to trudge,
trust long, not to penny, to have him thy drudge.

Evening Works

Time drawing to night,
See all things go right.

When hens go to roost go in hand to dress meat,
serve hogs and to milking and some to serve neat.

Where twain be enough, be not served with three,
more knaves in a company worser they be.

Make lackey to trudge,
Make servant thy drudge.

For every trifle leave jaunting thy nag,[3]
but rather make lackey of Jack boy thy wag.[4]

Make servant at night lug in wood or a log,
let none come in empty but slut and thy dog.

False knave ready pressed,
All safe is the best.

Where pullen[5] use nightly to perch in the yard,
there two-legged foxes keep watches and ward.

[3] don't tire your horse out for every trifle [4] boy, fellow [5] poultry

See cattle well served, without and within,
and all thing quiet ere supper begin.

Take heed it is needful
True pity is meedful.

No clothes in garden, no trinkets without,
no door leave unbolted, for fear of a doubt.

Thou woman whom pity becometh the best,
grant all that hath laboured time to take rest.

from *The Five Hundred Points of Good Husbandry*

POSIES FOR THE GUEST'S CHAMBER

The sloven and the careless man, the roinish[1] nothing nice,
To lodge in chamber comely decked, is seldom suffered twice.

With curtain some make scabbard clean, with coverlet their shoe,
All dirt and mire some wallow bed, as spaniels use to do.

Though boots and spurs be ne'er so foul, what passeth some thereon?
What place they foul, what thing they tear, by tumbling thereupon.

Foul mail some cast on fair board, be carpet ne'er so clean,
What manners careless master hath, by knave his man is seen.

Some make the chimney chamber pot to smell like filthy sink,
Yet who so bold, so soon to say, fough, how these houses stink?

They therefore such as make no force what comely thing they spill,
Must have a cabin like themselves, although against their will.

But gentlemen will gently do where gentleness is shewed,
Observing this, with love abide, or else hence all beshrewed.

from *The Five Hundred Points of Good Husbandry*

[1] scurvy

GEORGE GASCOYNE

A SHIPWRECK

In March it was, that cannot I forget,
In this last March upon the nineteenth day,
When from Gravesend in a boat I 'gan to jette
To board our ship in Quinborough that lay,
From whence the very twentieth day we set
Our sails abroad to slice the salt sea foam,
And anchors weighed against the trustless flood:
That day and night amid the waves we roam
To seek the coast of Holland where it stood.
And on the next when we were far from home,
And near the haven whereto we sought to sail,
A fearly chance (whereon alone to think
My hand now quakes, and all my senses fail)
'Gan us befall; the Pilot 'gan to shrink,
And all aghast his courage seemed to quail.
Whereat amazed, the Master and his mate
'Gan ask the cause of his so sudden change,
And from aloft the steward of our state
(The sounding plumb) in haste post haste must range,
To try the depth and goodness of our gate.[1]
Me thinks even yet I hear his heavy voice,
'Fathom three, four, foot more, foot less' that cried:
Me thinks I hear the fearful whispering noise
Of such as said full softly, me beside,
'God grant this journey cause us to rejoice'
When I, poor soul, which close in cabin lay,
And there had retched till gall was well-near burst,
With giddy head, my stumbling steps must stay
To look abroad as boldly as I durst.
And whiles I hearken what the sailors say,
The sounder sings 'Fathom, two full, no more'.
'Aloft, aloft', then cried the Master out,
The steersman strives to send us from the shore,

[1] way

And trusts the stream, whereof we erst had doubt,
'Tween two extremes thus were we tossed sore,
And went to hull,[2] until we leisure had
To talk at large, and eke to know the cause
What mood had made our Pilot look so sad.
At last the Dutch with butterbitten jaws
(For so he was a Dutch, a devil, a swad,[3]
A fool, a drunkard, or a traitor tone)
'Gan answer thus: '*Gy zijt te vroegh*[4] here come,
'Tis *niet goet tijt*',[5] and standing all alone,
'Gan preach to us, which fools were all and some
To trust him, fool in whom there skill was none.

*

Why stay I long to end a woeful tale?
We trust his Dutch, and up the foresail goes,
We fall on knees amid the happy gale
Which by God's will full kind and calmly blows,
And unto him we there unfold our bale,
Whereon I think I write and weep for joy,
That pleasant song the hundred and seventh psalm
There did we read to comfort our annoy,
Which in my soul, methought, was sweet as balm,
Yea far more sweet than any worldly toy.
And when he had with prayers praised the Lord,
Our *edell bloetts*[6] 'gan fall to eat and drink,
And for their sauce, at taking up the board
The ship so struck (as we all thought to sink)
Against the ground. Then all with one accord
We fell again on knees to pray apace,
And therewithal even at the second blow
(The number cannot from my mind outpace)
Our helm struck off, and we must fleet and flow
Where wind and waves would guide us by their grace.
The wind waxed calm, as I have said before
(O mighty God so did'st thou 'suage our woes)
The silly ship was soused[7] and smitten sore

[2] drift with sails furled [3] clodhopper [4] Thou art too early [5] not good tide [i.e., the tide is wrong] [6] fine fellows [lit., 'noble bloods'] [7] struck

With counter-buffets, blows and double blows.
At last the keel, which might endure no more,
'Gan rend in twain and sucked the water in:
Then might you see pale looks and woeful cheer,
Then might you hear loud cries amid deadly din:
Well noble minds in perils best appear,
And boldest hearts in bale will never blinn.[8]
For there were some (of whom I will not say
That I was one) which never changed hue,
But pumped apace, and laboured every way
To save themselves, and all their lovely crew;
Which cast the best freight overboard away,
Both corn and cloth, and all that was of weight;
Which hauled and pulled at every helping cord,
Which prayed to God and made their conscience straight.
As for myself, here I protest, my Lord,
My words were these: 'O God, in heaven on height,
Behold me not as now a wicked wight,
A sack of sin, a wretch y-wrapped in wrath,
Let no fault past, O Lord, offend Thy sight,
But weigh my will which now those faults doth loath,
And of Thy mercy pity this our plight.
Even Thou, good God, which of Thy grace didst say
That for one good, Thou would'st all Sodom save,
Behold us all: Thy shining beams display.
Some here, I trust, Thy goodness shall engrave,
To be chaste vessels unto Thee alway,
And so to live in honour of Thy Name:
Believe me, Lord', thus to the Lord I said.
But there were some (alas the more their blame)
Which in the pump their only comfort laid,
And trusted that to turn our grief to game.
'Alas,' quoth I, 'our pump good God must be,
Our sail, our stern, our tackling, and our trust.'
Some other cried to clear the shipboat free,
To save the chief and leave the rest in dust.
Which word once spoke (a wondrous thing to see)

[8] fail

All haste post haste was made to have it done:
And up it comes in haste much more than speed.
There did I see a woeful work begun
Which now, even now, doth make my heart to bleed.
Some made such haste that in the boat they won,
Before it was above the hatches brought.
Strange tale to tell, what haste some men shall make
To find their death before the same be sought.
Some 'twixt the boat and ship their bane do take,
Both drowned and slain with brains for haste crushed out.
At last the boat half freighted in the air
Is hoist aloft, and on the seas down set,
When I that yet in God could not despair
Still plied the pump, and patiently did let
All such take boat as thither made repair.
And herewithal I safely may protest
I might have won the boat as well as one,
And had that seemed a safety for the rest
I should percase[9] even with the first have gone.
But when I saw the boat was over pressed
And pestered full with more than it might bear,
And therewithal with cheerful look might see
My chief companions whom I held most dear
(Whose company had thither trained me)
Abiding still aboard our ship y-fear:
'Nay then,' quoth I, 'good God, Thy will be done,
For with my feres[10] I will both live and die.'
And ere the boat far from our sight was gone
The wave so wrought, that they which sought to flee
And so to 'scape, with waves were overrun.
Lo how he strives in vain that strives with God!
For there we lost the flower of the band,
And of our crew full twenty souls and odd
The sea sucks up, whilst we on hatches stand
In smarting fear to feel that selfsame rod.
Well on (as yet) our battered bark did pass,
And brought the rest within a mile of land.

[9] perhaps [10] companions

Then thought I, 'Sure now need I not to pass,
For I can swim and so escape this sand.'
Thus did I deem, all careless like an ass,
When suddenly the wind our foresail took,
And turned about and brought us eft to seas.
Then cried we all, 'Cast out the anchor hook,
And here let bide such help as God may please.'
Which anchor cast, we soon the same forsook,
And cut it off, for fear lest thereupon
Our ship should bouge,[11] then called we fast for fire
And so discharged our great guns every one
To warn the town thereby of our desire:
But all in vain, for succour sent they none.
But when this hoy 'gan well-near board our bark,
And might perceive what peril we were in,
It turned away and left us still in cark –
This tale is true (for now to lie were sin):
It left us there in dread and dangers dark.
It left us so, and that within the sight
And hearing both of all the pier at Breyll.
Now ply thee pen, and paint the foul despite
Of drunken Dutchmen standing there even still,
For whom we came for their cause for to fight,
For whom we came their state for to defend,
For whom we came as friends to grieve their foes:
They now disdained (in this distress) to lend
One helping boat for to assuage our woes.
They saw our harms the which they would not mend,
And had not been that God even then did raise
Some instruments to succour us at need,
We had been sunk and swallowed all in seas.
But God's will was (in way of our good speed)
That on the pier, lamenting our misease,
Some English were, whose naked swords did force
The drunken Dutch, the cankered churls to come,
And so at last, not moved by remorse
But forced by fear, they sent us succour some.
Some I must say: and for to tell the course,

[11] spring a leak

They sent us succour sauced with sour despite;
They saved our lives and spoiled us of the rest,
They stole our goods by day and eke by night;
They showed the worst and closely kept the best.
And in this time (this treason I must write)
Our Pilot fled – but how? – not empty-handed:
He fled from us, and with him did convey
A hoy full fraught (whiles we meanwhile were landed)
With powder, shot, and all our best array:
This skill he had, for all he set us sanded.

from *Gascoyne's Voyage into Holland, 1572*

THOMAS DELONEY

THE CLOTHIER'S HOUSE

Within one room, being large and long,
There stood two hundred looms full strong,
Two hundred men, the truth is so,
Wrought in these looms all in a row.
By every one a pretty boy
Sat making quilts with mickle joy,
And in another place hard by
A hundred women merrily
Were carding hard with joyful cheer
Who singing sate with voices clear,
And in a chamber close beside
Two hundred maidens did abide,
In petticoats of stammel[1] red,
And milk-white kerchers on their head.
And each sleeve with a silken band
Was featly tied at the hand.
These pretty maids did never lin[2]
But in that place all day did spin,
And spinning so with voices meet
Like nightingales they sang full sweet.
Then to another room came they
Where children were in poor array;

[1] coarse cloth [2] cease

And every one sate picking wool
The finest from the coarse to cull:
The number was sevenscore and ten,
The children of poor silly men:
And these their labours to requite
Had every one a penny at night,
Beside their meat and drink all day,
Which was to them a wondrous stay.
Within another place likewise
Full fifty proper men he spies
And these were sheremen[3] every one,
Whose skill and cunning there was shown:
And hard by them there did remain
Full four-score rowers[4] taking pain.
A Dye-house likewise had he then,
Wherein he kept full forty men:
And likewise in his fulling-mill
Full twenty persons kept he still.
Each week ten good fat oxen he
Spent in his house for certainty,
Beside good butter, cheese and fish
And many another wholesome dish.
He kept a butcher all the year,
A brewer eke for ale and beer;
A baker for to bake his bread,
Which stood his household in good stead.
Five cooks within his kitchen great
Were all the year to dress his meat.
Six scullion boys unto their hands,
To make clean dishes, pots and pans,
Besides poor children that did stay
To turn the broaches every day.
The old man that did see this sight
Was much amaz'd, as well he might:
This was a gallant Clothier sure,
Whose fame forever shall endure.

from *Jack of Newbury*

[3] shearers of cloth [4] those who put a nap on cloth

THOMAS BRICE

THE REGISTER OF THE MARTYRS

1555
February

When raging reign of tyrants stout,
Causeless, did cruelly conspire
To rend and root the simple out,
With furious force of sword and fire;
When man and wife were put to death:
We wished for our Queen ELIZABETH.

February

4 When ROGERS ruefully was brent;
8 When SAUNDERS did the like sustain;
When faithful FARRAR forth was sent
His life to lose, with grievous pain;
22 When constant HOOPER died the death:
We wished for our ELIZABETH.

*

August

23 When LAURENCE, COLLIER, COKER, and STERE,
At Canterbury, were causeless slain,
23 With HOPPER and WRIGHT; six in one fire,
Converted flesh to earth again;
24 When ROGER CORRIAR was done to death:
We wished for our ELIZABETH.

*

October

When learned RIDLEY, and LATIMER,
16 Without regard, were swiftly slain;
When furious foes could not confer
But with revenge and mortal pain.
When these two Fathers were put to death:
We wished for our ELIZABETH.

1556

February

When two women in Ipswich town,
19 Joyfully did the fire embrace;
When they sang out with cheerful sound,
Their fixed foes for to deface;
When NORWICH NO-BODY put them to death,
We wished for our ELIZABETH.

March

12 When constant CRANMER lost his life
And held his hand into the fire;
When streams of tears for him were rife
And yet did miss their just desire:
When Popish power put him to death,
We wished for our ELIZABETH.

*

1557

July

2 When GEORGE EGLES, at Chelmsford town,
Was hanged, drawn, and quarterèd;
His quarters carried up and down,
And on a pole they set his head.
When wrestèd law put him to death,
We wished for our ELIZABETH.

*

1558

July

14 When WILLIAM PECKES, COTTON, and WREIGHT,
The Popish power did sore invade;
To Burning School, they were sent straight,
14 And with them went, constant JOHN SLADE:
When these, at Brainford, were put to death,
We wished for our ELIZABETH.

Thomas Brice (d. 1570)

November

4 When ALEXANDER GECHE was brent,
4 And with him ELIZABETH LAUNSON;
When they with joy, did both consent
To do as their brethren had done;
When these, at Ipswich, were put to death,
We wished for our ELIZABETH.

November

5 When JOHN DAVY, and eke his brother,
5 With PHILIP HUMFREY kissed the cross;
When they did comfort one another
Against all fear, and worldy loss;
When these, at Bury, were put to death,
We wished for our ELIZABETH.

November

When, last of all (to take their leave!),
At Canterbury, they did some consume,
Who constantly to CHRIST did cleave;
Therefore were fried with fiery fume:
But, six days after these were put to death,
GOD sent us our ELIZABETH!

Our wished wealth hath brought us peace.
Our joy is full; our hope obtained;
The blazing brands of fire do cease,
The slaying sword also restrained.
The simple sheep, preserved from death
By our good Queen, ELIZABETH.

As Hope hath here obtained her prey,
By GOD's good will and Providence;
So Trust doth truly look for stay,
Through His heavenly influence,
That great GOLIATH shall be put to death
By our good Queen, ELIZABETH.

That GOD's true Word shall placèd be,
The hungry souls, for to sustain;
That Perfect Love and Unity
Shall be set in their seat again:
That no more good men shall be put to death;
Seeing GOD hath sent ELIZABETH.

Pray we, therefore, both night and day,
For Her Highness, as we be bound.
O LORD, preserve this Branch of Bay!
(And all her foes, with force confound)
Here, long to live! and, after death,
Receive our Queen, ELIZABETH!

Amen

Apoc. 6. How long tarriest thou, O LORD, holy and true! to judge, and avenge our blood on them that dwell on the earth.

FINIS

ROBERT SOUTHWELL

A LAMENT FOR OUR LADY'S SHRINE AT WALSINGHAM

In the wracks of Walsingham
Whom should I choose
But the Queen of Walsingham
To be guide to my muse?
Then thou Prince of Walsingham
Grant me to frame,
Bitter plaints to rue thy wrong,
Bitter woe for thy name.
Bitter was it so to see
The silly sheep
Murdered by ravening wolves
While the shepherds did sleep.

Robert Southwell (1561?–1595)

Bitter was it oh to view
  The sacred vine,
Whiles the gardeners played all close,
  Rooted up by the swine.
Bitter bitter oh to behold
  The grass to grow
Where the walls of Walsingham
  So stately did show.
Such were the works of Walsingham
  While she did stand
Such are the wracks that now do show
  Of that holy land.
Level level with the ground
  The towers do lie
Which with their golden glittering tops
  Pierced once to the sky.
Where were gates no gates are now,
  The ways unknowen
Where the press of peers did pass
  While her fame was far blowen.
Owls do scrike where the sweetest hymns
  Lately were sung;
Toads and serpents hold their dens
  Where the palmers did throng.
Weep weep O Walsingham
  Whose days are nights,
Blessings turned to blasphemies,
  Holy deeds to despites.
Sin is where our Lady sat,
  Heaven turned is to Hell.
Satan sits where our Lord did sway,
  Walsingham O farewell.

HENRY FITZSIMON

SWEARING

In elder times an ancient custom 'twas
To swear in weighty matters by the Mass.
But when Mass was put down, as old men note,
They swore then by the Cross of this grey groat.
And when the Cross was held likewise in scorn,
Then Faith, and Truth, for common oaths were sworn.
But now men banished have both Faith and Truth,
So that 'God damn me' is the common oath.
So custom keeps decorum, by gradation
Losing Mass, Cross, Faith, Truth, followeth Damnation.

ANONYMOUS

A NEW COURTLY SONNET OF THE LADY GREENSLEEVES

Greensleeves was all my joy,
Greensleeves was my delight;
Greensleeves was my heart of gold,
And who but Lady Greensleeves.

Alas, my Love! ye do me wrong
To cast me off discourteously;
And I have loved you so long,
Delighting in your company.
Greensleeves was all my joy, &c.

I have been ready at your hand,
To grant whatever you would crave;
I have both waged[1] life and land,
Your love and goodwill for to have.
Greensleeves was all my joy, &c.

[1] risked

I bought thee kerchers to thy head,
  That were wrought fine and gallantly;
I kept thee both at board and bed,
  Which cost my purse well favouredly.
    Greensleeves was all my joy, &c.

I bought thee petticoats of the best,
  The cloth so fine as fine might be;
I gave thee jewels for thy chest,
  And all this cost I spent on thee.
    Greensleeves was all my joy, &c.

Thy smock of silk, both fair and white,
  With gold embroidered gorgeously;
Thy petticoat of sendal[2] right;
  And thus I bought thee gladly.
    Greensleeves was all my joy, &c.

Thy girdle of gold so red,
  With pearls bedecked sumptuously;
The like no other lasses had,
  And yet thou wouldst not love me.
    Greensleeves was all my joy, &c.

Thy purse and eke thy gay gilt knives,
  Thy pincase gallant to the eye;
No better wore the burgess wives,
  And yet thou wouldst not love me.
    Greensleeves was all my joy, &c.

Thy crimson stockings all of silk,
  With gold all wrought above the knee;
Thy pumps as white as was the milk,
  And yet thou wouldst not love me.
    Greensleeves was all my joy, &c.

Thy gown was of the grassy green,
  Thy sleeves of satin hanging by,
Which made thee be our harvest queen,
  And yet thou wouldst not love me.
    Greensleeves was all my joy, &c.

[2] fine silk

Thy garters fringed with the gold,
  And silver aglets[3] hanging by,
Which made thee blithe for to behold,
  And yet thou wouldst not love me.
    Greensleeves was all my joy, &c.

My gayest gelding I thee gave,
  To ride wherever liked thee;
No lady ever was so brave,
  And yet thou wouldst not love me.
    Greensleeves was all my joy, &c.

My men were clothed all in green,
  And they did ever wait on thee;
All this was gallant to be seen,
  And yet thou wouldst not love me.
    Greensleeves was all my joy, &c.

They set thee up, they took thee down,
  They served thee with humility;
Thy foot might not once touch the ground,
  And yet thou wouldst not love me.
    Greensleeves was all my joy, &c.

For every morning when thou rose,
  I sent thee dainties orderly,
To cheer thy stomach from all woes,
  And yet thou wouldst not love me.
    Greensleeves was all my joy, &c.

Thou couldst desire no earthly thing
  But still thou hadst it readily;
Thy music still to play and sing,
  And yet thou wouldst not love me.
    Greensleeves was all my joy, &c.

And who did pay for all this gear
  That thou didst spend when pleased thee?
Even I that am rejected here,
  And thou disdain'st to love me.
    Greensleeves was all my joy, &c.

[3] spangles

Well, I will pray to God on high,
  That thou my constancy mayst see,
And that yet once before I die,
  Thou wilt vouchsafe to love me.
    Greensleeves was all my joy, &c.

Greensleeves, now farewell! adieu!
  God I pray to prosper thee;
For I am still thy lover true.
  Come once again and love me.
Greensleeves was all my joy,
  Greensleeves was my delight;
Greensleeves was my heart of gold,
  And who but Lady Greensleeves.

MICHAEL DRAYTON

THE COTSWOLDS

Few Vales (as I suppose) like Evesham hapt to find:
Nor any other Wold, like Cotswold ever sped
So fair and rich a Vale by fortuning to wed.
He hath the goodly wool, and she the wealthy grain:
Through which they wisely seem their household to maintain.
He hath pure wholesome air, and dainty crystal springs.
To those delights of his, she daily profit brings:
As to his large expense, she multiplies her heaps:
Nor can his flocks devour th' aboundance that she reaps;
As th' one with what it hath, the other strove to grace.
  And, now that everything may in the proper place
Most aptly be contriv'd, the sheep our Wold doth breed
(The simplest though it seem) shall our description need,
And shepherd-like, the Muse thus of that kind doth speak:
No brown, nor sullied black the face or legs doth streak,
Like those of Moreland, Cank, or of the Cambrian Hills
That lightly laden are: but Cotswold wisely fills
Her with the whitest kind: whose brows so woolly be,
As men in her fair sheep no emptiness should see.

The staple deep and thick, through, to the very grain,
Most strongly keepeth out the violentest rain:
A body long and large, the buttocks equal broad;
As fit to undergo the full and weighty load.
And of the fleecy face, the flank doth nothing lack,
But everywhere is stor'd; the belly, as the back.
The fair and goodly flock, the shepherd's only pride,
As white as winter's snow, when from the river's side
He drives his new-wash'd sheep; or on the shearing-day,
When as the lusty ram, with those rich spoils of May
His crooked horns hath crown'd; the bell-wether, so brave
As none in all the flock they like themselves would have.
  But Muse, return to tell, how there the Shepherds' King,
Whose flock hath chanc'd that year the earliest lamb to bring,
In his gay bauldric sits at his low grassy board,
With flawns, curds, clouted-cream, and country dainties stor'd:
And, whilst the bag-pipe plays, each lusty jocund swain
Quaffs sillibubs in cans, to all upon the plain,
And to their country-girls, whose nosegays they do wear,
Some roundelays do sing: the rest, the burthen bear.

from *Polyolbion*

HAWKING

  When making for the brook, the Falconer doth espy
On river, plash, or mere, where store of fowl doth lie:
Whence forcéd over land, by skilful Falconers' trade:
A fair convenient flight, may easily be made.
He whistleth off his hawks, whose nimble pinions straight,
Do work themselves by turns, into a stately height:
And if that after check, the one or both do go,
Sometimes he them the lure, sometimes doth water show;
The trembling fowl that hear the jigging hawk-bells ring,
And find it is too late to trust then to their wing,
Lie flat upon the flood, whilst the high-mounted hawks,
Then being lords alone, in their etherial walks,

Aloft so bravely stir, their bells so thick that shake;
Which when the Falconer sees, that scarce one plane[1] they make,
The gallant'st birds, saith he, that ever flew on wing,
And swears there is a flight, were worthy of a King.
  Then making to the flood, to cause the fowls to rise,
The fierce and eager hawks, down thrilling from the skies,
Make sundry canceleers[2] e'er they the fowl can reach,
Which then to save their lives, their wings do lively stretch.
But when the whizzing bells the silent air do cleave,
And that their greatest speed, them vainly do deceive,
And the sharp cruel hawks, they at their backs do view,
Themselves for very fear they instantly ineawe.[3]
  The hawks get up again into their former place,
And ranging here and there, in that their airy race,
Still as the fearful fowl attempt to 'scape away,
With many a stooping brave, them in again they lay.
But when the Falconers take their hawking-poles in hand,
And crossing of the brook, do put it over land,
The hawk gives it a souse,[4] that makes it to rebound,
Well-near the height of man, sometime above the ground;
Oft takes a leg, or wing, oft takes away the head,
And oft from neck to tail, the back in two doth shred.
With many a Wo-ho-ho, and jocond lure again,
When he his quarry makes upon the grassy plain.

from *Polyolbion*

THE PLEASURES OF THE FENS

The buzzing Bittern sits, which through his hollow bill,
A sudden bellowing sends, which many times doth fill
The neighbouring marsh with noise, as though a bull did roar;
But scarcely have I yet recited half my store:
And with my wondrous flocks of Wild-geese come I then,
Which look as though alone they peopled all the fen,
Which here in winter time, when all is overflow'd,
And want of solid sward enforceth them abroad,

[1] soaring flight [2] swerves or turns [3] plunge into water [4] swoops on it

Th' abundance then is seen, that my full fens do yield,
That almost through the Isle, do pester every field.
The Barnacles with them, which wheresoe'er they breed,
On trees, or rotten ships, yet to my fens for feed
Continually they come, and chief abode do make,
And very hardly forc'd my plenty to forsake:
Who almost all this kind do challenge as mine own,
Whose like I dare aver, is elsewhere hardly known.
For sure, unless in me, no one yet ever saw
The multitudes of fowl, in mooting time they draw:
From which to many a one, much profit doth accrue.
  Now such as flying feed, next these I must pursue;
The Sea-mew, Sea-pie, Gull, and Curlew here do keep,
As searching every shoal, and watching every deep,
To find the floating fry, with their sharp-piercing sight,
Which suddenly they take, by stooping from their height.
The Cormorant then comes, (by his devouring kind)
Which flying o'er the fen, immediately doth find
The fleet best stor'd of fish, when from his wings at full,
As though he shot himself into the thick'ned skull,
He under water goes, and so the shoal pursues,
Which into creeks do fly, when quickly he doth choose,
The fin that likes him best, and rising, flying feeds.
The Osprey oft here seen, though seldom here it breeds,
Which over them the fish no sooner do espy,
But (betwixt him and them, by an antipathy)
Turning their bellies up, as though their death they saw,
They at his pleasure lie, to stuff his glutt'nous maw.
  The toiling fisher here is tewing[1] of his net:
The fowler is employ'd his limed twigs to set.
One underneath his horse, to get a shoot doth stalk;
Another over dykes upon his stilts doth walk:
There other with their spades, the peats are squaring out,
And others from their cars, are busily about,
To draw out sedge and reed, for thatch and stover fit,
That whosoever would a landskip rightly hit,
Beholding but my fens, shall with more shapes be stor'd,
Than Germany, or France, or Thuscan can afford:

[1] towing.

And for that part of me, which men High Holland call,
Where Boston seated is, by plenteous Wytham's fall,
I peremptory am, large Neptune's liquid field,
Doth to no other tract the like abundance yield.
For that of all the Seas environing this Isle,
Our Irish, Spanish, French, howe'er we them enstyle,
The German is the great'st, and it is only I,
That do upon the same with most advantage lie.
What fish can any shore, or British sea-town show,
That's eatable to us, that it doth not bestow
Abundantly thereon? the Herring, King of Sea,
The faster-feeding Cod, the Mackrell brought by May,
The dainty Sole, and Plaice, the Dab, as of their blood;
The Conger finely sous'd, hot summer's coollest food;
The Whiting known to all, a general wholesome dish;
The Gurnet, Rochet, Maid, and Mullet, dainty fish;
The Haddock, Turbet, Bert, fish nourishing and strong;
The Thornback, and the Skate, provocative among:
The Weaver, which although his prickles venom be,
By fishers cut away, which buyers seldom see,
Yet for the fish he bears, 'tis not accounted bad;
The Sea-Flounder is here as common as the Shad;
The Sturgeon cut to kegs, (too big to handle whole)
Gives many a dainty bit out of his lusty jole.[2]
Yet of rich Neptune's store, whilst thus I idly chat,
Think not that all betwixt the Wherpoole and the Sprat,
I go about to name, that were to take in hand,
The atomy to tell, or to cast up the sand;
But on the English coast, those most that usual are,
Wherewith the stalls from thence do furnish us for far;
Amongst whose sundry sorts, since thus far I am in,
I'll of our Shell-Fish speak, with these of scale and fin:
  The sperm-increasing Crab, much cooking that doth ask,
The big-legg'd Lobster, fit for wanton Venus' task,
Voluptuaries oft take rather than for food,
And that the same effect which worketh in the blood
The rough long Oyster is, much like the Lobster limb'd:
The Oyster hot as they, the Mussel often trimm'd

[2] jowl

With Orient pearl within, as thereby Nature show'd,
That she some secret good had on that shell bestow'd:
The Scallop cordial judg'd, the dainty Whelk and Limp;
The Periwinkle, Prawn, the Cockle, and the Shrimp,
For wanton women's tastes, or for weak stomachs bought.

from *Polyolbion*

LANCASHIRE

To give to this her Town, what rightly doth belong,
Of this most famous Shire, our Lun thus frames her Song:
  First, that most precious thing, and pleasing most to man,
Who from him (made of earth) immediately began,
His she-self woman, which the goodliest of this Isle,
This country hath brought forth, that much doth grace my style;
Why should those ancients else, which so much-knowing were,
When they the blazons gave to every several Shire,
Fair women as mine own, have titled due to me?
Besides in all this Isle, there no such cattle be,
For largeness, horn, and hair, as these of Lancashire;
So that from every part of England far and near,
Men haunt her marts for store, as from her race to breed.
And for the third, wherein she doth all Shires exceed,
Be those great race of hounds, the deepest-mouth'd of all
The other of this kind, which we our hunters call,
Which from their bellowing throats upon a scent so roar,
That you would surely think, that the firm earth they tore
With their wide yawning chaps, or rent the clouds in sunder,
As though by their loud cry they meant to mock the thunder.
Besides, her natives have been anciently esteem'd,
For bowmen near our best, and ever have been deem'd
So loyal, that the guard of our preceding kings,
Of them did most consist; but yet 'mongst all these things,
Even almost ever since the English crown was set
Upon the lawful head, of our Plantagenet,
In honour, next the first, our Dukedom was allow'd,
And always with the great'st revenues was endow'd:

And after when it hapt, France-conquering Edward's blood
Divided in itself, here for the Garland stood;
The right Lancastrian Line, it from York's issue bare;
The Red-Rose, our brave badge, which in their helmets ware,
In many a bloody field; at many a doubtful fight,
Against the House of York, which bare for theirs the White.
  And for myself there's not the Tivy, nor the Wye,
Nor any of those nymphs, that to the southward lie,
For salmon me excels; and for this name of Lun,
That I am christ'ned by, the Britons it begun,
Which fulness doth import, of waters still increase;
To Neptune louting low, when crystal Lun doth cease,
And Conder coming in, conducts her by the hand,
Till lastly she salute the point of Sunderland,
And leaves our dainty Lun to Amphitrite's care.
  So blithe and bonny now the lads and lasses are,
That ever as anon the bag-pipe up doth blow,
Cast in a gallant round about the hearth they go,
And at each pause they kiss, was never seen such rule
In any place but here, at Boon-fire, or at Yule;
And every village smokes at Wakes with lusty cheer,
Then 'Hey' they cry 'for Lun', and 'Hey for Lancashire';
That one high hill was heard to tell it to his brother,
That instantly again to tell it to some other:
From hill again to vale, from vale to hill it went,
The high-lands they again, it to the lower sent,
The mud-exhausted meres, add mosses deep among,
With the report thereof, each road, and harbour rung.

from *Polyolbion*

THE SHEPHERD'S LIFE

Melanthus. Well, fisher, you have done, and forester, for you,
Your tale is neatly told – s' are both's, to give you due,
And now my turn comes next, then hear a shepherd speak:
My watchfulness and care gives day scarce leave to break
But to the fields I haste, my folded flock to see,
Where, when I find nor wolf nor fox hath injured me,

I to my bottle straight, and soundly baste my throat;
Which done, some country song or roundelay I rote
So merrily that to the music that I make
I force the lark to sing ere she be well awake;
Then Baull, my cut-tailed cur, and I begin to play,
He o'er my sheephook leaps, now th' one, now th' other way,
Then on his hinder feet he doth himself advance,
I tune, and to my note my lively dog doth dance;
Then whistle in my fist, my fellow swains to call,
Down go our hooks and scrips, and we to nine-holes fall,
At dust-point or at quoits else are we at it hard,
All false and cheating games we shepherds are debarred.
Surveying of my sheep, if ewe or wether look
As though it were amiss, or with my cur or crook
I take it, and when once I find what it doth ail,
It hardly hath that hurt but that my skill can heal;
And when my careful eye I cast upon my sheep,
I sort them in my pens, and sorted so I keep;
Those that are big'st of bone I still reserve for breed,
My cullings I put off, or for the chapman feed.
When the evening doth approach I to my bagpipe take,
And to my grazing flocks such music then I make
That they forbear to feed; then me a king you see,
I playing go before, my subjects follow me.
My bell-wether most brave before the rest doth stalk,
The father of the flock, and after him doth walk
My writhen-headed ram with posies crowned in pride,
Fast to his crooked horns with ribands neatly tied.
And at our shepherds' board that's cut out of the ground,
My fellow swains and I together at it round,
With green-cheese, clouted cream, with flawns[1] and custards stored,
Whig,[2] cider, and with whey, I domineer, a lord.
When shearing time is come I to the river drive
My goodly well-fleeced flocks (by pleasure thus I thrive)
Which being washed at will, upon the shearing day
My wool I forth in locks fit for the winder lay,
Which upon lusty heaps into my cote I heave,
That in the handling feels as soft as any sleave;

[1] cheesecakes [2] buttermilk

When every ewe two lambs that yeaned hath that year,
About her new-shorn neck a chaplet then doth wear.
My tarbox and my scrip, my bagpipe at my back,
My sheephook in my hand, what can I say I lack?
He that a scepter swayed, a sheephook in his hand
Hath not disdained to have, for shepherds then I stand;
Then forester, and you, my fisher, cease your strife,
I say your shepherd leads your only merry life.

from *The Muses' Elizium: The Sixt Nymphall*

BEN JONSON

TO MY BOOKSELLER

Thou that mak'st gain thy end, and wisely well
  Call'st a book good or bad as it doth sell,
Use mine so too, I give thee leave; but crave,
  For the luck's sake, it thus much favour have,
To lie upon thy stall till it be sought,
  Not offered, as it made suit to be bought;
Nor have my title-leaf on posts or walls,
  Or in cleft-sticks, advanced to make calls
For termers, or some clerk-like servingman
  Who scarce can spell th' hard names, whose knight less can.
If, without these vile arts, it will not sell,
  Send it to Bucklersbury,[1] there 'twill well.

INVITING A FRIEND TO SUPPER

To-night, grave sir, both my poor house and I
  Do equally desire your company;
Not that we think us worthy such a guest,
  But that your worth will dignify our feast

[1] [the grocers' quarter of London – where it would be used for wrapping-paper]

With those that come, whose grace may make that seem
  Something, which else could hope for no esteem.
It is the fair acceptance, sir, creates
  The entertainment perfect, not the cates.
Yet shall you have, to rectify your palate,
  An olive, capers, or some better salad
Ush'ring the mutton; with a short-legged hen,
  If we can get her, full of eggs, and then
Lemons and wine for sauce; to these, a coney
  Is not to be despaired of, for our money;
And though fowl now be scarce, yet there are clerks,
  The sky not falling, think we may have larks.
I'll tell you of more, and lie, so you will come,
  Of partridge, pheasant, woodcock, of which some
May yet be there; and godwit, if we can,
  Gnat, rail, and ruff too. Howsoe'er, my man
Shall read a piece of Virgil, Tacitus,
  Livy, or of some better book to us,
Of which we'll speak our minds amidst our meat;
  And I'll profess no verses to repeat;
To this, if aught appear which I know not of,
  That will the pastry, not my paper, show of.
Digestive cheese, and fruit there sure will be;
  But that which most doth take my muse, and me,
Is a pure cup of rich Canary wine,
  Which is the Mermaid's now, but shall be mine;
Of which had Horace or Anacreon tasted,
  Their lives, as do their lines, till now had lasted.
Tobacco, nectar, or the Thespian springs
  Are all but Luther's beer to this I sing.
Of this we will sup free, but moderately,
  And we will have no polly, or parrot by;
Nor shall our cups make any guilty men,
  But at our parting we will be as when
We innocently met. No simple word
  That shall be uttered at our mirthful board
Shall make us sad next morning, or affright
  The liberty that we'll enjoy to-night.

TO PENSHURST

Thou art not, Penshurst, built to envious show
  Of touch or marble, nor canst boast a row
Of polished pillars, or a roof of gold;
  Thou hast no lantern whereof tales are told,
Or stairs or courts; but stand'st an ancient pile,
  And these, grudged at, art reverenced the while.
Thou joy'st in better marks, of soil, of air,
  Of wood, of water; therein thou art fair.
Thou hast thy walks for health as well as sport;
  Thy mount, to which the Dryads do resort,
Where Pan and Bacchus their high feasts have made
  Beneath the broad beech, and the chestnut shade,
That taller tree, which of a nut was set
  At his great birth, where all the Muses met.
There in the writhed bark are cut the names
  Of many a sylvan, taken with his flames;
And thence the ruddy satyrs oft provoke
  The lighter fauns to reach thy Lady's oak.
Thy copse too, named of Gamage, thou hast there,
  That never fails to serve thee seasoned deer
When thou wouldst feast, or exercise thy friends.
  The lower land, that to the river bends,
Thy sheep, thy bullocks, kine, and calves do feed;
  The middle grounds thy mares and horses breed.
Each bank doth yield thee conies; and the tops,
  Fertile of wood, Ashore and Sidney's copse,
To crown thy open table, doth provide
  The purpled pheasant with the speckled side;
The painted partridge lies in every field,
  And, for thy mess, is willing to be killed.
And if the high-swollen Medway fail thy dish,
  Thou hast thy ponds that pay thee tribute fish,
Fat aged carps that run into thy net,
  And pikes, now weary their own kind to eat,
As loath the second draught or cast to stay,
  Officiously at first themselves betray;

Bright eels that emulate them, and leap on land
  Before the fisher, or into his hand.
Then hath thy orchard fruit, thy garden flowers
  Fresh as the air, and new as are the hours.
The early cherry, with the later plum,
  Fig, grape, and quince, each in his time doth come;
The blushing apricot and woolly peach
  Hang on thy walls, that every child may reach.
And though thy walls be of the country stone,
  They're reared with no man's ruin, no man's groan;
There's none that dwell about them wish them down,
  But all come in, the farmer and the clown,
And no one empty handed, to salute
  Thy lord and lady, though they have no suit.
Some bring a capon, some a rural cake,
  Some nuts, some apples; some that think they make
The better cheeses bring 'em, or else send
  By their ripe daughters whom they would commend
This way to husbands, and whose baskets bear
  An emblem of themselves in plum or pear.
But what can this, more than express their love,
  Add to thy free provisions, far above
The need of such, whose liberal board doth flow
  With all that hospitality doth know?
Where comes no guest but is allowed to eat
  Without his fear, and of thy lord's own meat;
Where the same beer and bread, and self-same wine
  That is his lordship's shall be also mine.
And I not fain to sit, as some this day
  At great men's tables, and yet dine away.
Here no man tells my cups, nor, standing by,
  A waiter doth my gluttony envy,
But gives me what I call and lets me eat;
  He knows below he shall find plenty of meat.
Thy tables hoard not up for the next day,
  Nor when I take my lodging need I pray
For fire or lights or livery; all is there
  As if thou then wert mine, or I reigned here;

There's nothing I can wish, for which I stay.
  That found King James, when hunting late this way
With his brave son, the prince, they saw thy fires
  Shine bright on every hearth as the desires
Of thy Penates had been set on flame
  To entertain them, or the country came
With all their zeal to warm their welcome here.
  What great I will not say, but sudden cheer
Didst thou then make 'em! and what praise was heaped
  On thy good lady then! who therein reaped
The just reward of her high huswifery;
  To have her linen, plate, and all things nigh
When she was far, and not a room but dressed
  As if it had expected such a guest!
These, Penshurst, are thy praise, and yet not all.
  Thy lady's noble, fruitful, chaste withal;
His children thy great lord may call his own,
  A fortune in this age but rarely known.
They are and have been taught religion; thence
  Their gentler spirits have sucked innocence.
Each morn and even they are taught to pray
  With the whole household, and may every day
Read, in their virtuous parents' noble parts,
  The mysteries of manners, arms, and arts.
Now, Penshurst, they that will proportion thee
  With other edifices when they see
Those proud, ambitious heaps and nothing else,
  May say, their lords have built, but thy lord dwells.

THE GOODWIFE'S ALE

When shall we meet again, and have a taste
Of that transcendent Ale, we drank of last?
What wild ingredients did the woman choose
To mad her drink with all; it made me lose
My wits before I quenched my thirst: there came
Such whimsies in my head, and such a flame

Of fiery drunkenness had singed my nose,
My beard shrunk in for fear. There were of those
That took me for a comet; some a far
Distance remote thought me a blazing star.
The earth methought just as it was it went
Round in a wheeling course of merriment.
My head was ever drooping, and my nose
Offering to be a suitor to my toes.
My mouth did stand awry just as it were
Lab'ring to whisper something in mine ear.
My pockholed face, they say, appeared to some
Most like a dry and burning honeycomb.
My tongue did swim in ale, and joyed to boast
Himself a better seaman than the toast.
My guts were mines of sulphur, and my set
Of parched teeth, struck fire as they met.
Nay, when I pissed, my urine was so hot
It burnt a hole quite through the chamber-pot.
Each brewer that I met I kissed and made
Suitor to be apprentice to the trade.
One did approve the motion when he saw
That mine own legs did the indenture draw.
Well, Sir, I grew stark mad, as you may see
By this adventure upon poetry.
You easily may guess, I am not quite
Grown sober yet, by these poor lines I write.
I only do't for this, that you may see
That though you paid for th'ale, yet it paid me.

JOHN DONNE

A TALE OF A CITIZEN AND HIS WIFE

I sing no harm good sooth to any wight,
To lord or fool, cuckold, beggar or knight,
To peace-teaching lawyer, proctor, or brave
Reformed or reduced captain, knave,

Officer, juggler, or justice of peace,
Juror or judge; I touch no fat sow's grease,
I am no libeller, nor will be any,
But (like a true man) say there are too many.
I fear not *ore tenus*; for my tale,
Nor Count nor counsellor will red or pale.
   A citizen and his wife the other day
Both riding on one horse, upon the way
I overtook, the wench a pretty peat,[1]
And (by her eye) well fitting for the feat.
I saw the lecherous citizen turn back
His head, and on his wife's lip steal a smack,
Whence apprehending that the man was kind,
Riding before, to kiss his wife behind,
To get acquaintance with him I began
To sort discourse fit for so fine a man:
I asked the number of the Plaguy Bill,
Asked if the Custom Farmers held out still,
Of the Virginian plot, and whether Ward
The traffic of the Midland seas had marred,
Whether the Britain Bourse did fill apace,
And likely were to give th' Exchange disgrace;
Of new-built Aldgate, and the Moorfield crosses,
Of store of bankrupts, and poor merchants' losses
I urged him to speak; but he (as mute
As an old courtier worn to his last suit)
Replied with only yeas and nays; at last
(To fit his element) my theme I cast
On tradesmen's gains; that set his tongue a-going:
Alas, good sir (quoth he), 'There is no doing
In Court nor City now'; she smiled and I,
And (in my conscience) both gave him the lie
In one met thought: but he went on apace,
And at the present time with such a face
He railed as frayed me; for he gave no praise ,
To any but my Lord of Essex' days;

[1] girl

Called those the age of action; 'true' (quoth he)
'There's now as great an itch of bravery,
And heat of taking up, but cold lay down,
For, put to push of pay, away they run;
Our only City trades of hope now are
Bawd, tavern-keeper, whore and scrivener;
The much of privileged kingsmen, and the store
Of fresh protections make the rest all poor;
In the first state of their creation,
Though many stoutly stand, yet proves not one
A righteous paymaster.' Thus ran he on
In a continued rage: so void of reason
Seemed his harsh talk, I sweat for fear of treason.
And (troth) how could I less? when in the prayer
For the protection of the wise Lord Mayor,
And his wise brethren's worships, when one pray'th,
He swore that none could say Amen with faith.
To get him off from what I glowed to hear,
(In happy time) an angel did appear,
The bright sign of a loved and well-tried inn,
Where many citizens with their wives have been
Well used and often; here I prayed him stay,
To take some due refreshment by the way.
Look how he looked that hid the gold (his hope)
And at return found nothing but a rope,
So he on me, refused and made away,
Though willing she pleaded a weary day:
I found my miss, shook hands, yet prayed him tell
(To hold acquaintance still) where he did dwell;
He barely named the street, promised the wine.
But his kind wife gave me the very sign.

Elegy XIV

JOSEPH HALL

A TUTOR

A gentle squire would gladly entertain
Into his house some trencher-chaplain,
Some willing man that might instruct his sons
And that would stand to good conditions.
First, that he lie upon the truckle-bed
Whiles his young master lieth o'er his head.
Second, that he do on no default
Ever presume to sit above the salt.
Third, that he never change his trencher twice.
Fourth, that he use all common courtesies,
Sit bare at meals, and one half rise and wait.
Last, that he never his young master beat
But he must ask his mother to define
How many jerks she would his breech should line.
All these observed, he could contented be
To give five marks and winter livery.

Satire VI

JOHN MARSTON

A FINE LADY

Peace, Cynic; see, what yonder doth approach;
A cart? a tumbrel? No, a badged coach.[1]
What's in't? Some man. No, nor yet womankind,
But a celestial angel, fair, refined.
The devil as soon! Her mask so hinders me,
I cannot see her beauty's deity.
Now that is off, she is so vizarded,
So steep'd in lemon's juice, so surphuled,[2]

[1] i.e., with armorial bearings [2] painted with cosmetics

I cannot see her face. Under one hood
Two faces; but I never understood
Or saw one face under two hoods till now:
'Tis the right resemblance of old Janus' brow.
Her mask, her vizard, her loose hanging gown
For her loose-lying body, her bright spangled crown,
Her long slit sleeve, stiff busk, puff verdingal[3]
Is all that makes her thus angelical.
Alas! her soul struts round about her neck;
Her seat of sense is her rebato[4] set;
Her intellectual is a feigned niceness,
Nothing but clothes and simpering preciseness.

from *The Scourge of Villainy*

THOMAS CAMPION

JACK AND JOAN

Jack and Joan they think no ill,
But loving live, and merry still;
Do their week-days' work and pray
Devoutly on the holy day;
Skip and trip it on the green,
And help to choose the summer queen;
Lash out, at a country feast,
Their silver penny with the best.

Well can they judge of nappy ale,
And tell at large a winter tale;
Climb up to the apple loft,
And turn the crabs till they be soft.
Tib is all the father's joy,
And little Tom the mother's boy.
All their pleasure is content,
And care, to pay their yearly rent.

Joan can call by name her cows,
And deck her windows with green boughs;

[3] farthingale [4] a kind of stiff collar

She can wreaths and tutties[1] make,
And trim with plums a bridal cake.
Jack knows what brings gain or loss,
And his long flail can stoutly toss;
Make the hedge, which others break,
And ever thinks what he doth speak.

Now, you courtly dames and knights,
That study only strange delights,
Though you scorn the home-spun gray,
And revel in your rich array;
Though your tongues dissemble deep,
And can your heads from danger keep;
Yet for all your pomp and train,
Securer lives the silly swain.

WINTER NIGHTS

Now winter nights enlarge
  The number of their hours,
And clouds their storms discharge
  Upon the airy towers.

Let now the chimneys blaze
  And cups o'erflow with wine;
Let well-tuned words amaze
  With harmony divine.

Now yellow waxen lights
  Shall wait on honey love,
While youthful revels, masks, and courtly sights
  Sleep's leaden spells remove.

This time doth well dispense
  With lovers' long discourse;
Much speech hath some defence,
  Though beauty no remorse.

All do not all things well:
  Some measures comely tread;

[1] nosegays

Some knotted riddles tell;
  Some poems smoothly read.

The summer hath his joys,
  And winter his delights;
Though love and all his pleasures are but toys,
  They shorten tedious nights.

ANONYMOUS

OF CORNELIUS

See you him yonder who sits o'er the stage
With the tobacco-pipe now at his mouth?
It is Cornelius, that brave gallant youth,
Who is new printed to this fangled age.
  He wears a jerkin cudgeled[1] with gold lace,
  A profound slop,[2] a hat scarce pipkin-high;
  For boots a pair of dagge cases; his face
  Furred with cad's-beard,[3] his poniard on his thigh.
He wallows in his walk, his slop to grace;
Swears by the Lord, deigns no salutation
But to some jade that's sick of his own fashion,
As, Farewell, sweet captain, or, Boy, come apace.
  Yet this Sir Bevis or the fairy knight
  Put up the lie because he durst not fight.

from *Skialethia* (1598)

A SONNET UPON THE PITIFUL BURNING OF THE GLOBE PLAYHOUSE IN LONDON

Now sit thee down, Melpomene,
Wrapped in a sea-coal robe,
And tell the doleful tragedy
That late was played at Globe;

[1] heavily trimmed [2] pair of loose breeches [3] caddis-beard [caddis=cotton wool]

For no man that can sing and say
Was scared on St Peter's Day.
Oh sorrow, pitiful sorrow, and yet all this is true.

All you that please to understand,
Come listen to my story;
To see Death with his raking brand
'Mongst such an auditory;
Regarding neither Cardinal's might,
Nor yet the rugged face of Henry the eight.
Oh sorrow, etc.

This fearful fire began above,
A wonder strange and true,
And to the stage-house did remove,
As round as tailor's clew;
And burnt down both beam and snag,
And did not spare the silken flag.
Oh sorrow, etc.

Out run the knights, out run the lords,
And there was great ado;
Some lost their hats and some their swords,
Then out run Burbage too;
The reprobates, though drunk on Monday,
Prayed for the fool and Henry Condye.
Oh sorrow, etc.

The periwigs and drum-heads fry,
Like to a butter firkin;
A woeful burning did betide
To many a good buff jerkin.
Then with swollen eyes, like drunken Flemings,
Distressed stood old stuttering Hemings.
Oh sorrow, etc.

No shower his rain did there down force,
In all that sunshine weather,
To save that great renowned house,
Nor thou, O ale-house, neither.
Had it begun below, *sans doute*,

Their wives for fear had pissed it out.
Oh sorrow, etc.

Be warned, you stage strutters all,
Lest you again be catched,
And such a burning do befall
As to them whose house was thatched;
Forbear your whoring, breeding biles,
And lay up that expense for tiles.
Oh sorrow, etc.

Go draw you a petition,
And do you not abhor it,
And get, with low submission,
A license to beg for it
In churches, *sans* churchwardens' checks,
In Surrey and in Middlesex.
Oh sorrow, pitiful sorrow, and yet all this is true.

Broadsheet Ballad

FRANCIS BEAUMONT

MR FRANCIS BEAUMONT'S LETTER TO BEN JONSON

The sun, which doth the greatest comfort bring
To absent friends (because the self-same thing
They know they see, however absent), is
Here our best hay-maker (forgive me this,
It is our country style); in this warm shine
I lie, and dream of your full Mermaid wine.
Oh, we have water mixed with claret-lees,
Drink apt to bring in drier heresies
Than beer, good only for a sonnet strain,
With fustian metaphors to stuff the brain;
So mixed that given to the thirstiest one
'Twill not prove alms unless he have the stone.

'Tis sold by Puritans, mixed with intent
To make it serve for either sacrament.
I think with one draught man's invention fades,
Two cups had quite marred Homer's *Iliads*;
'Tis liquor that will find out Sutcliffe's wit,
Lie where it will, and make him write worse yet.
Filled with such moisture, in a grievous qualm,
Did Robert Wisdom write his singing psalm;
And so must I do this, and yet I think
It is a potion sent us down to drink
By special providence, keeps us from fights,
Makes us not laugh when we make legs to knights;
'Tis this that keeps our minds fit for our states,
A med'cine to obey our magistrates.
For we do live more free than you; no hate,
No envy of another's happy state
Moves us, we are all equal, every whit;
Of land, that God gives men here, is their wit,
If we consider fully, for our best
And gravest man will, with his main house-jest,
Scarce please you; we want subtlety to do
The city tricks – lie, hate, and flatter too.
Here are none that can bear a painted show,
Strike when you wink, and then lament the blow,
Who, like mills set the right way to grind,
Can make their gains alike with every wind.
Only some fellow with the subtlest pate
Amongst us, may perchance equivocate
At selling of a horse, and that's the most.
Methinks the little wit I had is lost
Since I saw you; for wit is like a rest
Held up at tennis, which men do the best
With the best gamesters. What things have we seen
Done at the Mermaid! heard words that have been
So nimble and so full of subtle flame,
As if that everyone from whom they came
Had meant to put his whole wit in a jest,
And had resolved to live a fool the rest

Of his dull life; then when there has been thrown
Wit able to justify the town
For three days past, wit that might warrant be
For the whole city to talk foolishly
Till that were cancelled, and when we were gone
We left an air behind, which was alone
Able to make the two next companies
Right witty, though they were downright cockneys.
When I remember this, and see that now
The country gentlemen begin to allow
My wit for dry-bobs, then I needs must cry,
I see my days of ballading are nigh;
I can already riddle, and can sing
Catches, sell bargains, and I fear shall bring
Myself to speak the hardest words I find
Over as fast as any, with one wind
That takes no medicines. But one thought of thee
Makes me remember all these things to be
The wit of our young men, fellows that show
No part of good, yet utter all they know;
Who like trees and the guard have growing souls
Only; strong destiny, which all controls,
I hope hath left a better fate in store
For me, thy friend, than to live evermore
Banished unto this home; 'twill once again
Bring me to thee, who wilt make smooth and plain
The way of knowledge for me, and then I
Who have no good in me but simplicity,
Know that it will my greatest comfort be
To acknowledge all the rest to come from thee.

ROBERT SEMPILL OF BELTREES

THE LIFE AND DEATH OF HABBIE SIMSON, THE PIPER OF KILBARCHAN

Kilbarchan now may say alas!
For she hath lost her game and grace,
Both *Trixie* and *The Maiden Trace*;
But what remead?
For no man can supply his place:
Hab Simson's dead.

Now who shall play *The Day it Dawis*,
Or *Hunt's Up*, when the cock he craws?
Or who can for our kirk-town cause
Stand us in stead?
On bagpipes now nobody blaws
Sen[1] Habbie's dead.

Or wha will cause our shearers shear?
Wha will bend up the brags of weir,[2]
Bring in the bells, or good play-meir
In time of need?
Hab Simson could, what needs you speir?[3]
But now he's dead.

So kindly to his neighbours neist[4]
At Beltan and St Barchan's feast
He blew, and then held up his breast,
As he were weid:[5]
But now we need not him arrest,
For Habbie's dead.

At fairs he play'd before the spear-men,
All gaily graithed[6] in their gear men:
Steel bonnets, jacks, and swords so clear then
Like any bead:
Now wha shall play before such weir-men[7]
Sen Habbie's dead?

[1] since [2] play this tune [3] ask [4] beside [5] mad [6] dressed [7] warriors

At clark-plays when he wont to come,
His Pipe played trimly to the drum;
Like bikes[8] of bees he gart it bum,[9]
  And tun'd his reed:
Now all our pipers may sing dumb,
  Sen Habbie's dead.

And at horse races many a day,
Before the black, the brown, the gray,
He gart his pipe, when he did play,
  Baith skirl and skreed:[10]
Now all such pastime's quite away
  Sen Habbie's dead.

He counted was a waled wight-man,[11]
And fiercely at football he ran:
At every game the gree[12] he wan
  For pith[13] and speed.
The like of Habbie was na than,
  But now he's dead.

And then, besides his valiant acts,
At bridals he wan many placks;[14]
He bobbit ay behind folk's backs
  And shook his head.
Now we want many merry cracks[15]
  Sen Habbie's dead.

He was convoyer of the bride,
With Kittock hinging[16] at his side;
About the kirk he thought a pride
  The ring to lead:
But now we may gae but[17] a guide,
  For Habbie's dead.

So well's he keepèd his decorum,
And all the stots[18] of *Whig-meg-morum*;[19]

[8] hives [9] made it buzz [10] screech [11] chosen stalwart [12] prize [13] power [14] coins
[15] capers [16] purse hanging [17] go without [18] bullocks [19] politics

He slew a man, and wae's me for him,
  And bure the fead![20]
But yet the man wan hame before him,
  And was not dead.

Ay whan he play'd, the lasses leugh[21]
To see him teethless, auld, and teugh,
He wan his pipes besides Barcleugh,
  Withouten dread!
Which after wan him gear[22] eneugh;
  But now he's dead.

Ay when he play'd the gaitlings[23] gedder'd,[24]
And when he spake the carl bleddered,[25]
On Sabbath days his cap was fedder'd,[26]
  A seemly weid;[27]
In the kirk-yeard his mare stood tedder'd
  Where he lies dead.

Alas! for him my heart is sair,
For of his spring I gat a skair,[28]
At every play, race, feast, and fair,
  But guile or greed;
We need not look for piping mair,
  Sen Habbie's dead.

ROBERT HERRICK

A NEW-YEAR'S GIFT SENT TO SIR SIMON STEWARD

No news of navies burnt at seas;
No noise of late-spawn'd tittyries;[1]
No closet plot, or open vent,
That frights men with a parliament;

[20] bore the feud [21] laughed [22] wealth [23] children [24] gathered [25] old man gossiped [26] feathered [27] garment [28] share

[1] roisterers

No new device or late-found trick
To read by the stars the kingdom's sick;
No gin to catch the state, or wring
The freeborn nostril of the king,
We send to you; but here a jolly
Verse, crown'd with ivy and with holly,
That tells of winter's tales and mirth,
That milkmaids make about the hearth,
Of Christmas sports, the wassail-bowl,
That's tost up, after fox-i'-th'-hole;
Of blind-man-buff, and of the care
That young men have to shoe the mare;
Of Twelfth-tide cakes, of peas and beans,
Wherewith you make those merry scenes,
Whenas ye choose your king and queen,
And cry out: *Hey, for our town green*;
Of ash-heaps, in the which ye use
Husbands and wives by streaks to choose;
Of crackling laurel, which fore-sounds
A plenteous harvest to your grounds:
Of these and such-like things for shift,
We send instead of New-Year's gift.
Read then, and when your faces shine
With buxom[2] meat and cap'ring wine,
Remember us in cups full crown'd,
And let our city-health go round,
Quite through the young maids and the men
To the ninth number, if not ten;
Until the fired chestnuts leap
For joy to see the fruits ye reap
From the plump chalice and the cup,
That tempts till it be tossed up;
Then as ye sit about your embers,
Call not to mind those fled Decembers,
But think on these that are t' appear
As daughters to the instant year:

[2] tender

Sit crown'd with rosebuds, and carouse
Till Liber Pater[3] twirls the house
About your ears; and lay upon
The year your cares that's fled and gone.
And let the russet swains the plough
And harrow hang up, resting now;
And to the bagpipe all address,
Till sleep takes place of weariness.
And thus, throughout, with Christmas plays
Frolic the full twelve holidays.

THE COUNTRY LIFE

Sweet country life, to such unknown
Whose lives are others', not their own!
But serving courts and cities, be
Less happy, less enjoying thee.
Thou never plough'st the ocean's foam
To seek and bring rough pepper home;
Nor to the Eastern Ind dost rove
To bring from thence the scorchéd clove;
Nor, with the loss of thy lov'd rest,
Bring'st home the ingot from the West.
No, thy ambition's masterpiece
Flies no thought higher than a fleece;
Or how to pay thy hinds, and clear
All scores, and so to end the year:
But walk'st about thine own dear bounds,
Not envying others larger grounds:
For well thou know'st *'tis not th' extent*
Of land makes life, but sweet content.
When now the cock (the ploughman's horn)
Calls forth the lily-wristed morn,
Then to thy corn-fields thou dost go,
Which though well soil'd,[1] yet thou dost know
That the best compost for the lands
Is the wise master's feet and hands.

[3] Father Bacchus

[1] manured

There at the plough thou find'st thy team
With a hind whistling there to them;
And cheer'st them up by singing how
The kingdom's portion is the plough.
This done, then to th' enamelled meads
Thou go'st, and as thy foot there treads,
Thou see'st a present God-like power
Imprinted in each herb and flower;
And smell'st the breath of great-ey'd kine,
Sweet as the blossoms of the vine.
Here thou behold'st thy large sleek neat
Unto the dew-laps up in meat;
And, as thou look'st, the wanton steer,
The heifer, cow, and ox draw near
To make a pleasing pastime there.
These seen, thou go'st to view thy flocks
Of sheep, safe from the wolf and fox,
And find'st their bellies there as full
Of short sweet grass as backs with wool,
And leav'st them, as they feed and fill,
A shepherd piping on a hill.
For sports, for pageantry and plays
Thou hast thy eves and holidays;
On which the young men and maids meet
To exercise their dancing feet;
Tripping the comely country round,
With daffodils and daisies crown'd.
Thy wakes, thy quintels here thou hast,
Thy May poles, too, with garlands grac'd;
Thy morris dance, thy Whitsun ale,
Thy shearing feast which never fail;
Thy harvest-home, thy wassail bowl,
That's toss'd up after fox i' th' hole;
Thy mummeries, thy Twelfth-tide kings
And queens, thy Christmas revellings,
Thy nut-brown mirth, thy russet wit,
And no man pays too dear for it.
To these, thou hast thy times to go
And trace the hare i' th' treacherous snow;

Thy witty wiles to draw, and get
The lark into the trammel net;
Thou hast thy cockrood[2] and thy glade
To take the precious pheasant made;
Thy lime-twigs, snares and pit-falls then
To catch the pilfering birds, not men.
O happy life! if that their good
The husbandmen but understood!
Who all the day themselves do please,
And younglings, with such sports as these,
And lying down have nought t' affright
Sweet sleep, that makes more short the night.

Cætera desunt –

THOMAS RANDOLPH

AN ODE TO MR ANTHONY STAFFORD TO HASTEN HIM INTO THE COUNTRY

Come, spur away,
I have no patience for a longer stay,
But must go down
And leave the chargeable noise of this great town.
I will the country see,
Where old simplicity
Though hid in grey
Doth look more gay
Than foppery in plush and scarlet clad.
Farewell, you city wits that are
Almost at civil war;
'Tis time that I grow wise, when all the world grows mad.

More of my days
I will not spend to gain an idiot's praise,
Or to make sport
For some slight puny of the Inns of Court.

[2] run for snaring woodcocks

Then, worthy Stafford, say
How shall we spend the day;
With what delights
Shorten the nights?
When from this tumult we are got secure
Where mirth with all her freedom goes,
Yet shall no finger lose,
Where every word is thought, and every thought is pure.

There from the tree
We'll cherries pluck, and pick the strawberry.
And every day
Go see the wholesome country girls make hay,
Whose brown hath lovelier grace
Than any painted face
That I do know
Hyde Park can show;
Where I had rather gain a kiss than meet
(Though some of them in greater state
Might court my love with plate)
The beauties of the Cheap, and wives of Lombard street.

But think upon
Some other pleasures, these to me are none;
Why do I prate
Of women, that are things against my fate?
I never mean to wed
That torture to my bed;
My muse is she
My love shall be.
Let clowns get wealth and heirs; when I am gone,
And the great bugbear, grisly death,
Shall take this idle breath,
If I a poem leave, that poem is my son.

Of this, no more;
We'll rather taste the bright Pomona's store, –
No fruit shall 'scape
Our palates, from the damson to the grape.

Then full we'll seek a shade,
And hear what music's made;
How Philomel
Her tale doth tell,
And how the other birds do fill the choir;
The thrush and blackbird lend their throats,
Warbling melodious notes;
We will all sports enjoy, which others but desire.

Ours is the sky,
Where at what fowl we please our hawk shall fly;
Nor will we spare
To hunt the crafty fox or timorous hare;
But let our hounds run loose
In any ground they'll choose,
The buck shall fall,
The stag and all;
Our pleasures must from their own warrants be,
For to my muse, if not to me,
I'm sure all game is free;
Heaven, earth, are all but parts of her great royalty.

And when we mean
To taste of Bacchus' blessings now and then,
And drink by stealth
A cup or two to noble Berkeley's health,
I'll take my pipe and try
The Phrygian melody,
Which he that hears
Lets through his ears
A madness to distemper all the brain.
Then I another pipe will take
And Doric music make,
To civilize with graver notes our wits again.

ANONYMOUS

AN OLD SOLDIER OF THE QUEEN'S

Of an old Soldier of the Queen's,
With an old motley coat, and a Malmsey nose,
And an old jerkin that's out at the elbows,
And an old pair of boots, drawn on without hose
Stuft with rags instead of toes;
  And an old Soldier of the Queen's,
  And the Queen's old Soldier.

With an old rusty sword that's hackt with blows,
And an old dagger to scare away the crows,
And an old horse that reels as he goes,
And an old saddle that no man knows,
  And an old Soldier of the Queen's,
  And the Queen's old Soldier.

With his old wounds in Eighty Eight,
Which he recover'd, at Tilbury fight;
With an old Passport that never was read,
That in his old travels stood him in great stead;
  And an old Soldier of the Queen's,
  And the Queen's old Soldier.

With his old gun, and his bandeliers,
And an old head-piece to keep warm his ears,
With an old shirt is grown to wrack,
With a huge louse, with a great list on his back,
Is able to carry a pedlar and his pack;
  And an old Soldier of the Queen's,
  And the Queen's old Soldier.

THE OLD AND THE NEW COURTIER

Old Courtier

An old song made by an old aged Pate,
Of an old worshipful gentleman, had a wealthy estate,
That kept an old house at a bountiful rate,
And an old Porter to relieve poor people at his gate,
Like an old Courtier of the Queen's,
And the Queen's old Courtier.

With an old Lady whose anger one word assuageth,
Who every quarter paid his old Servants their wages,
Who never knew what belonged to coachmen, footmen, nor pages,
But kept two and fifty men in blue caps and badges.
Like an old Courtier of the Queen's, etc.

With an old study, stuff full of old learned books,
And an old Parson, you may know him by his looks;
And an old butt'ry-hatch worn quite off the old hooks,
And an old kitchen that maintain'd half a dozen old cooks.
Like an old Courtier of the Queen's, etc.

With an old hall hung with pikes, guns, and bows,
And old blades and bucklers, had borne many shrewd blows,
With an old freezadoe coat to cover his trunk hose,
With an old cup of sherry to comfort his old nose.
Like an old Courtier of the Queen's, etc.

With an old fashion, when Christmas was come,
To call in all his old neighbours with a bagpipe or a drum,
And good cheer enough to furnish out every old room,
And beer and ale would make a cat to speak, and a wise man dumb.
Like an old Courtier of the Queen's, etc.

With an old falconer, a huntsman, and a kennel of hounds,
That never hawked nor hunted but in his grand-father's old grounds,
Who like a wise man kept himself in his own old bounds.
And when he died gave each child a thousand old pounds.
Like an old Courtier of the Queen's, etc.

But to his son and heir his lands he assign'd,
With an old will to charge him to keep the same bountiful mind,
To be good to his old tenants, and to his old neighbours kind,
But in the next ditty you shall hear how he was inclined.
Like a new Courtier of the King's,
And the King's new Courtier.

New Courtier

With a new flourishing gallant, who is newly come to his land,
Who keeps a brace of painted creatures at his own command,
And can take up readily a thousand pounds on his new bond,
And drink in a new tavern, till he can neither go nor stand,
Like a new Courtier of the King's, and the King's new Courtier.

With a new lady whose face is beautiful and fair,
Who never knew what belong'd to house-keeping nor care,
But purchas'd seven colour'd fans to play with the wanton air,
And seventeen new dressings of other women's hair,
Like a new Courtier of the King's, etc.

With a new study full of pamphlets and plays,
With a new chaplain, that drinks oftener than he prays,
With a new butt'ry-hatch opens once in five or six days,
With a new French cook to devise kickshaws and toys,
For the new Courtier of the King's, etc.

With a new hall builded where an old hall stood,
Hung round with new pictures, does the poor little good,
With a new shovel-board whereon never stood food,
With 22 fair chimnies never burnt coals nor wood.
For the new Courtier of the King's, etc.

With a new fashion when Christmas was drawing on,
Upon a new journey they must all to London be gone,
And leave none to keep house in the country, but their new man John,
Who relieves all his neighbours with a great thump on the back with a cold stone,
Like a new Courtier of the King's, etc.

With a new gentleman-usher whose carriage is complete,
With a new coachman, and two footmen to carry up the meat,

With a new waiting gentlewoman whose dressing is very neat,
Who when her lady hath dined gives her fellows very little meat,
Like a new Courtier of the King's, etc.

With new titles of honour bought with his grand-father's old gold,
For which most of his father's manors were all sold,
And that's one cause housekeeping is grown so cold,
Yet this is the new course most of our new gallants hold,
Like new Courtiers of the King's, and the King's new Courtiers.

Thus have you heard of the old courtiers and the new,
And for the last I could wish never a word were true,
With these rude lines which I dedicate to you,
And these rude verses I present to your view,
By the poor Courtier of the King's, and the King's poor Courtier.

WILL BAGNALL'S BALLET

A ballet, a ballet! let every poet,
A ballet make with speed:
And he that has wit, now let him shew it,
For never was greater need:
And I that never made ballet before,
Will make one now, though I never make more.
O women, monstrous women,
What do you mean to do?

It is their pride, and strange attire,
Which binds me to this task;
Which king, and court, did much admire,
At the last Christmas mask,
But by your entertainment then,
You should have small cause to come there again.
O women, etc.

You cannot be contented to go,
As did the women of old:
But you are all for pride and show,
As they were for weather and cold.

O women, women! fie, fie, fie,
I wonder you are not ashamed, I.
        O women, etc.

Where is the decency become
  Which your fore-mother had?
With gowns of cloth, and caps of thrum,[1]
  They went full meanly clad.
But you must jet it in silks and gold;
Your pride, though in winter, is never a cold.
        O women, etc.

Your faces trick'd and painted be,
  Your breasts all open bare;
So far that a man may almost see
  Unto your lady ware:
And in the church, to tell you true,
Men cannot serve God for looking on you.
        O women, etc.

And at the devil's shops you buy,
  A dress of powdered hair,
On which your feathers flaunt and fly;
  But I'd wish you have a care,
Lest Lucifer's self, who is not prouder,
Do one day dress up your hair with a powder.
        O women, etc.

And many there are of those that go
  Attir'd from head to heel,
That them from men you cannot know
  Unless you do them feel;
But, oh, for shame, though they have none,
'Tis better believe, and let them alone.
        O women, etc.

Both round and short they cut their hair,
  Whose length should women grace;
Loose, like themselves, their hats they wear;
  And when they come in place,

[1] waste thread on yarn

Where courtship and compliments must be,
They do it like men with cap and knee.
        O women, etc.

They at their sides, against our laws,
  With little poniards go;
Which surely is, I think, because
  They love men's weapons so;
Or else it is they'll stab all men,
That do refuse to stab them agen.
        O women, etc.

Doublets, like to men, they wear,
  As if they meant to flout us,
Trust round with points, and ribbons fair,
  But, I pray, let's look about us;
For since the doublet so well doth fit 'um,
They will have the breeches, and if they can get 'um.
        O women, etc.

Nor do they care what a wise man saith,
  Or preachers in their defame,
But jeer, and hold him an ass; but i' faith
  They'd blush if they had any shame:
For city and country do both deride 'em,
And our king, God bless him, cannot abide 'em.
        O women, etc.

And when the mask was at the court,
  Before the king to be shown,
They got upon seats to see the sport,
  But soon they were pull'd down;
And many were thrust out of doors,
Their coats well cudgel'd, and they call'd whores.
        O king, religious king,
        God save thy majesty.

And so with prayers to God on high,
  To grant his highness peace,
We hope we shall find remedy
  To make this mischief cease:

Since he in court hath ta'en so good order,
The city leave to the mayor and recorder.
O king, religious king,
God bless thy majesty.

And women, all whom this concerns,
Though you offended be;
And now in foul and railing terms
Do swagger and scold at me;
I tell you, if you mind not your ways,
The devil will fetch you all, one of these days.
O women, monstrous women,
What do you mean to do?

Musarium Deliciae (1655)

DIALOGUE BETWEEN CAPTAIN LONG-HAIR AND ALDERMAN SHORT-HAIR

C. L. Ask me no more why I do wear
My hair so far below mine ear;
For the first man that e'er was made
Did never know the barber trade.

A. S. Ask me no more where all the day,
The foolish owl doth make her stay;
'Tis in your locks, for, tak't from me,
She thinks your hair an ivy-tree.

C. L. Tell me no more that length of hair,
Can make the visage seem less fair;
For know, howe'er my hair doth sit,
I'm sure that yours comes *short* of it.

A. S. Tell me no more men wear long hair
To chase away the coldest air;
For by experience we may see,
Long hair will but a backwind be.

C. L. Tell me no more that long hair can
Argue deboystness[1] in a man;

[1] debauchery

For 'tis religious, being inclined,
To keep the temples from the wind.

A. S. Tell me no more that roarers wear
Their hair extent below their ear:
For having mortgaged their land
They'd fain obscure th' appearing band.

C. L. Ask me no more why hair may be,
Th' expression of gentility;
'Tis that which, being largely grown,
Derives its pedigree from the crown.

THE TIME'S ABUSES

Attend, my masters, and give ear,
  Whilst here I do relate
The base injurious slanders
  Are thrown on me in hate:
My wrongs and great abuses
  So commonly are known,
As in a song, to right my wrong,
  Shall instantly be shown.
They call me fuddling Muld-Sack,
  When drink I have got none:
Cannot they look to their business,
  And let Muld-sack alone?

If I sometimes a pot or so
  Do drink for recreation,
My reckoning paid, away I go,
  And follow my vocation;
Not any good man grieving,
  Offensive for to be,
By rooking or deceiving;
  From that my thoughts are free.
They call me fuddling Muld-sack,
  When drink I have got none;
Cannot they think on the black-jack,
  And let Muld-sack alone?

As I along the streets do sing,
  The people flock about me;
No harm to any one I mean,
  Yet jeeringly they flout me;
The bar-boys and the tapsters
  Leave drawing of their beer,
And, running forth in haste, they cry,
  'See where Muld-sack comes here!'
Thus am I jeered by them,
  Though harm I do them none;
Cannot they look to their small cans,
  And let Muld-sack alone?

The jeering cunning courtesan,
  And rooking roaring boy,
Which day and night do take delight,
  In drunkenness to joy;
They, with their pimps and panders,
  Decoys, and cheating knaves,
Which runs to whores, and drinks and roars,
  And simple men deceives:
They have no grace to guide well,
  And conscience they have none;
Cannot they take heed of Bridewell,
  And let Muld-sack alone?

The glutton rich, that feedeth
  Of beef and mutton store,
And hates the poor that needeth –
  Which goes from door to door –
And will not spend his money
  But for the love of drink,
And grieves to give a penny –
  So well he loves his chink; –
Too many such alive is,
  Of whom I am sure he's one;
Cannot he remember Dives,
  And let Muld-sack alone?

II

Term-trotting petty-foggers,
  Which are so fine and nice,
Will drink, if they meet rightly,
  A cup of ale and spice;
Yet must they take their chamber
  Before they do begin,
And, if they can but hide it,
  They think it is no sin:
When I in the streets walk open
  To the view of every one;
Cannot they look to their clients,
  And let Muld-sack alone?

The jeering fleering coxcomb,
  With hands behind his back,
All day, which stands from morn till night
  To cry 'What do you lack?'
With scoffing, and with taunting,
  Will by the sleeve me pull;
'What is't you'll buy?' he'll to me cry,
  Yet, like a brainless gull,
He'll cast on me a scornful look,
  Though harm I do him none;
Cannot he look to his shop-book,
  And let Muld-sack alone?

The tailor's saucy prentices,
  As I do pass along,
They at my head will cast their shreds,
  Though I do them no wrong;
The saying old hath oft been told,
  It plain doth verify,
'Poor and proud, still tailor-like';
  For they most jeeringly
Do call me fuddling Muld-sack,
  Though drink I have got none:
Cannot they keep their fingers true,
  And let Muld-sack alone?

Also the jeering tripe-wives,
  Which puddings sell and souse,
Cries, 'There goes fuddling Muld-sack,
  Doth wine and beer carouse!'
And with disdainful speeches,
  Having no cause at all,
Will taunt and scoff and jeer and laugh,
  And basely me miscall;
And calls me fuddling Muld-sack,
  Though I am no such one:
Cannot she scrape well her greasy tripes,
  And let Muld-sack alone?

The clownish country carter
  Will likewise, with a jeer,
Point at me as I go along,
  His head being fill'd with beer;
Yet for his jeers I care not,
  But laughing let him pass,
To follow his cart with 'Gee, gee ho,'
  Most like a witless ass:
They have no grace to guide well,
  And conscience they have none;
Cannot they take heed of Bridewell,
  And let Muld-sack alone?

The glutton rich, that feedeth
  Of beef and mutton store,
And hates the poor that needeth –
  Which goes from door to door –
And will not spend his money
  But for the love of drink,
And grieves to give a penny –
  So well he loves his chink; –
Too many such alive is,
  Of whom I am sure he's one;
Cannot he remember Dives,
  And let Muld-sack alone?

SIR WILLIAM DAVENANT

THE LONG VACATION IN LONDON

Now Town-wit says to witty friend,
Transcribe apace all thou hast penn'd;
For I in journey hold it fit
To cry thee up to Country-wit.
Our mules are come! dissolve the club!
The word, till Term, is rub, O rub!
  Now Gamester poor, in cloak of stammel,[1]
Mounted on steed as slow as camel,
Baton of crab[2] in luckless hand
(Which serves for bilbo[3] and for wand)
Early in morn does sneak from town
Lest landlord's wife should seize on crown;
On crown which he in pouch does keep,
When day is done to pay for sleep;
For he in journey nought does eat.
Host spies him come, cries, 'Sir, what meat?'
He calls for room, and down he lies.
Quoth host, 'No supper, sir?' He cries
'I eat no supper, fling on rug!
I'm sick, d'you hear, yet bring a jug!'
  Now damsel young that dwells in Cheap,
For very joy begins to leap;
Her elbow small she oft does rub,
Tickled with hope of syllabub!
For mother (who does gold maintain
On thumb, and keys in silver chain)
In snow white clout wrapped nook[4] of pie,
Fat capon's wing, and rabbit's thigh,
And said to hackney coachman: 'Go,
Take shillings six, say I, or no.'
'Whither?' says he. Quoth she, 'Thy team
Shall drive to place where groweth cream.'

[1] coarse red cloth [2] crab-tree wood [3] sword [4] corner

But husband grey now comes to stall,
For prentice notch'd he straight does call.
'Where's dame?' quoth he. Quoth son of shop
'She's gone her cake in milk to sop:
Ho, ho! to Islington!' 'Enough!
Fetch Job my son, and our dog Ruff!
For there in pond, through mire and muck,
We'll cry, hay duck, there Ruff, hay duck!'
Now Turnbull-dame,[5] by starving paunch,
Bates[6] two stone weight in either haunch:
On bran and liver she must dine,
And sits at door instead of sign.
She softly says to roaring swash,[7]
Who wears long whiskers: 'Go, fetch cash!
There's gown,' quoth she, 'speak broker fair,
Till term brings up weak country heir
Whom kirtle red will much amaze,
Whilst Clown his man on signs does gaze,
In livery short, galloon[8] on cape,
With cloak-bag mounting high as nape.'
Now man that trusts, with weary thighs,
Seeks garret where small poet lies:
He comes to lane, finds garret shut,
Then not with knuckle, but with foot,
He rudely thrusts, would enter doors.
Though poet sleeps not, yet he snores:
Cit chafes like beast of Libya then,
Swears he'll not come nor send again.
From little lump triangular[9]
Poor poet's sighs are heard afar.
Quoth he, 'Do noble numbers choose
To walk on feet that have no shoes?'
Then he does wish with fervent breath,
And as his last request ere death,
Each ode a bond, each madrigal
A lease from Haberdashers' Hall;

[5] bawd [6] takes off [7] swashbuckler [8] braided ribbon [9] the heart

Or that he had protected been
At court, in list of Chamberlain;
For wights near thrones care not an ace
For Wood Street friend that wieldeth mace.[10]
Courts pay no score but when they list,
And treasurer still has cramp in fist.
Then forth he steals; to Globe does run;
And smiles, and vows four acts are done:
Finis to bring he does protest,
Tells every player his part is best.
And all to get (as poets use)
Some crown in pouch to solace Muse.
  Now wight that acts on stage of Bull,
In sculler's bark does lie at hull,[11]
Which he for pennies two does rig
All day on Thames to bob for grig:[12]
Whilst fencer poor does by him stand
In old dung-lighter,[13] hook in hand,
Between knees rod, with canvas crib
To girdle tide close under rib;[14]
Where worms are put which must small fish
Betray at night to earthen dish.
  Now London's chief, on saddle new,
Rides into fair of Bartholomew;
He twirls his chain, and looketh big,
As if to fright the head of pig
That gaping lies on greasy stall,
Till female with great belly call.
  Now alderman in field doth stand,
With foot on trig,[15] a quoit in hand:
'I'm seven,' quoth he, 'the game is up!
Nothing I pay, and yet I sup.'
To alderman quoth neighbour then,
'I lost but mutton, play for hen'.
But wealthy blade cries out: 'At rate
Of kings, thou'ldst play; let's go, 'tis late.'

[10] i.e., the sergeant outside the debtors' prison [11] with sails furled [12] fish for eels [13] barge for carrying dung [14] with canvas bag to catch the tide flowing under the boat's ribs [15] starting-line

Now lean attorney, that his cheese
Ne'er pared, nor verses took for fees,
And aged proctor, that controls
The feats of punk[16] in court of Paul's,
Do each with solemn oath agree
To meet in fields of Finsbury:
With loins in canvas bow-case tied,
Where arrows stick with mickle pride,
With hats pinn'd up, and bow in hand,
All day so fiercely there they stand
Like ghosts of Adam Bell, and Clym,
Sol sets for fear they'll shoot at him.
Now spiny[17] Ralph, and Gregory small,
And short-haired Stephen, whey-faced Paul
(Whose times are out, indentures torn,
Who seven long years did never scorn
To fetch up coals for maid to use,
Wipe mistress's and children's shoes)
Do jump for joy they are made free;
Hire meagre steeds to ride and see
Their parents old, who dwell as near
As place called Peak in Derbyshire.
There they alight, old crones are mild;
Each weeps on cragg[18] of pretty child:
They portions give, trades up to set,
That babes may live, serve God and cheat.
Near house of law by Temple Bar
Now man of mace cares not how far
In stockings blue he marcheth on,
With velvet cape his cloak upon;
In girdle, scrolls, where names of some
Are written down, whom touch of thumb
On shoulder left must safe convoy,
Annoying wights with name of Roy.[19]
Poor prisoner's friend that sees the touch
Cries out aloud, 'I thought as much'.

[16] prostitute [17] skinny [18] neck [19] 'annoying fellows in the king's name'

Now vaulter good, and dancing lass
On rope, and man that cries 'Hey, pass',
And tumbler young that needs but stoop,
Lay head to heel, to creep through hoop;
And man in chimney hid to dress
Puppet that acts our old *Queen Bess*,[20]
And man that whilst the puppets play
Through nose expoundeth what they say:
And man that does in chest include
Old *Sodom and Gomorrah*[20] lewd;
And white oat-eater[21] that does dwell
In stable small at sign of Bell,
That lifts up hoof to show the pranks
Taught by magician, styled Banks;
And ape led captive still in chain
Till he renounce the Pope and Spain.
All these on hoof now trudge from town
To cheat poor turnip-eating clown.
Now man of war with visage red
Grows choleric and swears for bread.
He sendeth note to man of kin,
But man leaves word: 'I'm not within.'
He meets in street with friend called Will:
And cries, 'Old rogue! What, living still?'
But ere that street they quite are past,
He softly asks: 'What money hast?'
Quoth friend, 'A crown'. He cries, 'Dear heart!
O base, no more? Sweet, lend me part!'
But stay, my frighted pen is fled,
Myself through fear creep under bed:
For just as Muse would scribble more,
Fierce city dun did rap at door.

[20] names of puppet plays [21] horse

JOHN MILTON

ON THE UNIVERSITY CARRIER WHO SICKENED IN THE TIME OF HIS VACANCY, BEING FORBID TO GO TO LONDON, BY REASON OF THE PLAGUE

Here lies old Hobson, Death hath broke his girt,
And here alas, hath laid him in the dirt,
Or else the ways being foul, twenty to one,
He's here stuck in a slough, and overthrown.
'Twas such a shifter, that if truth were known,
Death was half glad when he had got him down;
For he had any time this ten years full,
Dodg'd with him, betwixt Cambridge and the Bull.
And surely, Death could never have prevail'd,
Had not his weekly course of carriage fail'd;
But lately finding him so long at home,
And thinking now his journey's end was come,
And that he had ta'en up his latest Inn,
In the kind office of a Chamberlain
Shew'd him his room where he must lodge that night,
Pull'd off his Boots, and took away the light:
If any ask for him, it shall be said,
Hobson has supt, and 's newly gone to bed.

HENRY VAUGHAN

LONDON AT NIGHT

Should we go now a-wandering, we should meet
With catchpoles, whores, and carts in every street:
Now when each narrow lane, each nook and cave,
Sign-posts, and shop-doors, pimp for every knave,
When riotous sinful plush, and tell-tale spurs
Walk Fleet Street, and the Strand, when the soft stirs

Of bawdy, ruffled silks turn night to day;
And the loud whip, and coach scolds all the way;
When lust of all sorts, and each itchy blood
From Tower-wharf to Cymbeline, and Lud,
Hunts for a mate, and the tired footman reels
'Twixt chairmen, torches, and the hackney wheels . . .

from *A Rhapsodie*

ANDREW MARVELL

AN HORATIAN ODE
UPON CROMWELL'S RETURN FROM IRELAND

The forward youth that would appear
Must now forsake his Muses dear,
    Nor in the shadows sing
    His numbers languishing.

'Tis time to leave the books in dust,
And oil the unused armour's rust,
    Removing from the wall
    The corslet of the hall.

So restless Cromwell could not cease
In the inglorious arts of peace,
    But through adventurous war
    Urged his active star.

And like the three-fork'd lightning, first
Breaking the clouds where it was nurst,
    Did thorough his own side
    His fiery way divide.

For 'tis all one to courage high,
The emulous or enemy;
    And with such to enclose
    Is more than to oppose.

Then burning through the air he went
And palaces and temples rent;
    And Cæsar's head at last
    Did through his laurels blast.

'Tis madness to resist or blame
The face of angry Heaven's flame:
    And if we would speak true,
    Much to the man is due.

Who, from his private gardens, where
He lived reservèd and austere,
    As if his highest plot
    To plant the bergamot,

Could by industrious valour climb
To ruin the great work of time,
    And cast the Kingdoms old
    Into another mould.

Though Justice against Fate complain,
And plead the ancient rights in vain:
    But those do hold or break
    As men are strong or weak.

Nature that hateth emptiness,
Allows of penetration less:
    And therefore must make room
    Where greater spirits come.

What field of all the civil wars
Where his were not the deepest scars?
    And Hampton shows what part
    He had of wiser art.

Where, twining subtle fears with hope,
He wove a net of such a scope
    That Charles himself might chase
    To Caresbrooke's narrow case.

That thence the Royal actor borne
The tragic scaffold might adorn:
    While round the armèd bands
    Did clap their bloody hands.

He nothing common did or mean
Upon that memorable scene:
    But with his keener eye
    The axe's edge did try:

Nor call'd the gods with vulgar spite
To vindicate his helpless right,
    But bow'd his comely head
    Down, as upon a bed.

This was that memorable hour
Which first assured the forced power.
    So when they did design
    The Capitol's first line,

A Bleeding Head where they begun,
Did fright the architects to run;
    And yet in that the State
    Foresaw its happy fate.

And now the Irish are ashamed
To see themselves in one year tamed:
    So much one man can do
    That does both act and know.

They can affirm his praises best,
And have, though overcome, confest
    How good he is, how just,
    And fit for highest trust.

Nor yet grown stiffer with command,
But still in the republic's hand:
    How fit he is to sway
    That can so well obey.

He to the Commons' feet presents
A Kingdom for his first year's rents:
    And, what he may, forbears
    His fame, to make it theirs:

And has his sword and spoils ungirt
To lay them at the public's skirt.
    So when the falcon high
    Falls heavy from the sky,

She, having kill'd, no more doth search
But on the next green bough to perch;
    Where, when he first does lure,
    The falconer has her sure.

What may not then our Isle presume
While victory his crest does plume!
    What may not others fear,
    If thus he crowns each year!

As Cæsar he ere long to Gaul,
To Italy an Hannibal,
    And to all States not free
    Shall climacteric be.

The Pict no shelter now shall find
Within his particolour'd mind;
    But, from this valour, sad
    Shrink underneath the plaid:

Happy, if in the tufted brake
The English hunter him mistake,
    Nor lay his hounds in near
    The Caledonian deer.

But thou, the war's and fortune's son,
March indefatigably on:
    And for the last effect,
    Still keep the sword erect;

Besides the force it has to fright
The spirits of the shady night,
    The same arts that did gain
    A power must it maintain.

ANONYMOUS

THE COACHES' OVERTHROW

The world no more shall run on wheels
  With coach-men, as 't has done;
But they must take them to their heels,
  And try how they can run.
Heigh, down dery, dery down,
  With the hackney coaches down!
    We thought they'd burst
    Their pride, since first
Swell'd so within the town.

The Sedan does, like Atlas, hope
  To carry heaven pick-a-pack;
And likewise, since he has such scope,
  To bear the town at 's back.
Heigh, down dery, dery down,
  With the hackney coach-men down!
    Arise, Sedan!
    Thou shalt be the man
To bear us about the town.

I love Sedans, 'cause they do plod
  And amble everywhere,
Which prancers are with leather shod,
  And ne'er disturb the ear.
Heigh, down dery, dery down,
  With the hackney coaches down!
    Their jumpings make
    The pavement shake,
Their noise doth mad the town.

The elder brother shall take place,
  The youngest brother rise;
The middle brother's out of grace,
  And every tradesman cries,

'Heigh, down dery, dery down,
With the hackney coaches down!
'Twould save much hurt,
Spare dust and dirt,
Were they clean out of town.'

The sick, the weak, the lame also,
A coach for ease might beg;
When they on foot might lightly go,
That are as right 's my leg.
Heigh, down dery, dery down,
With the hackney coaches down!
Let's foot it out,
Ere the year comes about,
'Twill save us many a crown.

What though we trip o'er boots and shoes
'Twill ease the price of leather:
We shall get twice what once we lose,
When they do fall together.
Heigh, down dery, dery down,
With the hackney coaches down!
Though one trade fall,
Yet, in general,
'Tis a good to all the town.

'Tis an undoing unto none
That a profession use:
'Tis good for all, not hurt to one,
Considering the abuse.
Then heigh, down dery, dery down,
With the hackney coaches down!
'Tis so decreed
By a royal deed,
To make 't a happy town.

Coach-makers may use many trades,
And get enough of means;
And coach-men may turn off their jades,
And help to drain the fens.

Heigh, down dery, dery down,
With the hackney coaches down!
The scythe and flail,
Cart and plough-tail,
Do want them out of town.

But, to conclude, 'tis true, I hear,
They'll soon be out of fashion;
'Tis thought they very likely are
To have a long vacation.
Heigh, down dery, dery down,
With the hackney coaches down!
Their term's near done,
And shall be begun
No more in London town.

JOHN DRYDEN

THE BURNING OF LONDON

The diligence of trades, and noiseful gain,
And luxury, more late, asleep were laid;
All was the Night's, and in her silent reign
No sound the rest of Nature did invade.

In this deep quiet, from what source unknown,
Those seeds of fire their fatal birth disclose;
And first few scattering sparks about were blown,
Big with the flames that to our ruin rose.

Then in some close-pent room it crept along
And, smouldering as it went, in silence fed;
Till the infant monster, with devouring strong,
Walked boldly upright with exalted head.

Now, like some rich or mighty murderer,
Too great for prison which he breaks with gold,
Who fresher for new mischiefs does appear
And dares the world to tax him with the old,

So scapes the insulting fire his narrow jail
And makes small outlets into open air;
There the fierce winds his tender force assail
And beat him downward to his first repair.

The winds, like crafty courtesans, withheld
His flames from burning but to blow them more:
And, every fresh attempt, he is repelled
With faint denials, weaker than before.

And now, no longer letted of his prey,
He leaps up at it with enraged desire,
O'erlooks the neighbours with a wide survey,
And nods at every house his threatening fire.

The ghosts of traitors from the Bridge descend,
With bold fanatic spectres to rejoice;
About the fire into a dance they bend
And sing their sabbath notes with feeble voice.

Our guardian angel saw them where they sate,
Above the palace of our slumbering King;
He sighed, abandoning his charge to Fate,
And drooping oft looked back upon the wing.

At length the crackling noise and dreadful blaze
Called up some waking lover to the sight;
And long it was ere he the rest could raise,
Whose heavy eyelids yet were full of night.

The next to danger, hot pursued by fate,
Half-clothed, half naked, hastily retire;
And frighted mothers strike their breasts too late
For helpless infants left amidst the fire.

Their cries soon waken all the dwellers near;
Now murmuring noises rise in every street;
The more remote run stumbling with their fear,
And in the dark men justle as they meet.

So weary bees in little cells repose;
But if night-robbers lift the well-stored hive,
An humming through their waxen city grows,
And out upon each other's wings they drive.

Now streets grow thronged and busy as by day;
  Some run for buckets to the hallowed quire;
Some cut the pipes, and some the engines play,
  And some more bold mount ladders to the fire.

In vain; for from the east a Belgian wind
  His hostile breath through the dry rafters sent;
The flames impelled soon left their foes behind
  And forward with a wanton fury went.

A key of fire ran all along the shore
  And lightened all the river with a blaze;
The wakened tides began again to roar,
  And wondering fish in shining waters gaze.

Old Father Thames raised up his reverend head,
  But feared the fate of Simois would return;
Deep in his ooze he sought his sedgy bed
  And shrank his waters back into his urn.

The fire meantime walks in a broader gross;
  To either hand his wings he opens wide;
He wades the streets, and straight he reaches cross
  And plays his longing flames on the other side.

At first they warm, then scorch, and then they take;
  Now with long necks from side to side they feed;
At length, grown strong, their mother-fire forsake,
  And a new colony of flames succeed.

To every nobler portion of the town
  The curling billows roll their restless tide;
In parties now they straggle up and down,
  As armies unopposed for prey divide.

One mighty squadron, with a sidewind sped,
  Through narrow lanes his cumbered fire does haste,
By powerful charms of gold and silver led
  The Lombard bankers and the Change to waste.

Another backward to the Tower would go
  And slowly eats his way against the wind;
But the main body of the marching foe
  Against the imperial palace is designed.

John Dryden (1631–1700)

Now day appears; and with the day the King,
  Whose early care had robbed him of his rest;
Far off the cracks of falling houses ring
  And shrieks of subjects pierce his tender breast.

Near as he draws, thick harbingers of smoke
  With gloomy pillars cover all the place;
Whose little intervals of night are broke
  By sparks that drive against his sacred face.

More than his guards his sorrows made him known
  And pious tears which down his cheeks did shower;
The wretched in his grief forgot their own;
  So much the pity of a king has power.

He wept the flames of what he loved so well
  And what so well had merited his love;
For never prince in grace did more excel
  Or royal city more in duty strove.

Nor with an idle care did he behold:
  Subjects may grieve, but monarchs must redress;
He cheers the fearful and commends the bold
  And makes despairers hope for good success.

Himself directs what first is to be done
  And orders all the succours which they bring;
The helpful and the good about him run
  And form an army worthy such a King.

He sees the dire contagion spread so fast
  That, where it seizes, all relief is vain.
And therefore must unwillingly lay waste
  That country which would else the foe maintain.

The powder blows up all before the fire;
  The amazed flames stand gathered on a heap,
And from the precipice's brink retire,
  Afraid to venture on so large a leap.

Thus fighting fires a while themselves consume,
  But straight, like Turks forced on to win or die,
They first lay tender bridges of their fume
  And o'er the breach in unctuous vapours fly.

Part stays for passage, till a gust of wind
  Ships o'er their forces in a shining sheet;
Part, creeping under ground, their journey blind
  And, climbing from below, their fellows meet.

Thus to some desert plain or old wood-side
  Dire night-hags come from far to dance their round,
And o'er broad rivers on their fiends they ride
  Or sweep in clouds above the blasted ground.

No help avails: for, hydra-like, the fire
  Lifts up his hundred heads to aim his way;
And scarce the wealthy can one half retire
  Before he rushes in to share the prey.

The rich grow suppliant and the poor grow proud:
  Those offer mighty gain and these ask more;
So void of pity is the ignoble crowd,
  When others' ruin may increase their store.

As those who live by shores with joy behold
  Some wealthy vessel split or stranded nigh,
And from the rocks leap down for shipwracked gold
  And seek the tempest which the others fly:

So these but wait the owners' last despair
  And what's permitted to the flames invade;
Even from their jaws they hungry morsels tear
  And on their backs the spoils of Vulcan lade.

The days were all in this lost labour spent;
  And when the weary King gave place to night
His beams he to his royal brother lent,
  And so shone still in his reflective light.

Night came, but without darkness or repose,
  A dismal picture of the general doom;
Where souls distracted, when the trumpet blows,
  And half unready with their bodies come.

Those who have homes, when home they do repair,
  To a lodging call their wandering friends:
Their short uneasy sleeps are broke with care,
  To look how near their own destruction tends:

Those who have none sit round where once it was
  And with full eyes each wonted room require,
Haunting the yet warm ashes of the place,
  As murdered men walk where they did expire.

Some stir up coals and watch the vestal fire,
  Others in vain from sight of ruin run
And, while through burning labyrinths they retire,
  With loathing eyes repeat what they would shun.

The most in fields like herded beasts lie down,
  To dews obnoxious on the grassy floor;
And while their babes in sleep their sorrows drown,
  Sad parents watch the remnants of their store.

While by the motion of the flames they guess
  What streets are burning now, and what are near,
An infant, waking, to the paps would press
  And meets instead of milk a falling tear.

from *Annus Mirabilis*

JOHN WILMOT, EARL OF ROCHESTER

AT TUNBRIDGE WELLS

  Amidst the crowd next I myself conveyed,
For now were come, whitewash and paint being laid,
Mother and daughter, mistress and the maid,
And squire with wig and pantaloon displayed.
But ne'er could conventicle, play, or fair
For a true medley, with this herd compare.
Here lords, knights, squires, ladies and countesses,
Chandlers, mum-bacon women, sempstresses
Were mixed together, nor did they agree
More in their humors than their quality.
  Here waiting for gallant, young damsel stood,
Leaning on cane, and muffled up in hood.

The would-be wit, whose business was to woo,
With hat removed and solemn scrape of shoe
Advanceth bowing, then genteelly shrugs,
And ruffled foretop into order tugs,
And thus accosts her: 'Madam, methinks the weather
Is grown much more serene since you came hither.
You influence the heavens; but should the sun
Withdraw himself to see his rays outdone
By your bright eyes, they would supply the morn,
And make a day before the day be born.'
With mouth screwed up, conceited winking eyes,
And breasts thrust forward, 'Lord, sir!' she replies,
'It is your goodness, and not my deserts,
Which makes you show this learning, wit, and parts.'
He, puzzled, bites his nail, both to display
The sparkling ring, and think what next to say,
And thus breaks forth afresh: 'Madam, egad!
Your luck at cards last night was very bad:
At cribbage fifty-nine, and the next show
To make the game, and yet to want those two.
God damn me, madam, I'm the son of a whore
If in my life I saw the like before!'
To peddler's stall he drags her, and her breast
With hearts and such-like foolish toys he dressed;
And then, more smartly to expound the riddle
Of all his prattle, gives her a Scotch fiddle.[1]
  Tired with this dismal stuff, away I ran
Where were two wives, with girl just fit for man –
Short-breathed, with pallid lips and visage wan.
Some curtsies past, and the old compliment
Of being glad to see each other, spent,
With hand in hand they lovingly did walk,
And one began thus to renew the talk:
'I pray, good madam, if it may be thought
No rudeness, what cause was it hither brought
Your ladyship?' She soon replying, smiled,
'We have a good estate, but have no child,

[1] the itch

And I'm informed these wells will make a barren
Woman as fruitful as a cony warren.'
The first returned, 'For this cause I am come,
For I can have no quietness at home.
My husband grumbles though we have got one,
This poor young girl, and mutters for a son.
And this is grieved with headache, pangs, and throes;
Is full sixteen, and never yet had *those*.'
She soon replied, 'Get her a husband, madam:
I married at that age, and ne'er had had 'em;
Was just like her. Steel waters let alone:
A back of steel will bring 'em better down.'
And ten to one but they themselves will try
The same means to increase their family.
Poor foolish fribble, who by subtlety
Of midwife, truest friend to lechery,
Persuaded art to be at pains and charge
To give thy wife occasion to enlarge
Thy silly head! For here walk Cuff and Kick,
With brawny back and legs and potent prick,
Who more substantially will cure thy wife,
And on her half-dead womb bestow new life.
From these the waters got the reputation
Of good assistants unto generation.
  Some warlike men were now got into th' throng,
With hair tied back, singing a bawdy song.
Not much afraid, I got a nearer view,
And 'twas my chance to know the dreadful crew.
They were cadets, that seldom can appear:
Damned to the stint of thirty pounds a year.
With hawk on fist, or greyhound led in hand,
The dogs and footboys sometimes they command.
But now, having trimmed a cast-off spavined horse,
With three hard-pinched-for guineas in their purse,
Two rusty pistols, scarf about the arse,
Coat lined with red, they here presume to swell:
This goes for captain, that for colonel.
So the Bear Garden ape, on his steed mounted,
No longer is a jackanapes accounted,

But is, by virtue of his trumpery, then
Called by the name of 'the young gentleman'.
  Bless me! thought I, what thing is man, that thus
In all his shapes, he is ridiculous?
Ourselves with noise of reason we do please
In vain: humanity's our worst disease.
Thrice happy beasts are, who, because they be
Of reason void, are so of foppery.
Faith, I was so ashamed that with remorse
I used the insolence to mount my horse;
For he, doing only things fit for his nature,
Did seem to me by much the wiser creature.

JOHN OLDHAM

REASONS FOR NOT LIVING IN LONDON

  ''Tis hard for any man to rise, that feels
His virtue clogged with poverty at heels;
But harder 'tis by much in London, where
A sorry lodging, coarse and slender fare,
Fire, water, breathing, everything is dear;
Yet such as these an earthen dish disdain,
With which their ancestors, in Edgar's reign
Were served, and thought it no disgrace to dine,
Though they were rich, had store of leather coin.
Low as their fortune is, yet they despise
A man that walks the streets in homely frieze;
To speak the truth, great part of England now,
In their own cloth will scarce vouchsafe to go;
Only, the statute's penalty to save,
Some few perhaps wear woollen in the grave.
Here all go daily dressed, although it be
Above their means, their rank, and quality;
The most in borrowed gallantry are clad,
For which the tradesmen's books are still unpaid;

This fault is common in the meaner sort,
That they must needs affect to bear the port
Of gentlemen, though they want income for't.
'Sir, to be short, in this expensive town
There's nothing without money to be done;
What will you give to be admitted there,
And brought to speech of some court minister?
What will you give to have the quarter-face,
The squint and nodding go-by of his Grace?
His porter, groom, and steward must have fees,
And you may see the Tombs, and Tower for less;
Hard fate of suitors! who must pay, and pray
To livery-slaves, yet oft go scorned away.
'Whoe'er at Barnet, or St Albans, fears
To have his lodging drop about his ears,
Unless a sudden hurricane befall,
Or such a wind as blew old Noll to hell?
Here we build slight, what scarce outlasts the lease,
Without the help of props and buttresses;
And houses now-a-days as much require
To be ensured from falling, as from fire.
There, buildings are substantial, though less neat,
And kept with care both wind and water tight;
There, you in safe security are blessed,
And nought, but conscience, to disturb your rest.
'I am for living where no fires affright,
No bells rung backward break my sleep at night;
I scarce lie down, and draw my curtains here,
But straight I'm roused by the next house on fire;
Pale, and half dead with fear, myself I raise,
And find my room all over in a blaze;
By this 't has seized on the third stairs, and I
Can now discern no other remedy,
But leaping out at window to get free;
For if the mischief from the cellar came,
Be sure the garret is the last takes flame.
'The moveables of Pordage were a bed
For him and 's wife, a basin by its side,
A looking-glass upon the cupboard's head,

A comb-case, candlestick, and pewter spoon
For want of plate, a desk to write upon;
A box without a lid served to contain
Few authors, which made up his Vatican;
And there his own immortal works were laid,
On which the barbarous mice for hunger preyed;
Pordage had nothing, all the world does know,
And yet should he have lost this nothing too,
No one the wretched bard would have supplied
With lodging, house-room, or a crust of bread.
'But if the fire burn down some great man's house,
All straight are interested in the loss;
The court is straight in mourning sure enough,
The act, commencement, and the term put off;
Then we mischances of the town lament,
And fasts are kept, like judgments to prevent.
Out comes a brief immediately, with speed
To gather charity as far as Tweed.
Nay, while 'tis burning, some will send him in
Timber, and stone to build his house again;
Others choice furniture; some rare piece
Of Rubens, or Vandyke presented is;
There a rich suit of Mortlack tapestry,
A bed of damask or embroidery;
One gives a fine scrutoire, or cabinet,
Another a huge massy dish of plate,
Or bag of gold: thus he at length gets more
By kind misfortune than he had before;
And all suspect it for a laid design,
As if he did himself the fire begin.
Could you but be advised to leave the town,
And from dear plays, and drinking friends be drawn,
A handsome dwelling might be had in Kent,
Surrey, or Essex, at a cheaper rent
Than what you're forced to give for one half year
To lie, like lumber, in a garret here.
A garden there, and well, that needs no rope,
Engine, or pains to crane its waters up;

Water is there through Nature's pipes conveyed,
For which no custom or excise is paid.
Had I the smallest spot of ground, which scarce
Would summer half a dozen grasshoppers,
Not larger than my grave, though hence remote
Far as St Michael's Mount, I would go to't,
Dwell there content, and thank the Fates to boot.
'Here want of rest a-nights more people kills
Than all the college, and the weekly bills;
Where none have privilege to sleep, but those
Whose purses can compound for their repose.
In vain I go to bed, or close my eyes,
Methinks the place the middle region is,
Where I lie down in storms, in thunder rise;
The restless bells such din in steeples keep,
That scarce the dead can in their churchyards sleep;
Huzzas of drunkards, bellmen's midnight rhymes,
The noise of shops, with hawker's early screams,
Besides the brawls of coachmen, when they meet,
And stop in turnings of a narrow street,
Such a loud medley of confusion make,
As drowsy Archer on the bench would wake.
'If you walk out in business ne'er so great,
Ten thousand stops you must expect to meet;
Thick crowds in every place you must charge through,
And storm your passage wheresoe'er you go;
While tides of followers behind you throng,
And, pressing on your heels, shove you along;
One with a board, or rafter, hits your head,
Another with his elbow bores your side;
Some tread upon your corns, perhaps in sport,
Meanwhile your legs are cased all o'er with dirt;
Here, you the march of a slow funeral wait,
Advancing to the church with solemn state;
There, a sedan and lackeys stop your way,
That bears some punk of honour to the play;
Now, you some mighty piece of timber meet,
Which tottering threatens ruin to the street;

Next, a huge Portland stone, for building Paul's,
Itself almost a rock, on carriage rolls;
Which, if it fall, would cause a massacre,
And serve at once to murder, and inter.
  'If what I've said can't from the town affright,
Consider other dangers of the night:
When brickbats are from upper stories thrown,
And empty chamber-pots come pouring down
From garret windows; you have cause to bless
The gentle stars, if you come off with piss;
So many fates attend, a man had need,
Ne'er walk without a surgeon by his side;
And he can hardly now discreet be thought,
That does not make his will ere he go out.
  'If this you 'scape, twenty to one you meet
Some of the drunken scourers of the street,
Flushed with success of warlike deeds performed,
Of constables subdued, and brothels stormed,
These, if a quarrel or a fray be missed,
Are ill at ease a-nights, and want their rest;
For mischief is a lechery to some,
And serves to make them sleep like laudanum.
Yet heated, as they are, with youth and wine,
If they discern a train of flambeaux shine,
If a great man with his gilt coach appear,
And a strong guard of footboys in the rear,
The rascals sneak and shrink their heads for fear.
Poor me, who use no light to walk about,
Save what the parish, or the skies hang out,
They value not; 'tis worth your while to hear
The scuffle, if that be a scuffle, where
Another gives the blows I only bear;
He bids me stand; of force I must give way,
For 'twere a senseless thing to disobey,
And struggle here, where I'd as good oppose
Myself to Preston[1] and his mastiffs loose.

[1] Keeper of the Bear-Garden in Hockley Hole

"Who's there?" he cries, and takes you by the throat;
"Dog! are you dumb? Speak quickly, else my foot
Shall march about your buttocks; whence d'ye come?
From what bulk-ridden strumpet reeking home?
Saving your reverend pimpship, where d'ye ply?
How may one have a job of lechery?"
If you say anything, or hold your peace,
And silently go off, 'tis all a case;
Still he lays on; nay well, if you 'scape so;
Perhaps he'll clap an action on you too
Of battery, nor need he fear to meet
A jury to his turn, shall do him right,
And bring him in large damage for a shoe
Worn out, besides the pains in kicking you.
A poor man must expect nought of redress,
But patience; his best course in such a case
Is to be thankful for the drubs, and beg
That they would mercifully spare one leg,
Or arm unbroke, and let him go away
With teeth enough to eat his meat next day.
'Nor is this all which you have cause to fear;
Oft we encounter midnight padders here,
When the exchanges and the shops are close,
And the rich tradesman in his counting-house
To view the profits of the day withdraws.
Hither in flocks from Shooter's Hill they come,
To seek their prize and booty nearer home:
"Your purse!" they cry; 'tis madness to resist,
Or strive, with a cocked pistol at your breast.
And these each day so strong and numerous grow,
The town can scarce afford them jail-room now.'

from *A Satire in Imitation of the Third of Juvenal*

ANONYMOUS

THE BEAU'S CHARACTER

A wig that's full,
An empty skull,
A box of bergamot;
A hat ne'er made
To fit his head,
No more than that to plot.
A hand that's white,
A ring that's right,
A sword-knot, patch and feather;
A gracious smile,
And grounds and oil,
Do very well together.

A smatch of French,
And none of sense,
All conquering airs and graces;
A tune that thrills,
A leer that kills,
Stol'n flights and borrow'd phrases.
A chariot gilt,
To wait on jilt,
An awkward pace and carriage;
A foreign tour,
Domestick whore,
And mercenary marriage.

A limber ham,
God damn ye, m'am,
A smock-face, tho' a tann'd one;
A peaceful sword,
Not one wise word,
But state and prate at random.
Duns, bastards, craps,
And am'rous scraps

Of *Cœlia* and *Amadis*,
  Toss up a beau,
  That grand ragout,
That hodge-podge for the ladies.

from D'Urfey's *Wit and Mirth,*
or Pills to Purge Character

JONATHAN SWIFT

WRITTEN IN A LADY'S IVORY TABLE-BOOK, 1698

Peruse my leaves thro' ev'ry part,
And think thou seest my owner's heart,
Scrawl'd o'er with trifles thus, and quite
As hard, as senseless, and as light;
Expos'd to ev'ry coxcomb's eyes,
But hid with caution from the wise.
Here you may read, 'Dear charming saint';
Beneath, 'A new receipt for paint':
Here, in beau-spelling, 'Tru tel deth';
There, in her own, 'For an el breth':
Here, 'Lovely nymph, pronounce my doom!'
There, 'A safe way to use perfume':
Here, a page fill'd with billets-doux;
On t'other side, 'Laid out for shoes' –
'Madam, I die without your grace' –
'Item, for half a yard of lace.'
Who that had wit would place it here,
For every peeping fop to jeer?
In pow'r of spittle and a clout,
Whene'er he please, to blot it out;
And then, to heighten the disgrace,
Clap his own nonsense in the place.
Whoe'er expects to hold his part
In such a book, and such a heart,

If he be wealthy, and a fool,
Is in all points the fittest tool;
Of whom it may be justly said,
He's a gold pencil tipp'd with lead.

BAUCIS AND PHILEMON

On the ever-lamented loss of the two yew-trees in the Parish of Chilthorne, Somerset, 1706. Imitated from the Eighth Book of Ovid.

In ancient time, as story tells,
The saints would often leave their cells,
And stroll about, but hide their quality,
To try good people's hospitality.
  It happen'd on a winter's night,
As authors of the legend write,
Two brother hermits, saints by trade,
Taking their tour in masquerade,
Came to a village hard by Rixham,
Ragged and not a groat betwixt 'em.
It rain'd as hard as it could pour,
Yet they were forced to walk an hour
From house to house, wet to the skin,
Before one soul would let 'em in.
They call'd at every door: 'Good people,
My comrade's blind, and I'm a creeple!
Here we lie starving in the street,
'Twould grieve a body's heart to see't,
No Christian would turn out a beast,
In such a dreadful night at least;
Give us but straw and let us lie
In yonder barn to keep us dry.'
Thus in the stroller's usual cant,
They begg'd relief, which none would grant.
No creature valued what they said,
One family was gone to bed:

The master bawled out half asleep,
'You fellows, what a noise you keep!
So many beggars pass this way,
We can't be quiet, night nor day;
We cannot serve you every one;
Pray take your answer, and be gone.'
One swore he'd send 'em to the stocks;
A third could not forbear his mocks;
But bawl'd as loud as he could roar
'You're on the wrong side of the door!'
One surly clown look't out and said,
'I'll fling the p—pot on your head:
You sha'nt come here, nor get a sous!
You look like rogues would rob a house.
Can't you go work, or serve the King?
You blind and lame! 'Tis no such thing.
That's but a counterfeit sore leg!
For shame! two sturdy rascals beg!
If I come down, I'll spoil your trick,
And cure you both with a good stick.'
  Our wand'ring saints, in woful state,
Treated at this ungodly rate,
Having thro' all the village past,
To a small cottage came at last
Where dwelt a good old honest ye'man,
Call'd thereabout good man Philemon;
Who kindly did the saints invite
In his poor house to pass the night;
And then the hospitable sire
Bid Goody Baucis mend the fire;
Whilst he from out the chimney took
A flitch of bacon off the hook,
And freely from the fattest side
Cut out large slices to be fry'd;
Which tost up in a pan with batter,
And served up in an earthen platter,
Quoth Baucis, 'This is wholesome fare,
Eat, honest friends, and never spare,

And if we find our victuals fail,
We can but make it out in ale.'
   To a small kilderkin of beer,
Brew'd for the good time of the year,
Philemon, by his wife's consent,
Stept with a jug, and made a vent,
And having fill'd it to the brink,
Invited both the saints to drink.
When they had took a second draught,
Behold, a miracle was wrought;
For, Baucis with amazement found,
Although the jug had twice gone round,
It still was full up to the top,
As they ne'er had drunk a drop.
You may be sure so strange a sight,
Put the old people in a fright:
Philemon whisper'd to his wife,
'These men are – Saints – I'll lay my life!'
The strangers overheard, and said,
'You're in the right – but be'nt afraid:
No hurt shall come to you or yours:
But for that pack of churlish boors,
Not fit to live on Christian ground,
They and their village shall be drown'd;
Whilst you shall see your cottage rise,
And grow a church before your eyes.'
   Scarce had they spoke, when fair and soft,
The roof began to mount aloft;
Aloft rose ev'ry beam and rafter;
The heavy wall went clambering after.
The chimney widen'd, and grew higher,
Became a steeple with a spire.
The kettle to the top was hoist,
And there stood fastened to a joist,
But with the upside down, to show
Its inclination for below:
In vain; for a superior force
Applied at bottom stops its course:

Doom'd ever in suspense to dwell,
'Tis now no kettle, but a bell.
  The wooden jack, which had almost
Lost by disuse the art to roast,
A sudden alteration feels,
Increas'd by new intestine wheels;
But what adds to the wonder more,
The number made the motion slower.
The flyer, altho't had leaden feet,
Would turn so quick you scarce could see't;
But, now stopt by some hidden powers,
Moves round but twice in twice twelve hours,
While in the station of a jack,
'Twas never known to turn its back,
A friend in turns and windings tried,
Nor ever left the chimney's side.
The chimney to a steeple grown,
The jack would not be left alone;
But, up against the steeple rear'd,
Became a clock, and still adher'd;
And still its love to household cares,
By a shrill voice at noon declares,
Warning the cookmaid not to burn
That roast meat, which it cannot turn.
  The groaning-chair began to crawl,
Like a huge insect, up the wall;
There stuck, and to a pulpit grew,
But kept its matter and its hue,
And mindful of its ancient state,
Still groans while tattling gossips prate.
The mortar only chang'd its name,
In its old shape a font became.
  The porringers, that in a row,
Hung high, and made a glitt'ring show,
To a less noble substance chang'd,
Were now but leathern buckets rang'd.
  The ballads, pasted on the wall,
Of Chevy Chase, and English Mall,

Fair Rosamond, and Robin Hood,
The little Children in the Wood,
Enlarged in picture, size, and letter,
And painted, lookt abundance better,
And now the heraldry describe
Of a churchwarden, or a tribe.
A bedstead of the antique mode,
Composed of timber many a load,
Such as our grandfathers did use,
Was metamorphos'd into pews;
Which yet their former virtue keep
By lodging folk disposed to sleep.
  The cottage, with such feats as these,
Grown to a church by just degrees,
The holy men desired their host
To ask for what he fancied most.
Philemon, having paused a while,
Replied in complimental style:
'Your goodness, more than my desert,
Makes you take all things in good part:
You've raised a church here in a minute,
And I would fain continue in it;
I'm good for little at my days,
Make me the parson if you please.'
  He spoke, and presently he feels
His grazier's coat reach down his heels;
The sleeves new border'd with a list,
Widen'd and gather'd at his wrist,
But, being old, continued just
As threadbare, and as full of dust.
A shambling awkward gait he took,
With a demure dejected look,
Talk't of his offerings, tithes, and dues,
Could smoke and drink and read the news,
Or sell a goose at the next town,
Decently hid beneath his gown.
Contriv'd to preach old sermons next,
Chang'd in the preface and the text.

At christ'nings well could act his part,
And had the service all by heart;
Wish'd women might have children fast,
And thought whose sow had farrow'd last;
Against dissenters would repine,
And stood up firm for 'right divine';
Carried it to his equals higher,
But most obedient to the squire.
Found his head fill'd with many a system;
But classic authors, – he ne'er mist 'em.
  Thus having furbish'd up a parson,
Dame Baucis next they play'd their farce on.
Instead of homespun coifs, were seen
Good pinners edg'd with colberteen;[1]
Her petticoat, transform'd apace,
Became black satin, flounced with lace.
'Plain Goody' would no longer down,
'Twas 'Madam', in her grogram gown.
Philemon was in great surprise,
And hardly could believe his eyes.
Amaz'd to see her look so prim,
And she admir'd as much at him.
  Thus happy in their change of life,
Were several years this man and wife:
When on a day, which prov'd their last,
Discoursing o'er old stories past,
They went by chance, amidst their talk,
To the churchyard, to take a walk;
When Baucis hastily cry'd out,
'My dear, I see your forehead sprout!' –
'Sprout'; quoth the man; 'what's this you tell us?
I hope you don't believe me jealous!
But yet, methinks, I feel it true,
And really yours is budding too –
Nay, – now I cannot stir my foot;
It feels as if 'twere taking root.'
  Description would but tire my Muse,
In short, they both were turn'd to yews.

[1] Kind of open lace

Old Goodman Dobson of the Green
Remembers he the trees has seen;
He'll talk of them from noon till night,
And goes with folk to show the sight;
On Sundays, after evening prayer,
He gathers all the parish there;
Points out the place of either yew,
Here Baucis, there Philemon, grew:
Till once a parson of our town,
To mend his barn, cut Baucis down;
At which, 'tis hard to be believ'd
How much the other tree was griev'd,
Grew scrubby, dy'd a-top, was stunted,
So the next parson stubb'd and burnt it.

A DESCRIPTION OF THE MORNING

Now hardly here and there an hackney-coach
Appearing, show'd the ruddy morn's approach.
Now Betty from her master's bed had flown,
And softly stole to discompose her own;
The slip-shod 'prentice from his master's door
Had pared the dirt, and sprinkled round the floor.
Now Moll had whirl'd her mop with dext'rous airs,
Prepared to scrub the entry and the stairs.
The youth with broomy stumps began to trace
The kennel's edge, where wheels had worn the place.
The small-coal man was heard with cadence deep,
Till drown'd in shriller notes of chimney-sweep:
Duns at his lordship's gate began to meet;
And brickdust Moll had scream'd through half the street.
The turnkey now his flock returning sees,
Duly let out a-nights to steal for fees:
The watchful bailiffs take their silent stands,
And schoolboys lag with satchels in their hands.

Jonathan Swift (1667–1745)

A DESCRIPTION OF A CITY SHOWER

Careful observers may foretell the hour,
(By sure prognostics,) when to dread a shower.
While rain depends, the pensive cat gives o'er
Her frolics, and pursues her tail no more.
Returning home at night, you'll find the sink
Strike your offended sense with double stink.
If you be wise, then, go not far to dine:
You'll spend in coach-hire more than save in wine.
A coming shower your shooting corns presage,
Old aches throb, your hollow tooth will rage;
Sauntering in coffeehouse is Dulman seen;
He damns the climate, and complains of spleen.
Meanwhile the South, rising with dabbled wings,
A sable cloud athwart the welkin flings,
That swill'd more liquor than it could contain,
And, like a drunkard, gives it up again.
Brisk Susan whips her linen from the rope,
While the first drizzling shower is borne aslope;
Such is that sprinkling which some careless quean
Flirts on you from her mop, but not so clean:
You fly, invoke the gods; then, turning, stop
To rail; she singing, still whirls on her mop.
Not yet the dust had shunn'd the unequal strife,
But, aided by the wind, fought still for life,
And wafted with its foe by violent gust,
'Twas doubtful which was rain, and which was dust.
Ah! where must needy poet seek for aid,
When dust and rain at once his coat invade?
Sole coat! where dust, cemented by the rain,
Erects the nap, and leaves a cloudy stain!
Now in contiguous drops the flood comes down,
Threatening with deluge this *devoted* town.
To shops in crowds the daggled females fly,
Pretend to cheapen goods, but nothing buy.
The Templar spruce, while every spout's abroach,
Stays till 'tis fair, yet seems to call a coach.

The tuck'd-up sempstress walks with hasty strides,
While streams run down her oil'd umbrella's sides.
Here various kinds, by various fortunes led,
Commence acquaintance underneath a shed.
Triumphant Tories, and desponding Whigs,
Forget their feuds, and join to save their wigs.
Box'd in a chair the beau impatient sits,
While spouts run clattering o'er the roof by fits,
And ever and anon with frightful din
The leather sounds; he trembles from within.
So when Troy chairmen bore the wooden steed,
Pregnant with Greeks impatient to be freed,
(Those bully Greeks, who, as the moderns do,
Instead of paying chairmen, ran them through,)
Laocoon struck the outside with his spear,
And each imprison'd hero quaked for fear.
  Now from all parts the swelling kennels flow,
And bear their trophies with them as they go:
Filth of all hues and odour, seem to tell
What street they sail'd from, by their sight and smell.
They, as each torrent drives with rapid force,
From Smithfield to St Pulchre's shape their course,
And in huge confluence join'd at Snowhill ridge,
Fall from the conduit prone to Holborn bridge.
Sweeping from butchers' stalls, dung, guts, and blood,
Drown'd puppies, stinking sprats, all drench'd in mud,
Dead cats, and turnip-tops, come tumbling down the flood.

From THE PROGRESS OF MARRIAGE

Aetatis suae fifty-two,
A rich Divine began to woo
A handsome, young, imperious girl,
Nearly related to an earl.
Her parents and her friends consent;
The couple to the temple went:
They first invite the Cyprian queen;
'Twas answer'd, 'She would not be seen';

The Graces next, and all the Muses,
Were bid in form, but sent excuses.
Juno attended at the porch,
With farthing candle for a torch;
While mistress Iris held her train,
The faded bow bedropt with rain.
Then Hebe came, and took her place,
But show'd no more than half her face.
  Whate'er these dire forebodings meant,
In joy the marriage-day was spent;
The marriage-*day*, you take me right,
I promise nothing for the night.
The bridegroom, drest to make a figure,
Assumes an artificial vigour;
A flourish'd nightcap on, to grace
His ruddy, wrinkled, smirking face;
Like the faint red upon a pippin,
Half wither'd by a winter's keeping.
  And thus set out this happy pair,
The swain is rich, the nymph is fair;
But, what I gladly would forget,
The swain is old, the nymph coquette.
Both from the goal together start;
Scarce run a step before they part;
No common ligament that binds
The various textures of their minds;
Their thoughts and actions, hopes and fears,
Less corresponding than their years.
Her spouse desires his coffee soon,
She rises to her tea at noon.
While he goes out to cheapen books,
She at the glass consults her looks;
While Betty's buzzing at her ear,
Lord, what a dress these parsons wear!
So odd a choice how could she make!
Wish'd him a colonel for her sake.
Then, on her finger ends she counts,
Exact, to what his age amounts.

The Dean, she heard her uncle say,
Is fifty, if he be a day;
His ruddy cheeks are no disguise;
You see the crow's feet round his eyes.
  At one she rambles to the shops,
To cheapen tea, and talk with fops;
Or calls a council of her maids,
And tradesmen, to compare brocades.
Her weighty morning business o'er,
Sits down to dinner just at four;
Minds nothing that is done or said,
Her evening work so fills her head.
The Dean, who used to dine at one,
Is mawkish, and his stomach's gone;
In threadbare gown, would scarce a louse hold,
Looks like the chaplain of the household;
Beholds her, from the chaplain's place,
In French brocades, and Flanders lace;
He wonders what employs her brain,
But never asks, or asks in vain;
His mind is full of other cares,
And, in the sneaking parson's airs,
Computes, that half a parish dues
Will hardly find his wife in shoes.
  Canst thou imagine, dull divine,
'Twill gain her love, to make her fine?
Hath she no other wants beside?
You raise desire as well as pride,
Enticing coxcombs to adore,
And teach her to despise thee more.
  If in her coach she'll condescend
To place him at the hinder end,
Her hoop is hoist above his nose,
His odious gown would soil her clothes.
She drops him at the church, to pray,
While she drives on to see the play.
He like an orderly divine,
Comes home a quarter after nine,

And meets her hasting to the ball:
Her chairmen push him from the wall.
He enters in and walk up stairs,
And calls the family to prayers;
Then goes alone to take his rest
In bed, where he can spare her best.
At five the footmen make a din,
Her ladyship is just come in;
The masquerade began at two,
She stole away with much ado;
And shall be chid this afternoon,
For leaving company so soon:
She'll say, and she may truly say't,
She can't abide to stay out late.

CLEVER TOM CLINCH GOING TO BE HANGED

As clever Tom Clinch, while the rabble was bawling,
Rode stately through Holborn, to die in his calling;
He stopped at the George for a bottle of sack,
And promised to pay for it when he'd come back.
His waistcoat and stockings and breeches were white,
His cap had a new cherry ribbon to tie't.
The maids to the doors and the balconies ran,
And said, 'Lack-a-day! He's a proper young man!'
But, as from the windows the ladies he spied,
Like a beau in a box, he bowed low to each side;
And when his last speech the loud hawkers did cry,
He swore from his cart, it was all a damned lie.
The hangman for pardon fell down on his knee;
Tom gave him a kick in the guts for his fee.
Then said, 'I must speak to the people a little,
But I'll see you all damned before I will whittle.[1]
My honest friend Wild,[2] may he long hold his place,
He lengthened my life with a whole year of grace.

[1] confess at the gallows [cant term] [2] Jonathan Wild, the noted thief-taker

Take courage, dear comrades, and be not afraid,
Nor slip this occasion to follow your trade.
My conscience is clear, and my spirits are calm,
And thus I go off without prayer-book or psalm.
Then follow the practice of clever Tom Clinch,
Who hung like a hero, and never would flinch.'

A BEAUTIFUL YOUNG NYMPH GOING TO BED

Corinna, pride of Drury Lane,
For whom no shepherd sighs in vain;
Never did Covent Garden boast
So bright a batter'd strolling toast!
No drunken rake to pick her up,
No cellar where on tick to sup;
Returning at the midnight hour,
Four stories climbing to her bower;
Then, seated on a three-legg'd chair,
Takes off her artificial hair;
Now picking out a crystal eye,
She wipes it clean, and lays it by.
Her eyebrows from a mouse's hide
Stuck on with art on either side,
Pulls off with care, and first displays 'em,
Then in a play-book smoothly lays 'em.
Now dext'rously her plumpers draws,
That serve to fill her hollow jaws,
Untwists a wire, and from her gums
A set of teeth completely comes;
Pulls out the rags contrived to prop
Her flabby dugs, and down they drop.
Proceeding on, the lovely goddess
Unlaces next her steel-ribb'd bodice,
Which, by the operator's skill,
Press down the lumps, the hollows fill.
Up goes her hand, and off she slips
The bolsters that supply her hips;

With gentlest touch she next explores
Her chancres, issues, running sores;
Effects of many a sad disaster,
And then to each applies a plaster:
But must, before she goes to bed,
Rub off the daubs of white and red,
And smooth the furrows in her front
With greasy paper stuck upon't.
She takes a bolus ere she sleeps;
And then between two blankets creeps.
With pains of love tormented lies;
Or, if she chance to close her eyes,
Of Bridewell and the Compter dreams,
And feels the lash, and faintly screams;
Or, by a faithless bully drawn,
At some hedge-tavern lies in pawn;
Or to Jamaica seems transported
Alone, and by no planter courted;
Or, near Fleet-ditch's oozy brinks,
Surrounded with a hundred stinks,
Belated, seems on watch to lie,
And snap some cully passing by;
Or, struck with fear, her fancy runs
On watchmen, constables, and duns,
From whom she meets with frequent rubs;
But never from religious clubs;
Whose favour she is sure to find,
Because she pays them all in kind.
Corinna wakes. A dreadful sight!
Behold the ruins of the night!
A wicked rat her plaster stole,
Half eat, and dragg'd it to his hole.
The crystal eye, alas! was miss'd;
And puss had on her plumpers piss'd,
A pigeon pick'd her issue-pease:
And Shock her tresses fill'd with fleas.
The nymph, though in this mangled plight
Must ev'ry morn her limbs unite.

But how shall I describe her arts
To re-collect the scatter'd parts?
Or show the anguish, toil, and pain,
Of gath'ring up herself again?
The bashful Muse will never bear
In such a scene to interfere.
Corinna, in the morning dizen'd,
Who sees, will spew; who smells, be poison'd.

EDWARD YOUNG

THE LANGUID LADY

The languid lady next appears in state,
Who was not born to carry her own weight;
She lolls, reels, staggers, till some foreign aid
To her own stature lifts the feeble maid.
Then, if ordained to so severe a doom,
She, by just stages, journeys round the room:
But, knowing her own weakness, she despairs
To scale the Alps – that is, ascend the stairs.
My fan! let others say, who laugh at toil;
Fan! hood! glove! scarf! is her laconic style;
And that is spoke with such a dying fall,
That Betty rather sees, than hears the call:
The motion of her lips, and meaning eye,
Piece out th'idea her faint words deny.
O listen with attention most profound!
Her voice is but the shadow of a sound.
And help! oh help! her spirits are so dead,
One hand scarce lifts the other to her head.
If, there, a stubborn pin it triumphs o'er,
She pants! she sinks away! and is no more.
Let the robust and the gigantic carve,
Life is not worth so much, she'd rather starve:
But chew she must herself; ah cruel fate!
That Rosalinda can't by proxy eat.

from *Satire V: On Women*

JOHN GAY

A TOWNSMAN'S GUIDE TO THE WEATHER

Nor do less certain signs the town advise,
Of milder weather, and serener skies.
The ladies gaily dress'd, the Mall adorn
With various dyes, and paint the sunny morn;
The wanton fawns with frisking pleasure range,
And chirping sparrows greet the welcome change:
Not that their minds with greater skill are fraught,
Endu'd by instinct, or by reason taught,
The seasons operate on ev'ry breast;
'Tis hence that fawns are brisk, and ladies drest.
When on his box the nodding coachman snores,
And dreams of fancy'd fares; when tavern doors
The chairmen idly crowd; then ne'er refuse
To trust thy busy steps in thinner shoes.
But when the swinging signs your ears offend
With creaking noise, then rainy floods impend;
Soon shall the kennels swell with rapid streams,
And rush in muddy torrents to the Thames.
The bookseller, whose shop's an open square,
Foresees the tempest, and with early care
Of learning strips the rails; the towing crew
To tempt a fare, clothe all their tilts in blue:
On hosiers' poles depending stockings tied,
Flag with the slacken'd gale, from side to side;
Church-monuments foretell the changing air;
Then Niobe dissolves into a tear
And sweats with secret grief: you'll hear the sounds
Of whistling winds, e'er kennels break their bounds;
Ungrateful odours common-shores diffuse,
And dropping vaults distil unwholesome dews,
E'er the tiles rattle with the smoking show'r,
And spouts on heedless men their torrents pour.

Trivia: or The Art of Walking the Streets of London

John Gay (1685–1732)

PLEASURES AND INCONVENIENCES OF WALKING IN LONDON

Who would of Watling-street the dangers share,
When the broad pavement of Cheapside is near?
Or who that rugged street[1] would traverse o'er,
That stretches, O Fleet-ditch, from thy black shore
To the Tow'r's moated walls? Here steams ascend
That, in mix'd fumes, the wrinkled nose offend.
Where chandlers' cauldrons boil; where fishy prey
Hide the wet stall, long absent from the sea;
And where the cleaver chops the heifer's spoil,
And where huge hogsheads sweat with trainy oil,
Thy breathing nostril hold; but how shall I
Pass, where in piles Cornavian cheeses lie;
Cheese, that the table's closing rites denies,
And bids me with th' unwilling chaplain rise.
O bear me to the paths of fair Pell-mell,
Safe are thy pavements, grateful is thy smell!
At distance rolls along the gilded coach,
Nor sturdy carmen on thy walks encroach;
No lets would bar thy ways were chairs denied
The soft supports of laziness and pride;
Shops breathe perfumes, thro' sashes ribbons glow,
The mutual arms of ladies, and the beau.
Yet still ev'n here, when rains the passage hide,
Oft' the loose stone spirts up a muddy tide
Beneath thy careless foot; and from on high,
Where masons mount the ladder, fragments fly;
Mortar, and crumbled lime in show'rs descend,
And o'er thy head destructive tiles impend.
But sometimes let me leave the noisy roads,
And silent wander in the close abodes
Where wheels ne'er shake the ground; there pensive stray,
In studious thought, the long uncrowded way.
Here I remark each walker's diff'rent face,
And in their look their various bus'ness trace.

[1] Thames Street

The broker here his spacious beaver wears,
Upon his brow sit jealousies and cares;
Bent on some mortgage (to avoid reproach)
He seeks bye streets, and saves th' expensive coach.
Soft, at low doors, old letchers tap their cane,
For fair recluse, who travels Drury-lane;
Here roams uncomb'd the lavish rake, to shun
His Fleet-street draper's everlasting dun.
  Careful observers, studious of the town,
Shun the misfortunes that disgrace the clown;
Untempted, they contemn the juggler's feats,
Pass by the Meuse, nor try the thimble's cheats.
When drays bound high, they never cross behind,
Where bubbling yeast is blown by gusts of wind:
And when up Ludgate-hill huge carts move slow,
Far from the straining steeds securely go,
Whose dashing hoofs behind them fling the mire,
And mark with muddy blots the gazing 'squire.
The Parthian thus his javelin backward throws,
And as he flies infests pursuing foes.
  The thoughtless wits shall frequent forfeits pay,
Who 'gainst the sentry's box discharge their tea.
Do thou some court, or secret corner seek,
Nor flush with shame the passing virgin's cheek.

Trivia: or The Art of Walking the Streets of London

THE GREAT FROST

  Winter my theme confines; whose nitry wind
Shall crust the slabby mire, and kennels bind;
She bids the snow descend in flaky sheets,
And in her hoary mantle clothe the streets.
Let not the virgin tread these slippery roads,
The gathering fleece the hollow patten loads;
But if thy footstep slide with clotted frost,
Strike off the breaking balls against the post.

On silent wheels the passing coaches roll;
Oft look behind, and ward the threatening pole.
In hardened orbs the school-boy moulds the snow,
To mark the coachman with a dexterous throw.
Why do ye, boys, the kennel's surface spread,
To tempt with faithless pass the matron's tread?
How can you laugh to see the damsel spurn,
Sink in your frauds, and her green stocking mourn?
At White's the harnessed chairman idly stands,
And swings around his waist his tingling hands;
The sempstress speeds to Change with red-tipped nose;
The Belgian stove beneath her footstool glows;
In half-whipped muslin needles useless lie,
And shuttlecocks across the counter fly.
These sports warm harmless; why then will ye prove,
Deluded maids, the dangerous flame of love?
  Where Covent-garden's famous temple stands,
That boasts the work of Jones' immortal hands;
Columns with plain magnificence appear,
And graceful porches lead along the square:
Here oft my course I bend; when, lo! from far
I spy the furies of the football war:
The 'prentice quits his shop, to join the crew,
Increasing crowds the flying game pursue.
Thus, as you roll the ball o'er snowy ground,
The gathering globe augments with every round.
But whither shall I run? the throng draws nigh,
The ball now skims the street, now soars on high;
The dexterous glazier strong returns the bound,
And jingling sashes on the pent-house sound.
  O, roving Muse! recall that wondrous year,
When winter reigned in bleak Britannia's air;
When hoary Thames, with frosted osiers crowned,
Was three long moons in icy fetters bound.
The waterman, forlorn, along the shore,
Pensive reclines upon his useless oar;
See harnessed steeds desert the stony town,
And wander roads unstable, not their own;

Wheels o'er the hardened waters smoothly glide,
And raze with whitened tracks the slippery tide;
Here the fat cook piles high the blazing fire,
And scarce the spit can turn the steer entire;
Booths sudden hide the Thames, long streets appear,
And numerous games proclaim the crowded fair.

Trivia: or The Art of Walking the Streets of London

THE HAPPINESS OF WALKERS

O ye associate walkers, O my friends,
Upon your state what happiness attends!
What, though no coach to frequent visit rolls,
Nor for your shilling chairmen sling their poles;
Yet still your nerves rheumatic pains defy,
Nor lazy jaundice dulls your saffron eye;
No wasting cough discharges sounds of death,
Nor wheezing asthma heaves in vain for breath;
Nor from your restless couch is heard the groan
Of burning gout, or sedentary stone.
Let others in the jolting coach confide,
Or in the leaky boat the Thames divide;
Or, box'd within the chair, contemn the street,
And trust their safety to another's feet,
Still let me walk; for oft the sudden gale
Ruffles the tide, and shifts the dang'rous sail.
Then shall the passenger too late deplore
The whelming billow, and the faithless oar;
The drunken chairman in the kennel spurns,
The glasses shatters, and his charge o'erturns.
Who can recount the coach's various harms,
The legs disjointed, and the broken arms?
I've seen a beau, in some ill-fated hour,
When o'er the stones chok'd kennels swell the show'r
In gilded chariot loll; he with disdain
Views spatter'd passengers all drench'd in rain;

With mud fill'd high, the rumbling cart draws near,
Now rule thy prancing steeds, lac'd charioteer!
The dust-man lashes on with spiteful rage,
His pond'rous spokes thy painted wheel engage,
Crush'd is thy pride, down falls the shrieking beau,
The slabby pavement crystal fragments strow,
Black floods of mire th' embroider'd coat disgrace,
And mud enwraps the honours of his face.

Trivia: or The Art of Walking the Streets of London

PERILS OF THE NIGHT

Who can the various city frauds recite,
With all the petty rapines of the night?
Who now the guinea-dropper's bait regards,
Tricked by the sharper's dice, or juggler's cards?
Why should I warn thee, ne'er to join the fray,
Where the sham quarrel interrupts the way?
Lives there in these our days so soft a clown,
Braved by the bully's oaths, or threatening frown?
I need not strict enjoin the pocket's care,
When from the crowded play thou lead'st the fair;
Who has not here or watch or snuff-box lost,
Or handkerchiefs that India's shuttle boast?
O! may thy virtue guard thee through the roads
Of Drury's mazy courts and dark abodes!
The harlots' guileful paths, who nightly stand
Where Catharine Street descends into the Strand!
Say, vagrant Muse, their wiles and subtle arts,
To lure the strangers' unsuspecting hearts:
So shall our youth on healthful sinews tread,
And city cheeks grow warm with rural red.
'Tis she who nightly strolls with sauntering pace,
No stubborn stays her yielding shape embrace;
Beneath the lamp her tawdry ribbons glare,
The new-scoured manteau, and the slattern air;
High-draggled petticoats her travels show,

And hollow cheeks with artful blushes glow;
With flattering sounds she soothes the credulous ear,
'My noble captain! charmer! love! my dear!'
In riding-hood near tavern-doors she plies,
Or muffled pinners hide her livid eyes.
With empty bandbox she delights to range,
And feigns a distant errand from the 'Change;
Nay, she will oft the quaker's hood profane,
And trudge demure the rounds of Drury Lane.
She darts from sarsenet ambush wily leers,
Twitches thy sleeve, or with familiar airs
Her fan will pat thy cheek; these snares disdain,
Nor gaze behind thee, when she turns again.

Trivia: or The Art of Walking the Streets of London

ANONYMOUS

THE JOLLY TRADESMEN

Sometimes I am a Tapster new,
And skilful in my trade Sir,
I fill my pots most duly,
Without deceit or froth Sir:
A spicket[1] of two handfuls long,
I use to occupy Sir:
And when I set a butt abroach,
Then shall no beer run by Sir.

Sometimes I am a butcher,
And then I feel fat ware Sir;
And if the flank be fleshed well,
I take no farther care Sir:
But in I thrust my slaughtering-knife,
Up to the haft with speed Sir;
For all that ever I can do,
I cannot make it bleed Sir.

[1] spigot

Sometimes I am a Baker,
And bake both white and brown Sir;
I have as fine a wriggling-pole,
As any is in all this town Sir:
But if my oven be over-hot,
I dare not thrust in it Sir;
For burning of my wriggling-pole,
My skill's not worth a pin Sir.

Sometimes I am a Glover,
And can do passing well Sir;
In dressing of a doe-skin,
I know I do excel Sir:
But if by chance a flaw I find,
In dressing of the leather;
I straightway whip my needle out,
And I tack 'em close together.

Sometimes I am a Cook,
And in Fleet-Street I do dwell Sir:
At the sign of the Sugar-loaf,
As it is known full well Sir:
And if a dainty lass comes by,
And wants a dainty bit Sir;
I take four quarters in my arms,
And put them on my spit Sir.

In weavering and in fulling,
I have such passing skill Sir;
And underneath my weavering-beam,
There stands a fulling-mill Sir:
To have good wives' displeasure,
I would be very loath Sir;
The water runs so near my hand,
It over-thicks my cloth Sir.

Sometimes I am a Shoe-maker,
And work with silly bones Sir;
To make my Leather soft and moist,
I use a pair of stones Sir:

My lasts for and my lasting sticks,
Are fit for every size Sir;
I know the length of lasses feet,
By handling of their thighs Sir.

The Tanner's trade I practice,
Sometimes amongst the rest Sir;
Yet I could never get a hair,
Of any hide I dress'd Sir:
For I have been tanning of a hide,
This long seven years and more Sir;
And yet it is as hairy still,
As ever it was before Sir.

Sometimes I am a Tailor,
And work with thread that's strong Sir;
I have a fine great needle,
About two handfuls long Sir;
The finest Sempster in this town,
That works by line or leisure;
May use my needle at a pinch,
And do themselves great pleasure.

from D'Urfey's *Pills to Purge Melancholy*

ALEXANDER POPE

EPISTLE TO MISS MARTHA BLOUNT, ON HER LEAVING THE TOWN AFTER THE CORONATION

As some fond virgin, whom her mother's care
Drags from the town to wholesome country air,
Just when she learns to roll a melting eye,
And hear a spark, yet think no danger nigh;
From the dear man unwilling she must sever,
Yet takes one kiss before she parts for ever:
Thus from the world fair Zephalinda flew,
Saw others happy, and with sighs withdrew;

Not that their pleasures caused her discontent,
She sigh'd not that they stay'd, but that she went.
She went to plain-work, and to purling brooks,
Old-fashion'd halls, dull aunts, and croaking rooks:
She went from opera, park, assembly, play,
To morning walks, and prayers three hours a-day;
To part her time 'twixt reading and bohea,
To muse, and spill her solitary tea,
Or o'er cold coffee trifle with the spoon,
Count the slow clock, and dine exact at noon;
Divert her eyes with pictures in the fire,
Hum half a tune, tell stories to the 'squire;
Up to her godly garret after seven,
There starve and pray, for that's the way to Heaven.
Some 'squire, perhaps, you take delight to rack;
Whose game is whisk, whose treat a toast in sack;
Who visits with a gun, presents you birds,
Then gives a smacking buss and cries, – No words!
Or with his hound comes hallooing from the stable,
Makes love with nods, and knees beneath a table;
Whose laughs are hearty, though his jests are coarse,
And loves you best of all things – but his horse.
In some fair ev'ning, on your elbow laid,
You dream of triumphs in the rural shade;
In pensive thought recall the fancied scene,
See coronations rise on ev'ry green;
Before you pass th' imaginary sights
Of lords, and earls, and dukes, and garter'd knights,
While the spread fan o'ershades your closing eyes;
Then give one flirt, and all the vision flies.
Thus vanish sceptres, coronets, and balls,
And leave you in lone woods, or empty walls!
So when your slave, at some dear idle time,
(Not plagued with head-aches, or the want of rhyme)
Stands in the streets, abstracted from the crew,
And while he seems to study, thinks of you;
Just when his fancy points your sprightly eyes,
Or sees the blush of soft Parthenia rise,

Gay pats my shoulder, and you vanish quite,
Streets, chairs, and coxcombs rush upon my sight;
Vex'd to be still in town, I knit my brow,
Look sour, and hum a tune as you may now.

EPISTLE TO RICHARD BOYLE, EARL OF BURLINGTON

'Tis strange, the miser should his cares employ
To gain those riches he can ne'er enjoy:
Is it less strange, the prodigal should waste
His wealth to purchase what he ne'er can taste?
Not for himself he sees, or hears, or eats;
Artists must choose his pictures, music, meats:
He buys for Topham drawings and designs,
For Pembroke statues, dirty gods, and coins;
Rare monkish manuscripts for Hearne alone,
And books for Mead, and butterflies for Sloane.
Think we all these are for himself? no more
Than his fine wife, alas! or finer whore.
  For what has Virro painted, built, and planted?
Only to show how many tastes he wanted.
What brought Sir Visto's ill-got wealth to waste?
Some demon whisper'd, 'Visto! have a taste.'
Heaven visits with a taste the wealthy fool,
And needs no rod but Ripley with a rule.
See! sportive Fate, to punish awkward pride,
Bids Bubo build, and sends him such a guide:
A standing sermon, at each year's expense,
That never coxcomb reach'd magnificence!
  You show us Rome was glorious, not profuse,
And pompous buildings once were things of use.
Yet shall (my lord) your just, your noble rules
Fill half the land with imitating fools;
Who random drawings from your sheets shall take,
And of one beauty many blunders make;
Load some vain church with old theatric state,
Turn acts of triumph to a garden-gate;

Reverse your ornaments, and hang them all
On some patch'd dog-hole eked with ends of wall;
Then clap four slices of pilaster on't,
That, laced with bits of rustic, makes a front.
Shall call the winds through long arcades to roar,
Proud to catch cold at a Venetian door;
Conscious they act a true Palladian part,
And, if they starve, they starve by rules of art.
  Oft have you hinted to your brother peer
A certain truth, which many buy too dear:
Something there is more needful than expense,
And something previous even to taste – 'tis sense:
Good sense, which only is the gift of Heaven,
And, though no science, fairly worth the seven:
A light, which in yourself you must perceive;
Jones and Le Nôtre have it not to give.
  To build, to plant, whatever you intend,
To rear the column, or the arch to bend,
To swell the terrace, or to sink the grot,
In all, let Nature never be forgot,
But treat the goddess like a modest fair,
Nor over-dress, nor leave her wholly bare;
Let not each beauty everywhere be spied,
Where half the skill is decently to hide.
He gains all points, who pleasingly confounds,
Surprises, varies, and conceals the bounds.
  Consult the genius of the place in all:
That tells the waters or to rise or fall;
Or helps the ambitious hill the heavens to scale,
Or scoops in circling theatres the vale;
Calls in the country, catches opening glades,
Joins willing woods, and varies shades from shades;
Now breaks, or now directs, the intending lines;
Paints, as you plant, and, as you work, designs.
Still follow sense, of every art the soul,
Parts answering parts shall slide into a whole,
Spontaneous beauties all around advance,
Start ev'n from difficulty, strike from chance;

Nature shall join you; Time shall make it grow
A work to wonder at – perhaps a Stowe.
  Without it, proud Versailles! thy glory falls;
And Nero's terraces desert their walls:
The vast parterres a thousand hands shall make,
Lo! Cobham comes, and floats them with a lake;
Or cut wide views through mountains to the plain,
You'll wish your hill or shelter'd seat again.
Even in an ornament its place remark,
Nor in an hermitage set Dr Clarke.
Behold Villario's ten years' toil complete;
His quincunx darkens, his espaliers meet;
The wood supports the plain, the parts unite,
And strength of shade contends with strength of light;
A waving glow the bloomy beds display,
Blushing in bright diversities of day,
With silver-quivering rills meander'd o'er –
Enjoy then, you! Villario can no more:
Tired of the scene parterres and fountains yield,
He finds at last he better likes a field.
  Through his young woods how pleased Sabinus stray'd,
Or sate delighted in the thickening shade,
With annual joy the reddening shoots to greet,
Or see the stretching branches long to meet!
His son's fine taste an opener vista loves,
Foe to the Dryads of his father's groves;
One boundless green, or flourish'd carpet views,
With all the mournful family of yews:
The thriving plants, ignoble broomsticks made,
Now sweep those alleys they were born to shade.
  At Timon's villa let us pass a day,
Where all cry out, 'What sums are thrown away!'
So proud, so grand: of that stupendous air,
Soft and agreeable come never there.
Greatness, with Timon, dwells in such a draught
As brings all Brobdignag before your thought.
To compass this, his building is a town,
His pond an ocean, his parterre a down:

Who but must laugh, the master when he sees,
A puny insect, shivering at a breeze!
Lo, what huge heaps of littleness around!
The whole, a labour'd quarry above ground,
Two cupids squirt before: a lake behind
Improves the keenness of the northern wind.
His gardens next your admiration call,
On every side you look, behold the wall!
No pleasing intricacies intervene,
No artful wildness to perplex the scene:
Grove nods at grove, each alley has a brother,
And half the platform just reflects the other.
The suffering eye inverted Nature sees,
Trees cut to statues, statues thick as trees;
With here a fountain, never to be play'd;
And there a summer-house, that knows no shade:
Here Amphitrite sails through myrtle bowers;
There gladiators fight, or die in flowers;
Unwater'd see the drooping sea-horse mourn,
And swallows roost in Nilus' dusty urn.
  My Lord advances with majestic mien,
Smit with the mighty pleasure to be seen:
But soft – by regular approach – not yet –
First through the length of yon hot terrace sweat;
And when up ten steep slopes you've dragg'd your thighs,
Just at his study-door he'll bless your eyes.
  His study! with what authors is it stored?
In books, not authors, curious is my Lord;
To all their dated backs he turns you round;
These Aldus printed, those Du Sueïl has bound.
Lo, some are vellum, and the rest as good
For all his Lordship knows, but they are wood.
For Locke or Milton 'tis in vain to look,
These shelves admit not any modern book.
  And now the chapel's silver bell you hear,
That summons you to all the pride of prayer:
Light quirks of music, broken and uneven,
Make the soul dance upon a jig to Heaven.

On painted ceilings you devoutly stare,
Where sprawl the saints of Verrio or Laguerre,
Or gilded clouds in fair expansion lie,
And bring all Paradise before your eye.
To rest, the cushion and soft dean invite,
Who never mentions Hell to ears polite.
   But hark! the chiming clocks to dinner call;
A hundred footsteps scrape the marble hall:
The rich buffet well-coloured serpents grace,
And gaping Tritons spew to wash your face.
Is this a dinner? this a genial room?
No, 'tis a temple, and a hecatomb.
A solemn sacrifice, perform'd in state,
You drink by measure, and to minutes eat.
So quick retires each flying course, you'd swear
Sancho's dread doctor and his wand were there.
Between each act the trembling salvers ring,
From soup to sweet-wine, and God bless the king.
In plenty starving, tantalized in state,
And complaisantly help'd to all I hate,
Treated, caress'd, and tired, I take my leave,
Sick of his civil pride from morn to eve;
I curse such lavish cost, and little skill,
And swear no day was ever pass'd so ill.
   Yet hence the poor are clothed, the hungry fed;
Health to himself, and to his infants bread,
The labourer bears: what his hard heart denies,
His charitable vanity supplies.
   Another age shall see the golden ear
Imbrown the slope, and nod on the parterre,
Deep harvest bury all his pride has plann'd,
And laughing Ceres reassume the land.
   Who then shall grace, or who improve the soil? –
Who plants like Bathurst, or who builds like Boyle.
'Tis use alone that sanctifies expense,
And splendour borrows all her rays from sense.
   His father's acres who enjoys in peace,
Or makes his neighbours glad, if he increase:

Whose cheerful tenants bless their yearly toil,
Yet to their lord owe more than to the soil;
Whose ample lawns are not ashamed to feed
The milky heifer and deserving steed;
Whose rising forests, not for pride or show,
But future buildings, future navies grow:
Let his plantations stretch from down to down,
First shade a country, and then raise a town.
You too proceed! make falling arts your care,
Erect new wonders, and the old repair;
Jones and Palladio to themselves restore,
And be whate'er Vitruvius was before:
'Till kings call forth the ideas of your mind
(Proud to accomplish what such hands design'd),
Bid harbours open, public ways extend,
Bid temples, worthier of the god, ascend;
Bid the broad arch the dangerous flood contain,
The mole projected break the roaring main;
Back to his bounds their subject sea command,
And roll obedient rivers through the land;
These honours Peace to happy Britain brings,
These are imperial works, and worthy kings.

PHILIP DORMER STANHOPE, EARL OF CHESTERFIELD

ADVICE TO A LADY IN AUTUMN

Asses milk, half a pint, take at seven, or before;
Then sleep for an hour or two, and no more.
At nine stretch your arms, and oh! think when alone,
There's no pleasure in bed. – Mary, bring me my gown:
Slip on that ere you rise; let your caution be such,
Keep all cold from your breast, there's already too much.
Your pinners set right, your twitcher tied on,
Your prayers at an end, and your breakfast quite done,

Retire to some author improving and gay,
And with sense like your own, set your mind for the day.
At twelve you may walk, for at this time o'the year,
The sun, like your wit, is as mild as 'tis clear:
But mark in the meadows the ruin of time;
Take the hint, and let life be improv'd in its prime.
Return not in haste, nor of dressing take heed;
For beauty like yours, no assistance can need.
With an appetite, thus, down to dinner you sit,
Where the chief of the feast, is the flow of your wit:
Let this be indulg'd, and let laughter go round;
As it pleases your mind, to your health 'twill redound.
After dinner two glasses at least, I approve;
Name the first to the king, and the last to your love:
Thus cheerful with wisdom, with innocence gay,
And calm with your joys gently glide thro' the day.
The dews of the evening most carefully shun;
Those tears of the sky for the loss of the sun.
Then in chat, or at play, with a dance, or a song,
Let the night, like the day, pass with pleasure along.
All cares, but of love, banish far from your mind;
And those you may end, when you please to be kind.

EDWARD CHICKEN

THE COLLIER'S WEDDING

In former days, when trade was good,
And men got money, clothes and food,
When landlords were not too severe,
And tenants broke not every year,
Then collier lads got money fast,
Had merry days when it did last,
Did feast and drink and game and play,
And swore when they had nought to say.

They came to church but very rare,
Yet missed not when a bride was there,

But rested on the Sabbath day
From everything but drink and play;
And slept that day, but not before
Their head and tail could hold no more.
Then like true cocks that love the game,
They'd rise, and drink, and sleep again.
And thus the colliers and their wives
Lived drunken, honest working lives.
The sons and daughters of this sort
Were always fond of country sport,
And all the young unmarried fry
Did strive each other to outvie,
And would on Hopping-days be dressed
Genteel and in their very best,
Look smart, be clean from tip to toe,
As all that would be married do.

A collier's daughter, brisk and clean,
Once at a country wake was seen.
The maid was born in Benwell Town,
Was not too fair, yet not too brown;
Of beauty she had got her part,
Enough to wound a collier's heart.
And then her name was up for this,
She loved to spin, but blushed to kiss.
Her pliant limbs, when music played,
Could humour everything it said;
For when she tripped it on the plain
To *Jocky's Lost His Fellow Swain*,
Her easy steps and airy wheels
Showed she had music in her heels.
She danced so well, so very long,
She won the smock and pleased the throng.

A collier lad was standing by,
And viewed her with a lover's eye.
He scratched his head, and then he swore
That none had danced so well before,
Then made a brush up to the maid.
'How do ye, lass?' the lover said.

'I'm glad to see ye, by my saul,
For sink my heart, thou's beat 'em all.
Thou's warmed their stomachs for 'em now,
By God, thou is a tuing sow.
Zoons, lass, come go, I'll warr'nt thou's dry.
Come, fool, what makes ye look so shy?'
Then seized her hand and being strong
He lugged the willing maid along.
She had not many words to say,
But hung an arse the country way,
Then gave a modest blush, and so
In silence gave consent to go.

He led her to an inn hard by,
Where drink was good, if she was dry.
In private they were o'er a pot,
With other cheer the house had got.
He plied her all the afternoon,
And kept her warm to melt her down.
He stroked her neck and squeezed her hand,
And pressed her till she could not stand;
And then she struggled in his arms
With sweet, disordered, homely charms,
Till fear and love with equal grace
Did vary colours in her face.

Her pulse beat quick, her breath went slow,
She just could say: 'Oh, let me go.
I'm spent, undone. Oh lack-a-day,
What can I either do or say?
Was ever lass in my condition?
For heaven's sake, hear my petition,
Unfold your arms and give me air,
And let me rest upon my chair.
I faint. Oh, Tommy, cut my lace,
And throw my apron o'er my face!'

With amorous looks he calls her jewel,
And said: 'How can ye be so cruel?
Come, ease my mind and speak, my life,
And give consent to be my wife,

For I can never love another.
Come, I'll go with you to your mother,
Have her consent, hear what she'll say,
And then we'll fix our wedding day.'
They trudged along, got home at last,
And found old goody smoking fast,
Placed on a cracket[1] near the fire.
Her spinning-wheel was standing by her,
Her skirts laid up for fear of burning;
She loved all warm, but hated turning.
An earthen pot with humming beer
Stood on a table very near,
For she would funk,[2] smoke, fart and drink,
And sometimes raise a hellish stink.

Our old wife turned her head about,
And spied at last her daughter out.
She cried: 'Lass, where the de'il hast thou been?
I thought thou would no more be seen.
You've got your belly full of play,
I'll warr'nt ye've had a merry day.
For now it will be twelve o'clock
And more, for I've spun off my rock.
Lass, whe's that wi' ye?' 'Whe should it be?
Sit still,' says Tom. ''Tis none but me.
I've come to have a little clash.'
'Hout, lad, get hame; ye're nought but fash.
De'il scratch your arse, what brought ye here?
Ye've kept our daughter up, I fear.'

Tom rose, and came where Bessy sat,
And fanned the fire with his hat,
Played with her pipe till it was broke,
And grinned and laughed, and then he spoke:
'Your Jenny is my heart's delight.
De'il rive their sarks gang hame tonight.
I'll have her, had she not a smock.
If ye'll consent, we'll call up Jock

[1] stool [2] blow smoke

And raise up Doll to fetch a drink.
Come, Bessy, speak. What do ye think?'

Her daughter Jane, with modest grace,
And fingers spread before her face,
Cried: 'Mother, Tommy's won my heart.
If you're content, we'll never part.
I love him as I do my life,
And would be glad to be his wife.'
When Bessy heard her daughter Jane
Declare herself so very plain,
The house was in an instant raised,
Greybeard was washed, the fire blazed,
Strong beer was fetched, tobacco too,
Old Bessy drank till she was fou,[3]
Then reeled to Tom with her consent,
And spewed her liquor as she went.
Old Jock and Doll lay on the floor,
For they could drink and spew no more.
Our lovers now have all the play.
They bill, and fix the wedding day.

Long wished for now has come at last.
The day appears, the bride is dressed,
The music makes the village ring,
The children shout, the old wives sing.
Tom comes in triumph o'er the plain
With collier lads, a jolly train.
They smoke along the dusty way,
Whips crack for joy, the horses play,
The bridegroom rides in state before,
Midst clouds of dust the bagpipes roar.
Like streamers in the painted sky,
At every breast the flavours fly.

Two lusty lads, well-dressed and strong,
Step out to lead the bride along,
And two maids of equal size
As soon the bridegroom's hands surprise.

[3] drunk

The pipers wind and take their post,
And go before to clear the coast.
Then all the vast promiscuous crowd,
With thundering tongues, and feet as loud,
Toss up their hats, clap hands and holler,
And mad with joy like Bedlam follow.
Some shout the bride and some the groom,
Till just as mad to church they come;
Knock, swear and rattle at the gate,
And vow to break the beadle's pate,
And call his wife a bitch and whore;
They will be in or break the door!
The gates fly open, all rush in;
The church is full with folks and din,
And all the crew, both great and small,
Behave as in a common hall;
For some perhaps that were three score
Were never in a church before.

They scamper, climb, and break the pews,
To see the couple make their vows.
With solemn face the priest draws near.
Poor Tom and Jenny quake for fear.
In decent order when they're got,
The priest proceeds to tie the knot.
Then hands are joined and loosed again,
And Tommy says: 'I take thee, Jane.'
And Jenny looks a little shy,
And kneels, and says: 'I take Tommy.'
And now they're fairly in for life.
The priest declares them man and wife.

Our couple now kneel down to pray,
Much unacquainted with the way.
Whole troops of colliers swarm around
And seize poor Jenny on the ground,
Put up their hands to loose her garters,
And work for pluck about her quarters,
Till ribbons from her legs are torn
And round the church in triumph borne.

Edward Chicken (1698–1746)

The wedding now is fairly o'er.
The fees are paid, but nothing more.
The bridegroom he comes foremost out.
He cocks his hat and looks about.
The pipers play for victory,
I'll Make Thee Fain to Follow Me.
Spruce Tommy now leads first away,
For Jenny's bound, and must obey.
Yet here our bride must have her due,
She stuck as close to Tom as glue,
Tucked up her skirts to mend her pace
And walked till sweat ran down her face.
Sturdy she raked along the plain
To keep in view her fellow swain.
Now they arrive all in a foam.
The old wife bids them welcome home,
Salutes her daughter and her son.
So now begins the merry fun.

The greasy cook at once appears
And thunders mischief in their ears.
She scolds and brawls and makes a noise,
And throws her fat among the boys;
Now runs to see the kettle boil;
Meanwhile she lets her butter oil,
Then boxes her who turns the spit
And cries: 'You jade, you'll burn the meat!
Fire, smoke and fury round her goes.
She's burnt her apron, singed her clothes.
'The dinner will be spoiled,' she cries.
'Good God, the baker's burnt the pies!
Come, take your seats and stand away,
My ladle has no room to play.
The hens and cocks are just laid down.
I never thought you'd come so soon!'
And thus, with suchlike noise and din,
The wedding banquet does begin.

Impatient for the want of meat,
They feak,[4] and cannot keep their seat,
Play with the plates, drum on the table,
And fast as long as they are able,
Then count the number of their knives,
And who is there that have not wives,
Unfold the napkins, lay them down,
Then tell the letters of a spoon,
Some eat the bread, some lick the salt,
Some drink, and other some find fault.
In short, they could no longer put,
For belly thinks that throat is cut.
They damn and sink and curse the cook,
And give her many a frightful look.
They call her bitch and jade and sow.
She says she does what fire could do.
And thus their guts disturb and vex 'em.
For want of patience doth perplex 'em.

At last the beef appears in sight.
The groom moves slow the ponderous weight.
Swift to the smoking beef they fly.
Some cut their passage through a pie.
Out streams the gravy on the cloth.
Some burn their tongue with scalding broth.
But rolling spices make them fain;
They shake their heads and sup again.
'Cut up the goose!' cries one below,
'And send us down a leg or so.'
An honest neighbour tries the point,
Works hard, but cannot hit a joint.
The bride sat nigh. She rose in prim,
And cut and tore it limb from limb.
Now geese, cocks, hens, the fury feel,
Extended jaws devour the veal,
Each rises and eats what he can get,
And all is fish that comes to net.

[4] twitch

Now all are full, the meat away,
The table drawn, the music play.
The bridegroom first assumes the floor
And dances all the maidens o'er,
Then rubs his face, and makes a bow,
And marches off when he can do.
He must not tire himself outright –
The bride expects a dance tonight.
In every room, both high and low,
The fiddlers play, the bagpipes blow.
Some shout the bride, and some the groom.
They roar the very music dumb.
Hand over head, and one through t'other,
They dance with sister and with brother.
Their common tune is *Get Her, Bo!*
The weary lass cries: 'Music O!'
Till tired in circling, round they wheel,
And beat the ground with toe and heel.

A collier lad of taller size,
With rings of dust about his eyes,
Laid down his pipe, rose from the table,
And swore he'd dance while was able,
He catched a partner by the hand,
And kissed her for to make her stand,
And then he bid the music play,
And said: 'Now, lass, come dance away!'
He led her off. Just when begun,
She stopped, and cried: 'Some other tune!'
Then whispered in the piper's ear
So loud that every one could hear:
'I'd have you play out *Jumping John.*'
He tuned his reed and tried his drone,
The pipes scream out her favourite jig.
She knacked[5] her thumbs and stood her trig,[6]
Then cocked her belly up a little,
Then wet her fingers with her spittle;

[5] snapped [6] took up her position

So off she goes. The collier lad
Sprung from the floor and danced like mad.
They sweep each corner of the room,
And all stand clear where'er they come.
They dance, and tire the piper out,
And all's concluded with a shout.

Old Bessy next was taken in.
She curled her nose and cocked her chin,
Then held her skirts on either side,
And kneeled and cried: 'Up with the bride!'
'Come, piper,' says the good old woman,
'Play me *The Joyful Days are Comin.*
I'll dance for joy, upon my life,
For now my daughter's made a wife.'
The old wife did what limbs could do.
'Well danced, old Bessy!' cried the crew.
The goody laughed, and showed her teeth,
And said: 'Ah, sirs, I have no breath.
I once was thought right good at this.'
So bowed and mumbled up a kiss.

The gladsome night doth now approach.
The barrel's found no more's to broach.
There's but a pipe for everyone;
The dear tobacco's almost gone.
The candles in their sockets wink,
Now sweat, now drop, then die and stink.
Intoxicating fumes arise.
They reel, and rub their drowsy eyes.
Dead drunk, some tumble on the floor,
And swim in what they'd drunk before.
'Hiccup,' cries one. 'Reach me your hand.
The house turns round. I cannot stand.'
So now the drunken senseless crew
Break pipes, spill drink, piss, shit and spew.
The sleepy hens now mount their balk,
Ducks quack, flap wings, and homewards walk.
The labouring peasant, weary grown,
Embraces night and trudges home.

Edward Chicken (1698–1746)

The posset made, the bride is led
In great procession to her bed.
The females with an edict come
That all the men depart the room.
When young and old and all are out,
They shut the doors and spy about.
A general search is quickly made
Lest any lie in ambuscade.
So when they think all places sure,
And holes and corners all secure,
That none could see nor none could hear,
Nor none rush in to make them fear,
Then one far wiser than the rest,
Who knew their way of bedding best,
Steps up to Jenny, bathed in tears,
And thus with counsel fills her ears:

'Come, wipe your face; for shame, don't cry.
We were all made with men to lie.
And Tommy, if I guess but right,
Will make you have a merry night.
Be courteous, kind, lie in his arms,
And let him rifle all your charms.
If he should rise, do you lie still,
He'll fall again, give him his will.
Lie close and keep your husband warm,
And, as I live, you'll get no harm.
Be mannerly in every posture.
Take this advice from Nanny Forster.'

Thus spoke, she ran and catched the bowl
Where currant cakes in ale did roll,
Then with a smile said: 'Jenny lass,
Come, here's thy health without a glass.'
Her arm supports it to her head,
She drinks, and gobbles up the bread.
So everyone their courses took.
Some watch for fear the men should look.
And some prepare t'undress the bride,
While others tame the posset's pride.

Some loose her head, and some her stays
And so undress her sundry ways;
Then quickly lay the bride in bed,
And bind a ribbon round her head.
Her neck and breasts are both displayed
And every charm in order laid,
Now all being ready for Tom's coming,
The doors are opened by the women.
Impatient Tommy rushes in,
And thinks that they have longsome been.
The maids unwilling to withdraw,
They must go out, for it's the law.
Now Tommy next must be undressed,
But which of them can do it best?
It is no matter, all assist,
Some at his feet, some at his breast.
Soon they undress the jolly blade,
And into bed he's fairly laid.

Between the sheets now view this pair,
And think what merry work was there.
The stocking thrown, the company gone,
And Tom and Jenny both alone.
No light was there but Jenny's charms,
And Tom all those in his own arms.
Now he is master of his wishes,
And treats her with a thousand kisses.
Young Tommy cocked, and Jenny spread,
So here I leave them both in bed.

JOHN DYER

THE LOOM AND FULLING-MILL

Next the industrious youth employs his care
To store soft yarn; and now he strains the warp
Along the garden-walk, or highway side,
Smoothing each thread; now fits it to the loom,

And sits before the work: from hand to hand
The thready shuttle glides along the lines,
Which open to the woof and shut altern;
And ever and anon, to firm the work,
Against the web is driv'n the noisy frame,
That o'er the level rushes, like a surge
Which, often dashing on the sandy beach,
Compacts the traveller's road: from hand to hand
Again, across the lines oft op'ning, glides
The thready shuttle, while the web apace
Increases, as the light of eastern skies,
Spread by the rosy fingers of the morn,
And all the fair expanse with beauty glows.
   Or if the broader mantle be the task,
He chuses some companion to his toil.
From side to side, with amicable aim,
Each to the other darts the nimble bolt,
While friendly converse, prompted by the work,
Kindles improvement in the op'ning mind.
   What need we name the sev'ral kinds of looms?
Those delicate, to whose fair-colour'd threads
Hang figur'd weights, whose various numbers guide
The artist's hand: he, unseen, flowr's, and trees,
And vales, and azure hills, unerring works:
Or that whose num'rous needles, glitt'ring bright,
Weave the warm hose to cover tender limbs;
Modern invention; modern is the want.
   Next from the slacken'd beam the woof, unroll'd,
Near some clear-sliding river, Aire or Stroud,
Is by the noisy fulling-mill receiv'd,
Where tumbling waters turn enormous wheels,
And hammers, rising and descending, learn
To imitate the industry of man.
   Oft the wet web is steep'd, and often rais'd,
Fast dripping, to the river's grassy bank,
And sinewy arms of men, with full-strain'd strength
Wring out the latent water: then up-hung
On rugged tenters, to the fervid sun
Its level surface, reeking, it expands,

Still brightening in each rigid discipline,
And gathering worth, as human life in pains,
Conflicts, and troubles. Soon the clothier's shears
And burler's thistle skim the surface sheen.

from *The Fleece*

THE BUILDING OF LEEDS

. . . Take we now our eastward course
To the rich fields of Burstal. Wide around
Hillock and valley, farm and village, smile;
And ruddy roofs and chimney-tops appear
Of busy Leeds, up-wafting to the clouds
The incense of thanksgiving: all is joy;
And trade and bus'ness guide the living scene,
Roll the full cars, adown the winding Aire
Load the slow-sailing barges, pile the pack
On the long tinkling train of slow-pac'd steeds.
As when a sunny day invites abroad
The sedulous ants, they issue from their cells
In bands unnumber'd, eager for their work,
O'er high o'er low they lift, they draw, they haste
With warm affection to each other's aid,
Repeat their virtuous efforts, and succeed.
Thus all is here in motion, all is life:
The creaking wain brings copious store of corn;
The grazier's sleeky kine obstruct the roads;
The neat-dress'd housewives, for the festal board
Crown'd with full baskets, in the field-way paths
Come tripping on; the echoing hills repeat
The stroke of axe and hammer; scaffolds rise,
And growing edifices; heaps of stone,
Beneath the chisel, beauteous shapes assume
Of frieze and column. Some, with even line,
New streets are marking in the neighb'ring fields,
And sacred domes of worship. Industry,
Which dignifies the artist, lifts the swain,

And the straw cottage to a palace turns,
Over the work presides. Such was the scene
Of hurrying Carthage, when the Trojan chief
First view'd her growing turrets: so appear
Th' increasing walls of busy Manchester,
Sheffield, and Birmingham, whose reddening fields
Rise and enlarge their suburbs. Lo! in throngs,
For every realm, the careful factors meet,
Whispering each other. In long ranks the bales,
Like War's bright files, beyond the sight extend.

from *The Fleece*

SOAME JENYNS

LIVING IN THE COUNTRY

But I, my lord, who, as you know,
Care little how these matters go,
And equally detest the strife
And usual joys of country life,
Have by good fortune little share
Of its diversions, or its care;
For seldom I with 'squires unite
Who hunt all day and drink all night;
Nor reckon wonderful inviting
A quarter-sessions, or cock-fighting.
But then no farm I occupy,
With sheep to rot, or cows to die:
Nor rage I much, or much despair,
Though in my hedge I find a snare;
Nor view I, with due admiration,
All the high honours here in fashion;
The great commissions of the quorum,
Terrors to all who come before them;
Militia scarlet-edg'd with gold,
Or the white staff high-sherriffs hold;

The representative's caressing,
The judge's bow, the bishop's blessing;
Nor can I for my soul delight
In the dull feast of neighbouring knight,
Who, if you send three days before,
In white gloves meets you at the door,
With superfluity of breeding
First makes you sick, and then with feeding:
Or if, with ceremony cloyed,
You would next time such plagues avoid,
And visit without previous notice,
'John, John, a coach! – I can't think who 'tis,'
My lady cries, who spies your coach,
Ere you the avenue approach;
'Lord, how unlucky! – washing day!
And all the men are in the hay!'
Entrance to gain is something hard,
The dogs all bark, the gates are barred;
The yard's with lines of linen crossed,
The hall door's locked, the key is lost:
These difficulties all o'ercome,
We reach at length the drawing-room;
Then there's such trampling overhead,
Madam you'd swear was brought to bed;
Miss in a hurry bursts her lock,
To get clean sleeves to hide her smock;
The servants run, the pewter clatters,
My lady dresses, calls, and chatters;
The cook-maid raves for want of butter,
Pigs squeak, fowls scream, and green geese flutter.
Now after three hours tedious waiting,
On all our neighbours' faults debating,
And having nine times viewed the garden,
In which there's nothing worth a farthing,
In comes my lady and the pudden:
'You will excuse, sir, – on a sudden' –
Then, that we may have four and four,
The bacon, fowls, and cauliflower

Their ancient unity divide,
The top one graces, one each side;
And by and by, the second course
Comes lagging like a distanced horse;
A salver then to church and king,
The butler swears, the glasses ring;
The cloth removed, the toasts go round,
Bawdy and politics abound;
And as the knight more tipsy waxes,
We damn all ministers and taxes.
At last the ruddy sun quite sunk,
The coachman tolerably drunk,
Whirling o'er hillocks, ruts, and stones,
Enough to dislocate one's bones,
We home return, a wondrous token
Of Heaven's kind care, with limbs unbroken.
Afflict us not, ye gods, though sinners,
With many days like this, or dinners!

from *An Epistle from the Country*

STEPHEN DUCK

THRESHING

Soon as the harvest hath laid bare the plains,
And barns well fill'd reward the farmer's pains;
What corn each sheaf will yield, intent to hear,
And guess from thence the profits of the year;
Or else impending ruin to prevent,
By paying, timely, threat'ning landlord's rent,
He calls his threshers forth: Around we stand,
With deep attention waiting his command:
To each our tasks he readily divides,
And pointing, to our different stations guides.
As he directs, to different barns we go;
Here two for wheat, and there for barley two.

But first, to shew what he expects to find,
These words, or words like these, disclose his mind:
'So dry the corn was carried from the field,
So easily 'twill thresh, so well 'twill yield;
Sure large day's work I well may hope for now;
Come strip, and try, let's see what you can do.'
Divested of our clothes, with flail in hand,
At a just distance, front to front we stand;
And first the threshall's[1] gently swung, to prove,
Whether with just exactness it will move:
That once secure, more quick we whirl them round,
From the strong plank our crab-tree staves rebound,
And echoing barns return the rattling sound.
Now in the air our knotty weapons fly;
And now with equal force descend from high:
Down one, one up, so well they keep the time,
The Cyclops' hammers could not truer chime;
Not with more heavy strokes could Etna groan,
When Vulcan forged the arms for Thetis' son.
In briny streams our sweat descends apace,
Drops from our locks, or trickles down our face
No intermission in our works we know;
The noisy threshall must for ever go.
Their master absent, others safely play:
The sleeping threshall doth itself betray.

from *The Thresher's Labour*

SCYTHING

The birds salute us as to work we go,
And a new life seems in our breasts to glow.
Across one's shoulder hangs a scythe well steeled,
The weapon destined to unclothe the field:
T'other supports the whetstone, scrip, and beer;
That for our scythes, and these ourselves to cheer.

[1] flail

And now the field designed our strength to try
Appears, and meets at last our longing eye;
The grass and ground each cheerfully surveys,
Willing to see which way th'advantage lays.
As the best man, each claims the foremost place,
And our first work seems but a sportive race:
With rapid force our well-whet blades we drive,
Strain every nerve, and blow for blow we give:
Tho' but this eminence the foremost gains,
Only t'excel the rest in toil and pains.
But when the scorching sun is mounted high,
And no kind barns with friendly shades are nigh,
Our weary scythes entangle in the grass,
And streams of sweat run trickling down apace;
Our sportive labour we too late lament,
And wish that strength again, we vainly spent.

*

With heat and labour tired, our scythes we quit,
Search out a shady tree, and down we sit;
From scrip and bottle hope new strength to gain;
But scrip and bottle too are tried in vain.
Down our parched throats we scarce the bread can get,
And quite o'er-spent with toil, but faintly eat;
Nor can the bottle only answer all,
Alas! the bottle and the beer's too small.
Our time slides on, we move from off the grass,
And each again betakes him to his place.
Not eager now, as late, our strength to prove,
But all contented regular to move:
Often we whet, as often view the sun,
To see how near his tedious race is run;
At length he veils his radiant face from sight,
And bids the weary traveller good night:
Homewards we move, but so much spent with toil,
We walk but slow, and rest at every stile.
Our good expecting wives, who think we stay,
Got to the door, soon eye us on the way;
Then from the pot the dumpling's catch'd in haste,
And homely by its side the bacon's placed.

Supper and sleep by morn new strength supply,
And out we set again our works to try:
But not so early quite, nor quite so fast,
As to our cost we did the morning past.

from *The Thresher's Labour*

CHRISTOPHER ANSTEY

A LETTER FROM BATH: IN WHICH MR BLUNDERHEAD GIVES A DESCRIPTION OF THE BATHING

This morning, dear mother, as soon as 'twas light,
I was waked by a noise that astonished me quite,
For in Tabitha's chamber I heard such a clatter,
I could not conceive what the deuce was the matter:
And, would you believe it? I went up and found her
In a blanket, with two lusty fellows around her,
Who both seemed a-going to carry her off in
A little black box just the size of a coffin:
Pray tell me, says I, what ye're doing of there?
'Why, masters, 'tis hard to be bilked of our fare,
And so we were thrusting her into a chair:
We don't see no reason for using us so,
For she bade us come hither, and now she won't go;
We've earned all the fare, for we both came and knocked her
Up, as soon as 'twas light, by advice of the doctor;
And this is a job that we often go after
For ladies that choose to go into the water.'
'But pray,' says I, 'Tabitha, what is your drift
To be covered in flannel instead of a shift?
'Tis all by the doctor's advice, I suppose,
That nothing is left to be seen but your nose:
I think if you really intend to go in,
'Twould do you more good if you stripped to the skin,
And if you've a mind for a frolic, i'faith
I'll just step and see you jump into the bath.'

So they hoisted her down just as safe and as well
And as snug as a Hod'mandod rides in his shell:
I fain would have gone to see Tabitha dip,
But they turned at a corner and gave me the slip,
Yet in searching about I had better success,
For I got to a place where the ladies undress;
Thinks I to myself they are after some fun,
And I'll see what they're doing as sure as a gun:
So I peeped at the door, and I saw a great mat
That covered a table, and got under that,
And laid myself down there, as snug and as still
(As a body may say) like a thief in a mill:
And of all the fine sights I have seen, my dear mother,
I never expect to behold such another:
How the ladies did giggle and set up their clacks,
All the while an old woman was rubbing their backs!
Oh! 'twas pretty to see them all put on their flannels,
And then take the water like so many spaniels,
And though all the while it grew hotter and hotter,
They swam just as if they were hunting an otter;
'Twas a glorious sight to behold the fair sex
All wading with gentlemen up to their necks,
And view them so prettily tumble and sprawl
In a great smoking kettle as big as our hall:
And today many persons of rank and condition
Were boiled by command of an able physician:
Dean Spavin, Dean Mangey, and Doctor de Squirt,
Were all sent from Cambridge to rub off their dirt;
Judge Scrub, and the worthy old Councillor Pest
Joined issue at once and went in with the rest:
And this they all said was exceedingly good
For strengthening the spirits, and mending the blood.
It pleased me to see how they all were inclined
To lengthen their lives for the good of mankind;
For I ne'er would believe that a bishop or judge
Can fancy old Satan may owe him a grudge,
Though some think the lawyer may choose to demur,
And the priest till another occasion defer,

And both to be better prepared for herea'ter,
Take a snack of the brimstone contained in the water.
But, what is surprising, no mortal e'er viewed
Any one of the physical gentlemen stewed;
Since the day that King Bladud first found out the bogs,
And thought them so good for himself and his hogs,
Not one of the faculty ever has tried
These excellent waters to cure his own hide:
Though many a skilful and learned physician,
With candour, good sense, and profound erudition,
Obliges the world with the fruits of his brain
Their nature and hidden effects to explain:
Thus Chiron advised Madam Thetis to take
And dip her poor child in the Stygian Lake,
But the worthy old doctor was not such an elf
As ever to venture his carcase himself:
So Jason's good wife used to set on a pot,
And put in at once all the patients she got,
But thought it sufficient to give her direction,
Without being coddled to mend her complexion:
And I never have heard that she wrote any treatise
To tell what the virtue of water and heat is.
You cannot conceive what a number of ladies
Were washed in the water the same as our maid is:
Old Baron Vanteazer, a man of great wealth,
Brought his lady the Baroness here for her health;
The Baroness bathes, and she says that her case
Has been hit to a hair, and is mending apace:
And this is a point all the learned agree on,
The Baron has met with the fate of Acteon;
Who while he peeped into the bath had the luck
To find himself suddenly changed to a buck.
Miss Scratchit went in and the Countess of Scales,
Both ladies of very great fashion in Wales;
Then all of a sudden two persons of worth
My Lady Pandora MacScurvey came forth,
With General Sulphur arrived from the north.
So Tabby, you see, had the honour of washing
With folk of distinction and very high fashion,

But in spite of good company, poor little soul,
She shook both her ears like a mouse in a bowl.

Odds bobs! how delighted I was unawares
With the fiddles I heard in the room above stairs,
For music is wholesome the doctors all think
For ladies that bathe, and for ladies that drink;
And that's the opinion of Robin our driver,
Who whistles his nags while they stand at the river:
They say it is right that for every glass
A tune you should take, that the water may pass:
So while little Tabby was washing her rump,
The ladies kept drinking it out of a pump.
I've a deal more to say, but am loath to intrude
On your time, my dear mother, so now I'll conclude.

Bath, 1766 *Simkin Blunderhead*

from *The New Bath Guide*

OLIVER GOLDSMITH

From THE DESERTED VILLAGE

i

Sweet smiling village, loveliest of the lawn,
Thy sports are fled, and all thy charms withdrawn;
Amidst thy bowers the tyrant's hand is seen,
And desolation saddens all thy green:
One only master grasps the whole domain,
And half a tillage stints thy smiling plain:
No more thy glassy brook reflects the day,
But chok'd with sedges, works its weedy way.
Along thy glades, a solitary guest,
The hollow-sounding bittern guards its nest;
Amidst thy desert walks the lapwing flies,
And tires their echoes with unvaried cries.

Sunk are thy bowers, in shapeless ruin all,
And the long grass o'ertops the mouldering wall;
And, trembling, shrinking from the spoiler's hand,
Far, far away, thy children leave the land.

Ill fares the land, to hastening ills a prey,
Where wealth accumulates, and men decay:
Princes and lords may flourish, or may fade;
A breath can make them, as a breath has made;
But a bold peasantry, their country's pride,
When once destroy'd, can never be supplied.

A time there was, ere England's griefs began,
When every rood of ground maintain'd its man;
For him light labour spread her wholesome store,
Just gave what life requir'd, but gave no more:
His best companions, innocence and health;
And his best riches, ignorance of wealth.

But times are alter'd; trade's unfeeling train
Usurp the land and dispossess the swain;
Along the lawn, where scatter'd hamlets rose,
Unwieldy wealth, and cumbrous pomp repose;
And every want to opulence allied,
And every pang that folly pays to pride.
Those gentle hours that plenty bade to bloom,
Those calm desires that ask'd but little room,
Those healthful sports that grac'd the peaceful scene,
Liv'd in each look, and brighten'd all the green;
These, far departing, seek a kinder shore,
And rural mirth and manners are no more.

ii

Sweet was the sound, when oft at evening's close
Up yonder hill the village murmur rose;
There, as I pass'd with careless steps and slow,
The mingling notes came soften'd from below;
The swain responsive as the milkmaid sung,
The sober herd that low'd to meet their young;

The noisy geese that gabbled o'er the pool,
The playful children just let loose from school;
The watchdog's voice that bay'd the whisp'ring wind,
And the loud laugh that spoke the vacant mind;
These all in sweet confusion sought the shade,
And fill'd each pause the nightingale had made.
But now the sounds of population fail,
No cheerful murmurs fluctuate in the gale,
No busy steps the grass-grown footway tread,
For all the bloomy flush of life is fled.
All but yon widow'd, solitary thing,
That feebly bends beside the plashy spring:
She, wretched matron, forc'd in age, for bread,
To strip the brook with mantling cresses spread,
To pick her wintry faggot from the thorn,
To seek her nightly shed, and weep till morn;
She only left of all the harmless train,
The sad historian of the pensive plain.

Near yonder copse, where once the garden smil'd,
And still where many a garden flower grows wild;
There, where a few torn shrubs the place disclose,
The village preacher's modest mansion rose.
A man he was to all the country dear,
And passing rich with forty pounds a year;
Remote from towns he ran his godly race,
Nor e'er had chang'd, nor wished to change his place;
Unpractis'd he to fawn, or seek for power,
By doctrines fashion'd to the varying hour;
Far other aims his heart had learn'd to prize,
More skill'd to raise the wretched than to rise.
His house was known to all the vagrant train,
He chid their wanderings, but reliev'd their pain;
The long remember'd beggar was his guest,
Whose beard descending swept his aged breast;
The ruin'd spendthrift, now no longer proud,
Claim'd kindred there, and had his claims allow'd;
The broken soldier, kindly bade to stay,
Sat by his fire, and talk'd the night away;

Wept o'er his wounds, or tales of sorrow done,
Shoulder'd his crutch, and show'd how fields were won.
Pleas'd with his guests, the good man learned to glow,
And quite forgot their vices in their woe;
Careless their merits, or their faults to scan,
His pity gave ere charity began.

iii

Beside yon straggling fence that skirts the way,
With blossom'd furze unprofitably gay,
There, in his noisy mansion, skill'd to rule,
The village master taught his little school;
A man severe he was, and stern to view;
I knew him well, and every truant knew;
Well had the boding tremblers learn'd to trace
The day's disasters in his morning face;
Full well they laugh'd, with counterfeited glee,
At all his jokes, for many a joke had he;
Full well the busy whisper, circling round,
Convey'd the dismal tidings when he frown'd;
Yet he was kind; or if severe in aught,
The love he bore to learning was in fault;
The village all declar'd how much he knew;
'Twas certain he could write, and cypher too;
Lands he could measure, terms and tides presage,
And even the story ran that he could gauge.
In arguing too, the parson own'd his skill,
For e'en though vanquish'd, he could argue still;
While words of learned length and thundering sound
Amaz'd the gazing rustics rang'd around,
And still they gaz'd, and still the wonder grew,
That one small head could carry all he knew.

But past is all his fame. The very spot
Where many a time he triumph'd, is forgot.
Near yonder thorn, that lifts its head on high,
Where once the sign-post caught the passing eye,
Low lies that house where nut-brown draughts inspir'd,
Where grey-beard mirth and smiling toil retir'd,

Where village statesmen talk'd with looks profound,
And news much older than their ale went round.
Imagination fondly stoops to trace
The parlour splendours of that festive place;
The white-wash'd wall, the nicely sanded floor,
The varnish'd clock that click'd behind the door;
The chest contriv'd a double debt to pay,
A bed by night, a chest of drawers by day;
The pictures plac'd for ornament and use,
The twelve good rules, the royal game of goose;
The hearth, except when winter chill'd the day,
With aspen boughs, and flowers, and fennel gay;
While broken tea-cups, wisely kept for show,
Rang'd o'er the chimney, glisten'd in a row.

Vain transitory splendours! could not all
Reprieve the tottering mansion from its fall!
Obscure it sinks, nor shall it more impart
An hour's importance to the poor man's heart;
Thither no more the peasant shall repair
To sweet oblivion of his daily care;
No more the farmer's news, the barber's tale,
No more the wood-man's ballad shall prevail;
No more the smith his dusky brow shall clear,
Relax his ponderous strength, and lean to hear;
The host himself no longer shall be found
Careful to see the mantling bliss go round;
Nor the coy maid, half willing to be press'd,
Shall kiss the cup to pass it to the rest.

THE HAUNCH OF VENISON

Thanks, my Lord, for your venison, for finer or fatter
Never rang'd in a forest, or smok'd in a platter;
The haunch was a picture for painters to study,
The fat was so white, and the lean was so ruddy.
Though my stomach was sharp, I could scarce help regretting
To spoil such a delicate picture by eating;

I had thoughts, in my chambers, to place it in view,
To be shown to my friends as a piece of *virtù*;
As in some Irish houses, where things are so so,
One gammon of bacon hangs up for a show:
But for eating a rasher of what they take pride in,
They'd as soon think of eating the pan it is fried in.
But hold – let me pause – Don't I hear you pronounce
This tale of the bacon a damnable bounce?
Well, suppose it a bounce – sure a poet may try,
By a bounce now and then, to get courage to fly.

But, my Lord, it's no bounce: I protest in my turn,
It's a truth – and your Lordship may ask Mr Byrne.
To go on with my tale – as I gaz'd on the haunch,
I thought of a friend that was trusty and staunch;
So I cut it, and sent it to Reynolds undress'd,
To paint it, or eat it, just as he lik'd best.
Of the neck and the breast I had next to dispose;
'Twas a neck and a breast – that might rival Monroe's:—
But in parting with these I was puzzled again,
With the how, and the who, and the where, and the when.
There's Howard, and Coley, and Hogarth, and Hiff,
I think they love venison – I know they love beef;
There's my countryman Higgins – Oh! let him alone,
For making a blunder, or picking a bone.
But hang it – to poets who seldom can eat,
Your very good mutton's a very good treat;
Such dainties to them, their health it might hurt,
It's like sending them ruffles, when wanting a shirt.
While thus I debated, in reverie centred,
An acquaintance, a friend as he call'd himself, enter'd;
An under-bred, fine-spoken fellow was he,
And he smil'd as he look'd at the venison and me.
'What have we got here? – Why this is good eating!
Your own, I suppose – or is it in waiting?'
'Why, whose should it be?' cried I with a flounce,
'I get these things often;' – but that was a bounce:
'Some lords, my acquaintance, that settle the nation,
Are pleas'd to be kind – but I hate ostentation.'

*

'If that be the case, then,' cried he, very gay,
'I'm glad I have taken this house in my way.
Tomorrow you take a poor dinner with me;
No words – I insist on't – precisely at three:
We'll have Johnson, and Burke; all the wits will be there;
My acquaintance is slight, or I'd ask my Lord Clare.
And now that I think on't, as I am a sinner!
We wanted this venison to make out the dinner.
What say you – a pasty? it shall, and it must,
And my wife, little Kitty, is famous for crust.
Here, porter! – this venison with me to Mile-end;
No stirring – I beg – my dear friend – my dear friend!'
Thus snatching his hat, he brush'd off like the wind,
And the porter and eatables follow'd behind.

Left alone to reflect, having emptied my shelf,
'And nobody with me at sea but myself,'
Though I could not help thinking my gentleman hasty,
Yet Johnson, and Burke, and a good venison pasty,
Were things that I never dislik'd in my life,
Though clogg'd with a coxcomb, and Kitty his wife.
So next day, in due splendour to make my approach,
I drove to his door in my own hackney-coach.

When come to the place where we all were to dine,
(A chair-lumber'd closet just twelve feet by nine:)
My friend bade me welcome, but struck me quite dumb,
With tidings that Johnson and Burke would not come;
'For I knew it,' he cried, 'both eternally fail,
The one with his speeches, and t'other with Thrale;
But no matter, I'll warrant we'll make up the party
With two full as clever, and ten times as hearty.
The one is a Scotchman, the other a Jew,
They're both of them merry and authors like you:
The one writes the *Snarler*, the other the *Scourge*;
Some think he writes *Cinna* – he owns to *Panurge*.'
While thus he describ'd them by trade and by name,
They enter'd, and dinner was serv'd as they came.

At the top a fried liver and bacon were seen,
At the bottom was tripe in a swingeing tureen;

At the sides there was spinach and pudding made hot;
In the middle a place where the pasty – was not.
Now, my Lord, as for tripe, it's my utter aversion,
And your bacon I hate like a Turk or a Persian;
So there I sat stuck, like a horse in a pound,
While the bacon and liver went merrily round.
But what vex'd me most was that d—'d Scottish rogue,
With his long-winded speeches, his smiles and his brogue;
And, 'Madam,' quoth he, 'may this bite be my poison,
A prettier dinner I never set eyes on;
Pray a slice of your liver, though may I be curs'd,
But I've eat of your tripe till I'm ready to burst.'
'The tripe,' quoth the Jew, with his chocolate cheek,
'I could dine on this tripe seven days in the week:
I like these here dinners so pretty and small;
But your friend there, the Doctor, eats nothing at all.'
'O—Oh!' quoth my friend, 'he'll come on in a trice,
He's keeping a corner for something that's nice:
There's a pasty' – 'A pasty!' repeated the Jew,
'I don't care if I keep a corner for't too.'
'What the de'il, mon, a pasty!' re-echoed the Scot,
'Though splitting, I'll still keep a corner for thot.'
'We'll all keep a corner,' the lady cried out;
'We'll all keep a corner,' was echoed about.
While thus we resolv'd, and the pasty delay'd,
With looks that quite petrified, enter'd the maid;
A visage so sad, and so pale with affright,
Wak'd Priam in drawing his curtains by night.
But we quickly found out, for who could mistake her?
That she came with some terrible news from the baker:
And so it fell out, for that negligent sloven
Had shut out the pasty on shutting his oven.
Sad Philomel thus – but let similes drop –
And now that I think on't, the story may stop.
To be plain, my good Lord, it's but labour misplaced
To send such good verses to one of your taste;
You've got an odd something – a kind of discerning –
A relish – a taste – sicken'd over by learning;

At least it's your temper, as very well known,
That you think very slightly of all that's your own:
So, perhaps, in your habits of thinking amiss,
  You may make a mistake, and think slightly of this.

DESCRIPTION OF AN AUTHOR'S BEDCHAMBER

Where the Red Lion flaring o'er the way,
Invites each passing stranger that can pay;
Where Calvert's butt, and Parson's black champagne,
Regale the drabs and bloods of Drury-lane;
There in a lonely room, from bailiffs snug,
The Muse found Scroggen stretch'd beneath a rug;
A window, patch'd with paper, lent a ray,
That dimly show'd the state in which he lay;
The sanded floor that grits beneath the tread;
The humid wall with paltry pictures spread:
The royal game of goose was there in view,
And the twelve rules the royal martyr drew;
The seasons, fram'd with listing, found a place,
And above prince William show'd his lamp-black face;
The morn was cold, he views with keen desire
The rusty grate unconscious of a fire;
With beer and milk arrears the frieze was scor'd,
And five crack'd teacups dress'd the chimney board;
A nightcap deck'd his brows instead of bay,
A cap by night – a stocking all the day!

ANONYMOUS

MONSIEUR À-LA-MODE

Take a creature that nature has form'd without brains,
Whose skull nought but nonsense and sonnets contains;

With a mind where conceit with folly's ally'd,
Set off by assurance and unmeaning pride;
With common-place jests for to tickle the ear
With mirth, where no wisdom could ever appear;
That to the defenceless can strut and look brave,
Although he to cowardice shews he's a slave.
And now for to dress up my beau with a grace,
Let a well frizzled wig be set off from his face;
With a bag quite in taste, from Paris just come,
That was made and tied up by Monsieur Frisson:
With powder quite grey, then his head is complete;
If dress'd in the fashion, no matter for wit;
With a pretty black beaver tuck'd under his arm,
If plac'd on his head, it might keep it too warm;
Then a black solitaire his neck to adorn,
Like those of Versailles by the courtiers there worn;
His hands must be cover'd with fine Brussels lace,
With a sparkling brilliant his finger to grace;
Next a coat of embroidery from foreigners come,
'Twou'd be quite unpolite to have one wrought at home;
With cobweb silk stocking his legs to befriend,
Two pair underneath, his lank calves to amend;
With breeches in winter would cause one to freeze,
To add to his height, must not cover his knees;
A pair of smart pumps made up of grain'd leather;
So thin he can't venture to tread on a feather;
His buckles like diamonds must glitter and shine,
Should they cost fifty pounds they would not be too fine;
A repeater by Graham, which the hours reveals,
Almost over-balanc'd with knick-knacks and seals;
A mouchoir with musk his spirits to cheer,
Though he scents the whole room, that no soul can come near;
A gold-hilted sword with jewels inlaid,
So the scabbard's but cane, no matter for blade;
A word-knot of ribband to answer his dress,
Most completely tied up with tassles of lace;
Thus fully equipp'd and attir'd for show,
Observe, pray, ye belles, that fam'd thing call'd a beau.

WILLIAM COWPER

THE YEARLY DISTRESS, OR, TITHING TIME AT STOCK IN ESSEX

Come, ponder well, for 'tis no jest,
  To laugh it would be wrong;
The troubles of a worthy priest
  The burthen of my song.

This priest he merry is and blithe
  Three quarters of the year,
But oh! it cuts him like a scythe
  When tithing time draws near.

He then is full of frights and fears,
  As one at point to die,
And long before the day appears
  He heaves up many a sigh.

For then the farmers come jog, jog,
  Along the miry road,
Each heart as heavy as a log,
  To make their payments good.

In sooth, the sorrow of such days
  Is not to be express'd,
When he that takes and he that pays
  Are both alike distress'd.

Now all unwelcome, at his gates
  The clumsy swains alight,
With rueful faces and bald pates –
  He trembles at the sight.

And well he may, for well he knows
  Each bumpkin of the clan,
Instead of paying what he owes,
  Will cheat him if he can.

So in they come – each makes his leg,
  And flings his head before,
And looks as if he came to beg,
  And not to quit a score.

'And how does miss and madam do,
  The little boy and all?'
'All tight and well: and how do you,
  Good Mr What-d'ye-call?'

The dinner comes, and down they sit:
  Were e'er such hungry folk?
There's little talking and no wit;
  It is no time to joke.

One wipes his nose upon his sleeve,
  One spits upon the floor,
Yet, not to give offence or grieve,
  Holds up the cloth before.

The punch goes round, and they are dull
  And lumpish still as ever;
Like barrels with their bellies full,
  They only weigh the heavier.

At length the busy time begins,
  'Come, neighbours, we must wag' –
The money chinks, down drop their chins,
  Each lugging out his bag.

One talks of mildew and of frost,
  And one of storms of hail,
And one, of pigs that he has lost
  By maggots at the tail.

Quoth one, A rarer man than you
  In pulpit none shall hear:
But yet, methinks, to tell you true,
  You sell it plaguy dear.

Oh, why are farmers made so coarse,
  Or clergy made so fine!
A kick that scarce would move a horse
  May kill a sound divine.

Then let the boobies stay at home;
  'Twould cost him, I dare say,
Less trouble taking twice the sum,
  Without the clowns that pay.

SUBURBAN LIFE

  Suburban villas, highway-side retreats,
That dread th' encroachment of our growing streets,
Tight boxes, neatly sash'd, and in a blaze
With all a July sun's collected rays,
Delight the citizen, who, gasping there,
Breathes clouds of dust, and calls it country air.
Oh sweet retirement, who would balk the thought,
That could afford retirement, or could not?
'Tis such an easy walk, so smooth and straight,
The second milestone fronts the garden gate;
A step if fair, and, if a shower approach,
You find safe shelter in the next stage-coach.
There, prison'd in a parlour snug and small,
Like bottled wasps upon a southern wall,
The man of business and his friends compress'd,
Forget their labours, and yet find no rest;
But still 'tis rural – trees are to be seen
From ev'ry window, and the fields are green;
Ducks paddle in the pond before the door,
And what could a remoter scene show more?

from *Retirement*

CAPABILITY BROWN

Improvement too, the idol of the age,
Is fed with many a victim. Lo, he comes!
Th' omnipotent magician, Brown, appears!
Down falls the venerable pile, th' abode
Of our forefathers – a grave whisker'd race,

But tasteless. Springs a palace in its stead,
But in a distant spot; where, more expos'd,
It may enjoy th' advantage of the north,
And aguish east, till time shall have transform'd
Those naked acres to a shelt'ring grove.
He speaks. The lake in front becomes a lawn;
Woods vanish, hills subside, and valleys rise:
And streams, as if created for his use,
Pursue the track of his directing wand,
Sinuous or straight, now rapid and now slow,
Now murm'ring soft, now roaring in cascades –
Ev'n as he bids! Th' enraptur'd owner smiles.
'Tis finish'd, and yet, finish'd as it seems,
Still wants a grace, the loveliest it could show,
A mine to satisfy th' enormous cost.
Drain'd to the last poor item of his wealth,
He sighs, departs, and leaves th' accomplish'd plan
That he has touch'd, retouch'd, many a long day
Labour'd, and many a night pursu'd in dreams,
Just when it meets his hopes, and proves the heav'n
He wanted, for a wealthier to enjoy!

from *The Task*, Book III

ROBERT LLOYD

THE CIT'S COUNTRY BOX, 1757

The wealthy Cit, grown old in trade,
Now wishes for the rural shade,
And buckles to his one-horse chair,
Old Dobbin, or the founder'd mare;
While wedg'd in closely by his side,
Sits Madam, his unwieldy bride,
With Jacky on a stool before 'em,
And out they jog in due decorum.

Robert Lloyd (1733–1764)

Scarce past the turnpike half a mile,
How all the country seems to smile!
And as they slowly jog together,
The Cit commends the road and weather;
While Madam dotes upon the trees,
And longs for ev'ry house she sees,
Admires its views, its situation,
And thus she opens her oration.

What signify the loads of wealth,
Without that richest jewel, health?
Excuse the fondness of a wife,
Who dotes upon your precious life!
Such easeless toil, such constant care,
Is more than human strength can bear.
One may observe it in your face –
Indeed, my dear, you break apace:
And nothing can your health repair,
But exercise and country air.
Sir Traffic has a house, you know,
About a mile from Cheney-Row;
He's a *good* man, indeed 'tis true,
But not so *warm*, my dear, as you:
And folks are always apt to sneer –
One would not be out-done my dear!

Sir Traffic's name so well apply'd
Awak'd his brother merchant's pride;
And Thrifty, who had all his life
Paid utmost deference to his wife,
Confess'd her arguments had reason,
And by th' approaching summer season,
Draws a few hundreds from the stocks,
And purchases his Country Box.

Some three or four mile out of town,
(An hour's ride will bring you down,)
He fixes on his choice abode,
Not half a furlong from the road:
And so convenient does it lay,
The stages pass it ev'ry day:

And then so snug, so mighty pretty,
To have an house so near the city!
Take but your places at the Boar
You're set down at the very door.

Well then, suppose them fix'd at last,
White-washing, painting, scrubbing past,
Hugging themselves in ease and clover,
With all the fuss of moving over;
Lo, a new heap of whims are bred!
And wanton in my lady's head.

Well to be sure, it must be own'd,
It is a charming spot of ground;
So sweet a distance for a ride,
And all about so *countrified*!
'Twould come but to a trifling price
To make it quite a paradise;
I cannot bear those nasty rails,
Those ugly broken mouldy pales:
Suppose, my dear, instead of these,
We build a railing, all Chinese.
Although one hates to be expos'd;
'Tis dismal to be thus inclos'd;
One hardly any object sees –
I wish you'd fell those odious trees.
Objects continual passing by
Were something to amuse the eye,
But to be pent within the walls –
One might as well be at St Paul's.
Our house, beholders would adore,
Was there a level lawn before,
Nothing its views to incommode,
But quite laid open to the road;
While ev'ry trav'ler in amaze,
Should on our little mansion gaze,
And pointing to the choice retreat,
Cry, that's Sir Thrifty's country seat.

No doubt her arguments prevail,
For Madam's taste can never fail.

*

Robert Lloyd (1733–1764)

Blest age! when all men may procure,
The title of a Connoisseur;
When noble and ignoble herd,
Are govern'd by a single word;
Though, like the royal German dames,
It bears an hundred Christian names;
As Genius, Fancy, Judgement, Goût,
Whim, Caprice, Je-ne-scai-quoi, Virtù.
Which appellations all describe
Taste, and the modern tasteful tribe.

Now bricklay'rs, carpenters, and joiners,
With Chinese artists, and designers,
Produce their schemes of alteration,
To work this wond'rous reformation.
The useful dome, which secret stood,
Embosom'd in the yew-tree's wood,
The trav'ler with amazement sees
A temple, Gothic, or Chinese,
With many a bell, and tawdry rag on,
And crested with a sprawling dragon;
A wooden arch is bent astride
A ditch of water, four foot wide,
With angles, curves, and zigzag lines,
From Halfpenny's exact designs.
In front, a level lawn is seen,
Without a shrub upon the green,
Where Taste would want its first great law,
But for skulking, sly *ha-ha*,
By whose miraculous assistance,
You gain a prospect two fields distance.
And now from Hyde-Park Corner come
The Gods of Athens, and of Rome.
Here squabby Cupids take their places,
With Venus, and the clumsy Graces:
Apollo there, with aim so clever,
Stretches his leaden bow for ever;
And there, without the pow'r to fly,
Stands fix'd a tip-toe Mercury.

*

The villa thus completely grac'd,
All own that Thrifty has a Taste;
And Madam's female friends, and cousins,
With common-council-men, by dozens,
Flock every Sunday to the seat,
To stare about them, and to eat.

CHIT-CHAT

Mrs Brown
Is Mistress Scot at home, my dear?

Servant
Ma'm, is it you? I'm glad you're here.
My *Missess*, tho' resolv'd to wait,
Is quite *unpatient* – 'tis so late.
She fancy'd you would not come down,
– But pray walk in, Ma'm – Mrs Brown.

Mrs Scot
Your servant, Madam. Well, I swear
I'd giv'n you over – Child, a chair.
Pray, Ma'm, be seated.

Mrs Brown
Lard! my dear,
I vow I'm almost dead with fear.
There is such *scrouging* and such *squeeging*,
The folks are all so disobliging;
And then the waggons, carts and drays
So clog up all these narrow ways,
What with the bustle and the throng,
I wonder how I got along.
Besides the walk is so *immense* –
Not that I grudge a coach expense,
But then it jumbles me to death,
– And I was always short of breath.
How can you live so far, my dear?
It's quite a journey to come here.

Mrs Scot

Lard! Ma'm, I left it all to *Him*,
Husbands you know, will have their whim.
He took this house. – This house! this den. –
See but the temper of some men.
And I, forsooth, am hither hurl'd,
To live *quite out of all the world.*
Husband, indeed!

Mrs Brown

Hist! lower, pray,
The child hears every word you say.
See how he looks –

Mrs Scot

Jacky, come here,
There's a good boy, look up, my dear,
'Twas not papa we talk'd about.
– Surely he cannot find it out.

Mrs Brown

See how the urchin holds his hands.
Upon my life he understands.
– There's a sweet child, come, kiss me, come,
Will Jacky have a sugar-plumb?

Mrs Scot

This Person, Madam (call him so,
And then the child will never know)
From house to house would ramble out,
And every night a drunken-bout.
For at a tavern he will spend
His twenty shillings with a friend.
Your rabbits fricasseed and chicken,
With curious choice of dainty picking,
Each night got ready at the Crown,
With port and punch to wash 'em down,
Would scarcely serve this belly-glutton,
Whilst we must starve on mutton, mutton.

Mrs Brown

My good man, too – Lord bless us! Wives
Are born to lead unhappy lives,

Altho' his profits bring him clear
Almost two hundred pounds a year,
Keeps me of cash so short and bare,
That *I have not a gown to wear*;
Except my robe, and yellow sack,
And this old lutestring on my back.
– But we've no time, my dear, to waste.
Come, where's your cardinal, make haste.
The King, God bless his majesty, I say,
Goes to the House of Lords today,
In a fine painted coach and eight,
And rides along in all his state.
And then the Queen –

Mrs Scot

Aye, aye, you know,
Great folks can always make a show.
But tell me, do – I've never seen
Her present majesty, the Queen.

Mrs Brown

Lard! we've no time for talking now,
Hark! – one – two – three – 'tis *twelve* I vow.

Mrs Scot

Kitty, my things, – I'll soon have done,
It's time enough, you know, at *one*.
– Why, girl! see how the creature stands!
Some water here, to wash my hands.
– Be quick – why sure the gipsy sleeps!
– Look how the drawling dawdle creeps.
That basin there – why don't you pour,
Go on, I say – stop, stop – no more –
Lud – I could beat the hussey down,
She's pour'd it all upon my gown.
– Bring me my ruffles – can'st not mind?
And pin my handkerchief behind.
Sure thou hast awkwardness enough,
Go – fetch my gloves, and fan, and muff.

– Well, heav'n be prais'd – this work is done,
I'm ready now, my dear – let's run.
Girl, – put that bottle on the shelf,
And bring me back the key yourself.

Mrs Brown
That clouded silk becomes you much,
I wonder how you meet with such,
But you've a charming taste in dress.
What might it cost you, Madam?

Mrs Scot
Guess.

Mrs Brown
Oh! that's impossible – for I
Am in the world the worst to buy.

Mrs Scot
I never love to bargain hard,
Five shillings, as I think, a yard.
– I was afraid it should be gone –
'Twas what I'd set my heart upon.

Mrs Brown
Indeed you bargain'd with success,
For it's a most delightful dress.
Besides, it fits you to a hair,
And then 'tis slop'd with such an air.

Mrs Scot
I'm glad you think so, – Kitty, here,
Bring me my cardinal, my dear.
Jacky, my love, nay don't you cry,
Take *you* abroad! – indeed not I;
For all the Bugaboos to fright ye –
Besides, the naughty horse will bite ye;
With such a mob about the street,
Bless me, they'll tread you under feet.
Whine as you please, I'll have no blame,
You'd better blubber, than be lame.

The more you cry, the less you'll —
– Come, come then, give mamma a kiss,
Kitty, I say, here take the boy,
And fetch him down the last new toy,
Make him as merry as you can,
– There, go to Kitty – there's a *man.*
Call in the dog, and shut the door,
Now, Ma'm,

Mrs Brown
Oh Lard!

Mrs Scot
Pray go before.

Mrs Brown
I can't indeed, now.

Mrs Scot
Madam, pray.

Mrs Brown
Well then, for once, I'll lead the way.

Mrs Scot
Lard! what an uproar! what a throng!
How shall we do to get along?
What will become of us? – look here,
Here's all the king's horse-guards, my dear.
Let us cross over – haste, be quick,
– Pray sir, take care – your horse will kick.
He'll kill his rider – he's so wild.
– I'm glad I did not bring the child.

Mrs Brown
Don't be afraid, my dear, come on,
Why don't you see the guards are gone?

Mrs Scot
Well, I begin to draw my breath;
But I was almost scar'd to death.
For when a horse rears up and capers,
It always puts me in the vapours.
For as I live, – nay, don't you laugh,
I'd rather see a toad by half,

They kick and prance, and look so bold,
It makes my very blood run cold.
But let's go forward – come, be quick,
The crowd again grows vastly thick.

Mrs Brown
Come you from Palace-yard, old dame?

Old Woman
Troth, do I, my young ladies, why?

Mrs Brown
Was it much crowded when you came?

Mrs Scot
And is his majesty gone by?

Mrs Brown
Can we get in, old lady, pray
To see him robe himself to-day?

Mrs Scot
Can you direct us, dame?

Old Woman
Endeavour,
Troy could not stand a siege for ever.
By frequent trying, Troy was won,
All things, by trying, may be done.

Mrs Brown
Go thy ways, Proverbs – well – she's gone –
Shall we turn back, or venture on?
Look how the folks press on before,
And throng impatient at the door.

Mrs Scot
Perdigious! I can hardly stand,
Lord bless me, Mrs Brown, your hand;
And you, my dear, take hold of hers,
For we must stick as close as burrs,
Or in this racket, noise and pother,
We certainly shall lose each other.

– Good God! my cardinal and sack
Are almost torn from off my back.
Lard, I shall faint – Oh Lud – my breast –
I'm crush'd to atoms, I protest.
God bless me – I have dropt my fan,
– Pray did you see it, honest man?

Man

I, madam! no, – indeed, I fear
You'll meet with some misfortune here.
– Stand back, I say – pray, sir, forbear –
Why, don't you see the ladies there?
Put yourselves under my direction,
Ladies, I'll be your safe protection.

Mrs Scot

You're very kind, sir; truly few
Are half so complaisant as you.
We shall be glad at any day
This obligation to repay,
And you'll be always sure to meet
A welcome, sir, in – Lard! the street
Bears such a name, I can't tell how
To tell him where I live, I vow.
– Mercy! what's all this noise and stir?
Pray is the King a coming, sir?

Man

No – don't you hear the people shout?
'Tis Mr Pitt, just *going* out.

Mrs Brown

Aye, there he goes, pray heav'n bless him!
Well may the people all caress him.
– Lord, how my husband us'd to sit,
And drink success to honest Pitt,
And happy o'er his evening cheer,
Cry, you shall pledge this toast, my dear.

Man

Hist – silence – don't you hear the drumming?
Now, ladies, now, the King's a coming.

There, don't you see the guards approach?

Mrs Brown
Which is the King?

Mrs Scot
Which is the coach?

Scotchman
Which is the noble Earl of Bute,
Geud-faith, I'll *gi* him a salute.
For he's the Laird of aw our clan,
Troth, he's a bonny muckle man.

Man
Here comes the coach, so very slow
As if it ne'er was made to go,
In all the gingerbread of state,
And staggering under its own weight.

Mrs Scot
Upon my word, its *monstrous* fine!
Would half the gold upon't were mine!
How gaudy all the gilding shews!
It puts one's eyes out as it goes.
What a rich glare of various hues,
What shining yellows, scarlets, blues!
It must have cost a heavy price;
'Tis like a mountain drawn by mice.

Mrs Brown
So painted, gilded, and so large,
Bless me! 'tis like my lord mayor's barge.
And so it is – look how it reels!
'Tis nothing else – a barge on wheels.

Man
Large! it can't pass St James's gate,
So big the coach, the arch so strait.
It might be made to rumble thro'
And pass as other coaches do.
Could they a *body*-coachman get
So most preposterously fit,

Who'd undertake (and no rare thing)
Without a *head*, to drive the king.

Mrs Scot
Lard! what are those two ugly things
There – with their hands upon the springs,
Filthy, as ever eyes beheld,
With naked breasts, and faces swell'd?
What could the saucy maker mean,
To put such things to fright the Queen?

Man
Oh! they are Gods, Ma'm, which you see,
Of the Marine Society.
Tritons, which in the ocean dwell,
And only rise to blow their shell.

Mrs Scot
Gods, d'ye call those filthy men?
Why don't they go to sea again?
Pray, tell me, sir, you understand,
What do these Tritons do on land?

Mrs Brown
And what are they? those hindmost things,
Men, fish and birds, with flesh, scales, wings?

Man
Oh, they are Gods too, like the others,
All of one family and brothers,
Creatures, which seldom come ashore,
Nor seen about the King before.
For show, they wear the yellow hue,
Their proper colour is True-blue.

Mrs Scot
Lord bless us! what's this noise about?
Lord, what a tumult and a rout!
How the folks holla, hiss, and hoot!
Well – Heav'n preserve the Earl of Bute!
I cannot stay, indeed, not I,
If there's a riot I shall die.

Let's make for any house we can,
Do – give us shelter, honest man.

Mrs Brown
I wonder'd where you was, my dear,
I thought I should have died with fear.
This noise and racketing and hurry
Has put my nerves in such a flurry!
I could not think where you was got,
I thought I'd lost you, Mrs Scot;
Where's Mrs Tape, and Mr Grin?
Lard, I'm so glad we're all got in.

ROBERT FERGUSSON

From AULD REIKIE

Now Morn, with bonny purpie[1] smiles,
Kisses the air-cock[2] o' Saunt Giles;
Rakin their een, the servant lasses
Early begin their lies and clashes.
Ilk tells her friend of saddest distress,
That still she bruiks frae scoulin' mistress;
And wi' her joe in turnpike stair,
She'd rather snuff the stinkin air,
As be subjected to her tongue,
Whan justly censur'd i' the wrong.

On stair, wi' tub or pat[3] in hand,
The barefoot housemaids loe to stand,
That antrin fock[4] may ken how snell[5]
Auld Reikie will at mornin smell:
Then, with an inundation big as
The burn that 'neath the Nor' Loch brig is,
They kindly shower Edina's roses,
To quicken and regale our noses.

[1] crimson [2] weathercock [3] pot [4] chance people [5] pungent

Now some for this, wi' Satire's leese,[6]
Hae gien auld Edinbrough a creesh:[7]
But, without scourin nought is sweet;
The mornin smells that hail our street,
Prepare, and gently lead the way
To Simmer canty, braw, and gay.
Edina's sons mair eithly[8] share
Her spices and her dainties rare,
Than he that's never yet been call'd
Aff frae his plaidie or his fauld.

Now stairhead critics, senseless fools!
Censure their aim, and pride their rules,
In Luckenbooths, wi' glowrin[9] eye,
Their neebours'[10] sma'est faults descry.
If ony loun[11] shou'd dander there,
O' awkward gait, and foreign air,
They trace his steps, till they can tell
His pedigree as weel's himsel.

When Phœbus blinks wi' warmer ray,
And schools at noon-day get the play,
Then bus'ness, weighty bus'ness, comes;
The trader glowrs; he doubts, he hums.
The lawyers eke to cross repair,
Their wigs to shaw, and toss an air;
While busy agent closely plies,
And a' his kittle[12] cases tries.

Now night, that's cunzied[13] chief for fun,
Is wi' her usual rites begun;
Thro' ilka gate the torches blaze,
And globes send out their blinkin rays.
The usefu' cadie[14] plies in street,
To bide the profits o' his feet;
For, by thir lads Auld Reikie's fouk
Ken but a sample o' the stock

[6] lash [7] whipping [8] easily [9] staring [10] neighbours [11] lad [12] difficult [13] coined made [14] porter

O' thieves, that nightly wad oppress,
And mak baith goods and gear the less.
Near him the lazy chairman stands,
And wats na how to turn his hands,
Till some daft birky, rantin fou,[15]
Has matters somewhere else to do;
The chairman willing gies his light
To deeds o' darkness and o' night.

It's never saxpence for a lift
That gars thir lads wi' fu'ness rift;[16]
For they wi' better gear are paid,
And whores and culls[17] support their trade.

Near some lamp-post, wi' dowie[18] face,
Wi' heavy een, and sour grimace,
Stands she, that beauty lang had kend;
Whoredom her trade, and vice her end.
But, see whare now she wins her bread
By that which Nature ne'er decreed;
And sings sad music to the lugs,
'Mang bourachs[19] o' damn'd whores and rogues.
Whane'er we reputation lose,
Fair chastity's transparent gloss!
Redemption seenil[20] kens the name,
But a's black misery and shame.

Frae joyous tavern, reelin drunk,
We' fiery phiz, and een half sunk,
Behold the bruiser, fae to a'
That in the reek o' gardies fa'![21]
Close by his side, a feckless race
O' macaronies shaw their face,
And think, they're free frae skaith or harm,
While pith befriend's their leader's arm:
Yet fearfu' aften o' their maught,
They quit the glory o' the faught
To this same warrior wha led
Thae heroes to bright Honour's bed

[15] daft fellow, roaring drunk [16] belch [17] fools [18] doleful [19] crowds [20] seldom
[21] foe to all who rely on the reach of their fists

And aft the hack o' honour[22] shines
In bruiser's face wi' broken lines.
O' them sad tales he tells anon,
Whan ramble and whan fighting's done:
And, like Hectorian, ne'er impairs
The brag and glory o' his sairs.

Whan feet in dirty gutters plash
And fock to wale their fitstaps fash;[23]
At night, the macaroni drunk,
In pools and gutters aft-times sunk:
Heh! what a fright he now appears,
Whan he his corpse dejected rears!
Look at that head, and think if there
The pomet slaister'd up his hair![24]
The cheeks observe:— Where now cou'd shine
The scancin[25] glories o' carmine?
Ah, fegs![26] in vain the silk-worm there
Display'd to view her eident[27] care:
For stink, instead of perfumes, grow,
And clarty[28] odours fragrant flow.

Now, some to porter, some to punch –
Some to their wife, – and some their wench, –
Retire; – while noisy ten-hour's drum
Gars a' your trades gae danderin home.
Now, money a club, jocose and free,
Gie a' to merriment and glee:
Wi' sang, and glass, they fley the pow'r
O' Care, that wad harass the hour:
For wine and Bacchus still bear down
Our thrawart[29] fortune's wildest frown;
It maks you stark, and bauld, and brave,
Even whan descendin to the grave.

[22] honourable wound [23] take care to pick their way [24] his hair was smeared with pomatum [25] shining [26] faith! [27] diligent [28] filthy [29] adverse

GEORGE CRABBE

DESCRIPTION OF THE BOROUGH

'Describe the Borough' – though our idle tribe
May love description, can we so describe,
That you shall fairly streets and buildings trace,
And all that gives distinction to a place?
This cannot be; yet mov'd by your request,
A part I paint – let fancy form the rest.

Cities and towns, the various haunts of men,
Require the pencil: they defy the pen:
Could he, who sang so well the Grecian fleet,
So well have sung of alley, lane, or street?
Can measur'd lines these various buildings show,
The Town-hall Turning, or the Prospect Row?
Can I the seats of wealth and want explore,
And lengthen out my lays from door to door?

Then let thy fancy aid me – I repair
From this tall mansion of our last-year's Mayor,
Till we the outskirts of the Borough reach,
And these half-buried buildings next the beach;
Where hang at open doors, the net and cork,
While squalid sea-dames mend the meshy work;
Till comes the hour, when fishing through the tide,
The weary husband throws his freight aside;
A living mass, which now demands the wife,
Th' alternate labours of their humble life.

Can scenes like these withdraw thee from thy wood,
Thy upland forest or thy valley's flood?
Seek then thy garden's shrubby bound, and look,
As it steals by, upon the bordering brook;
That winding streamlet, limpid, lingering, slow,
Where the reeds whisper when the zephyrs blow;
Where in the midst, upon her throne of green,
Sits the large lily as the water's queen;

And makes the current, forc'd awhile to stay,
Murmur and bubble as it shoots away;
Draw then the strongest contrast to that stream,
And our broad river will before thee seem.

With ceaseless motion comes and goes the tide,
Flowing, it fills the channel vast and wide;
Then back to sea, with strong majestic sweep
It rolls, in ebb yet terrible and deep:
Here samphire-banks and salt-wort bound the flood,
There stakes and sea-weeds withering on the mud;
And higher up, a ridge of all things base,
Which some strong tide has roll'd upon the place.

Thy gentle river boasts its pigmy boat,
Urg'd on by pains, half grounded, half afloat;
While at her stern an angler takes his stand,
And marks the fish he purposes to land;
From that clear space, where in the cheerful ray
Of the warm sun the scaly people play.

Far other craft our prouder river shows,
Hoys, pinks and sloops; brigs, brigantines and snows:
Nor angler we on our wide stream descry
But one poor dredger where his oysters lie:
He cold and wet and driving with the tide,
Beats his weak arms against his tarry side,
Then drains the remnant of diluted gin,
To aid the warmth that languishes within;
Renewing oft his poor attempts to beat
His tingling fingers into gathering heat.

He shall again be seen when evening comes,
And social parties crowd their favourite rooms;
Where, on the table pipes and papers lie,
The steaming bowl or foaming tankard by;
'Tis then, with all these comforts spread around,
They hear the painful dredger's welcome sound;
And few themselves the savoury boon deny,
The food that feeds, the living luxury.

Yon is our quay! those smaller hoys from town,
Its various wares, for country-use, bring down;
Those laden waggons, in return, impart
The country produce to the city mart:
Hark! to the clamour in that miry road,
Bounded and narrow'd by yon vessels' load;
The lumbering wealth she empties round the place,
Package and parcel, hogshead, chest and case:
While the loud seaman and the angry hind,
Mingling in business, bellow to the wind.

Near these a crew amphibious in the docks,
Rear, for the sea, those castles on the stocks:
See! the long keel, which soon the waves must hide,
See! the strong ribs which form the roomy side,
Bolts yielding slowly to the sturdiest stroke,
And planks which curve and crackle in the smoke.
Around the whole rise cloudy wreaths, and far
Bear the warm pungence of o'er-boiling tar.

Dabbling on shore half-naked sea-boys crowd,
Swim round a ship, or swing upon the shroud;
Or in a boat purloin'd, with paddles play,
And grow familiar with the watery way:
Young though they be, they feel whose sons they are,
They know what British seamen do and dare;
Proud of that fame, they raise and they enjoy
The rustic wonder of the village-boy.

Before you bid these busy scenes adieu,
Behold the wealth that lies in public view,
Those far-extended heaps of coal and coke,
Where fresh-fill'd lime-kilns breathe their stifling smoke.
This shall pass off, and you behold instead,
The night-fire gleaming on its chalky bed;
When from the light-house brighter beams will rise,
To show the shipman where the shallow lies.

Thy walks are ever pleasant; every scene
Is rich in beauty, lively, or serene –

Rich – is that varied view with woods around,
Seen from the seat, within the shrubb'ry bound;
Where shines the distant lake, and where appear
From ruins bolting, unmolested deer;
Lively – the village-green, the inn, the place,
Where the good widow schools her infant-race.
Shops, whence are heard, the hammer and the saw,
And village-pleasures unreprov'd by law;
Then how serene! when in your favourite room,
Gales from your jasmines soothe the evening gloom;
When from your upland paddock you look down,
And just perceive the smoke which hides the town;
When weary peasants at the close of day
Walk to their cots, and part upon the way;
When cattle slowly cross the shallow brook,
And shepherds pen their folds, and rest upon their crook.

We prune our hedges, prime our slender trees,
And nothing looks untutor'd and at ease,
On the wide heath, or in the flow'ry vale,
We scent the vapours of the sea-born gale;
Broad-beaten paths lead on from stile to stile,
And sewers from streets, the road-side banks defile;
Our guarded fields a sense of danger show,
Where garden-crops with corn and clover grow;
Fences are form'd of wreck and plac'd around,
(With tenters tipp'd) a strong repulsive bound;
Wide and deep ditches by the gardens run,
And there in ambush lie the trap and gun;
Or yon broad board, which guards each tempting prize,
'Like a tall bully, lifts its head and lies.'

There stands a cottage with an open door,
Its garden undefended blooms before;
Her wheel is still, and overturn'd her stool,
While the lone widow seeks the neighb'ring pool;
This gives us hope, all views of town to shun –
No! here are tokens of the sailor-son;
That old blue jacket, and that shirt of check,
And silken kerchief for the seaman's neck;

Sea-spoils and shells from many a distant shore,
And furry robe from frozen Labrador.

Our busy streets and sylvan-walks between,
Fen, marshes, bog and heath all intervene;
Here pits of crag, with spongy, plashy base,
To some enrich th' uncultivated space;
For there are blossoms rare, and curious rush,
The gale's rich balm, and sundew's crimson blush,
Whose velvet leaf with radiant beauty drest,
Forms a gay pillow for the plover's breast.

Not distant far, an house commodious made,
(Lonely yet public stands) for Sunday-trade;
Thither for this day free, gay parties go,
Their tea-house walk, their tippling rendezvous;
There humble couples sit in corner-bowers
Or gaily ramble for th' allotted hours;
Sailors and lasses from the town attend,
The servant-lover, the apprentice-friend;
With all the idle social tribes who seek,
And find, their humble pleasures, once a week.

from *The Borough*

THE POOR AND THEIR DWELLINGS

Farewell to these; but all our poor to know,
Let's seek the winding lane, the narrow row,
Suburban prospects, where the traveller stops
To see the sloping tenement on props,
With building yards immix'd, and humble sheds and shops;
Where the Cross-Keys and Plumber's-Arms invite
Laborious men to taste their coarse delight;
Where the low porches, stretching from the door,
Gave some distinction in the days of yore,
Yet now neglected, more offend the eye,
By gloom and ruin than the cottage by:
Places like these the noblest town endures,
The gayest palace has its sinks and sewers.

Here is no pavement, no inviting shop,
To give us shelter when compell'd to stop;
But plashy puddles stand along the way,
Fill'd by the rain of one tempestuous day;
And these so closely to the buildings run,
That you must ford them, for you cannot shun;
Though here and there convenient bricks are laid,
And door-side heaps afford their dubious aid.

Lo! yonder shed; observe its garden-ground,
Which that low paling, form'd of wreck, surround;
There dwells a fisher; if you view his boat,
With bed and barrel – 'tis his house afloat;
Look at his house, where ropes, nets, blocks, abound,
Tar, pitch, and oakum – 'tis his boat aground:
That space enclos'd, but little he regards,
Spread o'er with relics of masts, sails, and yards:
Fish by the wall, on spit of elder, rest,
Of all his food, the cheapest and the best,
By his own labour caught, for his own hunger drest.

Here our reformers come not; none object
To paths polluted, or upbraid neglect;
None care that ashy heaps at doors are cast,
That coal-dust flies along the blinding blast:
None heed the stagnant pools on either side,
Where new-launch'd ships of infant-sailors ride:
Rodneys in rags, here British valour coast,
And lisping Nelsons fright the Gallic coast.
They fix the rudder, set the swelling sail,
They point the bowsprit, and they blow the gale:
True to her port, the frigate scuds away,
And o'er that frowning ocean finds her bay:
Her owner rigg'd her and he knows her worth,
And sees her, fearless, gunwale-deep go forth;
Dreadless he views his sea, by breezes curl'd,
When inch-high billows vex the watery world.

There, fed by food they love, to rankest size,
Around the dwellings docks and wormwood rise;

George Crabbe (1754–1832)

Here the strong mallow strikes her slimy root,
Here the dull nightshade hangs her deadly fruit;
On hills of dust the henbane's faded green,
And pencil'd flower of sickly scent is seen;
At the wall's base the fiery nettle springs,
With fruit globose and fierce with poison'd stings;
Above (the growth of many a year) is spread
The yellow level of the stone-crop's bed;
In every chink delights the fern to grow,
With glossy leaf and tawny bloom below:
These, with our sea-weeds, rolling up and down,
Form the contracted flora of the town.

Say, wilt thou more of scenes so sordid know?
Then will I lead thee down the dusty row;
By the warm alley and the long close lane, –
There mark the fractur'd door and paper'd pane,
Where flags the noon-tide air, and as we pass,
We fear to breathe the putrifying mass:
But fearless yonder matron; she disdains
To sigh for zephyrs from ambrosial plains;
But mends her meshes torn, and pours her lay
All in the stifling fervour of the day.

Her naked children round the alley run,
And roll'd in dust, are bronz'd beneath the sun;
Or gamble round the dame, who, loosely drest,
Woos the coy breeze to fan the open breast:
She, once an handmaid, strove by decent art
To charm her sailor's eye and touch his heart;
Her bosom then was veil'd in kerchief clean,
And fancy left to form the charms unseen.

But when a wife, she lost her former care,
Nor thought on charms, nor time for dress could spare;
Careless she found her friends who dwelt beside,
No rival beauty kept alive her pride:
Still in her bosom virtue keeps her place,
But decency is gone, the virtue's guard and grace.

See that long boarded building! – by these stairs
Each humble tenant to that home repairs –
By one large window lighted – it was made
For some bold project, some design in trade:
This fail'd, – and one, an humourist in his way,
(Ill was the humour,) bought it in decay;
Nor will he sell, repair, or take it down,
'Tis his, – what cares he for the talk of town:
'No! he will let it to the poor; – an home
Where he delights to see the creatures come:'
'They may be thieves;' – 'Well, so are richer men;'
'Or idlers, cheats, or prostitutes;' – 'What then?'
'Outcasts pursued by justice, vile and base,' –
'They need the more his pity and the place:'
Convert to system, his vain mind has built,
He gives asylum to deceit and guilt.

In this vast room, each place by habit fixed,
Are sexes, families, and ages mixt, –
To union forc'd by crime, by fear, by need,
And all in morals and in modes agreed;
Some ruin'd men, who from mankind remove,
Some ruin'd females, who yet talk of love,
And some grown old in idleness – the prey
To vicious spleen, still railing through the day;
And need and misery, vice and danger bind
In sad alliance each degraded mind.

That window view! – oil'd paper and old glass
Stain the strong rays, which, though impeded, pass,
And give a dusty warmth to that huge room,
The conquer'd sunshine's melancholy gloom;
When all those western rays, without so bright,
Within become a ghastly glimmering light,
As pale and faint upon the floor they fall,
Or feebly gleam on the opposing wall:
That floor, once oak, now piec'd with fir unplan'd,
Or, where not piec'd, in places bor'd and stain'd;
That wall once whiten'd, now an odious sight,
Stain'd with all hues, except its ancient white;

The only door is fasten'd by a pin,
Or stubborn bar, that none may hurry in:
For this poor room, like rooms of greater pride,
At times contains what prudent men would hide.

Where'er the floor allows an even space,
Chalking and marks of various games have place;
Boys, without foresight, pleas'd in halters swing;
On a fix'd hook men case a flying ring;
While gin and snuff their female neighbours share,
And the black beverage in the fractur'd ware.

On swinging shelf are things incongruous stor'd, –
Scraps of their food, – the cards and cribbage-board, –
With pipes and pouches; while on peg below,
Hang a lost member's fiddle and its bow:
That still reminds them how he'd dance and play,
E'er sent untimely to the convicts' bay.

Here by a curtain, by a blanket there,
Are various beds conceal'd, but none with care;
Where some by day and some by night, as best
Suit their employments, seek uncertain rest;
The drowsy children at their pleasure creep
To the known crib and there securely sleep.

Each end contains a grate, and these beside
Are hung utensils for their boil'd and fry'd –
All used at any hour, by night, by day,
As suit the purse, the person, or the prey.

Above the fire, the mantel-shelf contains
Of china-ware some poor unmatch'd remains;
There many a tea-cup's gaudy fragment stands,
All plac'd by vanity's unwearied hands;
For here she lives, e'en here she looks about,
To find some small consoling objects out:
Nor heed these Spartan dames their house, nor sit
'Mid cares domestic, – they nor sew nor knit;
But of their fate discourse, their ways, their wars,
With arm'd authorities, their 'scapes and scars:

These lead to present evils, and a cup,
If fortune grant it, winds description up.

High hung at either end, and next the wall,
Two ancient mirrors show the forms of all,
In all their force; – these aid them in their dress,
But with the good, the evils too express,
Doubling each look of care, each token of distress.

from *The Borough*

THE FARMER'S DAUGHTER

To farmer Moss, in Langar Vale, came down
His only daughter, from her school in town;
A tender, timid maid! who knew not how
To pass a pig-sty, or to face a cow:
Smiling she came, with petty talents graced,
A fair complexion, and a slender waist.
Used to spare meals, disposed in manner pure,
Her father's kitchen she could ill endure:
Where by the steaming beef he hungry sat,
And laid at once a pound upon his plate;
Hot from the field, her eager brother seized
An equal part, and hunger's rage appeased;
The air, surcharged with moisture, flagg'd around,
And the offended damsel sigh'd and frown'd;
The swelling fat in lumps conglomerate laid,
And fancy's sickness seized the loathing maid:
But when the men beside their station took,
The maidens with them, and with these the cook;
When one huge wooden bowl before them stood,
Fill'd with huge balls of farinaceous food;
With bacon, mass saline, where never lean
Beneath the brown and bristly rind was seen;
When from a single horn the party drew
Their copious draughts of heavy ale and new;
When the coarse cloth she saw, with many a stain,
Soil'd by rude hinds who cut and came again –

She could not breathe; but, with a heavy sigh,
Rein'd the fair neck, and shut th'offended eye;
She minced the sanguine flesh in frustums fine,
And wonder'd much to see the creatures dine:
When she resolved her father's heart to move,
If hearts of farmers were alive to love.
  She now entreated by herself to sit
In the small parlour, if papa thought fit,
And there to dine, to read, to work alone: –
'No!' said the farmer, in an angry tone;
'These are your school-taught airs; your mother's pride
Would send you there; but I am now your guide. –
Arise betimes, our early meal prepare,
And this despatch'd, let business be your care;
Look to the lasses, let there not be one
Who lacks attention, till her tasks be done;
In every household work your portion take,
And what you make not, see that others make:
At leisure times attend the wheel, and see
The whit'ning web be sprinkled on the Lea;
When thus employ'd, should our young neighbour view
An useful lass, you may have more to do.'

from *The Widow's Tale*

WILLIAM BLAKE

HOLY THURSDAY

'Twas on a Holy Thursday, their innocent faces clean,
The children walking two and two, in red and blue and green,
Grey headed beadles walk'd before, with wands as white as snow,
Till into the high dome of Paul's they like Thames' waters flow.

O what a multitude they seem'd, these flowers of London town!
Seated in companies they sit with radiance all their own.
The hum of multitudes was there, but multitudes of lambs,
Thousands of little boys and girls raising their innocent hands.

Now like a mighty wind they raise to heaven the voice of song,
Or like harmonious thunderings the seats of heaven among.
Beneath them sit the aged men, wise guardians of the poor;
Then cherish pity, lest you drive an angel from your door.

LONDON

I wander thro' each charter'd street
Near where the charter'd Thames does flow,
And mark in every face I meet
Marks of weakness, marks of woe.

In every cry of every Man,
In every Infant's cry of fear,
In every voice, in every ban,
The mind-forg'd manacles I hear.

How the Chimney-sweeper's cry
Every black'ning Church appalls,
And the hapless Soldier's sigh
Runs in blood down Palace walls.

But most thro' midnight streets I hear
How the youthful Harlot's curse
Blasts the new born Infant's tear,
And blights with plagues the Marriage hearse.

ROBERT BURNS

THE JOLLY BEGGARS

A Cantata

Recitativo

When lyart[1] leaves bestrow the yird,[2]
Or wavering like the bauckie-bird,[3]

[1] withered [2] ground [3] bat

Bedim cauld Boreas' blast;
When hailstanes drive wi' bitter skyte,[4]
And infant frosts begin to bite,
In hoary cranreuch[5] drest;
Ae night at e'en a merry core[6]
O' randie, gangrel bodies,[7]
In Poosie-Nansie's held the splore,[8]
To drink their orra duddies:[9]
Wi' quaffing and laughing,
They ranted an' they sang,
Wi' jumping an' thumping,
The vera girdle[10] rang.

First, niest the fire, in auld red rags,
Ane sat, weel brac'd wi' mealy bags,[11]
And knapsack a' in order;
His doxy lay within his arm;
Wi' usquebae[12] an' blankets warm
She blinket on her sodger:
An' ay he gies the tozie[13] drab
The tither skelpin[14] kiss,
While she held up her greedy gab,
Just like an aumous dish:[15]
Ilk smack still did crack still,
Just like a cadger's whip;
Then staggering an' swaggering,
He roar'd this ditty up –

Air

Tune: *Soldier's Joy*

I am a son of Mars who have been in many wars,
And show my cuts and scars wherever I come;
This here was for a wench, and that other in a trench,
When welcoming the French at the sound of the drum.
Lal de daudle, etc.

[4] slanting stroke [5] hoar-frost [6] party [7] disorderly, vagrant people [8] carouse [9] variegated rags [10] griddle [11] well-wrapped in mealbags [12] whisky [13] tipsy [14] smacking [15] almsdish

My prenticeship I past where my leader breath'd his last,
When the bloody die was cast on the heights of Abram:
And I servèd out my trade when the gallant game was play'd,
And the Moro low was laid at the sound of the drum.
Lal de daudle, etc.

I lastly was with Curtis among the floating batt'ries,
And there I left for witness an arm and a limb;
Yet let my country need me, with Elliot to head me,
I'd clatter on my stumps at the sound of a drum.
Lal de daudle, etc.

And now tho' I must beg, with a wooden arm and leg,
And many a tatter'd rag hanging over my bum,
I'm as happy with my wallet, my bottle and my callet,[16]
As when I used in scarlet to follow a drum.
Lal de daudle, etc.

What tho', with hoary locks, I must stand the winter shocks,
Beneath the woods and rocks, oftentimes for a home,
When the tother bag I sell, and the tother bottle tell,
I could meet a troop of hell, at the sound of a drum.
Lal de daudle, etc.

Recitativo

He ended; and the kebars[17] sheuk,
Aboon the chorus roar;
While frighted rattons[18] backward leuk,
An' seek the benmost bore:[19]
A fairy fiddler frae the neuk,[20]
He skirl'd out, encore!
But up arose the martial chuck,[21]
An' laid the loud uproar.

[16] whore [17] rafters [18] rats [19] innermost hole [20] corner [21] sweetheart

Robert Burns (1759–1796)

Air

Tune: *Sodger Laddie*

I once was a maid, tho' I cannot tell when,
And still my delight is in proper young men:
Some one of a troop of dragoons was my daddie,
No wonder I'm fond of a sodger laddie.
Sing, Lal de dal, etc.

The first of my loves was a swaggering blade,
To rattle the thundering drum was his trade:
His leg was so tight, and his cheek was so ruddy,
Transported I was with my sodger laddie.
Sing, Lal de dal, etc.

But the godly old chaplain left him in the lurch;
The sword I forsook for the sake of the church:
He ventur'd the soul, and I risket the body,
'Twas then I prov'd false to my sodger laddie.
Sing, Lal de dal, etc.

Full soon I grew sick of my sanctified sot,
The regiment at large for a husband I got;
From the gilded spontoon to the fife I was ready,
I askèd no more but a sodger laddie.
Sing, Lal de dal, etc.

But the peace it reduc'd me to beg in despair,
Till I met my old boy in a Cunningham fair;
His rags regimental they flutter'd so gaudy,
My heart it rejoic'd at a sodger laddie.
Sing, Lal de dal, etc.

And now I have liv'd – I know not how long,
And still I can join in a cup and a song;
But whilst with both hands I can hold the glass steady,
Here's to thee, my hero, my sodger laddie.
Sing, Lal de dal, etc.

Recitativo

Poor Merry-Andrew, in the neuk,
  Sat guzzling wi' a tinkler-hizzie;[22]
They mind't na wha the chorus teuk,
  Between themselves they were sae busy:
At length, wi' drink an' courting dizzy,
  He stoiter'd[23] up an' made a face;
Then turn'd, an' laid a smack[24] on Grizzie,
  Syne tun'd his pipes wi' grave grimace.

Air

Tune: *Auld Sir Symon*

Sir Wisdom's a fool when he's fou;[25]
  Sir Knave is a fool in a session;
He's there but a prentice I trow,
  But I am a fool by profession.

My grannie she bought me a beuk,
  An' I held awa to the school;
I fear I my talent misteuk,
  But what will ye hae of a fool?

For drink I would venture my neck;
  A hizzie's[26] the half of my craft;
But what could ye other expect,
  Of ane that's avowedly daft?

I ance was ty'd up like a stirk,[27]
  For civilly swearing and quaffing;
I ance was abus'd i' the kirk,
  For towsing[28] a lass i' my daffin.[29]

Poor Andrew that tumbles for sport,
  Let nae body name wi' a jeer;
There's even, I'm tauld, i' the Court
  A tumbler ca'd the Premier.

[22] tinker-wench [23] staggered [24] kiss
[25] drunk [26] wench [27] bullock [28] rumpling [29] fun

Observ'd ye yon reverend lad
  Mak faces to tickle the mob;
He rails at our mountebank squad,
  It's rivalship just i' the job.

And now my conclusion I'll tell,
  For faith I'm confoundedly dry:
The chiel that's a fool for himself,
  Guid L—d, he's far dafter than I.

Recitativo

Then niest outspak a raucle carlin,[30]
Wha kent fu' weel to cleek[31] the sterlin;
For mony a pursie she had hooked,
An' had in mony a well been douked:
Her love had been a Highland laddie,
But weary fa' the waefu' woodie![32]
Wi' sighs an' sobs she thus began
To wail her braw John Highlandman.

Air

Tune: *O an' ye were dead, Gudeman*

A Highland lad my love was born,
The lalland[33] laws he held in scorn;
But he still was faithfu' to his clan,
My gallant, braw John Highlandman.

Chorus

Sing hey my braw John Highlandman!
Sing ho my braw John Highlandman!
There's not a lad in a' the lan'
Was match for my John Highlandman.

With his philibeg[34] an' tartan plaid,
An' guid claymore down by his side,

[30] stout old woman [31] steal
[32] gallows [33] Lowland [34] kilt

The ladies' hearts he did trepan,
My gallant, braw John Highlandman.
Sing hey, etc.

We rangèd a' from Tweed to Spey,
An' liv'd like lords an' ladies gay;
For a lalland face he fearèd none,
My gallant, braw John Highlandman.
Sing hey, etc.

They banish'd him beyond the sea,
But ere the bud was on the tree,
Adown my cheeks the pearls ran,
Embracing my John Highlandman.
Sing hey, etc.

But Och! they catch'd him at the last,
And bound him in a dungeon fast,
My curse upon them every one,
They've hang'd my braw John Highlandman.
Sing hey, etc.

And now a widow I must mourn
The pleasures that will ne'er return;
No comfort but a hearty can,
When I think on John Highlandman.
Sing hey, etc.

Recitativo

A pigmy scraper wi' his fiddle,
Wha us'd at trystes an' fairs to driddle,[35]
Her strappin limb an' gausy[36] middle
(He reach'd nae higher)
Had hol'd his heartie like a riddle,[37]
An' blawn't on fire.

[35] play [36] buxom [37] sieve

Wi' hand on hainch,[38] and upward e'e,
He croon'd his gamut, one, two, three,
Then in an arioso key,
The wee Apollo
Set off wi' allegretto glee
His giga solo.

Air

Tune: *Whistle owre the lave o' 't*

Let me ryke[39] up to dight[40] that tear,
An' go wi' me an' be my dear;
An' then your every care an' fear
May whistle owre the lave[41] o' 't.

Chorus

I am a fiddler to my trade,
An' a' the tunes that e'er I play'd,
The sweetest still to wife or maid,
Was whistle owre the lave o' 't.

At kirns[42] an' weddins we'se be there,
An' O sae nicely's we will fare!
We'll bowse[43] about till Dadie Care
Sing whistle owre the lave o' 't.
I am, etc.

Sae merrily's the banes we'll pyke,[44]
An' sun oursells about the dyke;[45]
An' at our leisure, when ye like,
We'll whistle owre the lave o' 't.
I am, etc.

But bless me wi' your heav'n o' charms,
An' while I kittle hair on thairms,[46]
Hunger, cauld, an' a' sic harms
May whistle owre the lave o' 't.
I am, etc.

[38] haunch [39] reach [40] wipe [41] rest [42] Harvest Homes [43] booze [44] pick
[45] fence [46] apply hair to catgut

Recitativo

Her charms had struck a sturdy caird,[47]
  As weel as poor gutscraper;
He taks the fiddler by the beard,
  An' draws a roosty[48] rapier –
He swoor by a' was swearing worth
  To speet him like a pliver,[49]
Unless he would from that time forth
  Relinquish her for ever:

Wi' ghastly e'e poor tweedledee
  Upon his hunkers[50] bended,
An' pray'd for grace wi' ruefu' face,
  An' so the quarrel ended;
But tho' his little heart did grieve,
  When round the tinkler prest her,
He feign'd to snirtle[51] in his sleeve,
  When thus the caird address'd her:

Air

Tune: *Clout the Caudron*

My bonie lass, I work in brass,
  A tinkler is my station;
I've travell'd round all Christian ground
  In this my occupation;
I've ta'en the gold an' been enroll'd
  In many a noble squadron;
But vain they search'd when off I march'd
  To go an' clout[52] the caudron.
          I've ta'en the gold, etc.

Despise that shrimp, that withered imp,
  With a' his noise an' cap'rin;
An' take a share with those that bear
  The budget[53] and the apron!

[47] gipsy [48] rusty [49] spit him like a plover [50] knees [51] laugh [52] mend [53] bag of tools

And by that stowp! my faith an' houpe,
  And by that dear Kilbaigie,
If e'er ye want, or meet wi' scant,
  May I ne'er weet my craigie.[54]
            And by that stowp, etc.

Recitativo

The caird prevail'd – th' unblushing fair
  In his embraces sunk;
Partly wi' love o'ercome sae sair,
  An' partly she was drunk:
Sir Violino, with an air
  That show'd a man o' spunk,
Wish'd unison between the pair,
  An' made the bottle clunk
            To their health that night.

But hurchin Cupid shot a shaft,
  That play'd a dame a shavie –[55]
The fiddler rak'd her, fore and aft,
  Behint the chicken cavie.[56]
Her lord, a wight of Homer's craft,
  Tho' limpin wi' the spavie,[57]
He hirpl'd up, an' lap[58] like daft,
  An' shor'd[59] them *Dainty Davie*
            O' boot[60] that night.

He was a care-defying blade
  As ever Bacchus listed!
Tho' Fortune sair upon him laid,
  His heart she ever miss'd it.
He had no wish but – to be glad,
  Nor want but – when he thirsted;
He hated nought but – to be sad,
  An' thus the Muse suggested
            His sang that night.

[54] throat [55] trick [56] coop [57] spavin [58] leaped [59] promised [60] into the bargain

Robert Burns (1759–1796)

Air

Tune: *For a' that an' a' that*

I am a Bard of no regard,
  Wi' gentle folks an' a' that;
But Homer like, the glowrin byke,[61]
  Frae town to town I draw that.

Chorus

For a' that an' a' that,
  An' twice as muckle's a' that,
I've lost but ane, I've twa behin',
  I've wife eneugh for a' that.

I never drank the Muses' stank,[62]
  Castalia's burn an' a' that;
But there it streams an' richly reams,
  My Helicon I ca' that.
      For a' that, etc.

Great love I bear to all the fair,
  Their humble slave an' a' that;
But lordly will, I hold it still
  A mortal sin to thraw[63] that.
      For a' that, etc.

In raptures sweet this hour we meet,
  Wi' mutual love an' a' that;
But for how lang the flie may stang,
  Let inclination law that.
      For a' that, etc.

Their tricks an' craft hae put me daft,
  They've ta'en me in, an' a' that;
But clear your decks, an' here's the Sex!
  I like the jads for a' that.

[61] staring multitude [62] fountain [63] cross

Chorus

For a' that an' a' that,
  An' twice as muckle's a' that,
My dearest bluid, to do them guid,
  They're welcome till 't for a' that.

Recitativo

So sung the bard – and Nansie's wa's
Shook with a thunder of applause
  Re-echo'd from each mouth!
They toom'd[64] their pocks,[65] they pawn'd their duds,
They scarcely left to coor[66] their fuds,[67]
  To quench their lowin drouth,[68]
Then owre again the jovial thrang
  The poet did request
To lowse[69] his pack an' wale[70] a sang,
  A ballad o' the best;
    He, rising, rejoicing,
      Between his twa Deborahs,
    Looks round him, an' found them
      Impatient for the chorus.

Air

Tune: *Jolly Mortals, fill your glasses*

See the smoking bowl before us,
  Mark our jovial, ragged ring!
Round and round take up the chorus,
  And in raptures let us sing –

Chorus

A fig for those by law protected!
  Liberty's a glorious feast!
Courts for cowards were erected,
  Churches built to please the priest.

[64] emptied [65] bags [66] cover [67] posteriors [68] burning thirst [69] open [70] select

What is title, what is treasure,
  What is reputation's care?
If we lead a life of pleasure,
  'Tis no matter how or where.
        A fig, etc.

With the ready trick and fable,
  Round we wander all the day;
And at night, in barn or stable,
  Hug our doxies on the hay.
        A fig, etc.

Does the train-attended carriage
  Thro' the country lighter rove?
Does the sober bed of marriage
  Witness brighter scenes of love?
        A fig, etc.

Life is all a variorum,
  We regard not how it goes;
Let them cant about decorum,
  Who have character to lose.
        A fig, etc.

Here's to budgets, bags and wallets!
  Here's to all the wandering train!
Here's our ragged brats and callets![71]
  One and all cry out, Amen!
        A fig, etc.

ANONYMOUS

THE NIGHT BEFORE LARRY WAS STRETCHED

The night before Larry was stretched,
The boys they all paid him a visit;
A bit in their sacks, too, they fetched;
They sweated their duds till they riz it;

[71] wenches

For Larry was ever the lad,
When a boy was condemned to the squeezer,
Would fence all the duds that he had
To help a poor friend to a sneezer,
And warm his gob 'fore he died.

The boys they came crowding in fast,
They drew all their stools round about him,
Six glims round his trap-case were placed,
He couldn't be well waked without 'em.
When one of us asked could he die
Without having truly repented,
Says Larry, 'That's all in my eye,
And first by the clargy invented,
To get a fat bit for themselves.'

'I'm sorry, dear Larry,' says I,
'To see you in this situation;
And, blister my limbs if I lie,
I'd as lieve it had been my own station.'
'Ochone! it's all over,' says he,
'For the neck-cloth I'll be forced to put on,
And by this time tomorrow you'll see
Your poor Larry as dead as a mutton,
Because why, his courage was good.

'And I'll be cut up like a pie,
And my nob from my body be parted.'
'You're in the wrong box, then,' says I,
'For blast me if they're so hard-hearted;
A chalk on the back of your neck
Is all that Jack Ketch dares to give you;
Then mind not such trifles a feck,
For why should the likes of them grieve you?
And now, boys, come tip us the deck.'

The cards being called for, they played,
Till Larry found one of them cheated;
A dart at his napper he made
(The boy being easily heated);

'O, by the hokey, you thief,
I'll scuttle your nob with my daddle!
You cheat me because I'm in grief,
But soon I'll demolish your noddle,
And leave you your claret to drink.'

Then the clargy came in with his book,
He spoke him so smooth and so civil;
Larry tipped him a Kilmainham look,
And pitched his big wig to the devil;
Then sighing, he threw back his head,
To get a sweet drop of the bottle,
And pitiful sighing, he said:
'Oh, the hemp will be soon round my throttle,
And choke my poor windpipe to death.'

'Though sure it's the best way to die,
O! the devil a better a-livin'!
For when the gallows is high
Your journey is shorter to heaven:'
But what harasses Larry the most,
And makes his poor soul melancholy,
Is that he thinks of the time when his ghost
Will come in a sheet to sweet Molly;
'O, sure it will kill her alive!'

So moving these last words he spoke,
We all vented our tears in a shower;
For my part, I thought my heart broke,
To see him cut down like a flower.
On his travels we watched him next day;
O! the throttler, I thought I could kill him;
But Larry not one word did say,
Nor changed till he came to King William,
Then, musha, his colour grew white.

When we came to the numbing chit,
He was tucked up so neat and so pretty,
The rumbler jogged off from his feet,
And he died with his face to the city;

He kicked, too – but that was all pride,
For soon you might see 'twas all over;
Soon after the noose was untied,
And at darkee we waked him in clover,
And sent him to take a ground sweat.

ROBERT BLOOMFIELD

THE DAIRY

The chatt'ring dairy-maid immersed in steam,
Singing and scrubbing midst her milk and cream,
Bawls out, 'Go fetch the cows!' – he hears no more;
For pigs, and ducks, and turkeys, throng the door,
And sitting hens, for constant war prepared;
A concert strange to that which late he heard.
Straight to the meadow then he whistling goes;
With well-known halloo calls his lazy cows;
Down the rich pasture heedlessly they graze,
Or hear the summon with an idle gaze:
For well they know the cow-yard yields no more
Its tempting fragrance, nor its wintry store.
Reluctance marks their steps, sedate and slow;
The right of conquest all the law they know;
The strong press on, the weak by turns succeed,
And one superior always takes the lead,
Is ever foremost, whereso'er they stray;
Allow'd precedence, undisputed sway;
With jealous pride her station is maintain'd,
For many a broil that post of honour gain'd.
At home the yard affords a grateful scene;
For Spring makes e'en a miry cow-yard clean;
Thence from its chalky bed behold convey'd
The rich manure that drenching Winter made,
Which piled near home, grows green with many a weed,
A promised nutriment for Autumn's seed.

Forth comes the maid, and like the morning smiles;
The mistress too, and follow'd close by Giles.
A friendly tripod forms their humble seat,
With pails bright scour'd, and delicately sweet.
Where shadowing elms obstruct the morning ray,
Begins the work, begins the simple lay;
The full-charged udder yields its willing streams,
While Mary sings some lover's amorous dreams;
And crouching Giles beneath a neighbouring tree
Tugs o'er his pail and chants with equal glee;
Whose hat with tatter'd brim, of nap so bare,
From the cow's side purloins a coat of hair,
A mottled ensign of his harmless trade,
An unambitious, peaceable cockade.
As unambitious too that cheerful aid
The mistress yields beside her rosy maid;
With joy she views her plenteous reeking store,
And bears a brimmer to the dairy door;
Her cows dismiss'd, the luscious mead to roam,
Till eve again recall them loaded home.
And now the dairy claims her choicest care,
And half her household find employment there:
Slow rolls the churn, its load of clogging cream
At once foregoes its quality and name:
From knotty particles first floating wide
Congealing butter's dash'd from side to side;
Streams of new milk through flowing coolers stray,
And snow-white curd abounds, and wholesome whey.
Due north the unglaz'd windows, cold and clear,
For warming sunbeams are unwelcome here.
Brisk goes the work beneath each busy hand,
And Giles must trudge, whoever gives command;
A Gibeonite, that serves them all by turns:
He drains the pump, from him the faggot burns;
From him the noisy hogs demand their food;
While at his heels run many a chirping brood,
Or down his path in expectation stand,
With equal claims upon his strewing hand.

Thus wastes the morn, till each with pleasure sees
The bustle o'er, and press'd the new-made cheese.

from *The Farmer's Boy*

RICHARD ALFRED MILLIKEN

THE GROVES OF BLARNEY

The groves of Blarney they look so charming,
Down by the purling of sweet, silent streams,
Being banked with posies that spontaneous grow there,
Planted in order by the sweet rock close.
'Tis there's the daisy and the sweet carnation,
The blooming pink and the rose so fair,
The daffodowndilly, likewise the lily,
All flowers that scent the sweet, fragrant air.
O, ullagoane.

'Tis Lady Jeffers that owns this station;
Like Alexander, or Queen Helen fair,
There's no commander in all the nation,
For emulation, can with her compare.
Such walls surround her, that no nine-pounder
Could dare to plunder her place of strength;
But Oliver Cromwell he did her pommell,
And made a breach in her battlement.
O, ullagoane.

There's gravel walks there for speculation
And conversation in sweet solitude.
'Tis there the lover may hear the dove, or
The gentle plover in the afternoon;
And if a lady would be so engaging
As to walk alone in those shady bowers,
'Tis there the courtier he may transport her
Into some fort, or all under ground.
O, ullagoane.

'Tis there's the kitchen hangs many a flitch in
With the maids a stitching upon the stair;
The bread and biske', the beer and whisky,
Would make you frisky if you were there.
'Tis there you'd see Peg Murphy's daughter
A washing praties forenent the door,
With Roger Cleary, and Father Healy,
All blood relations to my Lord Donoughmore.
O, ullagoane.

For 'tis there's a cave where no daylight enters,
But cats and badgers are for ever bred;
Being mossed by nature, that makes it sweeter
Than a coach-and-six or a feather bed.
'Tis there the lake is, well stored with perches,
And comely eels in the verdant mud;
Besides the leeches, and groves of beeches,
Standing in order for to guard the flood.
O, ullagoane.

There's statues gracing this noble place in –
All heathen gods and nymphs so fair;
Bold Neptune, Plutarch, and Nicodemus,
All standing naked in the open air!
So now to finish this brave narration,
Which my poor geni' could not entwine;
But were I Homer, or Nebuchadnezzar,
'Tis in every feature I would make it shine.
O, ullagoane.

GEORGE CANNING

SAPPHICS: THE FRIEND OF HUMANITY AND THE KNIFE-GRINDER

Friend of Humanity

'Needy Knife-grinder! whither are you going?
Rough is the road, your Wheel is out of order –
Bleak blows the blast; – your hat has got a hole in't,
So have your breeches!

'Weary Knife-grinder! little think the proud ones,
Who in their coaches roll along the turnpike-
Road, what hard work 'tis crying all day "Knives and
Scissors to grind O!"

'Tell me, Knife-grinder, how you came to grind knives?
Did some rich man tyrannically use you?
Was it the 'Squire? or Parson of the Parish?
Or the Attorney?

'Was it the 'Squire for killing of his Game? or
Covetous Parson for his Tythes distraining?
Or roguish Lawyer made you lose your little
All in a law-suit?

'(Have you not read the Rights of Man, by Tom Paine?)
Drops of compassion tremble on my eye-lids,
Ready to fall, as soon as you have told your
Pitiful story.'

Knife-grinder

'Story! God bless you! I have none to tell, Sir,
Only last night a-drinking at the Chequers,
This poor old hat and breeches, as you see, were
Torn in a scuffle.

'Constables came up for to take me into
Custody; they took me before the Justice;
Justice Oldmixon put me in the Parish-
Stocks for a Vagrant.

'I should be glad to drink your Honour's health in
A Pot of Beer, if you would give me Sixpence;
But for my part, I never love to meddle
With Politics, Sir.'

Friend of Humanity

'*I* give thee Sixpence! I will see thee damn'd first –
Wretch! whom no sense of wrongs can rouse to vengeance –
Sordid, unfeeling, reprobate, degraded,
Spiritless outcast!'

(*Kicks the Knife-grinder, overturns his Wheel, and exit in a transport of republican enthusiasm and universal philanthropy.*)

WILLIAM WORDSWORTH

POWER OF MUSIC

An Orpheus! an Orpheus! yes, Faith may grow bold,
And take to herself all the wonders of old; –
Near the stately Pantheon you'll meet with the same
In the street that from Oxford hath borrowed its name.

His station is there; and he works on the crowd,
He sways them with harmony merry and loud;
He fills with his power all their hearts to the brim –
Was aught ever heard like his fiddle and him?

What an eager assembly! what an empire is this!
The weary have life, and the hungry have bliss;
The mourner is cheered, and the anxious have rest;
And the guilt-burdened soul is no longer opprest.

As the Moon brightens round her the clouds of the night,
So He, where he stands, is a centre of light;
It gleams on the face, there, of dusky-browed Jack,
And the pale-visaged Baker's, with basket on back.

That errand-bound 'Prentice was passing in haste –
What matter! he's caught – and his time runs to waste;
The Newsman is stopped, though he stops on the fret;
And the half-breathless Lamplighter – he's in the net!

The Porter sits down on the weight which he bore;
The Lass with her barrow wheels hither her store;
If a thief could be here he might pilfer at ease;
She sees the Musician, 'tis all that she sees!

He stands, backed by the wall; – he abates not his din;
His hat gives him vigour, with boons dropping in,
From the old and the young, from the poorest; and there!
The one-pennied Boy has his penny to spare.

O blest are the hearers, and proud be the hand
Of the pleasure it spreads through so thankful a band;

I am glad for him, blind as he is! – all the while
If they speak 'tis to praise, and they praise with a smile.

That tall Man, a giant in bulk and in height,
Not an inch of his body is free from delight;
Can he keep himself still, if he would? oh, not he!
The music stirs in him like the wind through a tree.

Mark that Cripple who leans on his crutch; like a tower
That long has leaned forward, leans hour after hour! –
That Mother, whose spirit in fetters is bound,
While she dandles the Babe in her arms to the sound.

Now, coaches and chariots! roar on like a stream;
Here are twenty souls happy as souls in a dream:
They are deaf to your murmurs – they care not for you,
Nor what ye are flying, nor what ye pursue!

SKATING

And in the frosty season, when the sun
Was set, and visible for many a mile
The cottage windows through the twilight blaz'd,
I heeded not the summons: – happy time
It was, indeed, for all of us; to me
It was a time of rapture: clear and loud
The village clock toll'd six; I wheel'd about,
Proud and exulting, like an untired horse,
That cares not for its home. – All shod with steel,
We hiss'd along the polish'd ice, in games
Confederate, imitative of the chase
And woodland pleasures, the resounding horn,
The pack loud bellowing, and the hunted hare.
So through the darkness and the cold we flew,
And not a voice was idle; with the din,
Meanwhile, the precipices rang aloud,
The leafless trees, and every icy crag

Tinkled like iron, while the distant hills
Into the tumult sent an alien sound
Of melancholy, not unnoticed, while the stars,
Eastward, were sparkling clear, and in the west
The orange sky of evening died away.

from *The Prelude* (1805 version)

COTTAGE AMUSEMENTS

Ye lowly cottages in which we dwelt,
A ministration of your own was yours,
A sanctity, a safeguard, and a love!
Can I forget you, being as ye were
So beautiful among the pleasant fields
In which ye stood? Or can I here forget
The plain and seemly countenance with which
Ye dealt out your plain comforts? Yet had ye
Delights and exultations of your own.
Eager and never weary we pursued
Our home amusements by the warm peat-fire
At evening; when with pencil and with slate,
In square divisions parcell'd out, and all
With crosses and with cyphers scribbled o'er,
We schemed and puzzled, head opposed to head
In strife too humble to be named in verse.
Or round the naked table, snow-white deal,
Cherry or maple, sate in close array,
And to the combat, Lu or Whist, led on
A thick-ribbed army; not as in the world
Neglected and ungratefully thrown by
Even for the very service they had wrought,
But husbanded through many a long campaign.
Uncouth assemblage was it, where no few
Had changed their functions, some, plebeian cards,
Which Fate beyond the promise of their birth
Had glorified, and call'd to represent
The persons of departed potentates.

Oh! with what echoes on the board they fell!
Ironic diamonds, clubs, hearts, diamonds, spades,
A congregation piteously akin.
Cheap matter did they give to boyish wit,
Those sooty knaves, precipitated down
With scoffs and taunts, like Vulcan out of heaven,
The paramount ace, a moon in her eclipse,
Queens, gleaming through their splendour's last decay,
And monarchs, surly at the wrongs sustain'd
By royal visages. Meanwhile, abroad
The heavy rain was falling, or the frost
Raged bitterly, with keen and silent tooth,
And, interrupting oft the impassion'd game,
From Esthwaite's neighbouring lake the splitting ice,
While it sank down towards the water, sent,
Among the meadows and the hills, its long
And dismal yellings, like the noise of wolves
When they are howling round the Bothnic main.

from *The Prelude* (1805 version)

A CAMBRIDGE UNDERGRADUATE

It was a dreary morning when the chaise
Roll'd over the flat plains of Huntingdon
And, through the open windows, first I saw
The long-back'd chapel of King's College rear
His pinnacles above the dusky groves.

Soon afterwards, we espied upon the road,
A student cloth'd in gown and tassell'd cap;
He pass'd; nor was I master of my eyes
Till he was left a hundred yards behind.
The place, as we approach'd, seem'd more and more
To have an eddy's force, and suck'd us in
More eagerly at every step we took.
Onward we drove beneath the castle, down
By Magdalene Bridge we went and cross'd the Cam,
And at the *Hoop* we landed, famous inn.

My spirit was up, my thoughts were full of hope;
Some friends I had, acquaintances who there
Seem'd friends, poor simple schoolboys, now hung round
With honour and importance; in a world
Of welcome faces up and down I rov'd;
Questions, directions, counsel and advice
Flow'd in upon me from all sides, fresh day
Of pride and pleasure! to myself I seem'd
A man of business and expense, and went
From shop to shop about my own affairs,
To tutors or to tailors, as befel,
From street to street with loose and careless heart.

I was the dreamer, they the dream; I roam'd
Delighted, through the motley spectacle;
Gowns grave or gaudy, doctors, students, streets,
Lamps, gateways, flocks of churches, courts and towers:
Strange transformation for a mountain youth,
A northern villager. As if by word
Of magic or some fairy's power, at once
Behold me rich in monies, and attir'd
In splendid clothes, with hose of silk, and hair
Glittering like rimy trees when frost is keen.
My lordly dressing-gown I pass it by,
With other signs of manhood which supplied
The lack of beard. – The weeks went roundly on,
With invitations, suppers, wine, and fruit,
Smooth housekeeping within, and all without
Liberal and suiting gentleman's array!

The Evangelist St John my patron was,
Three gloomy courts are his; and in the first
Was my abiding-place, a nook obscure!
Right underneath, the college kitchens made
A humming sound, less tuneable than bees,
But hardly less industrious; with shrill notes
Of sharp command and scolding intermix'd.
Near me was Trinity's loquacious clock,
Who never let the quarters, night or day,
Slip by him unproclaim'd, and told the hours

Twice over with a male and female voice.
Her pealing organ was my neighbour too;
And, from my bedroom, I in moonlight nights
Could see, right opposite, a few yards off,
The antechapel, where the statue stood
Of Newton, with his prism and silent face.

  Of college labours, of the lecturer's room,
All studded round, as thick as chairs could stand,
With loyal students, faithful to their books,
Half-and-half idlers, hardy recusants,
And honest dunces; – of important days,
Examinations, when the man was weigh'd
As in the balance, – of excessive hopes,
Tremblings withal, and commendable fears,
Small jealousies, and triumphs good or bad
I make short mention; things they were which then
I did not love, nor do I love them now.

from *The Prelude* (1805 version)

LONDON

  Oh, wond'rous power of words, how sweet they are
According to the meaning which they bring!
Vauxhall and Ranelagh, I then had heard
Of your green groves, and wilderness of lamps,
Your gorgeous ladies, fairy cataracts,
And pageant fireworks; nor must we forget
Those other wonders different in kind,
Though scarcely less illustrious in degree,
The river proudly bridged, the giddy top
And Whispering Gallery of St Paul's, the tombs
Of Westminster, the giants of Guildhall,
Bedlam, and the two maniacs at its gates,
Streets without end, and Churches numberless,
Statues, with flowery gardens in vast Squares,
The Monument, and Armoury of the Tower.

These fond imaginations of themselves
Had long before given way in season due,
Leaving a throng of others in their stead;
And now I looked upon the real scene,
Familiarly perus'd it day by day
With keen and lively pleasure even there
Where disappointment was the strongest, pleas'd
Through courteous self-submission, as a tax
Paid to the object by prescriptive right,
A thing that ought to be. Shall I give way,
Copying the impression of the memory,
Though things unnumber'd idly do half seem
The work of fancy, shall I, as the mood
Inclines me, here describe, for pastime's sake
Some portion of that motley imagery,
A vivid pleasure of my youth, and now
Among the lonely places that I love
A frequent day-dream for my riper mind?
– And first the look and aspect of the place
The broad high-way appearance, as it strikes
On strangers of all ages, the quick dance
Of colours, lights and forms, the Babel din
The endless stream of men, and moving things,
From hour to hour the illimitable walk
Still among streets with clouds and sky above,
The wealth, the bustle and the eagerness,
The glittering chariots with their pamper'd steeds,
Stalls, barrows, porters; midway in the street
The scavenger, who begs with hat in hand,
The labouring hackney coaches, the rash speed
Of coaches travelling far, whirl'd on with horn
Loud blowing, and the sturdy drayman's team,
Ascending from some alley of the Thames
And striking right across the crowded Strand
Till the fore horse veer round with punctual skill:
Here there and everywhere a weary throng
The comers and the goers face to face,
Face after face; the string of dazzling wares,

Shop after shop, with symbols, blazon'd names,
And all the tradesman's honours overhead;
Here, fronts of houses, like a title-page
With letters huge inscribed from top to toe;
Station'd above the door, like guardian saints,
There, allegoric shapes, female or male;
Or physiognomies of real men,
Land-Warriors, Kings, or Admirals of the sea,
Boyle, Shakespeare, Newton, or the attractive head
Of some Scotch doctor, famous in his day.

Meanwhile the roar continues, till at length,
Escaped as from an enemy, we turn
Abruptly into some sequester'd nook
Still as a shelter'd place when winds blow loud:
At leisure thence, through tracts of thin resort,
And sights and sounds that come at intervals,
We take our way: a raree-show is here
With children gather'd round, another street
Presents a company of dancing dogs,
Or dromedary, with an antic pair
Of monkeys on his back, a minstrel band
Of Savoyards, or, single and alone,
An English ballad-singer. Private courts,
Gloomy as coffins, and unsightly lanes
Thrill'd by some female vendor's scream, belike
The very shrillest of all London cries,
May then entangle us awhile,
Conducted through these labyrinths unawares
To privileg'd regions and inviolate,
Where from their airy lodges studious lawyers
Look out on waters, walks, and gardens green.

Thence back into the throng, until we reach,
Following the tide that slackens by degrees,
Some half-frequented scene where wider streets
Bring straggling breezes of suburban air;
Here files of ballads dangle from dead walls,
Advertisements of giant-size, from high
Press forward in all colours on the sight;

These, bold in conscious merit; lower down
That, fronted with a most imposing word,
Is, peradventure, one in masquerade.
As on the broadening causeway we advance,
Behold a face turn'd up towards us, strong
In lineaments, and red with over-toil;
'Tis one perhaps, already met elsewhere,
A travelling cripple, by the trunk cut short,
And stumping with his arms: in sailor's garb
Another lies at length beside a range
Of written characters, with chalk inscrib'd
Upon the smooth flat stones: the nurse is here,
The bachelor that loves to sun himself,
The military idler, and the dame,
That field-ward takes her walk in decency.

Now homeward through the thickening hubbub, where
See, among less distinguishable shapes,
The Italian, with his frame of images
Upon his head; with basket at his waist
The Jew; the stately and slow-moving Turk
With freight of slippers piled beneath his arm.
Briefly, we find, if tired of random sights
And haply to that search our thoughts should turn,
Among the crowd, conspicuous less or more,
As we proceed, all specimens of man
Through all the colours which the sun bestows,
And every character of form and face,
The Swede, the Russian; from the genial South,
The Frenchman and the Spaniard; from remote
America, the Hunter-Indian; Moors,
Malays, Lascars, the Tartar and Chinese,
And Negro ladies in white muslin gowns.

from *The Prelude* (1805 version)

A PREACHER

. . . Other public shows
The capital city teems with, of a kind
More light, and where but in the holy Church?
There have I seen a comely bachelor,
Fresh from a toilette of two hours, ascend
The pulpit, with seraphic glance look up,
And, in a tone elaborately low
Beginning, lead his voice through many a maze,
A minuet course, and winding up his mouth,
From time to time into an orifice
Most delicate, a lurking eyelet, small
And only not invisible, again
Open it out, diffusing thence a smile
Of rapt irradiation exquisite.
Meanwhile the Evangelists, Isaiah, Job,
Moses, and he who penn'd the other day
The death of Abel, Shakespeare, Doctor Young,
And Ossian, (doubt not, 'tis the naked truth)
Summon'd from streamy Morven, each and all
Must in their turn lend ornament and flowers
To entwine the crook of eloquence with which
This pretty shepherd, pride of all the plains,
Leads up and down his captivated flock.

from *The Prelude* (1805 version)

SAMUEL TAYLOR COLERIDGE

From THE DELINQUENT TRAVELLERS

Keep moving! Steam, or Gas, or Stage,
Hold, cabin, steerage, hencoop's cage –
Tour, Journey, Voyage, Lounge, Ride, Walk,
Skim, Sketch, Excursion, Travel-talk –

For move you must! 'Tis now the rage,
The law and fashion of the Age.
If you but perch, where Dover tallies,
So strangely with the coast of Calais,
With a good glass and knowing look,
You'll soon get matter for a book!
Or else, in Gas-car, take your chance
Like that adventurous king of France,
Who, once, with twenty thousand men
Went up – and then came down again;
At least, he moved if nothing more:
And if there's nought left to explore,
Yet while your well-greased wheels keep spinning,
The traveller's honoured name you're winning,
And, snug as Jonas in the Whale,
You may loll back and dream a tale.
Move, or be moved – there's no protection,
Our Mother Earth has ta'en the infection –
(That rogue Copernicus, 'tis said
First put the whirring in her head,)
A planet She, and can't endure
T'exist without her annual Tour:
The *name* were else a mere misnomer,
Since Planet is but Greek for *Roamer*.

JAMES and HORACE SMITH

BRIGHTON

Now fruitful autumn lifts his sunburnt head,
  The slighted Park few cambric muslins whiten,
The dry machines revisit Ocean's bed,
  And Horace quits awhile the town for Brighton.

The cit foregoes his box at Turnham Green,
  To pick up health and shells with Amphitrite,
Pleasure's frail daughters trip along the Steyne,
  Led by the dame the Greeks call Aphrodite.

Phœbus, the tanner, plies his fiery trade,
  The graceful nymphs ascend Judea's ponies,
Scale the west cliff, or visit the parade,
  While poor papa in town a patient drone is.

Loose trousers snatch the wreath from pantaloons;
  Nankeen of late were worn the sultry weather in;
But now, (so will the Prince's Light Dragoons,)
  White jean have triumph'd o'er their Indian brethren.

Here with choice food earth smiles and ocean yawns,
  Intent alike to please the London glutton,
This, for our breakfast proffers shrimps and prawns,
  That, for our dinner, South-down lamb and mutton.

Yet here, as elsewhere, death impartial reigns,
  Visits alike the cot and the Pavilion,
And for a bribe, with equal scorn disdains
  My half a crown, and Baring's half a million.

Alas, how short the span of human pride!
  Time flies, and hope's romantic schemes are undone;
Cosweller's coach, that carries four inside,
  Waits to take back the unwilling bard to London.

Ye circulating novelist, adieu!
  Long envious cords my black portmanteau tighten;
Billiards, begone! avaunt, illegal loo!
  Farewell old Ocean's bauble, glittering Brighton!

from *Horace in London*

NEW BUILDINGS

Saint George's Fields are fields no more,
  The trowel supersedes the plough;
Huge inundated swamps of yore,
  Are changed to civic villas now.

The builder's plank, the mason's hod,
  Wide, and more wide extending still,
Usurp the violated sod,
  From Lambeth Marsh, to Balaam Hill.

Pert poplars, yew trees, water tubs,
  No more at Clapham meet the eye,
But velvet lawns, Acacian shrubs,
  With perfume greet the passer-by.

Thy carpets, Persia, deck our floors,
  Chintz curtains shade the polish'd pane,
Verandahs guard the darken'd doors,
  Where dunning Phœbus knocks in vain.

Not thus acquir'd was Gresham's hoard,
  Who founded London's mart of trade,
Not such thy life, Grimalkins lord,
  Who Bow's recalling peal obey'd.

In Mark or Mincing Lane confin'd,
  In cheerful toil they pass'd the hours,
'Twas theirs to leave their wealth behind;
  To lavish, while we live, is ours.

They gave no treats to thankless kings;
  Many their gains, their wants were few;
They built no house with spacious wings,
  To give their riches pinions too.

Yet someone leaving in the lurch
  Sons, to luxurious folly prone,
Their funds rebuilt the parish church –
  Oh! pious waste, to us unknown.

We from our circle never roam,
  Nor ape our sires' eccentric sins;
Our charity begins at home,
  And mostly ends where it begins.

from *Horace in London*

EBENEZER ELLIOT

THE FOX-HUNTERS

What Gods are these? Bright red, or white and green,
Some of them jockey-capp'd and some in hats,
The gods of vermin have their runs, like rats.
Each has six legs, four moving, pendent two,
Like bottled tails, the tilting four between.
Behold Land-Interest's compound Man-and-Horse,
Which so enchants his outraged helot-crew,
Hedge-gapping, with his horn, and view-halloo,
O'er hunter's clover – glorious broom and gorse!
The only crop his godship ever grew:
Except his crop of hate, and smouldering ire,
And cloak'd contempt, of coward insult born,
And hard-faced labour, paid with straw for corn,
And fain to reap it with a scythe of fire.

GEORGE GORDON, LORD BYRON

THE APPROACH TO LONDON

What a delightful thing's a turnpike road!
  So smooth, so level, such a mode of shaving
The earth, as scarce the eagle in the broad
  Air can accomplish, with his wide wings waving.
Had such been cut in Phaeton's time, the god
  Had told his son to satisfy this craving
With the York Mail; – but onwards as we roll,
'*Surgit amari aliquid*' – the toll!

Alas! how deeply painful is all payment!
  Take lives, take wives, take aught except men's purses.
As Machiavel shows those in purple raiment,
  Such is the shortest way to general curses.

They hate a murderer much less than a claimant
  On that sweet ore which everybody nurses. –
Kill a man's family, and he may brook it,
But keep your hands out of his breeches' pocket:

So said the Florentine; ye monarchs, hearken
  To your instructor. Juan now was borne,
Just as the day began to wane and darken,
  O'er the high hill, which looks with pride or scorn
Toward the great city. – Ye who have a spark in
  Your veins of Cockney spirit, smile or mourn
According as you take things well or ill;
Bold Britons, we are now on Shooter's Hill!

The sun went down, the smoke rose up, as from
  A half-unquenched volcano, o'er a space
Which well beseem'd the 'Devil's drawing-room,'
  As some have qualified that wondrous place:
But Juan felt, though not approaching *home*,
  As one who, though he were not of the race,
Revered the soil, of those true sons the mother,
Who butcher'd half the earth, and bullied t'other.

A mighty mass of brick, and smoke, and shipping,
  Dirty and dusky, but as wide as eye
Could reach, with here and there a sail just skipping
  In sight, then lost amidst the forestry
Of masts; a wilderness of steeples peeping
  On tiptoe through their sea-coal canopy;
A huge, dun cupola, like a foolscap crown
On a fool's head – and there is London Town!

But Juan saw not this: each wreath of smoke
  Appear'd to him but as the magic vapour
Of some alchymic furnace, from whence broke
  The wealth of worlds (a wealth of tax and paper):
The gloomy clouds, which o'er it as a yoke
  Are bow'd, and put the sun out like a taper,
Were nothing but the natural atmosphere,
Extremely wholesome, though but rarely clear.

from *Don Juan* (Canto X)

ARRIVAL IN LONDON

Hail! Thamis, hail! Upon thy verge it is
That Juan's chariot, rolling like a drum
In thunder, holds the way it can't well miss,
Through Kennington and all the other 'tons',
Which makes us wish ourselves in town at once; –

Through Groves, so call'd as being void of trees,
(Like *lucus* from *no* light); through prospects named
Mount Pleasant, as containing nought to please,
Nor much to climb; through little boxes framed
Of bricks, to let the dust in at your ease,
With 'To be let', upon their doors proclaim'd;
Through 'Rows' most modestly call'd 'Paradise',
Which Eve might quit without much sacrifice; –

Through coaches, drays, choked turnpikes, and a whirl
Of wheels, and roar of voices, and confusion;
Here taverns wooing to a pint of 'purl',
There mails fast flying off like a delusion;
There barbers' block with periwigs in curl
In windows; here the lamplighter's infusion
Slowly distill'd into the glimmering glass
(For in those days we had not got to gas –);

Through this, and much, and more, is the approach
Of travellers to mighty Babylon:
Whether they come by horse, or chaise, or coach,
With slight exceptions, all the ways seem one.
I could say more, but do not choose to encroach
Upon the Guide-book's privilege. The sun
Had set some time, and night was on the ridge
Of twilight, as the party cross'd the bridge.

That's rather fine, the gentle sound of Thamis –
Who vindicates a moment, too, his stream –
Though hardly heard through multifarious 'damme's'.
The lamps of Westminster's more regular gleam,
The breadth of pavement, and yon shrine where fame is
A spectral resident – whose pallid beam

In shape of moonshine hovers o'er the pile –
Make this a sacred part of Albion's isle.

The Druid's groves are gone – so much the better:
  Stone-Henge is not – but what the devil is it? –
But Bedlam still exists with its sage fetter,
  That madmen may not bite you on a visit;
The Bench too seats or suits full many a debtor;
  The Mansion-House, too (though some people quiz it),
To me appears a stiff yet grand erection;
But then the Abbey's worth the whole collection.

The line of lights, too, up to Charing Cross,
  Pall Mall, and so forth, have a coruscation
Like gold as in comparison to dross,
  Match'd with the Continent's illumination.
Whose cities Night by no means deigns to gloss.
  The French were not yet a lamp-lighting nation,
And when they grew so – on their new-found lantern,
Instead of wicks, they made a wicked man turn.

A row of gentlemen along the streets
  Suspended, may illuminate mankind,
As also bonfires made of country-seats;
  But the old way is best for the purblind:
The other looks like phosphorus on sheets,
  A sort of ignis fatuus to the mind,
Which, though 'tis certain to perplex and frighten,
Must burn more mildly ere it can enlighten.

But London's so well lit, that if Diogenes
  Could recommence to hunt his *honest man*,
And found him not amidst the various progenies
  Of this enormous city's spreading spawn,
'Twere not for want of lamps to aid his dodging his
  Yet undiscover'd treasure. What *I* can,
I've done to find the same throughout life's journey,
But see the world is only one attorney.

Over the stones still rattling, up Pall Mall,
  Through crowds and carriages, but waxing thinner

As thunder'd knockers broke the long-seal'd spell
  Of doors 'gainst duns, and to an early dinner
Admitted a small party as night fell, –
  Don Juan, our young diplomatic sinner,
Pursued his path, and drove past some hotels,
St James's Palace and St James's 'Hells'.

They reach'd the hotel: forth stream'd from the front door
  A tide of well-clad waiters, and around
The mob stood, and as usual several score
  Of those pedestrian Paphians who abound
In decent London when the daylight's o'er;
  Commodious, but immoral, they are found
Useful, like Malthus, in promoting marriage. –
But Juan now is stepping from his carriage.

Into one of the sweetest hotels,
  Especially for foreigners – and mostly
For those whom favour or whom fortune swells,
  And cannot find a bill's small items costly.
There many an envoy either dwelt or dwells
  (The den of many a diplomatic lost lie),
Until to some conspicuous square they pass,
And blazon o'er the door their names in brass.

from *Don Juan* (Canto XI)

LIFE IN LONDON

His morns he pass'd in business – which dissected,
  Was like all business, a laborious nothing
That leads to lassitude, the most infected
  And Centaur Nessus garb of mortal clothing,
And on our sofas makes us lie dejected,
  And talk in tender horrors of our loathing
All kinds of toil, save for our country's good –
Which grows no better, though 'tis time it should.

His afternoons he pass'd in visits, luncheons,
  Lounging, and boxing, and the twilight hour
In riding round those vegetable puncheons
  Call'd 'Parks', where there is neither fruit nor flower
Enough to gratify a bee's slight munchings;
  But after all it is the only 'bower'
(In Moore's phrase) where the fashionable fair
Can form a slight acquaintance with fresh air.

Then dress, then dinner, then awakes the world!
  Then glare the lamps, then whirl the wheels, then roar
Through street and square fast flashing chariots hurl'd
  Like harness'd meteors; then along the floor
Chalk mimics painting; then festoons are twirl'd;
  Then roll the brazen thunders of the door,
Which opens to the thousand happy few
An earthly paradise of 'Or Molu'.

There stands the noble hostess, nor shall sink
  With the three-thousandth curtsy; there the waltz,
The only dance which teaches girls to think,
  Makes one in love even with its very faults.
Saloon, room, hall, o'erflow beyond their brink,
  And long the latest of arrivals halts,
'Midst royal dukes and dames condemn'd to climb,
And gain an inch of staircase at a time.

Thrice happy he who, after a survey
  Of the good company, can win a corner,
A door that's *in* or boudoir *out* of the way,
  Where he may fix himself like small 'Jack Horner',
And let the Babel round run as it may,
  And look on as a mourner, or a scorner,
Or an approver, or a mere spectator,
Yawning a little as the night grows later.

But this won't do, save by and by; and he
  Who, like Don Juan, takes an active share,
Must steer with care through all that glittering sea
  Of gems and plumes and pearls and silks, to where

He deems it is his proper place to be;
  Dissolving in the waltz to some soft air,
Or proudlier prancing with mercurial skill,
Where Science marshals forth her own quadrille.

Or, if he dance not, but hath higher views
  Upon an heiress or his neighbour's bride,
Let him take care that that which he pursues
  Is not at once too palpably descried.
Full many an eager gentleman oft rues
  His haste; impatience is a blundering guide,
Amongst a people famous for reflection,
Who like to play the fool with circumspection.

But, if you can contrive, get next at supper;
  Or if forestall'd, get opposite and ogle: –
Oh, ye ambrosial moments! always upper
  In mind, a sort of sentimental bogle,
Which sits for ever upon memory's crupper,
  The ghost of vanish'd pleasures once in vogue! Ill
Can tender souls relate the rise and fall
Of hopes and fears which shake a single ball.

from *Don Juan* (Canto XI)

DEPARTURE TO THE COUNTRY

The English winter – ending in July,
  To recommence in August – now was done.
'Tis the postilion's paradise: wheels fly;
  On roads, east, south, north, west, there is a run.
But for post-horses who finds sympathy?
  Man's pity for himself, or for his son,
Always premising that said son at college
Has not contracted much more debt than knowledge.

The London winter's ended in July –
  Sometimes a little later. I don't err
In this: whatever other blunders lie
  Upon my shoulders, here I must aver

My muse a glass of weatherology;
  For parliament is our barometer:
Let radicals its other acts attack,
Its sessions form our only almanack.

When its quicksilver's down at zero, – lo!
  Coach, chariot, luggage, baggage, equipage!
Wheels whirl from Carlton palace to Soho,
  And happiest they who horses can engage;
The turnpikes glow with dust; and Rotten Row
  Sleeps from the chivalry of this bright age;
And tradesmen, with long bills and longer faces,
Sigh – as the postboys fasten on the traces.

They and their bills, 'Arcadians both', are left
  To the Greek kalends of another session.
Alas! to them of ready cash bereft,
  What hope remains? Of *hope* the full possession
Of generous draft, conceded as a gift,
  At a long date – till they can get a fresh one –
Hawk'd about at a discount, small or large;
Also the solace of an overcharge.

But these are trifles. Downward flies my lord,
  Nodding beside my lady in his carriage.
Away! away! 'Fresh horses!' are the word,
  And changed as quickly as hearts after marriage;
The obsequious landlord hath the change restored;
  The postboys have no reason to disparage
Their fee; but ere the water'd wheels may hiss hence,
The ostler pleads too for a reminiscence.

'Tis granted; and the valet mounts the dickey –
  That gentleman of lords and gentlemen;
Also my lady's gentlewoman, tricky,
  Trick'd out, but modest more than poet's pen
Can paint, – '*Cosi viaggino i Ricchi!*'
  (Excuse a foreign slipslop now and then,
If but to show I've travell'd: and what's travel,
Unless it teaches one to quote and cavil?)

The London winter and the country summer
  Were well nigh over. 'Tis perhaps a pity,
When nature wears the gown that doth become her.
  To lose those best months in a sweaty city,
And wait until the nightingale grows dumber,
  Listening debates not very wise or witty,
Ere patriots their true *country* can remember; –
But there's no shooting (save grouse) till September.

from *Don Juan* (Canto XIII)

LIFE IN THE COUNTRY

Lord Henry and his lady were the hosts;
  The party we have touch'd on were the guests.
Their table was a board to tempt even ghosts
  To pass the Styx for more substantial feasts.
I will not dwell upon ragoûts or roasts,
  Albeit all human history attests
That happiness for man – the hungry sinner! –
Since Eve ate apples, much depends on dinner.

Witness the lands which 'flow'd with milk and honey',
  Held out unto the hungry Israelites:
To this we have added since, the love of money,
  The only sort of pleasure which requites.
Youth fades, and leaves our days no longer sunny;
  We tire of mistresses and parasites;
But oh, ambrosial cash! Ah! who would lose thee?
When we no more can use, or even abuse thee!

The gentlemen got up betimes to shoot,
  Or hunt: the young, because they liked the sport –
The first thing boys like after play and fruit;
  The middle-aged, to make the day more short;
For *ennui* is a growth of English root,
  Though nameless in our language: – we retort
The fact for words, and let the French translate
That awful yawn which sleep cannot abate.

The elderly walk'd through the library,
  And tumbled books, or criticized the pictures,
Or saunter'd through the gardens piteously,
  And made upon the hot-house several strictures,
Or rode a nag which trotted not too high,
  Or on the morning papers read their lectures,
Or on the watch their longing eyes would fix,
Longing at sixty for the hour of six.

But none were 'gêné': the great hour of union
  Was rung by dinner's knell; till then all were
Masters of their own time – or in communion,
  Or solitary, as they chose to bear
The hours, which how to pass is but to few known.
  Each rose up at his own, and had to spare
What time he chose for dress, and broke his fast
When, where, and how he chose for that repast.

The ladies – some rouged, some a little pale –
  Met the morn as they might. If fine, they rode,
Or walk'd; if foul, they read, or told a tale,
  Sung, or rehearsed the last dance from abroad;
Discuss'd the fashion which might next prevail,
  And settled bonnets by the newest code,
Or cramm'd twelve sheets into one little letter,
To make each correspondent a new debtor.

For some had absent lovers, all had friends.
  The earth has nothing like a she epistle,
And hardly heaven – because it never ends.
  I love the mystery of a female missal,
Which, like a creed, ne'er says all it intends,
  But full of cunning as Ulysses' whistle,
When he allured poor Dolon: – you had better
Take care what you reply to such a letter.

Then there were billiards; cards, too, but *no* dice; –
  Save in the clubs no man of honour plays; –
Boats when 'twas water, skating when 'twas ice,
  And the hard frost destroy'd the scenting days:

And angling, too, that solitary vice,
  Whatever Izaak Walton sings or says:
The quaint, old, cruel coxcomb, in his gullet
Should have a hook, and a small trout to pull it.

With evening came the banquet and the wine;
  The conversazione; the duet,
Attuned by voices more or less divine
  (My heart or head aches with the memory yet).
The four Miss Rawbolds in a glee would shine;
  But the two youngest loved more to be set
Down to the harp – because to music's charms
They added graceful necks, white hands and arms.

Sometimes a dance (though rarely on field days,
  For then the gentlemen were rather tired)
Display'd some sylph-like figures in its maze;
  Then there was small-talk ready when required;
Flirtation – but decorous; the mere praise
  Of charms that should or should not be admired.
The hunters fought their fox-hunt o'er again,
And then retreated soberly – at ten.

The politicians, in a nook apart,
  Discuss'd the world, and settled all the spheres;
The wits watch'd every loophole for their art,
  To introduce a bon-mot head and ears;
Small is the rest of those who would be smart,
  A moment's good thing may have cost them years
Before they find an hour to introduce it;
And then, even *then*, some bore may make them lose it.

But all was gentle and aristocratic
  In this our party; polish'd, smooth, and cold,
As Phidian forms cut out of marble Attic.
  There now are no Squire Westerns as of old;
And our Sophias are not so emphatic,
  But fair as then, or fairer to behold.
We have no accomplish'd blackguards, like Tom Jones,
But gentlemen in stays, as stiff as stones.

They separated at an early hour;
  That is, ere midnight – which is London's noon:
But in the country ladies seek their bower
  A little earlier than the waning moon.
Peace to the slumbers of each folded flower –
  May the rose call back its true colour soon!
Good hours of fair cheeks are the fairest tinters,
And lower the price of rouge – at least some winters.

from *Don Juan* (Canto XIII)

DINNER AT A COUNTRY HOUSE

Great things were now to be achieved at table,
  With massy plate for armour, knives and forks
For weapons; but what Muse since Homer's able
  (His feasts are not the worst part of his works)
To draw up in array a single day-bill
  Of modern dinners? where more mystery lurks,
In soups or sauces, or a sole ragoût,
Than witches, b—ches, or physicians, brew.

There was a goodly 'soupe à la *bonne femme*',
  Though God knows whence it came from; there was, too,
A turbot for relief of those who cram,
  Relieved with 'dindon à la Parigeux':
There also was – the sinner that I am!
  How shall I get this gourmand stanza through? –
'Soupe à la Beauveau', whose relief was dory,
Relieved itself by pork, for greater glory.

But I must crowd all into one grand mess,
  Or mass; for should I stretch into detail,
My Muse would run much more into excess,
  Than when some squeamish people deem her frail;
But though a 'bonne vivante', I must confess
  Her stomach's not her peccant part; this tale
However doth require some slight refection,
Just to relieve her spirits from dejection.

Fowls 'à la Condé', slices eke of salmon,
  With 'sauces Génévoises', and haunch of venison:
Wines, too, which might again have slain young Ammon –
  A man like whom I hope we shan't see many soon;
They also set a glazed Westphalian ham on,
  Whereupon Apicius would bestow his benison;
And then there was champagne with foaming whirls,
As white as Cleopatra's melted pearls.

Then there was God knows what 'à l'Allemande',
  'A l'Espagnole', 'timballe', and 'salpicon' –
With things I can't withstand or understand,
  Though swallow'd with much zest upon the whole;
And 'entremets' to piddle with at hand,
  Gently to lull down the subsiding soul;
While great Lucullus' *Rome triumphal* muffles –
(*There's fame*) – young partridge fillets, deck'd with truffles.

What are the *fillets* on the victor's brow
  To these? They are rags or dust. Where is the arch
Which nodded to the nation's spoils below?
  Where the triumphal chariots' haughty march?
Gone to where victories must like dinners go.
  Farther I shall not follow the research:
But oh! ye modern heroes with your cartridges,
When will your names lend lustre e'en to partridges?

Those truffles too are no bad accessaries,
  Follow'd by 'petits puits d'amour' – a dish
Of which perhaps the cookery rather varies,
  So every one may dress it to his wish,
According to the best of dictionaries,
  Which encyclopedize both flesh and fish;
But even sans 'confitures', it no less true is,
There's pretty picking in those 'petit puits'.

The mind is lost in mighty contemplation
  Of intellect expanded on two courses;
And indigestion's grand multiplication
  Requires arithmetic beyond my forces.

Who would suppose, from Adam's simple ration,
  That cookery could have call'd forth such resources,
As form a science and a nomenclature
From out the commonest demands of nature?

The glasses jingled, and the palates tingled;
  The diners of celebrity dined well;
The ladies with more moderation mingled
  In the feast, pecking less than I can tell;
Also the younger men too: for a springald
  Can't, like ripe age, in gormandise excel,
But thinks less of good eating than the whisper
(When seated next him) of some pretty lisper.

Alas! I must leave undescribed the gibier,
  The salmi, the consommé, the purée,
All which I use to make my rhymes run glibber
  Than could roast beef in our rough John Bull way:
I must not introduce even a spare rib here,
  'Bubble and squeak' would spoil my liquid lay,
But I have dined, and must forego, alas!
The chaste description even of a 'bécasse';

And fruits, and ice, and all that art refines
  From nature for the service of the goût –
Taste or the *gout*, – pronounce it as inclines
  Your stomach? Ere you dine, the French will do;
But *after*, there are sometimes certain signs
  Which prove plain English truer of the two.
Hast ever *had* the *gout*? I have not had it –
But I may have, and you too, reader, dread it.

from *Don Juan* (Canto XV)

JOHN CLARE

A SHEPHERD'S COTTAGE

The shutter closed, the lamp alight,
The faggot chopt and blazing bright –
The shepherd now, from labour free,
Dances his children on his knee;
While, underneath his master's seat,
The tired dog lies in slumbers sweet,
Starting and whimpering in his sleep,
Chasing still the straying sheep.
The cat's roll'd round in vacant chair
Or leaping children's knees to lair,
Or purring on the warmer hearth,
Sweet chorus to the cricket's mirth.

The redcap, hanging overhead,
In cage of wire is perch'd abed;
Slumbering in his painted feathers,
Unconscious of the outdoor weathers;
Ev'n things without the cottage walls
Meet comfort as the evening falls,
As happy in the winter's dearth
As those around the blazing hearth.
The ass (frost-driven from the moor,
Where storms through naked bushes roar,
And not a leaf or sprig of green,
On ground or quaking bush, is seen,
Save grey-vein'd ivy's hardy pride,
Round old trees by the common side),
Litter'd with straw, now dozes warm,
Beneath his shed, from snow and storm:
The swine are fed and in the sty;
And fowls snug perch'd in hovel nigh,
With head in feathers safe asleep,
Where foxes cannot hope to creep,
And geese are gabbling in their dreams
Of litter'd corn and thawing streams.

The sparrow, too, a daily guest,
Is in the cottage eaves at rest;
And robin small, and smaller wren,
Are in their warm holes safe agen
From falling snows, that winnow by
The hovels where they nightly lie,
And ague winds, that shake the tree
Where other birds are forc'd to be.

The housewife, busy night and day,
Clears the supper-things away;
The jumping cat starts from her seat;
And stretching up on weary feet,
The dog wakes at the welcome tones
That call him up to pick the bones.

On corner walls, a glittering row,
Hang fire-irons – less for use than show,
With horse-shoe brighten'd, as a spell,
Witchcraft's evil powers to quell,
And warming-pan, reflecting bright
The crackling blaze's flickering light,
That hangs the corner wall to grace,
Nor oft is taken from its place:
There in its mirror, bright as gold,
The children peep, and straight behold
Their laughing faces, whilst they pass,
Gleam on the lid as plain as glass.

from *The Shepherd's Calendar*

MAY

Come, Queen of Months! in company
With all thy merry minstrelsy:
The restless cuckoo, absent long,
And twittering swallows' chimney-song;
With hedgerow crickets' notes, that run
From every bank that fronts the sun;

And swarthy bees, about the grass,
That stop with every bloom they pass,
And every minute, every hour,
Keep teasing weeds that wear a flower;
And toil, and childhood's humming joys,
For there is music in the noise
When village children, wild for sport,
In school-time's leisure, ever short,
Alternate catch the bounding ball,
Or run along the churchyard wall,
Capp'd with rude figured slabs, whose claims
In time's bad memory have no names,
Or race around the nooky church,
Or raise loud echoes in the porch,
Throw pebbles o'er the weathercock,
Viewing with jealous eyes the clock,
Or leap o'er grave-stones' leaning heights,
Uncheck'd by melancholy sights,
Though green grass swells in many a heap
Where kin, and friends, and parents sleep.
They think not, in their jovial cry,
The time will come when they shall lie
As lowly and as still as they,
While other boys above them play,
Heedless, as they are now, to know
The unconscious dust that lies below.

The driving boy, beside his team,
Of May-month's beauty now will dream,
And cock his hat, and turn his eye
On flower, and tree, and deepening sky;
And oft burst loud in fits of song,
And whistle as he reels along,
Cracking his whip in starts of joy –
A happy, dirty, driving boy.
The youth, who leaves his corner stool
Betimes for neighbouring village-school,
Where, as a mark to guide him right,
The church spire's all the way in sight,

With cheerings from his parents given,
Beneath the joyous smiles of heaven
Saunters, with many an idle stand,
With satchel swinging in his hand,
And gazes, as he passes by,
On everything that meets his eye.
Young lambs seem tempting him to play,
Dancing and bleating in his way;
With trembling tails and pointed ears
They follow him, and lose their fears;
He smiles upon their sunny faces,
And fain would join their happy races.
The birds, that sing on bush and tree,
Seem chirping for his company;
And all – in fancy's idle whim –
Seem keeping holiday, but him.
He lolls upon each resting stile,
To see the fields so sweetly smile,
To see the wheat grow green and long;
And lists the weeder's toiling song,
Or short note of the changing thrush
Above him in the whitethorn bush,
That o'er the leaning stile bends low
Its blooming mockery of snow.

Each hedge is cover'd thick with green;
And where the hedger late hath been,
Young tender shoots begin to grow
From out the mossy stumps below.
But woodmen still on spring intrude,
And thin the shadow's solitude;
With sharpen'd axes felling down
The oak-trees budding into brown,
Which, as they crash upon the ground,
A crowd of labourers gather round.
These, mixing 'mong the shadows dark,
Rip off the crackling, staining bark,
Depriving yearly, when they come,
The green woodpecker of his home,

Who early in the spring began,
Far from the sight of troubling man,
To bore his round holes in each tree
In fancy's sweet security;
Now, startled by the woodman's noise,
He wakes from all his dreary joys.
The blue-bells too, that thickly bloom
Where man was never known to come;
And stooping lilies of the valley,
That love with shades and dews to dally,
And bending droop on slender threads,
With broad hood-leaves above their heads,
Like white-robed maids, in summer hours,
Beneath umbrellas shunning showers;
These, from the bark-men's crushing treads,
Oft perish in their blooming beds.
Stripp'd of its boughs and bark, in white
The trunk shines in the mellow light
Beneath the green surviving trees,
That wave above it in the breeze,
And, waking whispers, slowly bend,
As if they mourn'd their fallen friend.

Each morning, now, the weeders meet
To cut the thistle from the wheat,
And ruin, in the sunny hours,
Full many a wild weed with its flowers;
Corn-poppies, that in crimson dwell,
Call'd 'headaches', from their sickly smell;
And charlocks, yellow as the sun,
That o'er the May-fields quickly run;
And 'iron-weed', content to share
The meanest spot that spring can spare –
E'en roads, where danger hourly comes,
Are not without its purple blooms,
Whose leaves, with threat'ning thistles round
Thick set, that have no strength to wound,
Shrink into childhood's eager hold
Like hair; and, with its eye of gold

And scarlet-starry points of flowers,
Pimpernel, dreading nights and showers,
Oft call'd 'the shepherd's weather-glass',
That sleeps till suns have dried the grass,
Then wakes, and spreads its creeping bloom
Till clouds with threatening shadows come –
Then close it shuts to sleep again:
Which weeders see, and talk of rain;
And boys, that mark them shut so soon,
Call them 'John-go-to-bed-at-noon'.
And fumitory too – a name
That superstition holds to fame –
Whose red and purple mottled flowers
Are cropp'd by maids in weeding hours,
To boil in water, milk, and whey,
For washes on a holiday,
To make their beauty fair and sleek,
And scare the tan from summer's cheek;
And simple small 'forget-me-not',
Eyed with a pin's-head yellow spot
I' the middle of its tender blue,
That gains from poets notice due:
These flowers, that toil by crowds destroys,
Robbing them of their lowly joys,
Had met the May with hopes as sweet
As those her suns in gardens meet;
And oft the dame will feel inclined,
As childhood's memory comes to mind,
To turn her hook away, and spare
The blooms it loved to gather there.
– Now young girls whisper things of love,
And from the old dames' hearing move;
Oft making 'love-knots' in the shade,
Of blue-green oat or wheaten blade;
Or, trying simple charms and spells
Which rural superstition tells,
They pull the little blossom threads
From out the knotweed's button heads,

And put the husk, with many a smile,
In their white bosoms for a while –
Then, if they guess aright the swain
Their loves' sweet fancies try to gain,
'Tis said, that ere it lies an hour,
'Twill blossom with a second flower,
And from their bosom's handkerchief
Bloom as it ne'er had lost a leaf.
– But signs appear that token wet,
While they are 'neath the bushes met;
The girls are glad with hopes of play,
And harp upon the holiday:
A high blue bird is seen to swim
Along the wheat, when skies grow dim
With clouds; slow as the gales of spring
In motion, with dark-shadow'd wing
Beneath the coming storm he sails:
And lonely chirp the wheat-hid quails,
That come to live with spring again,
But leave when summer browns the grain;
They start the young girls' joys afloat,
With 'wet my foot' – their yearly note:
So fancy doth the sound explain,
And oft it proves a sign of rain!

The thresher, dull as winter days,
And lost to all that spring displays,
Still mid his barn-dust forced to stand,
Swings round his flail with weary hand;
While o'er his head shades thickly creep,
That hide the blinking owl asleep,
And bats, in cobweb-corners bred,
Sharing till night their murky bed.
The sunshine trickles on the floor
Through ev'ry crevice of the door:
This makes his barn, where shadows dwell,
As irksome as a prisoner's cell;
And, whilst he seeks his daily meal,
As schoolboys from their task will steal,

So will he stand with fond delay
To see the daisy in his way,
Or wild weeds flowering on the wall;
For these to memory still recall
The joys, the sports that come with spring –
The twirling top, the marble ring,
The jingling halfpence hustled up
At pitch-and-toss, the eager stoop
To pick up *heads*, the smuggled plays
'Neath hovels upon sabbath-days,
The sitting down, when school was o'er,
Upon the threshold of the door,
Picking from mallows, sport to please,
Each crumpled seed he call'd a cheese,
And hunting from the stack-yard sod
The stinking henbane's belted pod,
By youth's warm fancies sweetly led
To christen them his loaves of bread.
He sees, while rocking down the street
With weary hands and crimpling feet,
Young children at the self-same games,
And hears the self-same boyish names
Still floating on each happy tongue:
Touch'd with the simple scene so strong,
Tears almost start, and many a sigh
Regrets the happiness gone by;
Thus, in sweet Nature's holiday,
His heart is sad while all is gay.

How lovely now are lanes and balks,
For lovers in their Sunday walks!
The daisy and the buttercup –
For which the laughing children stoop
A hundred times throughout the day,
In their rude romping summer play –
So thickly now the pasture crowd,
In a gold and silver sheeted cloud,
As if the drops of April showers
Had woo'd the sun, and changed to flowers.

The brook resumes her summer dresses,
Purling 'neath grass and water-cresses,
And mint and flagleaf, swording high
Their blooms to the unheeding eye,
And taper, bow-bent, hanging rushes,
And horsetail, children's bottle-brushes;

The summer tracks about its brink
Are fresh again where cattle drink;
And on its sunny bank the swain
Stretches his idle length again;
While all that lives enjoys the birth
Of frolic summer's laughing mirth.

from *The Shepherd's Calendar*

HARVESTING

The fields are all alive with sultry noise
Of labour's sounds, and insects' busy joys.
The reapers o'er their glittering sickles stoop,
Starting full oft the partridge coveys up;
Some o'er the rustling scythe go bending on;
And shockers follow where their toils have gone,
Heaping the swaths that rustle in the sun,
Where mice from terror's dangers nimbly run,
Leaving their tender young in fear's alarm
Lapt up in nests of chimbled grasses warm,
Hoping for safety from their flight in vain;
While the rude boy, or churlish-hearted swain,
Pursues with lifted weapons o'er the ground,
And spreads an instant murder all around.
In vain the anxious maiden's tender prayer
Urges the clown their little lives to spare;
She sighs, while trailing the long rake along,
At scenes so cruel, and forgets her song.
When the sun stoops to meet the western sky,
And noon's hot hours have wander'd weary by,

Seeking a hawthorn bush or willow-tree
For resting-places that the coolest be,
Where baskets heaped and unbroached bottle lie,
Which dogs in absence watched with wary eye,
They catch their breath awhile, and share the boon
Which bevering-time allows their toil at noon.
Next to her favour'd swain the maiden steals,
Blushing at kindness which his love reveals;
Making a seat for her of sheaves around,
He drops beside her on the naked ground.
Then from its cool retreat the beer they bring,
And hand the stout-hoop'd bottle round the ring.
Each swain soaks hard; the maiden, ere she sips,
Shrieks at the bold wasp settling on her lips,
That seems determined only hers to greet,
As if it fancied they were cherries sweet!
The dog forgoes his sleep awhile, or play,
Springing at frogs that rustling jump away,
To watch each morsel carelessness bestows,
Or wait the bone or crust the shepherd throws;
For shepherds are no more of ease possest,
But share in harvest-labours with the rest.

from *The Shepherd's Calendar*

THE FODDERING BOY

The foddering boy along the crumping snows
With straw-band-belted legs and folded arm
Hastens, and on the blast that keenly blows
Oft turns for breath, and beats his fingers warm,
And shakes the lodging snows from off his clothes,
Buttoning his doublet closer from the storm
And slouching his brown beaver o'er his nose –
Then faces it agen, and seeks the stack
Within its circling fence where hungry lows
Expecting cattle, making many a track
About the snow, impatient for the sound
When in huge forkfuls trailing at his back

He litters the sweet hay about the ground
And brawls to call the staring cattle round.

BADGER

When midnight comes a host of dogs and men
Go out and track the badger to his den,
And put a sack within the hole, and lie
Till the old grunting badger passes by.
He comes and hears – they let the strongest loose.
The old fox hears the noise and drops the goose.
The poacher shoots and hurries from the cry,
And the old hare half wounded buzzes by.
They get a forkèd stick to bear him down
And clap the dogs and take him to the town,
And bait him all the day with many dogs,
And laugh and shout and fright the scampering hogs.
He runs along and bites at all he meets:
They shout and hollo down the noisy streets.

He turns about to face the loud uproar
And drives the rebels to their very door.
The frequent stone is hurled where'er they go;
When badgers fight, then every one's a foe.
The dogs are clapt and urged to join the fray;
The badger turns and drives them all away.
Though scarcely half as big, demure and small,
He fights with dogs for hours and beats them all.
The heavy mastiff, savage in the fray,
Lies down and licks his feet and turns away.
The bulldog knows his match and waxes cold,
The badger grins and never leaves his hold.
He drives the crowd and follows at their heels
And bites them through – the drunkard swears and reels.

The frighted women take the boys away,
The blackguard laughs and hurries on the fray.
He tries to reach the woods, an awkward race,
But sticks and cudgels quickly stop the chase.

He turns agen and drives the noisy crowd
And beats the many dogs in noises loud.
He drives away and beats them every one,
And then they loose them all and set them on.
He falls as dead and kicked by boys and men,
Then starts and grins and drives the crowd agen;
Till kicked and torn and beaten out he lies
And leaves his hold and cackles, groans, and dies.

FARM BREAKFAST

Maids shout to breakfast in a merry strife,
And the cat runs to hear the whetted knife,
And dogs are ever in the way to watch
The mouldy crust and falling bone to catch.
The wooden dishes round in haste are set,
And round the table all the boys are met;
All know their own save Hodge who would be first,
But every one his master leaves the worst.
On every wooden dish, a humble claim,
Two rude-cut letters mark the owner's name;
From every nook the smile of plenty calls,
And reasty flitches decorate the walls,
Moore's Almanack where wonders never cease –
All smeared with candle-snuff and bacon-grease.

THE POOL

Where the clear water rises to the brink,
Battered by cattle coming there to drink,
Boys bring the mower's bottle to the fore
And hold and fill it till it bubbles o'er;
And eager ploughmen with a ruddy face
Throw in a stone to reach the clearest place,
And take a hearty soak and haste away,
And cow-boys seek it twenty times a day;
And when the idle boy has had his fill
He sucks the bubbles with an oaten quill;

While ever shy the timid maiden stands
And stooping sips the water from her hands;
Content to be adry she goes agen,
Because she will not kneel before the men.

SONG

She tied up her few things,
And laced up her shoe-strings,
And put on her bonnet worn through at the crown;
Her apron tied tighter,
Than snow her cap whiter,
She lapt up her earnings and left our old town.

The dog barked again
All the length of his chain,
And licked her hand kindly, and huffed her good-bye;
Old hens prated loudly,
The cock strutted proudly,
And the horse at the gate turned to let her go by.

The threshing man, stopping
The old barn-floor whopping,
Wished o'er the door-cloth her luck and no harm;
Bees hummed round the thistle,
Where the red robins whistle,
And she just had one look on the old mossy farm.

'Twas Michaelmas season,
They'd got corn and peas in,
And all the fields cleared save some rakings and tithes;
Cote-pigeons muster
Round the beans' shelling cluster,
And done are the whettings of reap-hooks and scythes.

Next year's flowers a-springing
Will miss Jenny's singing:
She opened her Bible and turned a leaf down.
In her bosom's forewarnings
She lapt up her earnings
And ere the sun set will be in her own town.

TO JOHN CLARE

Well, honest John, how fare you now at home?
The spring is come, and birds are building nests;
The old cock-robin to the sty is come,
With olive feathers and its ruddy breast;
And the old cock, with wattles and red comb,
Struts with the hens, and seems to like some best,
Then crows, and looks about for little crumbs,
Swept out by little folks an hour ago;
The pigs sleep in the sty; the bookman comes –
The little boy lets home-close nesting go,
And pockets tops and taws, where daisies blow
To look at the new number just laid down,
With lots of pictures, and good stories too,
And Jack the Giant-killer's high renown.

ANONYMOUS

THE TIMES HAVE ALTERED

Come all you swaggering farmers, whoever you may be,
One moment pay attention and listen unto me;
It is concerning former times, as I to you declare,
So different to the present times if you with them compare.

Chorus: For lofty heads and paltry pride, I'm sure it's all the go,
For to distress poor servants and keep their wages low.

If you'd seen the farmers wives 'bout fifty years ago,
In home-spun russet linsey clad from top to toe;
But nowadays the farmer's wives are so puffed up with pride,
In a dandy habit and green veil unto the market they must ride.

Some years ago the farmer's sons were learnt to plough and sow,
And when the summer-time did come, likewise to reap and mow;

But now they dress like Squire's sons, their pride it knows no bounds,
They mount upon a fine blood horse to follow up the hounds.

The farmer's daughters formerly were learnt to card and spin,
And, by their own industry, good husbands they did win;
But now the card and spinning-wheel are forced to take their chance,
While they're hopped off to a boarding-school to learn to sing and dance.

In a decent black silk bonnet to church they used to go,
Black shoes, and handsome cotton gown, stockings as white as snow,
But now silk gowns and coloured shoes they must be bought for them,
Besides they are frizzed and furbelowed just like a freizland hen.

Each morning when at breakfast, the master and the dame
Down with the servants they would sit, and eat and drink the same,
But with such good old things, they've done them quite away;
Into the parlour they do go with coffee, toast, and tea.

At the kitchen table formerly, the farmer he would sit,
And carve for all his servants, both pudding and fine meat,
But now all in the dining-room so closely they're boxed in,
If a servant only was to peep, it would be thought a sin.

Now, in those good old fashion'd times, the truth I do declare,
The rent and taxes could be spared, and money for to spare
But now they keep the fashion up, they look so very nice,
Although they cut an outside show they are as poor as mice.

When Bonaparte was in vogue, poor servants could engage
For sixteen pounds a year, my boys, that was a handsome wage,
But now the wages are so low, and what is worse than all,
The masters cannot find the cash, which brings them to the wall.

When fifty acres they did rent, then money they could save,
But now for to support their pride, five hundred they must have;
If those great farms were taken and divided into ten,
Oh! we might see as happy days as ever we did then.

O TELL ME IN WHICH GIN SHOP MY DEAR

Oh, tell me in which Gin shop my dear,
That I shall meet you at Bartlemy Fair,
Oh, tell me at which Gin shop my dear,
  That I shall meet with thee,
I'll meet thee on September's night
When the Gin-palace shows a flare-up light
So fine to us but not too bright
  To tell who's lushing there.

You've told me when now tell me where,
That I shall meet you at Bartlemy Fair,
Where will you blow your cloud my dear,
  Until I come to thee,
I'll meet you where you know I saw,
The donkeys join in sweet He-Haw,
And on Fridays you so oft did draw
  Your Poll on market-day.

You say you'll meet me at Bartlemy Fair,
But how shall I know that you'll be there,
What chi-ock will you tip my dear
  That I may know 'tis you,
I'll chaunt aloud that charming air,
That costermongers sing so clear,
All around my hat the green willow I'll wear
  And then you'll know 'tis me.

Broadsheet Ballad

GALWAY RACES

It's there you'll see confectioners with sugar sticks and dainties,
The lozenges and oranges, lemonade and the raisins;
The gingerbread and spices to accommodate the ladies,
And a big crubeen for threepence to be picking while you're able.
It's there you'll see the gamblers, the thimbles and the garters,
And the sporting Wheel of Fortune with the four and twenty quarters,

There was others without scruple pelting wattles at poor Maggy,
And her father well contented and he looking at his daughter.

It's there you'll see the pipers and fiddlers competing,
And the nimble-footed dancers and they tripping on the daisies.
There was others crying segars and lights, and bills of all the races
With the colour of the jockeys, the prize and horses' ages.

It's there you'd see the jockeys and they mounted on most stately,
The pink and blue, the red and green, the Emblem of our nation,
When the bell was rung for starting, the horses seemed impatient,
Though they never stood on ground, their speed was so amazing.

There was half a million people there of all denominations,
The Catholic, the Protestant, the Jew and Prespetarian.
There was yet no animosity, no matter what persuasion,
But *failte* and hospitality, inducing fresh acquaintance.

Broadsheet Ballad

CALL THE HORSE, MARROW

Call the horse, marrow,[1]
For I can call nane,
The heart of my belly
Is hard as a stane:
As hard as a stane,
And as round as a cup,
Call the horse, marrow,
Till my hewer[2] comes up.

Me and my marrow,
And Christy Craw Hall,
Will play with any three in the pit
At the foot ball:
At the foot ball,
And at the coal tram,
We'll play with any three in the pit
For twelve-pence a gam.

Hewing and putting,[3]
And keep in the sticks,

[1] mate [2] man who cuts coal in a seam [3] pushing coal-trams

I never so laboured
Since I took the picks;
I'm going to my hewer's
House on Fell Side,
He hews his coals thick,
And drives his boards wide.

The rope and the roll,
And the long ower tree,
The devil has flown over
The heap with them all three:
The roll it hangs cross the shaft,
De'il but it fall,
And stick in the thil;[4]
Twenty-four horn'd owls run away with the mill.

I'm going to my hewer
Where ever he be,
He's hipt of a buddock,
And blind of an eye;
He's blind of an eye,
And lame of a leg;
My uncle Jack Fenwick,
He kiss'd my aunt Peg.

Broadsheet Ballad

THE SKIPPER'S WEDDING

Neighbours, I'm come for to tell ye,
  Our Skipper and Moll's to be wed,
And if it be true what they're saying,
  Egad, we'll be all rarely fed!
They've brought home a shoulder of mutton,
  Besides two thumping fat geese,
And when at the fire they're roasting,
  We're all to have sops in the grease.
    Blind Willy's to play on the fiddle.

[4] underclay below a coal-seam

And there'll be pies and spice dumplings,
  And there'll be bacon and pease;
Besides a great lump of beef boiled,
  And they may get crowdies who please:
To eat such good things as these are,
  I'm sure ye've but seldom the luck;
Besides, for to make us some pottage,
  There'll be a sheep's head and a pluck.
    Blind Willy's to play on the fiddle.

Of sausages there'll be plenty,
  Black puddings, sheep fat, and neats' tripes;
Besides, for to warm all your noses,
  Great store of tobacco and pipes:
A room, they say, there is provided
  For us at 'The Old Jacob's Well';
The bridegroom went there this morning
  And spoke for a barrel o' yell.
    Blind Willy's to play on the fiddle.

There's sure to be those things I've mention'd,
  And many things else; and I learn,
There's white bread and butter and sugar,
  To please every bonny young bairn;
Of each dish and glass you'll be welcome
  To eat and to drink till you stare;
I've told you what meat's to be at it,
  I'll tell you next who's to be there.
    Blind Willy's to play on the fiddle.

Why there'll be Peter the hangman,
  Who flogs folks at the cart tail,
And Bob, with his new sark and ruffle,
  Made out of an old keel sail!
And Tib on the Quay, who sells oysters,
  Whose mother oft strove to persuade
To keep her from the lads, but she wouldn't,
  Until she got by them betray'd.
    Blind Willy's to play on the fiddle.

And there'll be Sandy the cobbler,
  Whose belly's as round as a cag,[1]
And Doll, with her short petticoats,
  To display her white stocking and leg;
And Sall, who when snug in a corner,
  At sixpence they say won't refuse;
She curs'd when her father was drown'd,
  Because he had on his new shoes.
    Blind Willy's to play on the fiddle.

And there'll be Sam the quack doctor,
  Of skill and profession he'll crack;
And Jack who would fain be a soldier,
  But for a great hump on his back;
And Tom in the streets for his living,
  Who grinds razors, scissors, and knives;
And two or three merry old women,
  That call, 'Mugs and doublers, wives!'
    Blind Willy's to play on the fiddle.

But, neighbours, I'd almost forgot
  For to tell ye – exactly at one
The dinner will be on the table,
  And music will play till it's done:
When you'll all be heartily welcome,
  Of this merry feast for to share:
But if you won't come at this bidding,
  Why then – you may stay where you are.
    Blind Willy's to play on the fiddle.

Broadsheet Ballad

THE GREENLAND WHALE FISHERY

We can no longer stay on shore,
Since we're so deep in debt,
So a voyage to Greenland we will go,
Some money for to get – brave boys.

[1] keg

Now, when we lay at Liverpool,
Our good-like ship to man,
'Twas there our names were all wrote down,
And we're bound for Greenland – brave boys.

In eighteen hundred and twenty-four,
On March the twenty-third,
We hoisted our colours up to our mast head,
And for Greenland bore away – brave boys.

But when we came to Greenland,
Our good-like ship to moor,
Oh, then we wished ourselves back again
With our friends upon the shore – brave boys.

The boatswain went to the mast-head,
With his spy-glass in his hand,
Here's a whale, a whale, a whale, he cried,
And she blows on every spring – brave boys.

The Captain on the quarter deck,
(A very good man was he,)
Overhaul, overhaul, your boat tackle fall
And launch your boats to sea – brave boys.

The boats being launch'd, and the hands got in,
The whale fishes appeared in view,
Resolved was the whole boat's crew,
To steer where the whale fish blew – brave boys.

The whale being struck, and the whale paid on,
She gave a flash with her tail,
She capsized the boat, and lost five men,
Nor did we catch the whale – brave boys.

Bad news unto our captain brought,
That we had lost the 'prentice boys,
He, hearing of this dreadful news,
His colours down did haul – brave boys.

The losing of this whale, brave boys,
Did grieve his heart full sore,
But losing of his five brave men,
Did grieve him ten times more – brave boys.

Come, weigh your anchors, my brave boys,
For the winter star I see,
It's time we should leave this cold country,
And for England bear away – brave boys.

For Greenland is a barren place,
Neither light, nor day to be seen,
Nought but ice and snow where the whale-fish blow,
And the daylight seldom seen – brave boys.

Broadsheet Ballad

VAN DIEMAN'S LAND

Come all you gallant poachers, that ramble void of care
That walk out on moonlight night with your dog, gun and snare,
The lofty hare and pheasants you have at your command,
Not thinking of your last career upon Van Dieman's Land.

Poor Tom Browne, from Nottingham, Jack Williams, and Poor Joe,
We are three daring poachers, the country do well know.
At night we were trepann'd by the keepers hid in sand,
Who for fourteen years transported us into Van Dieman's Land.

The first day that we landed upon that fatal shore
The planters they came round us full twenty score or more,
They rank'd us up like horses, and sold us out of hand
Then yok'd us unto ploughs, my boys, to plow Van Dieman's Land.

Our cottages that we live in were built of clod and clay,
And rotten straw for bedding, and we dare not say nay
Our cots were fenc'd with fire, we slumber when we can,
To drive away wolves and tigers upon Van Dieman's Land.

Its often when in slumber I have a pleasant dream
With my sweet girl a setting down by a purling stream,
Thro' England I've been roaming with her at command
Now I awaken broken-hearted upon Van Dieman's Land.

God bless our wives and families likewise the happy shore,
That isle of great contentment which we shall see no more

As for our wretched females, see them we seldom can,
There's twenty to one woman upon Van Dieman's Land.

There was a girl from Birmingham, Susan Summers was her
  name,
For fourteen years transported, we all well know the same
Our planter bought her freedom, and married her out of hand
She gave to us good usage upon Van Dieman's Land.

So all young gallant poachers give ear unto my song
It is a bit of good advice, although it is not long
Throw by your dogs and snare, for to you I speak plain,
For if you knew our hardships you'd never poach again.

Broadsheet Ballad

WILLIAM MACKWORTH PRAED

ARRIVALS AT A WATERING-PLACE

'I play a spade. – Such strange new faces
  Are flocking in from near and far;
Such frights! – (Miss Dobbs holds all the aces) –
  One can't imagine who they are:
The lodgings at enormous prices, –
  New donkeys, and another fly;
And Madame Bonbon out of ices,
  Although we're scarcely in July:
We're quite as sociable as any,
  But one old horse can scarcely crawl;
And really, where there are so many,
  We can't tell where we ought to call.

'Pray who has seen the odd old fellow
  Who took the Doctor's house last week? –
A pretty chariot, – livery yellow,
  Almost as yellow as his cheek;
A widower, sixty-five, and surly,
  And stiffer than a poplar-tree;
Drinks rum and water, gets up early
  To dip his carcass in the sea;

He's always in a monstrous hurry,
  And always talking of Bengal;
They say his cook makes noble curry; –
  I think, Louisa, we should call.

'And so Miss Jones, the mantua-maker,
  Has let her cottage on the hill! –
The drollest man, – a sugar-baker
  Last year imported from the till;
Prates of his *'orses* and his *'oney*,
  Is quite in love with fields and farms;
A horrid Vandal, – but his money
  Will buy a glorious coat of arms;
Old Clyster makes him take the waters;
  Some say he means to give a ball;
And after all, with thirteen daughters,
  I think, Sir Thomas, you might call.

'That poor young man! – I'm sure and certain
  Despair is making up his shroud;
He walks all night beneath the curtain
  Of the dim sky and murky cloud;
Draws landscapes, – throws such mournful glances;
  Writes verses, – has such splendid eyes;
An ugly name, – but Laura fancies
  He's some great person in disguise! –
And since his dress is all the fashion,
  And since he's very dark and tall,
I think that out of pure compassion,
  I'll get Papa to go and call.

'So Lord St Ives is occupying
  The whole of Mr Ford's hotel!
Last Saturday his man was trying
  A little nag I want to sell.
He brought a lady in the carriage;
  Blue eyes, – eighteen, or thereabouts; –
Of course, you know, we *hope* it's marriage,
  But yet the *femme de chambre* doubts.

She looked so pensive when we met her,
  Poor thing! – and such a charming shawl! –
Well! till we understand it better,
  It's quite impossible to call!

'Old Mr Fund, the London Banker,
  Arrived today at Premium Court;
I would not, for the world, cast anchor
  In such a horrid dangerous port;
Such dust and rubbish, lath and plaster, –
  (Contractors play the meanest tricks) –
The roof's as crazy as its master,
  And he was born in fifty-six;
Stairs creaking – cracks in every landing, –
  The colonnade is sure to fall;
We shan't find post or pillar standing,
  Unless we make great haste to call.

'Who was that sweetest of sweet creatures
  Last Sunday in the Rector's seat?
The finest shape, – the loveliest features, –
  I never saw such tiny feet!
My brother, – (this is quite between us)
  Poor Arthur, – 'twas a sad affair;
Love at first sight! – she's quite a Venus,
  But then she's poorer far than fair;
And so my father and my mother
  Agreed it would not do at all;
And so, – I'm sorry for my brother! –
  It's settled that we're not to call.

'And there's an author, full of knowledge;
  And there's a captain on half-pay;
And there's a baronet from college,
  Who keeps a boy and rides a bay;
And sweet Sir Marcus from the Shannon,
  Fine specimen of brogue and bone;
And Doctor Calipee, the canon,
  Who weighs, I fancy, twenty stone:

A maiden lady is adorning
  The faded front of Lily Hall: –
Upon my word, the first fine morning,
  We'll make a round, my dear, and call.'

Alas! disturb not, maid and matron,
  The swallow in my humble thatch;
Your son may find a better patron,
  Your niece may meet a richer match:
I can't afford to give a dinner,
  I never was on Almack's list;
And, since I seldom rise a winner,
  I never like to play at whist:
Unknown to me the stocks are falling,
  Unwatched by me the glass may fall:
Let all the world pursue its calling, –
  I'm not at home if people call.

OUR BALL

You'll come to our Ball; – since we parted,
  I've thought of you more than I'll say;
Indeed, I was half broken-hearted
  For a week, when they took you away.
Fond fancy brought back to my slumbers
  Our walks on the Ness and the Den,
And echoed the musical numbers
  Which you used to sing to me then.
I know the romance, since it's over,
  'Twere idle, or worse, to recall;
I know you're a terrible rover;
  But Clarence, you'll come to our Ball!

It's only a year, since, at College,
  You put on your cap and your gown;
But, Clarence, you're grown out of knowledge,
  And changed from the spur to the crown:

The voice that was best when it faltered
  Is fuller and firmer in tone,
And the smile that should never have altered –
  Dear Clarence – it is not your own:
Your cravat was badly selected;
  Your coat don't become you at all;
And why is your hair so neglected?
  You must have it curled for our Ball.

I've often been out upon Haldon
  To look for a covey with pup;
I've often been over to Shaldon,
  To see how your boat is laid up:
In spite of the terrors of Aunty,
  I've ridden the filly you broke;
And I've studied your sweet little Dante
  In the shade of your favourite oak:
When I sat in July to Sir Lawrence,
  I sat in your love of a shawl;
And I'll wear what you brought me from Florence,
  Perhaps, if you'll come to our Ball.

You'll find us all changed since you vanished:
  We've set up a National School;
And waltzing is utterly banished,
  And Ellen has married a fool;
The Major is going to travel,
  Miss Hyacinth threatens a rout,
The walk is laid down with fresh gravel,
  Papa is laid up with the gout;
And Jane has gone on with her easels,
  And Anne has gone off with Sir Paul;
And Fanny is sick with the measles, –
  And I'll tell you the rest at the Ball.

You'll meet all your Beauties; the Lily,
  And the Fairy of Willowbrook Farm,
And Lucy, who made me so silly
  At Dawlish, by taking your arm;

Miss Manners, who always abused you
  For talking so much about Hock,
And her sister, who often amused you
  By raving of rebels and Rock;
And something which surely would answer,
  An heiress quite fresh from Bengal;
So, though you were seldom a dancer,
  You'll dance, just for once, at our Ball.

But out on the World! from the flowers
  It shuts out the sunshine of truth:
It blights the green leaves in the bowers,
  It makes an old age of our youth;
And the flow of our feeling, once in it,
  Like a streamlet beginning to freeze,
Though it cannot turn ice in a minute,
  Grows harder by sudden degrees:
Time treads o'er the graves of affection;
  Sweet honey is turned into gall;
Perhaps you have no recollection
  That you ever danced at our Ball!

You once could be pleased with our ballads, –
  To-day you have critical ears;
You once could be charmed with our salads –
  Alas! you've been dining with Peers;
You trifled and flirted with many, –
  You've forgotten the when and the how;
There was one you liked better than any, –
  Perhaps you've forgotten her now.
But of those you remember most newly,
  Of those who delight or enthrall,
None love you a quarter so truly
  As some you will find at our Ball.

They tell me you've many who flatter,
  Because of your wit and your song:
They tell me – and what does it matter? –
  You like to be praised by the throng:

They tell me you're shadowed with laurel:
  They tell me you're loved by a Blue:
They tell me you're sadly immoral –
  Dear Clarence, that cannot be true!
But to me, you are still what I found you,
  Before you grew clever and tall;
And you'll think of the spell that once bound you;
  And you'll come – won't you come? – to our Ball!

ELIZABETH BARRETT BROWNING

AN ENGLISHWOMAN'S EDUCATION

I learnt the collects and the catechism,
The creeds, from Athanasius back to Nice,
The Articles, the Tracts *against* the times
(By no means Buonaventure's 'Prick of Love'),
And various popular synopses of
Inhuman doctrines never taught by John,
Because she liked instructed piety.
I learnt my complement of classic French
(Kept pure of Balzac and neologism)
And German also, since she liked a range
Of liberal education, – tongues, not books.
I learned a little algebra, a little
Of the mathematics, – brushed with extreme flounce
The circle of the sciences, because
She misliked women who are frivolous.
I learnt the royal genealogies
Of Oviedo, the internal laws
Of the Burmese empire, – by how many feet
Mount Chimborazo outsoars Teneriffe,
What navigable river joins itself
To Lara, and what census of the year five
Was taken at Klagenfurt, – because she liked
A general insight into useful facts.

I learnt much music, – such as would have been
As quite impossible in Johnson's day
As still it might be wished – fine sleights of hand
And unimagined fingering, shuffling off
The hearer's soul through hurricanes of notes
To a noisy Tophet; and I drew . . . costumes
From French engravings, nereids neatly draped
(With smirks of simmering godship): I washed in
Landscapes from nature (rather say, washed out).
I danced the polka and Cellarius,
Spun glass, stuffed birds, and modelled flowers in wax,
Because she liked accomplishments in girls.
I read a score of books on womanhood
To prove, if women do not think at all,
They may teach thinking (to a maiden aunt
Or else the author), – books that boldly assert
Their right of comprehending husband's talk
When not too deep, and even of answering
With pretty 'may it please you', or 'so it is', –
Their rapid insight and fine aptitude,
Particular worth and general missionariness,
As long as they keep quiet by the fire
And never say 'no' when the world says 'ay',
For that is fatal, – their angelic reach
Of virtue, chiefly used to sit and darn,
And fatten household sinners, – their, in brief,
Potential faculty in everything
Of abdicating power in it: she owned
She liked a woman to be womanly,
And English women, she thanked God and sighed
(Some people always sigh in thanking God),
Were models to the universe. And last
I learnt cross-stitch, because she did not like
To see me wear the night with empty hands
A-doing nothing. So, my shepherdess
Was something after all (the pastoral saints
Be praised for't), leaning lovelorn with pink eyes
To match her shoes, when I mistook the silks;
Her head uncrushed by that round weight of hat

So strangely similar to the tortoise-shell
Which slew the tragic poet.
By the way,
The works of women are symbolical.
We sew, sew, prick our fingers, dull our sight,
Producing what? A pair of slippers, sir,
To put on when you're weary – or a stool
To stumble over and vex you . . . 'curse that stool!'
Or else at best, a cushion, where you lean
And sleep, and dream of something we are not
But would be for your sake. Alas, alas!
This hurts most, this – that, after all, we are paid
The worth of our work, perhaps.

from *Aurora Leigh*

WILLIAM BARNES

WHITSUNTIDE AN' CLUB WALKEN

Ees, last Whit-Monday, I an' Meäry
Got up betimes to mind the deäiry;[1]
An' gi'ed the milkèn païls a scrub,
An' dress'd, an' went to zee the club.
Vor up at public-house, by ten
O'clock the pleäce[2] wer vull o' men,
A-dress'd to goo to church, an' dine,
An' walk about the pleäce in line.
Zoo off they started, two an' two,
Wi' païnted poles an' knots o' blue,
An' girt silk flags, – I wish my box
'D a-got em all in ceäpes[3] an' frocks, –
A-weävèn wide an' flappèn loud
In playsome winds above the crowd;
While fifes did squeak an' drums did rumble
An' deep beäzzoons[4] did grunt an' grumble,

[1] dairy [2] place [3] capes [4] bassoons

An' all the vo'k in gath'rèn crowds
Kick'd up the doust[5] in smeechy[6] clouds,
That slowly rose an' spread abrode
In streamèn aïr above the road.
An' then at church there wer sich lots
O' hats a-hangèn up wi' knots,
An' poles a-stood so thick as iver,
The rushes stood beside a river.
An' Mr Goodman gi'ed em warnèn
To spend their evenèn lik' their mornèn;
An' not to pray wi' mornèn tongues,
An' then to zwear[7] wi' evenèn lungs;
Nor vu'st sheäke hands, to let the wrist
Lift up at last a bruisèn vist:[8]
Vor clubs were all a-meän'd vor friends,
He twold em, an' vor better ends
Than twitèn vo'k[9] an' pickèn quarrels,
An' tipplèn cups an' emptèn barrels, –
Vor meäkèn woone man do another
In need the kindness ov a brother.

An' after church they went to dine
'Ithin the long-wall'd room behine
The public-house, where you remember,
We had our dance back last December.
An' there they meäde sich stunnèn clatters
Wi' knives an' forks, an' pleätes an' platters;
An' waïters ran, an' beer did pass
Vrom tap to jug, vrom jug to glass:
An' when they took away the dishes,
They drink'd good healths, an' wish'd good wishes,
To all the girt vo'k o' the land,
An' all good things vo'k took in hand;
An' woone cried *hip*, *hip*, *hip!* an' hollow'd,
An' tothers all struck in, an' vollow'd;
An' grabb'd their drink wi' eager clutches,
An' swigg'd it wi' sich hearty glutches,[10]

[5] dust [6] smoky [7] swear [8] bruising fist [9] twitting people [10] swallows

As vo'k, stark mad wi' pweison stuff,
That thought theirzelves not mad enough.

An' after that they went all out
In rank ageän, an' walk'd about,
An' gi'ed zome parish vo'k a call;
An' then went down to Narley Hall
An' had zome beer, an' danc'd between
The elm trees upon the green.
An' down along the road they done
All sorts o' mad-cap things vor fun;
An' danc'd, a-pokèn out their poles,
An' pushèn bwoys down into holes:
An' Sammy Stubbs come out o' rank,
An' kiss'd me up ageän the bank,
A saucy chap; I ha'nt vor'gied en[11]
Not yet, – in short, I han't a-zeed en.
Zoo in the dusk ov evenèn, zome
Went back to drink, an' zome went hwome.

ECLOGUE: THE COMMON A-TOOK IN

Thomas an' John

Thomas
Good morn t'ye, John. How b'ye? how b'ye?
Zoo you be gwaïn to market,[1] I do zee.
Why, you be quite a-lwoaded wi' your geese.

John
Ees,[2] Thomas, ees.
Why, I'm a-gettèn rid ov ev'ry goose
An' goslèn I've a-got: an' what is woose,[3]
I fear that I must zell my little cow.

Thomas
How zoo, then, John? Why, what's the matter now?
What, can't ye get along? B'ye run a-ground?

[11] forgiven him

[1] So you're going to market [2] Yes [3] worse

An' can't paÿ twenty shillèns vor a pound?
What can't ye put a lwoaf on shelf?

John

Ees, now;
But I do fear I shan't 'ithout my cow.
No; they do mëan to teäke the moor in, I do hear,
An' 'twill be soon begun upon;
Zoo I must zell my bit o' stock to-year,
Because they woon't have any groun' to run upon.

Thomas

Why, what d'ye tell o'? I be very zorry
To hear what they be gwaïn about;
But yet I s'pose there 'll be a 'lotment[4] vor ye,
When they do come to mark it out.

John

No; not vor me, I fear. An' if there should,
Why 'twoulden be so handy as 'tis now;
Vor 'tis the common that do do me good,
The run for my vew geese, or vor my cow.

Thomas

Ees, that's the job; why 'tis a handy thing
To have a bit o' common, I do know,
To put a little cow upon in Spring,
The while woone's bit ov orcha'd grass do grow.

John

Aye, that's the thing, you zee.Now I do mow
My bit o' grass, an' meäke a little rick;
An' in the zummer, while do grow,
My cow do run in common vor to pick
A bleäde or two o' grass, if she can vind em,
Vor tother cattle don't leäve much behind em.
Zoo in the evenèn, we do put a lock
O' nice fresh grass avore the wicket;
An' she do come at vive or zix o'clock,
As constant as the zun, to pick it.

[4] allotment

An' then, bezides the cow, why we do let
Our geese run out among the emmet hills;[5]
An' then when we do pluck em, we do get
Vor zeäle[6] zome veathers an' zome quills;
An' in the winter we do fat em well,
An' car em to the market vor to zell
To gentlevo'ks, vor we don't oft avvword[7]
To put a goose a-top ov ouer bwoard;
But we do get our feäst, – vor we be eäble
To clap the giblets up a-top o' teäble.

Thomas
An' I don't know o' many better things,
Than geese's heads and gizzards, lags an' wings.

John
An' then, when I ha' nothèn else to do,
Why I can teäke my hook an' gloves, an' goo
To cut a lot o' vuzz and briars
Vor hetèn ovens, or vor lightèn viers.
An' when the childern be too young to eärn
A penny, they can g'out in zunny weather,
An' run about, an' get together
A bag o' cow-dung vor to burn.

Thomas
'Tis handy to live near a common;
But I've a-zeed, an' I've a-zaid,
That if a poor man got a bit o' bread,
They'll try to teäke it vrom en.
But I wer twold back tother day,
That they be got into a way
O' lettèn bits o' groun' out to the poor.

John
Well, I do hope 'tis true, I'm sure;
An' I do hope that they will do it here,
Or I must goo to workhouse, I do fear.

[5] anthills [6] for sale [7] afford

THE SETTLE AN' THE GIRT WOOD VIRE

Ah! naïghbour John, since I an' you
Wer youngsters, ev'ry thing is new.
My father's vires wer all o' logs
O' cleft-wood, down upon the dogs
Below our clavy,[1] high, an' brode
Enough to teäke a cart an' lwoad,
Where big an' little all zot down
At bwoth zides, an' bevore, all roun'.
An' when I zot among em, I
Could zee all up ageän the sky
Drough chimney, where our vo'k did hitch
The zalt-box an' the beäcon vlitch,[2]
An' watch the smoke on out o' vier,
All up an' out o' tun, an' higher.
An' there wer beäcon up on rack,
An' pleätes an' dishes on the tack;
An' roun' the walls wer heärbs a-stowed
In peäpern bags, an' blathers[3] blowed.
An' just above the clavy-bwoard
Wer father's spurs, an' gun, an' sword;
An' there wer then, our girtest pride,
The settle by the vier-zide.
    Ah! gi'e me, if I wer a squier,
    The settle an' the girt wood vier.

But they've a-wall'd up now wi' bricks
The vier pleäce vor dogs an' sticks,
An' only left a little hole
To teäke a little greäte o' coal,
So small that only twos or drees
Can jist push in an' warm their knees.
An' then the carpets they do use,
Ben't fit to tread wi' ouer shoes;
An' chairs an' couches be so neat,
You mussen teäke em vor a seat:

[1] mantelpiece [2] bacon flitch [3] bladders

They be so fine, that vo'k mus' pleäce
  All over em an' outer ceäse,
An' then the cover, when 'tis on,
Is still too fine to loll upon.
    Ah! gi'e me, if I wer a squier,
    The settle an' the girt wood vier.

Carpets indeed! You coulden hurt
The stwone-vloor wi' a little dirt;
Vor what wer brought in doors by men,
The women soon mopp'd out ageän.
Zoo we did come vrom muck an' mire,
An' walk in straïght avore the vier;
But now, a man's a-kept at door
At work a pirty while, avore
He's screäp'd an rubb'd, an' cleän and fit
To goo in where his wife do zit.
An' then if he should have a whiff
In there, 'twould only breed a miff:
He can't smoke there, vor smoke woon't goo
'Ithin the footy[4] little flue.
    Ah! gi'e me, if I were a squier,
    The settle an' the girt wood vier.

LYDLINCH BELLS

When skies wer peäle wi' twinklèn stars,
An' whislèn aïr a-risèn keen;
An' birds did leäve the icy bars
To vind, in woods, their mossy screen;
When vrozen grass, so white's a sheet,
Did scrunchy sharp below our veet,
An' water, that did sparkle red
At zunzet, wer a-vrozen dead;
The ringers then did spend an hour
A-ringèn changes up in tow'r;
Vor Lydlinch bells be good vor sound,
An' liked by all the naïghbours round.

[4] small, inadequate

An' while along the leafless boughs
O' ruslèn hedges, win's[1] did pass,
An' orts[2] ov haÿ, a-left by cows,
Did russle on the vrozen grass,
An' maïdens' païls, wi' all their work
A-done, did hang upon their vurk,[3]
An' they, avore the fleämèn[4] brand,
Did teäke their needle-work in hand,
The men did cheer their heart an hour
A ringèn changes up in tow'r;
Vor Lydlinch bells be good vor sound,
An' lik'd by all the naïghbours round.

There sons did pull the bells that rung
Their mothers' weddèn peals avore,
The while their fathers led em young
An' blushèn vrom the churches door,
An' still did cheem, wi' happy sound
As time did bring the Zundays round,
An' call em to the holy pleäce
Vor heavenly gifts o' peace an' greäce;
An' vo'k did come, a-streamèn slow
Along below the trees in row,
While they, in merry peals, did sound
The bells vor all the naïghbours round.

An' when the bells, wi' changèn peal,
Did smite their own vo'ks window-peänes,
Their sof'en'd sound did often steal
Wi' west winds drough the Bagber leänes;
Or, as the win' did shift, mid goo[5]
Where woody Stock do nessle lew,[6]
Or where the risèn moon did light
The walls o' Thornhill on the height;
An' zoo, whatever time mid bring
To meäke their vive clear vaices zing,
Still Lydlinch bells wer good vor sound
An' liked by all the naïghbours round.

[1] winds [2] remnants [3] fork [of a pail-stand] [4] flaming [5] even went [6] nestles in shelter

FANNY'S BE'TH-DAY

How merry, wi' the cider cup,
We kept poor Fanny's be'th-day up!
An' how our busy tongues did run
An' hands did wag, a-meäkèn fun!
What plaÿsome anticks zome ō's done!
  An' how, a-reelèn roun' an' roun',
  We beät the merry tuèn[1] down,
    While music wer a-soundèn!

The maïdens' eyes o' black an' blue
Did glisten lik' the mornèn dew;
An' while the cider-mug did stand
A-hissèn by the bleäzèn brand,
An' uncle's pipe wer in his hand,
  How little he or we did think
  How peäle the zettèn stars did blink
    While music wer a-soundèn.

An' Fanny's last young *teen* begun,
Poor maïd, wi' thik day's risèn zun,
An' we all wish'd her many mwore
Long years wi' happiness in store;
An' as she went an' stood avore
  The vier, by her father's zide,
  Her mother dropp'd a tear o' pride
    While music wer a-soundèn.

An' then we did all kinds o' tricks
Wi' han'kerchiefs, an' strings, an' sticks:
An' woone did try to overmatch
Another wi' zome cunnèn catch,
While tothers slyly tried to hatch
  Zome geäme; but yet, by chap an' maïd,
  The dancèn wer the mwost injaÿ'd,
    While music wer a-soundèn.

[1] tune

The briskest chap ov all the lot
Wer Tom, that danc'd hizzelf so hot,
He doff'd his cwoat an' jump'd about,
Wi' girt new shirt-sleeves all a-strout,[2]
Among the maïdens screamèn out,
  A-thinkèn, wi' his strides an' stamps,
  He'd squot[3] their veet wi' his girt clamps,
    While music wer a-soundèn.

Then up jump'd uncle vrom his chair,
An' pull'd out aunt to meäke a peäir;
An' off he zet upon his tooe.
So light's the best that beät a shoe,
Wi' aunt a-crièn 'Let me goo':
  While all ov us did laugh so loud,
  We drown'd the tuèn o' the croud,
    While music wer a-soundèn.

A-comèn out o' passage, Nan,
Wi' pipes an' cider in her han',
An' watchèn uncle up so sprack,[4]
Vorgot her veet, an' vell down smack
Athirt the house-dog's shaggy back,
  That wer in passage vor a snooze,
  Beyond the reach o' dancers' shoes,
    While music wer a-soundèn.

THE LEÄNE

They do zay that a travellèn chap
  Have a-put in the newspeäper now,
That the bit o' green ground on the knap
  Should be all a-took in vor the plough.
He do fancy 'tis easy to show
  That we can be but stunpolls[1] at best,
Vor to leäve a green spot where a flower can grow,
  Or a voot-weary walker mid rest.

[2] stiff-spread [3] squash [4] active

[1] blockheads

'Tis hedge-grubbèn, Thomas, an' ledge-grubbèn,
Never a-done
While a sov'rèn mwore's to be won.

The road, he do zay, is so wide
As 'tis wanted vor travellers' wheels,
As if all that did travel did ride,
An' did never get galls on their heels.
He would leäve sich a thin strip o' groun',
That, if a man's veet in his shoes
Wer a-burnèn an' zore, why he coulden zit down
But the wheels would run over his tooes.
Vor 'tis meäke money, Thomas, an' teäke money,
What's zwold an' bought
Is all that is worthy o' thought.

Years agoo the leäne-zides did bear grass,
Vor to pull wi' the geeses' red bills,
That did hiss at the vo'k that did pass,
Or the bwoys that pick'd up their white quills.
But shortly, if vower or vive
Ov our goslèns do creep vrom the agg,
They must mwope in the geärden, mwore dead than alive,
In a coop, or a-tied by the lag.
Vor to catch at land, Thomas, an' snatch at land,
Now is the plan;
Meäke money wherever you can.

The childern wull soon have noo pleäce
Vor to play in, an' if they do grow,
They wull have a thin musheroom feäce,
Wi' their bodies so sumple as dough.
But a man is a-meäde ov a child,
An' his limbs do grow worksome by plaÿ;
An' if the young child's little body's a-spweil'd,[2]
Why, the man's wull the sooner decaÿ.
But wealth is wo'th now mwore than health is wo'th;
Let it all goo,
If't 'ull bring but a sov'rèn or two.

[2] spoiled

Vor to breed the young fox or the heäre,
  We can gi'e up whole eäcres o' ground,
But the greens be a-grudg'd, vor to rear
  Our young childern up healthy an' sound,
Why, there woont be a-left the next age
  A green spot where their veet can goo free;
An' the goocoo[3] wull soon be committed to cage
  Vor a trespass in zomebody's tree.
Vor 'tis lockèn up, Thomas, an' blockèn up,
    Stranger or brother,
Men mussen[4] come nigh woone another.

Woone day I went in at a geäte,
  Wi' my child, where an echo did sound,
An' the owner come up, an' did reäte
  Me as if I would car off his ground.
But his vield an' the grass wer-a-let,
  An' the damage that he could a-took
Wer at mwost that the while I did open the geäte
  I did rub roun' the eye on the hook.
But 'tis drevèn out, Thomas, an' hevèn out.
    Trample noo grounds,
Unless you be after the hounds.

Ah! the Squiër o' Culver-dell Hall
  Wer as diff'rent as light is vrom dark,
Wi' zome vo'k that, as evenèn did vall,
  Had a-broke drough long grass in his park;
Vor he went, wi' a smile, vor to meet
  Wi' the trespassers while they did pass,
An' he zaid, 'I do fear you'll catch cwold in your veet,
  You've a-walk'd drough so much o' my grass.'
His mild words, Thomas, cut em like swords, Thomas,
    Newly a-whet,
An' went vurder wi' them than a dreat.[5]

[3] cuckoo [4] mustn't [5] threat

THE RAILROAD

I took a flight, awhile agoo,
Along the raïls, a stage or two,
An' while the heavy wheels did spin
An' rottle, wi' a deafnèn din,
In clouds o' steam, the zweepèn traïn
Did shoot along the hill-bound plaïn,
As sheädes o' birds in flight, do pass
Below em on the zunny grass.
An' as I zot, an' look'd abrode
On leänen land an' windèn road,
The ground a-spread along our flight
Did vlee behind us out o' zight;
The while the zun, our heav'nly guide,
Did ride on wi' us, zide by zide.
An' zoo, while time, vrom stage to stage,
Do car us on vrom youth to age,
The e'thly[1] pleasures we do vind
Be soon a-met, an' left behind;
But God, beholdèn vrom above
Our lowly road, wi' yearnèn love,
Do keep bezide us, stage by stage,
Vrom be'th[2] to youth, vrom youth to age.

THE DO'SET MILITIA

Hurrah! my lads, vor Do'set men!
A-muster'd here in red ageän;
All welcome to your ranks, a-spread
Up zide to zide, to stand, or wheel,
An' welcome to your files, to head
The steady march wi' tooe to heel;
Welcome to marches slow or quick!
Welcome to gath'rèns thin or thick;

[1] earthly [2] birth

God speed the Colonel on the hill,[1]
An' Mrs Bingham,[2] off o' drill.

When you've a-handled well your lock,
An' flung about your rifle stock
Vrom han' to shoulder, up an' down;
When you've a-lwoaded an' a-vired,
Till you do come back into town,
Wi' all your loppèn limbs a-tired,
An you be dry an' burnèn hot,
Why here's your tea an' coffee pot
At Mister Greenèn's penny till,
Wi' Mrs Bingham off o' drill.

Last year John Hinley's mother cried,
'Why my bwoy John is quite my pride!
Vor he've a-been so good to-year,
An' han't a-mell'd wi' any squabbles,
An' han't a-drown'd his wits in beer,
An' han't a-been in any hobbles.
I never thought he'd turn out bad,
He always wer so good a lad;
But now I'm sure he's better still,
Drough Mrs Bingham, off o' drill.'

Jeäne Hart, that's Joey Duntley's chaïce,
Do praise en up wi' her sweet vaïce,
Vor he's so strait's a hollyhock
(Vew hollyhocks be up so tall),
An' he do come so true's the clock
To Mrs Bingham's coffee-stall;
An' Jeäne do write, an' brag o' Joe
To teäke the young recruits in tow,
An' try, vor all their good, to bring em,
A-come from drill, to Mrs Bingham.

God speed the Colonel, toppèn high,
An' officers wi' sworded thigh,

[1] Poundbury, Dorchester, the drill ground [2] The colonel's wife, who opened a room with a coffee-stall and entertainments for the men off drill

An' all the sargeants that do bawl
All day enough to split their droats,
An' all the corporals, and all
The band a-playèn up their notes,
An' all the men vrom vur an' near
We'll gi'e em all a heartÿ cheer,
An' then another cheerèn still
Vor Mrs Bingham, off o' drill.

CHARLES TENNYSON-TURNER

THE STEAM THRESHING MACHINE

with the Straw Carrier

Flush with the pond the lurid furnace burned
At eve, while smoke and vapour filled the yard;
The gloomy winter sky was dimly starred,
The fly-wheel with a mellow murmur turned;
While, ever rising on its mystic stair
In the dim light, from secret chambers borne,
The straw of harvest, severed from the corn,
Climbed, and fell over, in the murky air.
I thought of mind and matter, will and law,
And then of him, who set his stately seal
Of Roman words on all the forms he saw
Of old-world husbandry; *I* could but feel
With what a rich precision *he* would draw
The endless ladder, and the booming wheel!

Did any seer of ancient time forbode
This mighty engine, which we daily see
Accepting our full harvests, like a god,
With clouds about his shoulders, – it might be
Some poet-husbandman, some lord of verse,
Old Hesiod, or the wizard Mantuan
Who catalogued in rich hexameters,
The Rake, the Roller, and the mystic Van;

Or else some priest of Ceres, it might seem,
Who witnessed, as he trod the silent fane,
The notes and auguries of coming change,
Of other ministrants in shrine and grange,
The sweating statue, – and her sacred wain
Low-booming with the prophecy of steam!

ALFRED, LORD TENNYSON

'BLACK BULL OF ALDGATE'

Black Bull of Aldgate, may thy horns rot from the sockets!
For, jingling threepence, porter's pay, in hungry pockets,
And thirty times at least beneath thy doorway stepping
I've waited for this lousy coach that runs to Epping.
Ill luck befall thee, that hast made me so splenetic,
Through all thy holes and closets up from tap to attic,
Through all thy boys and bootses, chambermaids, and waiters,
And yonder booking-office-clerk in fustian gaiters.
Black Bull of Aldgate! mayst thou more miscarry
Than ever hasty Clement's did with bloated Harry!

THE PICNIC

'The Bull, the Fleece are crammed, and not a room
For love or money. Let us picnic there
At Audley Court.'
                                I spoke, while Audley feast
Hummed like a hive all round the narrow quay,
To Francis, with a basket on his arm,
To Francis just alighted from the boat,
And breathing of the sea. 'With all my heart,'
Said Francis. Then we shouldered through the swarm,
And rounded by the stillness of the beach
To where the bay runs up its latest horn.

We left the dying ebb that faintly lipped
The flat red granite; so by many a sweep
Of meadow smooth from aftermath we reached
The griffin-guarded gates, and passed through all
The pillared dusk of sounding sycamores,
And crossed the garden to the gardener's lodge,
With all its casements bedded, and its walls
And chimneys muffled in the leafy vine.

There, on a slope of orchard, Francis laid
A damask napkin wrought with horse and hound,
Brought out a dusky loaf that smelt of home,
And, half-cut-down, a pasty costly-made,
Where quail and pigeon, lark and leveret lay,
Like fossils of the rock, with golden yolks
Imbedded and injellied; last, with these,
A flask of cider from his father's vats,
Prime, which I knew; and so we sat and eat.

from *Audley Court*

THE FÊTE

Sir Walter Vivian all a summer's day
Gave his broad lawns until the set of sun
Up to the people: thither flocked at noon
His tenants, wife and child, and thither half
The neighbouring borough with their Institute
Of which he was the patron. I was there
From college, visiting the son, – the son
A Walter too, – with others of our set,
Five others: we were seven at Vivian-place.

And me that morning Walter showed the house,
Greek, set with busts: from vases in the hall
Flowers of all heavens, and lovelier than their names,
Grew side by side; and on the pavement lay
Carved stones of the Abbey-ruin in the park,
Huge Ammonites, and the first bones of Time;

And on the tables every clime and age
Jumbled together; celts and calumets,
Claymore and snowshoe, toys in lava, fans
Of sandal, amber, ancient rosaries,
Laborious orient ivory sphere in sphere,
The cursed Malayan crease, and battle-clubs
From the isles of palm: and higher on the walls,
Betwixt the monstrous horns of elk and deer,
His own forefathers' arms and armour hung.

And 'this' he said 'was Hugh's at Agincourt;
And that was old Sir Ralph's at Ascalon:
A good knight he! we keep a chronicle
With all about him' – which he brought, and I
Dived in a hoard of tales that dealt with knights,
Half-legend, half-historic, counts and kings
Who laid about them at their wills and died;
And mixt with these, a lady, one that armed
Her own fair head, and sallying through the gate,
Had beat her foes with slaughter from her walls.

'O miracle of women,' said the book,
'O noble heart who, being strait-besieged
By this wild king to force her to his wish,
Nor bent, nor broke, nor shunned a soldier's death,
But now when all was lost or seemed as lost –
Her stature more than mortal in the burst
Of sunrise, her arm lifted, eyes on fire –
Brake with a blast of trumpets from the gate,
And, falling on them like a thunderbolt,
She trampled some beneath her horses' heels,
And some were whelmed with missiles of the wall,
And some were pushed with lances from the rock,
And part were drowned within the whirling brook:
O miracle of noble womanhood!'

So sang the gallant glorious chronicle;
And, I all rapt in this, 'Come out,' he said,
'To the Abbey: there is Aunt Elizabeth
And sister Lilia with the rest.' We went

(I kept the book and had my finger in it)
Down through the park: strange was the sight to me;
For all the sloping pasture murmured, sown
With happy faces and with holiday.
There moved the multitude, a thousand heads:
The patient leaders of their Institute
Taught them with facts. One reared a font of stone
And drew, from butts of water on the slope,
The fountain of the moment, playing, now
A twisted snake, and now a rain of pearls,
Or steep-up spout whereon the gilded ball
Danced like a wisp: and somewhat lower down
A man with knobs and wires and vials fired
A cannon: Echo answered in her sleep
From hollow fields: and here were telescopes
For azure views; and there a group of girls
In circle waited, whom the electric shock
Dislinked with shrieks and laughter: round the lake
A little clock-work steamer paddling plied
And shook the lilies: perched about the knolls
A dozen angry models jetted steam:
A petty railway ran: a fire-balloon
Rose gem-like up before the dusky groves
And dropt a fairy parachute and past:
And there through twenty posts of telegraph
They flashed a saucy message to and fro
Between the mimic stations; so that sport
Went hand in hand with Science; otherwhere
Pure sport: a herd of boys with clamour bowled
And stumped the wicket; babies rolled about
Like tumbled fruit in grass; and men and maids
Arranged a country dance, and flew through light
And shadow, while the twangling violin
Struck up with Soldier-laddie, and overhead
The broad ambrosial aisles of lofty lime
Made noise with bees and breeze from end to end.

from *The Princess*

THE CHURCH-WARDEN AND THE CURATE

Eh? good daäy! good daäy! thaw it bean't not mooch of a daäy,
Nasty, casselty[1] weather! an' mea haäfe down wi' my haäy![2]

How be the farm gittin on? noäways. Gittin on i'deeäd!
Why, tonups was haäfe on 'em fingers an' toäs,[3] an' the mare
brokken-kneeäd,
An' pigs didn't sell at fall, an' wa lost wer Haldeny cow,
An' it beäts ma to knaw wot she died on, but wool's looking
oop ony how.

An' soä they've maäde tha a parson, an' thou'll git along,
niver fear,
Fur I beän chuch-warden mysen i' the parish fur fifteen year.
Well – sin ther beä chuch-wardens, ther mun be parsons an' all,
An' if t'ōne stick alongside t'uther[4] the chuch weänt happen a fall.

Fur I wur a Baptis wonst, an' ageän the toithe an' the raäte,
Till I fun[5] that it warn't not the gaäinist[6] waäy to the narra Gaäte.
An' I can't abeär 'em, I can't, fur a lot on 'em coomed ta-year –[7]
I wur down wi' the rheumatis then – to *my* pond to wesh
thessens theere –
Sa I sticks like the ivin[8] as long as I lives to the owd chuch now,
Fur they weshed their sins i' *my* pond, an' I doubts they
poisoned the cow.

Ay, an' ya seed the Bishop. They says 'at he coomed fra nowt –
Burn i' traäde. Sa I warrants 'e niver said haafe wot 'e thowt,
But 'e creeäpt an' 'e crawled along, till 'e feeäld 'e could
howd 'is oän,
Then 'e married a greät Yerl's darter, an' sits o' the Bishop's
throän.

Now I'll gie tha a bit o' my mind an' tha weant be taakin' offence,
Fur thou be a big scholard now wi' a hoonderd haäcre o' sense –
But sich an obstropulous lad – naay, naay – fur I minds tha sa well,
Tha'd niver not hopple[9] thy tongue, an' the tongue's sit afire
o' Hell,

[1] casualty [chancy] [2] and my hay half-mown! [3] half the turnips were diseased [4] if the one hold by the other [5] found [6] nearest [7] this year [8] ivy [9] hobble

As I says to my missis todaay, when she hurled a plaäte at the cat
An' anoother ageän my noäse. Ya was niver sa bad as that.

But I minds when i' Howlaby beck won daäy ya was ticklin'
o' trout,
An' keeäper 'e seed ya an rooned, an' 'e bealed[10] to ya 'Lad
coom hout'
An' ya stood oop naäkt i' the beck, an' ya telled 'im to knaw
his awn plaäce
An' ya called 'im a clown, ya did, an' ya thrawed the fish i'
'is faäce,
An' 'e torned as red as a stag-tuckey's[11] wattles, but theer an' then
I coämbed 'im down, fur I promised y'd niver not do it ageän.

An' I cotched tha wonst i' my garden, when thou was a
height-year-howd,[12]
An' I fun thy pockets as full o' my pippins as iver they'd 'owd,[13]
An' thou was as peärky[14] as owt, an' tha maäde me as mad as mad,
But I says to that 'keeap 'em, an' welcome' fur thou was the
Parson's lad.

An' Parson 'e 'ears on it all, an' then taäkes kindly to me,
An' then I wur chose chuch-warden an' coomed to the top
o' the tree
Fur Qùoloty's hall my friends, an' they maäkes ma a help to
the poor,
When I gits the plaäte fuller o' Soondays nor ony chuch-
warden afoor,
Fur if iver thy feyther 'ed riled me I kep' mysen meeäk as a lamb,
An' saw by the Graäce o' the Lord, Mr Harry, I ham wot I ham.

But Parson 'e *will* speäk out, saw, now 'e be sixty-seven,
He'll niver swap Owlby an' Scratby fur owt but the
Kingdom o' Heaven;
An' thou'll be 'is Curate 'ere, but, if iver tha meäns to git 'igher,
Tha mun tackle the sins o' the Wo'ld,[15] an' not the faults
o' the Squire.

[10] bellowed [11] turkey-cock [12] eight-year-old [13] hold [14] pert [15] world

An' I reckons tha'll light of a livin' somewheers i' the Wowd[16]
or the Fen,
If tha cottons down to thy betters, an' keeäps thysen to thysen.
But niver not speäk plaain out, if tha wants to git forrards a bit,
But creeäp along the hedge-bottoms, an' thou'll be a Bishop yit.

Naäy, but tha *mun* speäk hout to the Baptises here i' the town,
Fur moäst on 'em talks ageän tithe, an' I'd like tha to preäch
'em down,
Fur *they*'ve bin a-preächin' *mea* down, they have, an' I haätes
'em now,
Fur they leäved their nasty sins i' *my* pond, an' it poisoned the
cow.

ROBERT BROWNING

THE ZION CHAPEL-MEETING

I

Out of the little chapel I burst
Into the fresh night air again.
I had waited a good five minutes first
In the doorway, to escape the rain
That drove in gusts down the common's centre,
At the edge of which the chapel stands,
Before I plucked up heart to enter:
Heaven knows how many sorts of hands
Reached past me, groping for the latch
Of the inner door that hung on catch,
More obstinate the more they fumbled,
Till, giving way at last with a scold
Of the crazy hinge, in squeezed or tumbled
One sheep more to the rest in fold,
And left me irresolute, standing sentry
In the sheepfold's lath-and-plaster entry,

[16] Wold

Four feet long by two feet wide,
Partitioned off from the vast inside –
I blocked up half of it at least.
No remedy; the rain kept driving:
They eyed me much as some wild beast,
The congregation, still arriving.
Some of them by the mainroad, white
A long way past me into the night,
Skirting the common, then diverging;
Not a few suddenly emerging
From the common's self thro' the paling-gaps,
  – They house in the gravel-pits perhaps,
Where the road stops short with its safeguard border
Of lamps, as tired of such disorder; –
But the most turned in yet more abruptly
From a certain squalid knot of alleys,
Where the town's bad blood once slept corruptly,
Which now the little chapel rallies
And leads into day again, – its priestliness
Lending itself to hide their beastliness
So cleverly (thanks in part to the mason),
And putting so cheery a whitewashed face on
Those neophytes too much in lack of it,
That, where you cross the common as I did,
And meet the party thus presided,
'Mount Zion', with Love-lane at the back of it,
They front you as little disconcerted,
As, bound for the hills, her fate averted
And her wicked people made to mind him,
Lot might have marched with Gomorrah behind him.

II

Well, from the road, the lanes or the common,
In came the flock: the fat weary woman,
Panting and bewildered, down-clapping
Her umbrella with a mighty report,
Grounded it by me, wry and flapping,
A wreck of whalebones; then, with a snort,

Like a startled horse, at the interloper
Who humbly knew himself improper,
But could not shrink up small enough,
Round to the door, and in, – the gruff
Hinge's invariable scold
Making your very blood run cold.
Prompt in the wake of her, up-pattered
On broken clogs, the many-tattered
Little old-faced, peaking sister-turned-mother
Of the sickly babe she tried to smother
Somehow up, with its spotted face,
From the cold, on her breast, the one warm place;
She too must stop, wring the poor suds dry
Of a draggled shawl, and add thereby
Her tribute to the door-mat, sopping
Already from my own clothes' dropping,
Which yet she seemed to grudge I should stand on;
Then stooping down to take off her pattens,
She bore them defiantly, in each hand one,
Planted together before her breast
And its babe, as good as a lance in rest.
Close on her heels, the dingy satins
Of a female something, past me flitted,
With lips as much too white, as a streak
Lay far too red on each hollow cheek;
And it seemed the very door-hinge pitied
All that was left of a woman once,
Holding at least its tongue for the nonce.
Then a tall yellow man, like the Penitent Thief,
With his jaw bound up in a handkerchief,
And eyelids screwed together tight,
Led himself in by some inner light.
And, except from him, from each that entered,
I had the same interrogation –
'What, you, the alien, you have ventured
To take with us, elect, your station?
A carer for none of it, a Gallio?' –
Thus, plain as print, I read the glance
At a common prey, in each countenance,

As of huntsman giving his hounds the tallyho:
And, when the door's cry drowned their wonder,
The draught, it always sent in shutting,
Made the flame of the single tallow candle
In the cracked square lanthorn I stood under,
Shoot its blue lip at me, rebutting,
As it were, the luckless cause of scandal:
I verily thought the zealous light
(In the chapel's secret, too!) for spite,
Would shudder itself clean off the wick,
With the air of a St John's Candlestick.
There was no standing it much longer.
'Good folks,' said I, as resolve grew stronger,
'This way you perform the Grand-Inquisitor,
When the weather sends you a chance visitor?
You are the men, and wisdom shall die with you,
And none of the old Seven Churches vie with you!
But still, despite the pretty perfection
To which you carry your trick of exclusiveness,
And, taking God's word under wise protection,
Correct its tendency to diffusiveness,
Bidding one reach it over hot ploughshares, –
Still, as I say, though you've found salvation,
If I should choose to cry – as now – "Shares!" –
See if the best of you bars me my ration!
Because I prefer for my expounder
Of the laws of the feast, the feast's own Founder:
Mine's the same right with your poorest and sickliest,
Supposing I don the marriage-vestiment;
So, shut your mouth, and open your Testament,
And carve me my portion at your quickliest!'
Accordingly, as a shoemaker's lad
With wizened face in want of soap,
And wet apron wound round his waist like a rope,
After stopping outside, for his cough was bad,
To get the fit over, poor gentle creature,
And so avoid disturbing the preacher,
Passed in, I sent my elbow spikewise
At the shutting door, and entered likewise, –

Received the hinge's accustomed greeting,
Crossed the threshold's magic pentacle,
And found myself in full conventicle,
– To wit, in Zion Chapel Meeting,
On the Christmas-Eve, of 'Forty-nine,
Which, calling its flock to their special clover,
Found them assembled and one sheep over,
Whose lot, as the weather pleased, was mine.

from *Christmas Eve and Easter Day*

ARTHUR HUGH CLOUGH

THE READING-PARTY IN THE HIGHLANDS

It was the afternoon; and the sports were now at the ending.
Long had the stone been put, tree cast, and thrown the hammer;
Up the perpendicular hill, Sir Hector so called it,
Eight stout gillies had run, with speed and agility wondrous;
Run too the course on the level had been; the leaping was over:
Last in the show of dress, a novelty recently added,
Noble ladies their prizes adjudged for costume that was perfect,
Turning the clansmen about, as they stood with upraised elbows;
Bowing their eye-glassed brows, and fingering kilt and sporran.
It was four of the clock, and the sports were come to the ending,
Therefore the Oxford party went off to adorn for the dinner.
Be it recorded in song who was first, who last, in dressing.
Hope was first, black-tied, white-waistcoated, simple, His Honour;
For the postman made out he was heir to the Earldom of Ilay,
(Being the younger son of the younger brother, the Colonel,)
Treated him therefore with special respect; doffed bonnet, and ever
Called him his Honour; his Honour he therefore was at the cottage.
Always his Honour at least, sometimes the Viscount of Ilay.

Hope was first, his Honour, and next to his Honour the Tutor.
Still more plain the Tutor, the grave man, nicknamed Adam,
White-tied, clerical, silent, with antique square-cut waistcoat
Formal, unchanged, of black cloth, but with sense and feeling beneath it;
Skilful in Ethics and Logic, in Pindar and Poets unrivalled;
Shady in Latin, said Lindsay, but *topping* in Plays and Aldrich.
Somewhat more splendid in dress, in a waistcoat work of a lady,
Lindsay succeeded; the lively, the cheery, cigar-loving Lindsay,
Lindsay the ready of speech, the Piper, the Dialectician,
This was his title from Adam because of the words he invented,
Who in three weeks had created a dialect new for the party;
This was his title from Adam, but mostly they called him the Piper.
Lindsay succeeded, the lively, the cheery, cigar-loving Lindsay.
Hewson and Hobbes were down at the *matutine* bathing; of course too
Arthur, the bather of bathers, *par excellence*, Audley by surname,
Arthur they called him for love and for euphony; they had been bathing,
Where in the morning was custom, where over a ledge of granite
Into a granite bason the amber torrent descended,
Only a step from the cottage, the road and larches between them.
Hewson and Hobbes followed quick upon Adam; on them followed Arthur.
Airlie descended the last, effulgent as god of Olympus;
Blue, perceptibly blue, was the coat that had white silk facings,
Waistcoat blue, coral-buttoned, the white-tie finely adjusted,
Coral moreover the studs on a shirt as of crochet of women:
When the fourwheel for ten minutes already had stood at the gateway,
He, like a god, came leaving his ample Olympian chamber.
And in the fourwheel they drove to the place of the clansmen's meeting.

So in the fourwheel they came; and Donald the innkeeper showed them
Up to the barn where the dinner should be. Four tables were in it;
Two at the top and the bottom, a little upraised from the level,
These for Chairman and Croupier, and gentry fit to be with them,
Two lengthways in the midst for keeper and gillie and peasant.
Here were clansmen many in kilt and bonnet assembled,
Keepers a dozen at least; the Marquis's targeted gillies;
Pipers five or six, among them the young one, the drunkard;
Many with silver brooches, and some with those brilliant crystals
Found amid granite-dust on the frosty scalp of the Cairn-Gorm;
But with snuff-boxes all, and all of them using the boxes.
Here too were Catholic Priest, and Established Minister standing;
Catholic Priest; for many still clung to the Ancient Worship,
And Sir Hector's father himself had built them a chapel;
So stood Priest and Minister, near to each other, but silent,
One to say grace before, the other after the dinner.
Hither anon too came the shrewd, ever-ciphering Factor,
Hither anon the Attaché, the Guardsman mute and stately,
Hither from lodge and bothie in all the adjoining shootings
Members of Parliament many, forgetful of votes and blue-books,
Here, amid heathery hills, upon beast and bird of the forest
Venting the murderous spleen of the endless Railway Committee.
Hither the Marquis of Ayr, and Dalgarnish Earl and Croupier,
And at their side, amid murmurs of welcome, long-looked for, himself too
Eager, the grey, but boy-hearted Sir Hector, the Chief and the Chairman.
Then was the dinner served, and the Minister prayed for a blessing,
And to the viands before them with knife and with fork they beset them;
Venison, the red and the roe, with mutton; and grouse succeeding;

Such was the feast, with whisky of course, and at top and bottom
Small decanters of Sherry, not overchoice, for the gentry.
So to the viands before them with laughter and chat they beset them.
And, when on flesh and on fowl had appetite duly been sated,
Up rose the Catholic Priest and returned God thanks for the dinner.
Then on all tables were set black bottles of well-mixed toddy,
And, with the bottles and glasses before them, they sat, digesting,
Talking, enjoying, but chiefly awaiting the toasts and speeches.

from *The Bothie of Tober-Na-Vuolich*

FREDERICK LOCKER-LAMPSON

AT HURLINGHAM

This was dear Willy's brief dispatch,
  A curt and yet a cordial summons; –
'Do come! I'm in to-morrow's match,
  And see us whip the *Faithful Commons.*'
We trundled out behind the bays,
  Through miles and miles of brick and garden;
Mama was dresst in mauve and maize, –
  Of course I wore my *Dolly Varden.*

A charming scene, and lovely too,
  The paddock's full, the band is playing
Boulotte's song in *Barbe bleu*;
  And what are all these people saying?
They flirt! they bet! there's Linda Reeves
  Too lovely! I'd give worlds to borrow
Her yellow rose with russet leaves! –
  I'll wear a yellow rose to-morrow!

And there are May and Algy Meade;
  How proud she looks on her promotion!
The ring must be amused indeed
  And edified by such devotion!
I wonder if she ever guess'd!
  I wonder if he'll call on Friday!
I often wonder which is best! –
  I only hope my hair is tidy!

Some girls repine, and some rejoice,
  And some get bored, but I'm contented
To make my destiny my choice, –
  I'll never dream that I've repented.
There's something sad in *lov'd and cross'd*,
  For all the fond, fond hope that rings it:
There's something sweet in 'Loved and lost' –
  And Oh, how sweetly Alfred sings it.

I'll own I'm bored with *handicaps*!
  Bluerocks! (they always are 'bluerock'-ing!) –
With May, a little bit, perhaps, –
  And yon Faust's *teufelshund* is shocking!
Bang . . . bang . . .! That's Willy! There's his bird,
  Blithely it cleaves the skies above me!
He's missed all ten! He's too absurd! –
  I hope he'll always, always love me!

We've lost! To tea, then back to town;
  The crowd is laughing, eating, drinking:
The moon's eternal eyes look down, –
  Of what can yon sad moon be thinking?
Oh, but for some good fairy's wand, –
  This pigeoncide is worse than silly,
But still I'm very, very fond
  Of Hurlingham, and tea, – and Willy.

COVENTRY PATMORE

THE CATHEDRAL CLOSE

Once more I came to Sarum Close,
  With joy half memory, half desire,
And breathed the sunny wind that rose
  And blew the shadows o'er the Spire,
And toss'd the lilac's scented plumes,
  And sway'd the chestnut's thousand cones,
And filled my nostrils with perfumes,
  And shaped the clouds in waifs and zones,
And wafted down the serious strain
  Of Sarum bells, when, true to time,
I reach'd the Dean's, with heart and brain
  That trembled to the trembling chime.

'Twas half my home, six years ago.
  The six years had not alter'd it:
Red-brick and ashlar, long and low,
  With dormers and with oriels lit.
Geranium, lychnis, rose array'd
  The windows, all wide open thrown;
And some one in the study play'd
  The Wedding-March of Mendelssohn.
And there it was I last took leave:
  'Twas Christmas: I remember'd now
The cruel girls, who feign'd to grieve,
  Took down the evergreens; and how
The holly into blazes woke
  The fire, lighting the large, low room,
A dim, rich lustre of old oak
  And crimson velvet's glowing gloom.

No change had touch'd Dean Churchill: kind,
  By widowhood more than winters bent,
And settled in a cheerful mind,
  As still forecasting heaven's content.

Well might his thoughts be fix'd on high,
  Now she was there! Within her face
Humility and dignity
  Were met in a most sweet embrace.
She seem'd expressly sent below
  To teach our erring minds to see
The rhythmic change of time's swift flow
  As part of still eternity.
Her life, all honour, observed, with awe
  Which cross experience could not mar,
The fiction of the Christian law
  That all men honourable are;
And so her smile at once conferr'd
  High flattery and benign reproof;
And I, a rude boy, strangely stirr'd,
  Grew courtly in my own behoof.
The years, so far from doing her wrong,
  Anointed her with gracious balm,
And made her brows more and more young
  With wreaths of amaranth and palm.

Was this her eldest, Honor; prude,
  Who would not let me pull the swing;
Who, kiss'd at Christmas, call'd me rude,
  And, sobbing low, refused to sing?
How changed! In shape no slender Grace,
  But Venus; milder than the dove;
Her mother's air; her Norman face;
  Her large sweet eyes, clear lakes of love.
Mary I knew. In former time
  Ailing and pale, she thought that bliss
Was only for a better clime,
  And, heavenly overmuch, scorn'd this.
I, rash with theories of the right,
  Which stretch'd the tether of my Creed,
But did not break it, held delight
  Half discipline. We disagreed.
She told the Dean I wanted grace.

  Now she was kindest of the three,
And soft wild roses deck'd her face.
  And, what, was this my Mildred, she
To herself and all a sweet surprise?
  My Pet, who romp'd and roll'd a hoop?
I wonder'd where those daisy eyes
  Had found their touching curve and droop.

Unmannerly times! But now we sat
  Stranger than strangers; till I caught
And answer'd Mildred's smile; and that
  Spread to the rest, and freedom brought.
The Dean talk'd little, looking on,
  Of three such daughters justly vain.
What letters they had had from Bonn,
  Said Mildred, and what plums from Spain!
By Honor I was kindly task'd
  To excuse my never coming down
From Cambridge; Mary smiled and ask'd
  Were Kant and Goethe yet outgrown?
And, pleased, we talk'd the old days o'er;
  And, parting, I for pleasure sigh'd.
  To be there as a friend, (since more),
  Seem'd then, seems still, excuse for pride;
For something that abode endued
  With temple-like repose, an air
Of life's kind purposes pursued
  With order'd freedom sweet and fair.
A tent pitch'd in a world not right
  It seem'd, whose inmates, every one,
On tranquil faces bore the light
  Of duties beautifully done,
And humbly, though they had few peers,
  Kept their own laws, which seem'd to be
The fair sum of six thousand years'
  Traditions of civility.

from *The Angel in the House*

Coventry Patmore (1823–1895)

HUSBAND AND WIFE

I, while the shop-girl fitted on
  The sand-shoes, look'd where, down the bay,
The sea glow'd with a shrouded sun.
  'I'm ready, Felix; will you pay?'
That was my first expense for this
  Sweet Stranger, now my three days' Wife.
How light the touches are that kiss
  The music from the chords of life!

Her feet, by half-a-mile of sea,
  In spotless sand left shapely prints;
With agates, then, she loaded me;
  (The lapidary call'd them flints);
Then, at her wish, I hail'd a boat,
  To take her to the ships-of-war,
At anchor, each a lazy mote
  Black in the brilliance, miles from shore.

The morning breeze the canvas fill'd,
  Lifting us o'er the bright-ridged gulf,
And every lurch my darling thrill'd
  With light fear smiling at itself;
And, dashing past the Arrogant,
  Asleep upon the restless wave,
After its cruise in the Levant,
  We reach'd the Wolf, and signal gave
For help to board: with caution meet,
  My bride was placed within the chair,
The red flag wrapp'd about her feet,
  And so swung laughing through the air.

'Look, Love,' she said, 'there's Frederick Graham,
  'My cousin, whom you met, you know.'
And seeing us, the brave man came,
  And made his frank and courteous bow,
And gave my hand a sailor's shake,
  And said: 'You ask'd me to the Hurst:
'I never thought my luck would make
  'Your wife and you my guests the first.'

And Honor, cruel, 'Nor did we:
  'Have you not lately changed your ship?'
'Yes: I'm Commander, now,' said he,
  With a slight quiver of the lip.
We saw the vessel, shown with pride;
  Took luncheon; I must eat his salt!
Parting he said, (I fear my bride
  Found him unselfish to a fault),
His wish, he saw, had come to pass,
  (And so, indeed, her face express'd),
That that should be, whatever 'twas,
  Which made his Cousin happiest.
We left him looking from above;
  Rich bankrupt! for he could afford
To say most proudly that his love
  Was virtue and its own reward.
But others loved as well as he,
  (Thought I, half-anger'd), and if fate,
Unfair, had only fashion'd me
  As hapless, I had been as great.

As souls, ambitious, but low-born,
  If raised past hope by luck or wit,
All pride of place will proudly scorn,
  And live as they'd been used to it,
So we two wore our strange estate:
  Familiar, unaffected, free,
We talk'd, until the dusk grew late,
  Of this and that; but, after tea,
As doubtful if a lot so sweet
  As ours was ours in very sooth,
Like children, to promote conceit,
  We feign'd that it was not the truth;
And she assumed the maiden coy,
  And I adored remorseless charms,
And then we clapp'd our hands for joy,
  And ran into each other's arms.

from *The Angel in the House*

WILLIAM JOHNSON CORY

HERSILIA

I see her stand with arms akimbo,
A blue and blonde *sub aureo nimbo*;
She scans her literary limbo,
The reliques of her teens;
Things like the chips of broken stilts,
Or tatters of embroidered quilts,
Or nosegays tossed away by jilts,
Notes, ballads, tales, and scenes.

Soon will she gambol like a lamb
Fenced, but not tethered, near the Cam.
Maybe she'll swim where Byron swam,
And chat between the limes,
Where Arthur, Alfred, Fitz, and Brooks
Lit thought by one another's looks,
Embraced their jests and kicked their books
In England's happier times;

Ere magic poets felt the gout,
Ere Darwin whelmed the Church in doubt,
Ere Apologia had found out
The round world must be right;
When Gladstone, bluest of the blue,
Read all Augustine's folios through;
When France was tame, and no one knew
We and the Czar would fight.

'Sixty years since' (said dear old Scott;
We're bound, you know, to quote Sir Wat)
This isle had not a sweeter spot
Than Neville's Court by Granta;
No Newnham then, no kirtled scribes,
No Celia to harangue the tribes,
No race for girls, no apple bribes
To tempt an Atalanta.

We males talked fast, we meant to be
World-betterers all at twenty-three,
But somehow failed to level thee,
Oh battered fort of Edom!
Into the breach our daughters press,
Brave patriots in unwarlike dress,
Adepts at thought-in-idleness,
Sweet devotees of freedom.

And now it is your turn, fair soul,
To see the fervent car-wheels roll,
Your rivals clashing past the goal,
Some sly Milaniòn leading.
Ah! with them may your Genius bring
Some Celia, some Miss Mannering;
For youthful friendship is a thing
More precious than succeeding.

ANONYMOUS

THE ONE HORSE CHAY

Mrs Bubb was gay and free, fair, fat and forty-three,
And blooming as a Peony in buxom May,
The toast she long had been of Farringdon Within,
And she filled the better half of a one horse chay.

Mrs Bubb said to her lord, 'You can, Bubb, well afford
Whate'er a Common Councilman in prudence may;
We've no brats to plague our lives and the soap concern it thrives,
Let us take a trip to Brighton in the one horse chay.'

Mr Bubb said to his wife, 'Now I think upon't, my life,
'Tis three weeks at least to next boiling day;
The dog days are set in and London's growing thin,
So I'll order out old Nobbs and the one horse chay.'

Now Nobbs, it must be told, was rather fat and old,
Its colour was white and it had been gray,
He was round as a scot and when roundly whipt would trot,
Full five miles an hour in a one horse chay.

When at Brighton they were housed and had stuffed
and caroused,
O'er a bowl of arrack Punch Mr Bubb did say:
'I've ascertained, my dear, the mode of dipping here,
From the ostler who is cleaning up my one horse chay.

You're shut in a box, ill convenient as the stocks,
And eighteen pence each time are obliged to pay;
Court corruption here, says I, makes everything so high
And I wish I had come without my one horse chay.'

'As I hope' says she 'to thrive, 'tis flaying folks alive,
The king and these extortioners are leagued, I say;
'Tis encouraging of such to go and pay so much,
So we'll set them at defiance with our one horse chay.

Old Nobbs I am sure and sartin you may trust with gig or
cart in,
He takes every matter in a very easy way;
He'll stand like a post while we dabble on the coast,
And return back and dress in our one horse chay.'

So out they drove all dressed so gaily in their best,
And finding in their rambles a nice little bay,
They uncased at their leisure, paddled out at their pleasure,
And left everything behind in their one horse chay.

But while so snugly sure that all things were secure,
They flounced about like porpoises or whales at play;
Some young unlucky imps who prowled about for shrimps
Stole up to reconnoitre the one horse chay.

Old Nobbs in quiet mood was sleeping as he stood,
(He might possibly be dreaming of his corn or hay):
Not a foot did he wag as they whipt out every rag
And gutted all the contents of the one horse chay.

When our pair were soused enough and returning in their buff,
Oh there was the vengeance and Old Nick to pay;
Madame shrieked in consternation, Mr Bubb he swore damnation,
To find the empty state of the one horse chay.

'Come bundle in with me, we must squeeze for once,' says he,
'And manage this here business as best we may.
We've no other way to choose, not a moment must we lose,
Or the tide will float us off in our one horse chay.'

So noses, sides and knees altogether did they squeeze
And packed in little compass they trotted it away;
As dismal as two dummies, heads and hands stuck out like mummies,
From beneath the little apron of the one horse chay.

Mr Bubb ge-upped in vain and strove to jerk the rein,
Nobbs found he had his option to work or play,
So he wouldn't mend his pace, though they fain would have run race
To escape the merry gazers at the one horse chay.

Now good people laugh your fill and fancy if you will,
(For I'm fairly out of breath and have had my say);
The trouble and the rout, to wrap and get them out,
When they drove to their lodgings in their one horse chay.

Broadsheet Ballad

DOWN BY THE DARK ARCHES

As I walked out one day in the month of July
A pretty young damsel I chanced for to spy,
Singing Vilikens and Dinah, so blithe and so gay,
Down by the dark arches under the railway.

Then I stepped up to her so gay and so free,
And for the same ballad I paid one halfpenny,
Will you be my sweetheart to her I did say,
Down by the dark arches under the railway.

Oh no, my gay young man that cannot be,
There is a chap here in blue and he is a-watching of me,
And if he should see me, what would he say,
Down by the dark arches under the railway.

At last she consented, away we both went,
Five shillings in lobsters and oysters I spent,
Six drops of brandy for her I did pay,
Down by the dark arches under the railway.

Then in came a chap with a black eye and a stick,
He drunk up my brandy and broke my Pickwick;
Pop goes the weasel to me he did say,
Down by the dark arches under the railway.

Then he squared up to me and pulled my watch out,
He spoiled my new beaver and damaged my snout,
He kicked me in the gutter and there I lay,
Down by the dark arches under the railway.

I lay in the gutter till four in the morn
As naked as ever a poor creature was born,
And when I awakened quite stiff there I lay,
Down by the dark arches under the railway.

Four bobbies came up and to my surprise
I found I had no shirt on to cover my thighs,
They put me on a stretcher and bore me away
From beneath the dark arches under the railway.

I sent to my mother for money and clothes,
Likewise to a doctor to patch up my nose,
You have not had fair play to me he did say
Down by the dark arches under the railway.

Now all you young chaps take a warning by me,
And never go a-courting when you are on the spree,
And never take those young ladies out of their way
Down by the dark arches under the railway.

Broadsheet Ballad

DRIVING IN THE PARK

Of all the pleasant ways
To pass an afternoon,
Is in a pony chaise
One sultry day in June.
To drive between the trees
In Hyde Park round and round,
It brings a pleasant sense of ease
In spinning o'er the ground.
The men raise hats to me,
I mean, the men I know,
They smile, kiss hands, then laugh to see
The flying pony go.
And then I come in sight
Of one against the rails
Whose handsome face lights up so bright
As he my presence hails.

Driving in the Park,
Driving in the Park;
Love may haunt the drive,
And no one ever mark.
Glances meet with joy,
Alighting with love's spark.
Sweet one. Naughty boy.
Driving in the Park.

And very nice it seems
Among the beats I know,
When early sunlight gleams,
To gallop round the Row.
At ten some breezy morn
All care away I fling,
Luxurious days of rest I scorn,
The gallop is the thing.
I challenge all my friends
To run a race with me,
And when the madcap scamper ends,
The blood flows fresh and free.

And nicer yet to walk
The horse while someone near
Engages me with tender talk,
So very sweet to hear.

Riding in the Park,
Riding in the Park;
Love may haunt the Row
And no one ever mark.
Love may bend his bow,
Make two hearts his mark,
No one ever know –
Riding in the Park.

WALKING IN THE ZOO

The Stilton, sir, the cheese, the O.K. thing to do,
On Sunday afternoon, is to toddle to the Zoo;
Week days may do for cads, but not for me and you,
So dress'd, right down the road we show them who is who.

Chorus

Walking in the Zoo, walking in the Zoo,
The O.K. thing on Sunday is walking in the Zoo.

So when there came to town my pretty cousin Loo,
I took her off to spend a Sunday at the Zoo;
I showed her the aquarium, the Tiger, the Zebu,
The Elephant, the Eland, and that cuss – the Kangaroo.
Oh! walking in the Zoo, walking in the Zoo,
The monkeys put us to the blush on Sunday in the Zoo.

So into the monkey house, going in to woo,
Piling up the agony, swearing to be true,
Agony, indeed, for the cheerful cockatoo
Caught my ear a nip and bit it through and through.
Oh! that cheerful cockatoo, that awful cockatoo,
The horror and the agony, that Sunday at the Zoo.

Broadsheet Ballad

ERNÉE CLARK

THE CHICKALEARY COVE

I'm a Chickaleary bloke[1] with my one, two, three,
Whitechapel was the village I was born in,
For to get me on the hop, or on my tibby drop,[2]
You must wake up very early in the morning.
I have a rorty[3] gal, also a knowing pal,
And merrily together we jog on,
I doesn't care a flatch, as long as I've got a tach,[4]
Some pannum[5] for my chest, and a tog on.

Chorus

I'm a Chickaleary bloke with my one, two, three,
Whitechapel was the village I was born in,
For to get me on the hop, or on my tibby drop,
You must wake up very early in the morning.

Now kool my downy kicksies[6] – the style for me,
Built on a plan werry naughty,
The stock around my squeeze[7] a guiver[8] colour see,
And the vestat with the bins[9] so rorty.
My tailor sews you well, from a perger[10] to a swell,
At Groves' you are safe to make a sure pitch,
For ready yenom[11] down, there ain't a shop in town,
Can lick Groves in the Cut as well as Shoreditch.

Off to Paris I shall go, to show a thing or two
To the dipping blokes[12] what hangs about the caffes,
How to do a cross-fam,[13] for a super,[14] or a slang,[15]
And to bustle[16] them grand'armes I'd give the office:
Now my pals I'm going to slope, see you soon again, I hope,
My young woman is avaiting, so be quick,
Now join in a chyike,[17] the jolly[18] we all like,
I'm off with a party to the 'Vic'.

[1] artful fellow [2] take me unawares [3] lively [4] hat [5] bread [6] look at my smart trousers [7] throat [8] smart, fashionable [9] waistcoat with pockets [10] teetotaller [11] money [12] pickpockets [13] to pick a pocket by masking the action [14] watch [15] watch-chain [16] confuse [17] hearty salute [18] praise

ANONYMOUS

POVERTY KNOCK

Poverty, poverty knock!
Me loom is a-sayin' all day.
Poverty, poverty knock!
Gaffer's too skinny to pay.
Poverty, poverty knock!
Keepin' one eye on the clock.
Ah know ah can guttle[1]
When ah hear me shuttle
Go: Poverty, poverty knock!

Up every mornin' at five.
Ah wonder that we keep alive.
Tired an' yawnin' on the cold mornin',
It's back to the dreary old drive.

Oh dear, we're goin' to be late.
Gaffer is stood at the gate.
We're out o' pocket, our wages they're docket;
We'll 'a' to buy grub on the slate.

An' when our wages they'll bring,
We're often short of a string.[2]
While we are fratchin'[3] wi' gaffer for snatchin',
We know to his brass he will cling.

We've got to wet our own yarn
By dippin' it into the tarn.
It's wet an' soggy an' makes us feel groggy,
An' there's mice in that dirty old barn.

Oh dear, me poor 'ead it sings.
Ah should have woven three strings,
But threads are breakin' and my back is achin'.
Oh dear, ah wish ah had wings.

[1] eat [2] length of cloth [3] quarrelling

Sometimes a shuttle flies out,
Gives some poor woman a clout.
Ther she lies bleedin', but nobody's 'eedin'.
Who's goin' t'carry her out?

Tuner[4] should tackle me loom.
'E'd rather sit on his bum.
'E's far too busy a-courtin' our Lizzie,
An' ah cannat get 'im to come.

Lizzie is so easy led.
Ah think that 'e teks her to bed.
She allus was skinny, now look at her pinny.
It's just about time they was wed.

Poverty, poverty knock!
Me loom is a-sayin' all day.
Poverty, poverty knock!
Gaffer's too skinny to pay.
Poverty, poverty knock!
Keepin' one eye on the clock.
Ah know ah can guttle
When ah hear me shuttle
Go: Poverty, poverty knock!

THE BANKS OF NEWFOUNDLAND

My bully boys of Liverpool, I'd have you to beware,
When you sail in a packet ship, no dungaree jumpers wear,
But have a good monkey-jacket all ready to your hand,
For there blows some cold nor'westers on the Banks of Newfoundland.
So we'll scrape her and we'll scrub her with holystone and sand,
And we'll think of them cold nor'westers on the Banks of Newfoundland.

[4] loom-maintenance man

There was Jack Lynch from Ballinahinch, Jim Murphy and
Sam Moore;
It was in the year of sixty-two those poor boys suffered sore,
For they'd pawned their clothes in Liverpool, and they sailed
as they did stand,
And there blows some cold nor'westers on the Banks of
Newfoundland.

The mate came up on the foc'sle head and loudly he did roar:
Come rattle her in, my lively lads, we're bound for America's shore.
Then lay aloft and shake her out and give her all she can stand,
And there blows some cold nor'westers on the Banks of
Newfoundland.

And now it's reef and reef, my boys, with the canvas frozen hard,
And it's mount and pass, you son of a gun, on a ninety-foot
tops'l yard,
Never mind your boots and oilskins, but haul to beat the band,
For there blows some cold nor'westers on the Banks of
Newfoundland.

And now we're off the Hook, my boys, and the land's all
covered in snow,
With the tug-boat due ahead of us, into New York we will tow,
And as we tie up at the dock them pretty girls will stand,
Crying: 'It's snugger with me than it is at sea on the Banks
of Newfoundland!'

So we'll scrape her and we'll scrub her with holystone
and sand,
And we'll bid farewell to the Virgin Rocks and the Banks
of Newfoundland.

JOSEPH SKIPSEY

THE HARTLEY CALAMITY

The Hartley men are noble, and ye'll hear a tale of woe,
I'll tell the doom of the Hartley men, the year of sixty-two.
'Twas on a Thursday morning in the first month of the year,
When there befell the thing that well may rend the heart to hear.

Ere chantecleer with music rare awakes the old homestead,
The Hartley men are up and off to earn their daily bread.
On, on they toil, with heat they broil, and streams of sweat do glue
The stour[1] into their skins till they are black as the coals they hew.

Now to and fro the putters go, the waggons to and fro,
And clang on clang of wheel and hoof ring in the mine below.
The din and strife of human life awakes in 'wall' and 'board',
When all at once a shock is felt which makes each heart-beat heard.

Each bosom thuds as each his duds then snatches and away,
And to the distant shaft he flees with all the speed he may.
Each, all they flee by two, by three, they seek the shaft to seek
An answer in each other's face to what they may not speak.

Are we entombed? they seem to ask, for the shaft is closed, and no
Escape have they to God's bright day from out the night below.
So stand in pain the Hartley men, and swiftly o'er them comes
The memory of home and all that binds us to our homes.

Despair at length renews their strength, and they the shaft must clear,
And soon the sound of mall and pick half drowns the voice of fear.
And hark, to the sound of mall below, do sounds above reply?
Hurrah, hurrah for the Hartley men, for now their rescue's nigh.

Their rescue nigh? The sounds of joy and hope have ceased, and ere
A breath is drawn, a rumble's heard that drives them to despair.
Together now behold them bow, their burdened souls unload
In cries that never rise in vain unto the living God.

[1] coal-dust

Whilst yet they kneel, again they feel their strength renewed again
For the swing and ring of the mall attest the might of Hartley men.
And hark, to the blow of the mall below, do sounds above reply?
Hurrah, hurrah for the Hartley men, for now their rescue's nigh!

But now that light, erewhile so bright, no longer lights the scene,
A cloud of mist the light has kissed and shorn it of its sheen.
A cloud of mist the light has kissed, and see, along does crawl,
Till one by one the lights are smote, and darkness covers all.

'Oh father, till the shaft is cleared, close, close beside me keep.
My eyelids are together glued, and I – and I must sleep.'
'Sleep, darling, sleep and I will keep close by – heigh ho –' To keep
Himself awake the father strives, but soon he too must sleep.

And fathers and mothers and sisters and brothers, the lover, the new-made bride,
A vigil kept for those who slept from eve to morning tide.
But they slept, still sleep, in silence dread, two hundred old and young,
To awake when heaven and earth have sped and the last dread trumpet sung.

'GET UP!'

'Get up!' the caller calls, 'Get up!'
    And in the dead of night,
To win the bairns their bite and sup,
    I rise a weary wight.

My flannel dudden donn'd, thrice o'er
    My birds are kiss'd, and then
I with a whistle shut the door
    I may not ope again.

JAMES THOMSON ('B.V.')

LOW LIFE

As Overheard in the Train.

The jolly old gentleman, bless his white hat!
Wouldn't come in to spoil our chat;
We are alone and we can speak, –
What have you done, Miss, all the week?

'Oh, all the day it's been fit and shew,
And all the night it's been trim and sew,
For the ladies are flocking to Exeter Hall
In lovely light dresses fit for a ball.'

Under your eye a little dark streak,
And a point of red on the top of your cheek,
And your temples quite dim against your hair;
This sha'n't last very much longer I swear.

And what is the news from the workroom now?
'The week began with a bit of a row;
Emmy Harley married young Earl
Just in the busy time!' – sensible girl!

'That was on Monday; Missis said
It was very ungrateful, very ill-bred,
And very unkind to us when she knew
The work so heavy, the hands so few.

'But this was nothing: the minute we woke
On Wednesday, before it seemed any one spoke,
We knew that poor Mary Challis was dead;
Kate Long had been sleeping in the same bed.

'Mary worked with us till twelve, when tea
Was brought in to keep us awake, but she
Was so ill then, Miss Cooper sent her to bed;
And there in the morning they found her dead;

'With Kate fast asleep by her side: they had come
To see how she was, and the sight struck them dumb:
At last they roused Kate and led her away;
She was sick and shuddering all the day.

'Kate says when she went up at four to their room
She was stupid with sleep; but she marked a faint bloom
On Mary's pale face, and she heard her breathe low –
A light fluttering breath now quick and now slow;

'And feared to disturb her, for *she* had a cough,
But the moment she laid her head down she was off,
And knew nothing more till they stood by the side
Of the bed: p'r'aps Mary slept on till she died.

'They buried her yesterday. Kate was there,
And she was the only one Missis could spare;
Some dresses were bound to be finished by night,
For the ladies to go in to Church all right.

'Poor Mary! she didn't fear dying, she said,
Her father drinks and her mother is dead;
But she hoped that in Heaven the white garments wear
For ever; no fashions and dressmaking There.'

My Love, if the ladies most pious of all
Who flock to the Church and to Exeter Hall
Find Heaven has but one dress for rich as for poor,
And no fashions, they'll very soon cut it I'm sure.

I saw you ten minutes on Tuesday night,
Then I took the 'bus home for I had to write;
And I wrote and I wrote like an engine till five,
When my fingers were dead and the letters alive.

A fair bill of costs from a deuce of a draft
In our Cashier's worst scrawl like Chinese ran daft;
With entries between, on the margin, the back,
And figures like short-hand marks put to the rack.

But our Common-law Clerk is going away,
And the Gov'nor had me in yesterday,

And said he would try me, he thought I might do;
And I jumped at the chance, for this child thinks so too.

Just fancy, each morning a jolly good walk,
And instead of the copying, bustle and talk!
And if I do well – and well I will do –
A couple of sovs. a week for my screw!

And then when I'm free of the desk and the stool,
Do you think you will keep to the nunnery rule
Of the shop, till you go off like Mary some night
Smothered in work from the air and the light?

We'll use our professional talents, my dear:
You shall make such a wedding dress, best of the year!
And a wonderful marriage-deed I will draw
With magnificent settlements perfect in law.

Thus doing our duties in those states of life
In which it has pleased God to call us, *my wife!*
'And how much a year will you settle on me?'
My body and soul and – what we shall see.

W. S. GILBERT

DOWN TO THE DERBY

Waggon and cart, ready to start,
  Early in morning at six six;
Gallons of beer, stowed away here,
  Twiggery, swiggery, quick sticks.
Empty before, fill 'em once more;
  Women look trim in their caps, caps;
Screaming in fun, never say done,
  Joking and poking the chaps, chaps.
Sweeps in a truck, swells out of luck,
  Laughery, chaffery, grin, grin,
Travelling show, dwarf hid below,
  Eye on his giantess' gin, gin.

Twiggery, swiggery, shinery, finery, laughery,
chaffery, pokery, jokery;
Down to the Derby as all of us go,
These are the sights that we each of us know;
Yet off to the Downs as we often have been,
Still every year is some novelty seen.

Ten of the clock, carriages flock
Round to the doors at the West-end;
People who seem, skimming the cream,
To have laid hold of life at the best end.
Phaeton and pair, baronet there,
Lovely young girl with a smile, smile;
Look all about, splendid turn out,
Everything done in good style, style.
Hampers retain lots of champagne,
Hungerly, vulgarly, prog, prog,
Nothing more seek, nice little shriek,
Missing him, kissing him, dog, dog.

Flunkeydom, monkeydom, finery, whinery, livery,
shivery, fowlery, growlery –
Down to the Derby as all of us go,
These are the sights that we each of us know;
Yet off to the Downs as we often have been,
Still every year is some novelty seen.

Clapham we pass, schools in a mass,
Up at the windows we go by
Playful as mice, governess nice,
Thinkery, winkery, oh, fie!
Balham the dull vote it a mull,
Marchery, starchery, slow, slow;
Tooting the next, sticks to its text,
Travelly, gravelly, Oh! oh!
Sutton a whet, thirsty we get,
Palery, alery, take, take;
Smart four-in-hand comes to a stand,
Legs of the longest ones ache, ache.

Drinkery, winkery, palery, alery, laughery, chaffery,
crash along, dash along –
Down to the Derby as all of us go,
These are the sights that we each of us know;
Yet off to the Downs as we often have been,
Still every year is some novelty seen.

*

Epsom at last, nearing it fast,
Smackery, crackery, whip, whip;
There's the Grand Stand, now close at hand,
Think it a nice little trip, trip.
Get a good view, this one will do,
Squeezing it, seizing it, rush, rush;
Downs looking smooth, Careless's Booth,
Go in and get a good brush, brush.
Every one here, seems to appear,
'How d'ye do?' 'How are you?' nod, nod,
Some friends about, can't find em out,
Look for them, hook for them, odd, odd.

Smackery, snackery, scenery, greenery, Leger bit,
hedge a bit, look about, shook about –
Down to the Derby as all of us go,
There are the sights that we each of us know;
Yet off to the Downs as we often have been,
Still every year is some novelty seen.

Now take your place, this is the race,
Universe, tune averse, fame, fame;
Cards to be sold, everything told,
Colours and riders and name, name.
Buzz! off they go, galloping so,
Bothery, dothery, eye, eye;
Look as they pass, out with the glass,
Can't find the focus to spy, spy.
Yonder they run, some horse has won,
Up with the number and see, see;
Whichever is in, hundreds may win,
But thousands will diddled like me be.

Cantering, bantering, cheering em, nearing em,
spy away, fly away, dothery, bothery –
Down to the Derby as all of us go,
These are the sights that we each of us know;
Yet off to the Downs as we often have been,
Still every year is some novelty seen.

Derby complete, something to eat,
Out with the provender, crush, crush;
Somebody walks, off with the forks,
Bring out the bottles and lush, lush.
Plenty of pie, salad is nigh,
Lettuces, let us seize, cool, cool;
Popkins an ass, broken a glass,
Grittling, victualling, fool, fool.
Take to the wine, your health and mine,
Drinkery, thinkery, nice, nice;
Off with the cup, finish it up,
Sopping it, mopping it, trice, trice.

Readily, saidily, rather unsteadily, trickling,
prickling, toiletty, spoiletty –
Down to the Derby as all of us go,
These are the sights that we each of us know;
Yet off to the Downs as we often have been,
Still every year is some novelty seen.

*

Eaten a snack, time to be back,
Hurrying, scurrying, start, start;
Road as before, crammed but the more,
With carriage and phaeton and cart, cart.
Out come the stars, light up cigars,
Brandy and soda you must, must;
Road dry again, where was the rain?
Smokery, chokery, dust, dust.
Come to a block, just at 'The Cock',
Famous inn, same as in past time;
Pale ale to boot, take a cheroot,
'Dal be, it shall be the last time.'

Hurrying, scurrying, hampering, scampering,
smokery, jokery, crash along, dash along –
Up from the Derby as all of us go,
These are the sights that we each of us know;
Yet off to the Downs as we often have been,
Still every year is some novelty seen.

Come to a pike, just what you like,
Ticketing, stick it in, stop, stop;
Plenty of fun, never say done,
Hattery, flattery, drop, drop.
Driving along, 'let's have a song,'
Mystery, history, none, none;
Dozens of keys, take which you please,
Blowing horns, showing horns – Lon-don.
Lamps down the road, near your abode,
Flare away, glare away, far, far;
Kennington gate, longer to wait,
Loud din and crowding at bar, bar.

Ticketing, stick it in, hattery, battery, flare away,
stare away, splashery, dashery,
Up from the Derby as all of us go,
These are the sights that we each of us know;
Yet off to the Downs as we often have been,
Still every year is some novelty seen.

Home get at last, going it fast,
Lifery, wifery, look, look;
Had no excess, buy a new dress,
Made it all right with your 'book, book'.
Wake the next day, think of the way,
How will the debts you incur be;
Or more to your mind, glad that you find,
You did pretty well on the Derby.
Anyhow you think it will do
Not going now to be vexed here;
Hoping to spend with a 'party' or friend,
A holiday, jolly day, next year.

Theatre, be at a, upper rooms, supper rooms,
choppery, moppery, steakery, rakery, singing too,
bringing too, holiday, jolly day;
Fun thus we see as of old on the road,
This is the channel through which it has flowed;
Often to Epsom as people have been,
These are the fancies that freshen the scene.

THOMAS HARDY

REMINISCENCES OF A DANCING MAN

Who now remembers Almack's balls –
Willis's sometime named –
In those two smooth-floored upper halls
For faded ones so famed?
Where as we trod to trilling sound
The fancied phantoms stood around,
Or joined us in the maze,
Of the powdered Dears from Georgian years,
Whose dust lay in sightless sealed-up biers,
The fairest of former days.

Who now remembers gay Cremorne,
And all its jaunty jills,
And those wild whirling figures born
Of Julien's grand quadrilles?
With hats on head and morning coats
There footed to his prancing notes
Our partner-girls and we;
And the gas-jets winked, and the lustres clinked,
And the platform throbbed as with arms enlinked
We moved to the minstrelsy.

Who now recalls those crowded rooms
Of old yclept 'The Argyle,'
Where to the deep Drum-polka's booms
We hopped in standard style?

Whither have danced those damsels now!
Is Death the partner who doth moue
	Their wormy chaps and bare?
Do their spectres spin like sparks within
The smoky halls of the Prince of Sin
	To a thunderous Jullien air?

ONE WE KNEW

(M. H. 1772–1857)

She told how they used to form for the country dances –
	'The Triumph', 'The New-rigged Ship' –
To the light of the guttering wax in the panelled manses,
	And in cots to the blink of a dip.

She spoke of the wild 'poussetting' and 'allemanding'
	On carpet, on oak, and on sod;
And the two long rows of ladies and gentlemen standing,
	And the figures the couples trod.

She showed us the spot where the maypole was yearly planted,
	And where the bandsmen stood
While breeched and kerchiefed partners whirled, and panted
	To choose each other for good.

She told of that far-back day when they learnt astounded
	Of the death of the King of France:
Of the Terror; and then of Bonaparte's unbounded
	Ambition and arrogance.

Of how his threats woke warlike preparations
	Along the southern strand,
And how each night brought tremors and trepidations
	Lest morning should see him land.

She said she had often heard the gibbet creaking
	As it swayed in the lightning flash,
Had caught from the neighbouring town a small child's shrieking
	At the cart-tail under the lash. . . .

With cap-framed face and long gaze into the embers –
    We seated around her knees –
She would dwell on such dead themes, not as one who remembers,
    But rather as one who sees.

She seemed one left behind of a band gone distant
    So far that no tongue could hail:
Past things retold were to her as things existent,
    Things present but as a tale.

IN A WAITING-ROOM

On a morning sick as the day of doom
    With the drizzling gray
    Of an English May,
There were few in the railway waiting-room.
About its walls were framed and varnished
Pictures of liners, fly-blown, tarnished.
The table bore a Testament
For travellers' reading, if suchwise bent.

    I read it on and on,
And, thronging the Gospel of Saint John,
Were figures – additions, multiplications –
By some one scrawled, with sundry emendations;
    Not scoffingly designed,
    But with an absent mind, –
Plainly a bagman's counts of cost,
What he had profited, what lost;
And whilst I wondered if there could have been
    Any particle of a soul
    In that poor man at all,
    To cypher rates of wage
    Upon that printed page,
    There joined in the charmless scene
And stood over me and the scribbled book
    (To lend the hour's mean hue
    A smear of tragedy too)
A soldier and wife, with haggard look

Subdued to stone by strong endeavour;
    And then I heard
    From a casual word
They were parting as they believed for ever.

    But next there came
    Like the eastern flame
Of some high altar, children – a pair –
Who laughed at the fly-blown pictures there.
'Here are the lovely ships that we,
Mother, are by and by going to see!
When we get there it's 'most sure to be fine,
And the band will play, and the sun will shine!'
It rained on the skylight with a din
As we waited and still no train came in;
But the words of the child in the squalid room
Had spread a glory through the gloom.

THE COUNTRY WEDDING

(A Fiddler's Story)

Little fogs were gathered in every hollow,
But the purple hillocks enjoyed fine weather
As we marched with our fiddles over the heather
– How it comes back! – to their wedding that day.

Our getting there brought our neighbours and all, O!
Till, two and two, the couples stood ready.
And her father said: 'Souls, for God's sake, be steady!'
And we strung up our fiddles, and sounded out 'A'.

The groomsman he stared, and said, 'You must follow!'
But we'd gone to fiddle in front of the party,
(Our feelings as friends being true and hearty)
And fiddle in front we did – all the way.

Yes, from their door by Mill-tail-Shallow,
And up Styles-Lane, and by Front-Street houses,
Where stood maids, bachelors, and spouses,
Who cheered the songs that we knew how to play.

I bowed the treble before her father,
Michael the tenor in front of the lady,
The bass-viol Reub – and right well played he! –
The serpent Jim; ay, to church and back.

I thought the bridegroom was flurried rather,
As we kept up the tune outside the chancel,
While they were swearing things none can cancel
Inside the walls to our drumstick's whack.

'Too gay!' she pleaded. 'Clouds may gather,
And sorrow come.' But she gave in, laughing,
And by supper-time when we'd got to the quaffing
Her fears were forgot, and her smiles weren't slack.

A grand wedding 'twas! And what would follow
We never thought. Or that we should have buried her
On the same day with the man that married her,
A day like the first, half hazy, half clear.

Yes: little fogs were in every hollow,
Though the purple hillocks enjoyed fine weather,
When we went to play 'em to church together,
And carried 'em there in an after year.

AN EAST-END CURATE

A small blind street off East Commercial Road;
    Window, door; window, door;
    Every house like the one before,
Is where the curate, Mr Dowle, has found a pinched abode.
Spectacled, pale, moustache straw-coloured, and with a long thin face,
Day or dark his lodgings' narrow doorstep does he pace.

A bleached pianoforte, with its drawn silk plaitings faded,
Stands in his room, its keys much yellowed, cyphering, and abraded,
'Novello's Anthems' lie at hand, and also a few glees,
And 'Laws of Heaven for Earth' in a frame upon the wall one sees.

He goes through his neighbours' houses as his own, and none regards,
And opens their back-doors off-hand, to look for them in their yards:
A man is threatening his wife on the other side of the wall,
But the curate lets it pass as knowing the history of it all.

Freely within his hearing the children skip and laugh and say:
'There's Mister Dow-well! There's Mister Dow-well!' in their play;
And the long, pallid, devoted face notes not,
But stoops along abstractedly, for good, or in vain, God wot!

A SHEEP FAIR

The day arrives of the autumn fair,
And torrents fall,
Though sheep in throngs are gathered there,
Ten thousand all,
Sodden, with hurdles round them reared:
And, lot by lot, the pens are cleared,
And the auctioneer wrings out his beard,
And wipes his book, bedrenched and smeared,
And rakes the rain from his face with the edge of his hand,
As torrents fall.

The wool of the ewes is like a sponge
With the daylong rain:
Jammed tight, to turn, or lie, or lunge,
They strive in vain.
Their horns are soft as finger-nails,
Their shepherds reek against the rails,
The tied dogs soak with tucked-in tails,
The buyers' hat-brims fill like pails,
Which spill small cascades when they shift their stand
In the daylong rain.

Postscript

Time has trailed lengthily since met
At Pummery Fair

Those panting thousands in their wet
And woolly wear:
And every flock long since has bled,
And all the dripping buyers have sped,
And the hoarse auctioneer is dead,
Who 'Going – going!' so often said,
As he consigned to doom each meek, mewed band
At Pummery Fair.

NO BUYERS

A load of brushes and baskets and cradles and chairs
Labours along the street in the rain:
With it a man, a woman, a pony with whiteybrown hairs. –
The man foots in front of the horse with a shambling sway
At a slower tread than a funeral train,
While to a dirge-like tune he chants his wares,
Swinging a Turk's-head brush (in a drum-major's way
When the bandsmen march and play).

A yard from the back of the man is the whiteybrown pony's nose:
He mirrors his master in every item of pace and pose:
He stops when the man stops, without being told,
And seems to be eased by a pause; too plainly he's old,
Indeed, not strength enough shows
To steer the disjointed waggon straight,
Which wriggles left and right in a rambling line,
Deflected thus by its own warp and weight,
And pushing the pony with it in each incline.

The woman walks on the pavement verge,
Parallel to the man:
She wears an apron white and wide in span,
And carries a like Turk's-head, but more in nursing-wise:
Now and then she joins in his dirge,
But as if her thoughts were on distant things
The rain clams her apron till it clings. –
So, step by step, they move with their merchandize,
And nobody buys.

John Davidson (1837–1909)

AT THE AQUATIC SPORTS

With their backs to the sea two fiddlers stand
Facing the concourse on the strand,
    And a third man who sings.
The sports proceed; there are crab-catchings;
The people laugh as levity spreads;
Yet these three do not turn their heads
    To see whence the merriment springs.

They cease their music, but even then
They stand as before, do those three men,
    Though pausing, nought to do:
They never face to the seaward view
To enjoy the contests, add their cheer,
So wholly is their being here
    A business they pursue.

JOHN DAVIDSON

THIRTY BOB A WEEK

I couldn't touch a stop and turn a screw,
  And set the blooming world a-work for me,
Like such as cut their teeth – I hope, like you –
  On the handle of a skeleton gold key;
I cut mine on a leek, which I eat it every week:
  I'm a clerk at thirty bob as you can see.

But I don't allow it's luck and all a toss;
  There's no such thing as being starred and crossed;
It's just the power of some to be a boss,
  And the bally power of others to be bossed:
I face the music, sir; you bet I ain't a cur;
  Strike me lucky if I don't believe I'm lost!

For like a mole I journey in the dark,
  A-travelling along the underground

From my Pillar'd Halls and broad Suburban Park,
  To come the daily dull official round;
And home again at night with my pipe all alight,
  A-scheming how to count ten bob a pound.

And it's often very cold and very wet,
  And my missis stitches towels for a hunks;
And the Pillar'd Halls is half of it to let –
  Three rooms about the size of travelling trunks.
And we cough, my wife and I, to dislocate a sigh,
  When the noisy little kids are in their bunks.

But you never hear her do a growl or whine,
  For she's made of flint and roses, very odd;
And I've got to cut my meaning rather fine,
  Or I'd blubber, for I'm made of greens and sod:
So p'r'aps we are in Hell for all that I can tell,
  And lost and damn'd and served up hot to God.

I ain't blaspheming, Mr Silver-tongue;
  I'm saying things a bit beyond your art:
Of all the rummy starts you ever sprung,
  Thirty bob a week's the rummiest start!
With your science and your books and your the'ries about spooks,
  Did you ever hear of looking in your heart?

I didn't mean your pocket, Mr, no:
  I mean that having children and a wife,
With thirty bob on which to come and go,
  Isn't dancing to the tabor and the fife:
When it doesn't make you drink, by Heaven! it makes you think,
  And notice curious items about life.

I step into my heart and there I meet
  A god-almighty devil singing small,
Who would like to shout and whistle in the street,
  And squelch the passers flat against the wall;
If the whole world was a cake he had the power to take,
  He would take it, ask for more, and eat it all.

And I meet a sort of simpleton beside,
  The kind that life is always giving beans;
With thirty bob a week to keep a bride
  He fell in love and married in his teens:
At thirty bob he stuck; but he knows it isn't luck:
  He knows the seas are deeper than tureens.

And the god-almighty devil and the fool
  That meet me in the High Street on the strike,
When I walk about my heart a-gathering wool,
  Are my good and evil angels if you like.
And both of them together in every kind of weather
  Ride me like a double-seated bike.

That's rough a bit and needs its meaning curled.
  But I have a high old hot 'un in my mind –
A most egregious notion of the world,
  That leaves your lightning 'rithmetic behind:
I give it at a glance when I say 'There ain't no chance,
  Nor nothing of the lucky-lottery kind.'

And it's this way that I make it out to be:
  No fathers, mothers, countries, climates – none;
Not Adam responsible for me,
  Nor society, nor systems, nary one:
A little sleeping seed, I woke – I did, indeed –
  A million years before the blooming sun.

I woke because I thought the time had come;
  Beyond my will there was no other cause;
And everywhere I found myself at home,
  Because I chose to be the thing I was;
And in whatever shape of mollusc or of ape
  I always went according to the laws.

I was the love that chose my mother out;
  I joined two lives and from the union burst;
My weakness and my strength without a doubt
  Are mine alone for ever from the first:
It's just the very same with a difference in the name
  As 'Thy will be done.' You say it if you durst!

They say it daily up and down the land
  As easy as you take a drink, it's true;
But the difficultest go to understand,
  And the difficultest job a man can do,
Is to come it brave and meek with thirty bob a week,
  And feel that that's the proper thing for you.

It's a naked child against a hungry wolf;
  It's playing bowls upon a splitting wreck;
It's walking on a string across a gulf
  With millstones fore-and-aft about your neck;
But the thing is daily done by many and many a one;
  And we fall, face forward, fighting, on the deck.

RUDYARD KIPLING

THE BALLAD OF THE 'BOLIVAR'

1890

Seven men from all the world back to Docks again,
Rolling down the Ratcliffe Road drunk and raising Cain.
Give the girls another drink 'fore we sign away –
We that took the 'Bolivar' *out across the Bay!*

We put out from Sunderland loaded down with rails;
  We put back to Sunderland 'cause our cargo shifted;
We put out from Sunderland – met the winter gales –
  Seven days and seven nights to the Start we drifted.

    Racketing her rivets loose, smoke-stack white as snow,
    All the coals adrift adeck, half the rails below,
    Leaking like a lobster-pot, steering like a dray –
    Out we took the *Bolivar*, out across the Bay!

One by one the Lights came up, winked and let us by;
  Mile by mile we waddled on, coal and fo'c'sle short;
Met a blow that laid us down, heard a bulkhead fly;
  Left The Wolf behind us with a two-foot list to port.

Trailing like a wounded duck, working out her soul;
Clanging like a smithy-shop after every roll;
Just a funnel and a mast lurching through the spray –
So we threshed the *Bolivar* out across the Bay!

Felt her hog and felt her sag, betted when she'd break;
Wondered every time she raced if she'd stand the shock;
Heard the seas like drunken men pounding at her strake;
Hoped the Lord 'ud keep his thumb on the plummer-block!

Banged against the iron decks, bilges choked with coal;
Flayed and frozen foot and hand, sick of heart and soul;
'Last we prayed she'd buck herself into Judgement Day –
Hi! we cursed the *Bolivar* knocking round the Bay!

O her nose flung up to sky, groaning to be still –
Up and down and back we went, never time for breath;
Then the money paid at Lloyd's caught her by the keel,
And the stars ran round and round dancin' at our death!

Aching for an hour's sleep, dozing off between;
'Heard the rotten rivets draw when she took it green;
Watched the compass chase its tail like a cat at play –
That was on the *Bolivar*, south across the Bay!

Once we saw between the squalls, lyin' head to swell –
Mad with work and weariness, wishin' they was we –
Some damned Liner's lights go by like a grand hotel;
'Cheered her from the *Bolivar* swampin' in the sea.

Then a greyback cleared us out, then the skipper laughed;
'Boys, the wheel has gone to Hell – rig the winches aft!
'Yoke the kicking rudder-head – get her under way!'
So we steered her, pully-haul, out across the Bay!

Just a pack o' rotten plates puttied up with tar,
In we came, an' time enough, 'cross Bilbao Bar.
Overloaded, undermanned, meant to founder, we
Euchred God Almighty's storm, bluffed the Eternal Sea!

Seven men from all the world back to town again,
Rollin' down the Ratcliffe Road drunk and raising Cain:
Seven men from out of Hell. Ain't the owners gay,
'Cause we took the 'Bolivar' *safe across the Bay?*

DANNY DEEVER

'What are the bugles blowin' for?' said Files-on-Parade.
'To turn you out, to turn you out,' the Colour-Sergeant said.
'What makes you look so white, so white?' said Files-on-Parade.
'I'm dreadin' what I've got to watch,' the Colour-Sergeant said.
  For they're hangin' Danny Deever, you can hear the Dead March play,
  The regiment's in 'ollow square – they're hangin' him to-day;
  They've taken of his buttons off an' cut his stripes away,
  An' they're hangin' Danny Deever in the mornin'.

'What makes the rear-rank breathe so 'ard?' said Files-on-Parade.
'It's bitter cold, it's bitter cold,' the Colour-Sergeant said.
'What makes that front-rank man fall down?' said Files-on-Parade.
'A touch o' sun, a touch o' sun,' the Colour-Sergeant said.
  They are hangin' Danny Deever, they are marchin' of 'im round,
  They 'ave 'alted Danny Deever by 'is coffin on the ground;
  An' 'e'll swing in 'arf a minute for a sneakin' shootin' hound –
  O they're hangin' Danny Deever in the mornin'!

''Is cot was right-'and cot to mine,' said Files-on-Parade.
''E's sleepin' out an' far to-night,' the Colour-Sergeant said.
'I've drunk 'is beer a score o' times,' said Files-on-Parade.
''E's drinkin' bitter beer alone,' the Colour-Sergeant said.
  They are hangin' Danny Deever, you must mark 'im to 'is place,
  For 'e shot a comrade sleepin' – you must look 'im in the face;
  Nine 'undred of 'is county an' the Regiment's disgrace,
  While they're hangin' Danny Deever in the mornin'.

'What's that so black agin the sun?' said Files-on-Parade.
'It's Danny fightin' 'ard for life,' the Colour-Sergeant said.
'What's that what whimpers over'ead?' said Files-on-Parade.
'It's Danny's soul that's passin' now,' the Colour-Sergeant said.

For they're done with Danny Deever, you can 'ear the quickstep play,
The regiment's in column, an' they're marchin' us away;
Ho! the young recruits are shakin', an' they'll want their beer to-day,
After hangin' Danny Deever in the mornin'!

M'ANDREW'S HYMN

1893

Lord, Thou hast made this world below the shadow of a dream,
An', taught by time, I tak' it so – exceptin' always Steam.
From coupler-flange to spindle-guide I see Thy Hand, O God –
Predestination in the stride o' yon connectin'-rod.
John Calvin might ha' forged the same – enorrmous, certain, slow –
Ay, wrought it in the furnace-flame – *my* 'Institutio'.
I cannot get my sleep tonight; old bones are hard to please;
I'll stand the middle watch up here – alone wi' God an' these
My engines, after ninety days o' race an' rack an' strain
Through all the seas of all Thy world, slam-bangin' home again.
Slam-bang too much – they knock a wee – the crosshead-gibs are loose,
But thirty thousand mile o' sea has gied them fair excuse . . .
Fine, clear an' dark – a full-draught breeze, wi' Ushant out o' sight,
An' Ferguson relievin' Hay. Old girl, ye'll walk tonight!
His wife's at Plymouth . . . Seventy – One – Two – Three since he began –
Three turns for Mistress Ferguson . . . and who's to blame the man?
There's none at any port for me, by drivin' fast or slow,
Since Elsie Campbell went to Thee, Lord, thirty years ago.
(The year the *Sarah Sands* was burned. Oh roads we used to tread,
Fra' Maryhill to Pollokshaws – fra' Govan to Parkhead!)
Not but they're ceevil on the Board. Ye'll hear Sir Kenneth say:
'Good morrn, McAndrew! Back again? An' how's your bilge today?'
Miscallin' technicalities but handin' me my chair
To drink Madeira wi' three Earls – the auld Fleet Engineer

That started as a boiler-whelp – when steam and he were low.
I mind the time we used to serve a broken pipe wi' tow!
Ten pound was all the pressure then – Eh! Eh! – a man wad drive;
An' here, our workin' gauges give one hunder sixty-five!
We're creepin' on wi' each new rig – less weight an' larger power:
There'll be the loco-boiler next an' thirty miles an hour!
Thirty an' more. What I ha' seen since ocean-steam began
Leaves me na doot for the machine: but what about the man?
The man that counts, wi' all his runs, one million mile o' sea:
Four time the span from earth to moon . . . How far, O Lord, from Thee
That wast beside him night an' day? Ye mind my first typhoon?
It scoughed the skipper on his way to jock wi' the saloon.
Three feet were on the stokehold-floor – just slappin' to an' fro –
An' cast me on a furnace-door. I have the marks to show.
Marks! I ha' marks o' more than burns – deep in my soul an' black,
An' times like this, when things go smooth, my wickudness comes back.
The sins o' four an' forty years, all up an' down the seas.
Clack an' repeat like valves half-fed . . . Forgie 's our trespasses!
Nights when I'd come on deck to mark, wi' envy in my gaze,
The couples kittlin' in the dark between the funnel-stays;
Years when I raked the Ports wi' pride to fill my cup o' wrong –
Judge not, O Lord, my steps aside at Gay Street in Hong-Kong!
Blot out the wastrel hours of mine in sin when I abode –
Jane Harrigan's an' Number Nine, The Reddick an' Grant Road!
An' waur than all – my crownin' sin – rank blasphemy an' wild.
I was not four and twenty then – Ye wadna judge a child?
I'd seen the Tropics first that run – new fruit, new smells, new air –
How could I tell – blind-fou wi' sun – the Deil was lurkin' there?
By day like playhouse-scenes the shore slid past our sleepy eyes;
By night those soft, lasceevious stars leered from those velvet skies,
In port (we used no cargo-steam) I'd daunder down the streets –
An ijjit grinnin' in a dream – for shells an' parrakeets,
An' walkin'-sticks o' carved bamboo an' blowfish stuffed an' dried –
Fillin' my bunk wi' rubbishry the Chief put overside.

Till, off Sambawa Head, Ye mind, I heard a land-breeze ca',
Milk-warm wi' breath o' spice an' bloom: 'McAndrew, come awa'!'
Firm, clear an' low – no haste, no hate – the ghostly whisper went,
Just statin' eevidential facts beyon' all argument:
'Your mither's God's a graspin' deil, the shadow o'yoursel',
Got out o' books by meenisters clean daft on Heaven an' Hell.
They mak' him in the Broomielaw, o' Glasgie cold an' dirt,
A jealous, pridefu' fetich, lad, that's only strong to hurt,
Ye'll not go back to Him again an' kiss His red-hot rod,
But come wi' Us' (Now, who were *They*?) 'an' know the Leevin' God,
That does not kipper souls for sport or break a life in jest,
But swells the ripenin' cocoanuts an' ripes the woman's breast.'
An' there it stopped: cut off: no more; that quiet, certain voice –
For me, six months o' twenty-four, to leave or take at choice.
'Twas on me like a thunderclap – it racked me though an' through –
Temptation past the show o' speech, unnameable an' new –
The Sin against the Holy Ghost?. . . An' under all, our screw.

That storm blew by but left behind her anchor-shiftin' swell.
Thou knowest all my heart an' mind, Thou knowest, Lord, I fell.
Third on the *Mary Gloster* then, and first that night in Hell!
Yet was Thy Hand beneath my head, about my feet Thy Care –
Fra' Deli clear to Torres Strait, the trial o' despair,
But when we touched the Barrier Reef Thy answer to my prayer! . . .
We dared na run that sea by night but lay an' held our fire,
An' I was drowsin' on the hatch – sick – sick wi' doubt an' tire:
'*Better the sight of eyes that see than wanderin' o' desire!*'
Ye mind that word? Clear as our gongs – again, an' once again,
When rippin' down through coral-trash ran out our moorin'-chain;
An', by Thy Grace, I had the Light to see my duty plain.
Light on the engine-room – no more – bright as our carbons burn.
I've lost it since a thousand times, but never past return!

*

Obsairve. Per annum we'll have here two thousand souls aboard –
Think not I dare to justify myself before The Lord,
But – average fifteen hunder souls safe-borne fra' port to port –
I *am* o' service to my kind. Ye wadna blame the thought?

Maybe they steam from Grace to Wrath – to sin by folly led –
It isna mine to judge their path – their lives are on my head.
Mine at the last – when all is done it all comes back to me,
The fault that leaves six thousand ton a log upon the sea.
We'll tak' one stretch – three weeks an' odd by ony road ye steer –
Fra' Cape Town east to Wellington – ye need an engineer.
Fail there – ye've time to weld your shaft – ay, eat it, ere ye're spoke;
Or make Kerguelen under sail – three jiggers burned wi' smoke!
An' home again – the Rio run: it's no child's play to go
Steamin' to bell for fourteen days o' snow an' floe an' blow.
The bergs like kelpies overside that girn an' turn an' shift
Whaur, grindin' like the Mills o' God, goes by the big South drift.
(Hail, Snow and Ice that praise the Lord. I've met them at their work,
An' wished we had anither route or they anither kirk.)
Yon's strain, hard strain, o' head an' hand, for though Thy Power brings
All skill to naught, Ye'll understand a man must think o' things.
Then, at the last, we'll get to port an' hoist their baggage clear –
The passengers, wi' gloves an' canes – an' this is what I'll hear;
'Well, thank ye for a pleasant voyage. The tender's comin' now.'
While I go testin' follower-bolts an' watch the skipper bow.
They've words for every one but me – shake hands wi' half the crew
Except the dour Scots engineer, the man they never knew.
An' yet I like the wark for all we've dam' few pickin's here –
No pension, an' the most we'll earn 's four hunder pound a year.
Better myself abroad? Maybe. *I'd* sooner starve than sail
Wi' such as call a snifter-rod *ross* . . . French for nightingale.
Commeesion on my stores? Some do; but I cannot afford
To lie like stewards wi' patty-pans. I'm older than the Board.
A bonus on the coal I save? Ou ay, the Scots are close,
But when I grudge the strength Ye gave I'll grudge their food to *those.*
(There's bricks that I might recommend – an' clink the firebars cruel.
No! Welsh – Wangarti at the worst – an' damn all patent fuel!)

Inventions? Ye must stay in port to mak' a patent pay.
My Deeferential Valve-Gear taught me how that business lay,
I blame no chaps wi' clearer heads for aught they make or sell.
I found that I could not invent an' look to these as well.
So, wrestled wi' Apollyon – Nah! – fretted like a bairn –
But burned the workin'-plans last run wi' all I hoped to earn.
Ye know how hard an Idol dies, an' what that meant to me –
E'en tak' it for a sacrifice acceptable to Thee . . .
Below there! Oiler! What's your wark? Ye find it runnin' hard?
Ye needn't swill the cup wi' oil – this isn't the Cunard!
Ye thought? Ye are not paid to think. Go, sweat that off again!
Tck! Tck! It's deeficult to sweer nor tak' The Name in vain!
Men, ay an' women, call me stern. Wi' these to oversee
Ye'll note I've little time to burn on social repartee.
The bairns see what their elders miss; they'll hunt me to an' fro,
Till for the sake of – well, a kiss – I tak' 'em down below.
That minds me of our Viscount loon – Sir Kenneth's kin – the chap
Wi' Russia leather tennis-shoon an' spar-decked yachtin'-cap.
I showed him round last week, o'er all – an' at the last says he:
'Mister McAndrew, don't you think steam spoils romance at sea?'
Damned ijjit! I'd been doon that morn to see what ailed the throws,
Manholin', on my back – the cranks three inches off my nose.
Romance! Those first-class passengers they like it very well,
Printed an' bound in little books; but why don't poets tell?
I'm sick of all their quirks an' turns – the loves an' doves they dream –
Lord, send a man like Robbie Burns to sing the Song o' Steam!
To match wi' Scotia's noblest speech yon orchestra sublime
Whaurto – uplifted like the Just – the tail-rods mark the time.
The crank-throws give the double-bass, the feed-pump sobs an' heaves,
An' now the main eccentrics start their quarrel on the sheaves:
Her time, her own appointed time, the rocking link-head bides,
Till – hear that note? – the rod's return whings glimmerin' through the guides.
They're all awa! True beat, full power, the clangin' chorus goes
Clear to the tunnel where they sit, my purrin' dynamoes.

Interdependence absolute, foreseen, ordained, decreed,
To work, Ye'll note, at any tilt an' every rate o' speed.
Fra skylight-lift to furnace-bars, backed, bolted, braced an' stayed.
An' singin' like the Mornin' Stars for joy that they are made;
While, out o' touch o' vanity, the sweatin' thrust-block says:
'Not unto us the praise, or man – not unto us the praise!'
Now, a' together, hear them lift their lesson – theirs an' mine:
'Law, Orrder, Duty an' Restraint, Obedience, Discipline!'
Mill, forge an' try-pit taught them that when roarin' they arose,
An' whiles I wonder if a soul was gied them wi' the blows.
Oh for a man to weld it then, in one trip-hammer strain,
Till even first-class passengers could tell the meanin' plain!
But no one cares except mysel' that serve an' understand
My seven thousand horse-power here. Eh, Lord! They're grand –
they're grand!
Uplift am I? When first in store the new-made beasties stood,
Were Ye cast down that breathed the Word declarin' all things
good?
Not so! O' that warld-liftin' joy no after-fall could vex,
Ye've left a glimmer still to cheer the Man – the Arrtifex!
That holds, in spite o' knock and scale, o' friction, waste an' slip,
An' by that light – now, mark my word – we'll build the
Perfect Ship.
I'll never last to judge her lines or take her curve – not I.
But I ha' lived an' I ha' worked. Be thanks to Thee, Most High!
An' I ha' done what I ha' done – judge Thou if ill or well –
Always Thy Grace preventin' me . . .
Losh! Yon's the 'Stand-by' bell.
Pilot so soon? His flare it is. The mornin'-watch is set.
Well, God be thanked, as I was sayin', I'm no Pelagian yet.
Now I'll tak' on. . .
'Morrn, Ferguson. Man, have ye ever thought
What your good leddy costs in coal?. . . I'll burn 'em down to port.

W. H. DAVIES

THE SLEEPERS

As I walked down the waterside
  This silent morning, wet and dark;
Before the cocks in farmyards crowed,
  Before the dogs began to bark;
Before the hour of five was struck
By old Westminster's mighty clock:

As I walked down the waterside
  This morning, in the cold damp air,
I saw a hundred women and men
  Huddled in rags and sleeping there:
These people have no work, thought I,
And long before their time they die.

That moment, on the waterside,
  A lighted car came at a bound;
I looked inside, and saw a score
  Of pale and weary men that frowned;
Each man sat in a huddled heap,
Carried to work while fast asleep.

Ten cars rushed down the waterside
  Like lighted coffins in the dark;
With twenty dead men in each car,
  That must be brought alive by work:
These people work too hard, thought I,
And long before their time they die.

EDWARD THOMAS

MAN AND DOG

''Twill take some getting.' 'Sir, I think 'twill so.'
The old man stared up at the mistletoe
That hung too high in the poplar's crest for plunder
Of any climber, though not for kissing under:
Then he went on against the north-east wind –
Straight but lame, leaning on a staff new-skinned,
Carrying a brolly, flag-basket, and old coat, –
Towards Alton, ten miles off. And he had not
Done less from Chilgrove where he pulled up docks.
'Twere best, if he had had 'a money-box',
To have waited there till the sheep cleared a field
For what a half-week's flint-picking would yield.
His mind was running on the work he had done
Since he left Christchurch in the New Forest, one
Spring in the 'seventies, – navvying on dock and line
From Southampton to Newcastle-on-Tyne, –
In 'seventy-four a year of soldiering
With the Berkshires, – hoeing and harvesting
In half the shires where corn and couch will grow.
His sons, three sons, were fighting, but the hoe
And reap-hook he liked, or anything to do with trees.
He fell once from a poplar tall as these:
The Flying Man they called him in hospital.
'If I flew now, to another world I'd fall.'
He laughed and whistled to the small brown bitch
With spots of blue that hunted in the ditch.
Her foxy Welsh grandfather must have paired
Beneath him. He kept sheep in Wales and scared
Strangers, I will warrant, with his pearl eye
And trick of shrinking off as he were shy,
Then following close in silence for – for what?
'No rabbit, never fear, she ever got,
Yet always hunts. Today she nearly had one:
She would and she wouldn't. 'Twas like that. The bad one!

She's not much use, but still she's company,
Though I'm not. She goes everywhere with me.
So Alton I must reach tonight somehow:
I'll get no shakedown with that bedfellow
From farmers. Many a man sleeps worse tonight
Than I shall.' 'In the trenches.' 'Yes, that's right.
But they'll be out of that – I hope they be –
This weather, marching after the enemy.'
'And so I hope. Good luck.' And there I nodded
'Goodnight. You keep straight on,' Stiffly he plodded;
And at his heels the crisp leaves scurried fast,
And the leaf-coloured robin watched. They passed,
The robin till next day, the man for good,
Together in the twilight of the wood.

AS THE TEAM'S HEAD-BRASS

As the team's head-brass flashed out on the turn
The lovers disappeared into the wood.
I sat among the boughs of the fallen elm
That strewed the angle of the fallow, and
Watched the plough narrowing a yellow square
Of charlock. Every time the horses turned
Instead of treading me down, the ploughman leaned
Upon the handles to say or ask a word,
About the weather, next about the war.
Scraping the share he faced towards the wood,
And screwed along the furrow till the brass flashed
Once more.
                    The blizzard felled the elm whose crest
I sat in, by a woodpecker's round hole,
The ploughman said. 'When will they take it away?'
'When the war's over.' So the talk began –
One minute and an interval of ten,
A minute more and the same interval.
'Have you been out?' 'No.' 'And don't want to, perhaps?'
'If I could only back again, I should.

Edward Thomas (1878–1917)

I could spare an arm. I shouldn't want to lose
A leg. If I should lose my head, why, so,
I should want nothing more . . . Have many gone
From here?' 'Yes.' 'Many lost?' 'Yes, a good few.
Only two teams work on the farm this year.
One of my mates is dead. The second day
In France they killed him. It was back in March,
The very night of the blizzard, too. Now if
He had stayed here we should have moved the tree.'
'And I should not have sat here. Everything
Would have been different. For it would have been
Another world.' 'Ay, and a better, though
If we could see all all might seem good.' Then
The lovers came out of the wood again:
The horses started and for the last time
I watched the clods crumble and topple over
After the ploughshare and the stumbling team.

SELECT BIBLIOGRAPHY

W. W. Skeat (ed.), *The Lay of Havelok the Dane*, revised K. Sisam (Oxford University Press, 1929)

M. Y. Offord (ed.), *The Parlement of the Thre Ages* (Early English Text Society 246, 1959)

I. Gollancz (ed.), *Winnere and Wastoure* (Roxburghe Club, 1897); second edition, revised Mabel Day (Oxford University Press, 1930)

J. A. Burrow (ed.), *Sir Gawain and the Green Knight* (Penguin, 1972)

William Langland, *Piers Plowman*: B Text, ed. W. W. Skeat (Early English Text Society 38, 1869); C Text, ed. W. W. Skeat (Early English Text Society 54, 1873); Passus I–VII, ed. J. A. W. Bennett (Oxford University Press, 1972)

Geoffrey Chaucer, *Works*, ed. F. N. Robinson, second edition (Oxford University Press, 1957)

John Hoccleve, *Minor Poems*, vol. 1, ed. F. J. Furnivall (Early English Text Society ES 61, 1892)

John Lydgate, *Minor Poems*, ed. H. N. McCracken (Early English Text Society 192, 1934)

John Russell, *The Boke of Nurture*, in *The Babees Book*, ed. F. J. Furnivall (Early English Text Society 32, 1868)

Mabel Day and Robert Steele (eds), *Mum and the Sothsegger* (Early English Text Society 199, 1936)

W. W. Skeat (ed.), *Pierce the Plowman's Crede* (Early English Text Society 30, 1867)

Sir David Lindsay, *Works*, ed. D. Hamer (Scottish Text Society, Edinburgh, 1931–6)

John Skelton, *Poems*, ed. R. S. Kinsman (Oxford University Press, 1969)

W. H. French and C. B. Hale (eds), *English Metrical Romances* (Russell & Russell, New York, 1964)

A. C. Cawley (ed.), *The Wakefield Pageants in the Towneley Cycle* (Manchester University Press, 1958)

F. J. Furnivall (ed.), *The Stacions of Rome*, etc. (Early English Text Society 25, 1867)

Joseph Ritson (ed.), *The Squyer of Low Degre*, in *Ancient Metrical Romances* (3 vols, 1802)

R. L. Greene (ed.), *The Early English Carols* (Oxford University Press, 1935)

K. Sisam (ed.), *Fourteenth Century Verse and Prose* (Oxford University Press, 1921)

R. H. Robbins (ed.), *Secular Lyrics of the Fourteenth and Fifteenth Centuries* (Oxford University Press, 1955)

J. W. Hebel and H. H. Hudson (eds), *Poetry of the English Renaissance* (Blackwell, 1929)

E. Arber (ed.), *An English Garner: Ingatherings from Our History and Literature*, second edition (12 vols, Constable, 1903–4), vol. 6, *Tudor Tracts, 1532–88*

F. W. Fairholt (ed.), *Satirical Songs and Poems on Costume* (Percy Society, 1849), vol. 27 of *Early English Poetry, Ballads, and Popular Literature of the Middle Ages* (31 vols).

J. W. Ebsworth (ed.), *The Roxburghe Ballads* (9 vols, Ballad Society, 1871–99)

Robert Bell (ed.), *Early Ballads and Songs of the Peasantry of England* (George Bell, 1877)

John Ashton (ed.), *Modern Street Ballads* (Chatto & Windus, 1888)
W. H. Auden (ed.), *The Oxford Book of Light Verse* (Oxford University Press, 1938)

V. de Sola Pinto and A. E. Rodway (eds), *The Common Muse* (Chatto & Windus, 1957; Penguin, 1965)

A. L. Lloyd, *Folk Song in England* (Lawrence & Wishart, 1967; Panther, 1969)

INDEX OF AUTHORS

INDEX OF TITLES AND FIRST LINES